A Special Issue of
Language and Cognitive Processes

Spoken Word Access Processes

Edited by

James M. McQueen and Anne Cutler
Max Planck Institute for Psycholinguistics

Psychology Press
Taylor & Francis Group
LONDON AND NEW YORK

Published in 2001 by Psychology Press Ltd
27 Church Road, Hove, East Sussex, BN3 2FA

Simultaneously published in the USA and Canada
by Taylor & Francis Inc.
711 Third Avenue, New York, NY 10017, USA

First issued in paperback 2015

*Psychology Press is an imprint of the Taylor & Francis Group,
an informa business*

British Library Cataloguing in Publication Data
A catalogue record for this book is available from the British Library

ISBN 13: 978-1-138-87785-6 (pbk)
ISBN 13: 978-1-84169-916-5 (hbk)

ISSN 0169-0965

Cover design by Jim Wilkie from an original design by Kees Oerlemans
Typeset in the UK by Mendip Communications Ltd., Frome, Somerset

Contents*

Preface
James M. McQueen and Anne Cutler   465

Spoken word access processes: An introduction
James M. McQueen and Anne Cutler   469

New evidence for prelexical phonological processing in word
recognition
*Emmanuel Dupoux, Christophe Pallier, Kazuhiko Kakehi
and Jacques Mehler*   491

Subcategorical mismatches and the time course of lexical access:
Evidence for lexical competition
*Delphine Dahan, James S. Magnuson, Michael K. Tanenhaus
and Ellen M. Hogan*   507

Variation and assimilation in German:
Consequences for lexical access and representation
Else Coenen, Pienie Zwitserlood and Jens Bölte   535

Phonotactics, density, and entropy in spoken word recognition
Paul A. Luce and Nathan R. Large   565

Bottom-up inhibition in lexical selection:
Phonological mismatch effects in spoken word recognition
Uli H. Frauenfelder, Mark Scholten and Alain Content   583

Sequence detection in pseudowords in French:
Where is the syllable effect?
Alain Content, Christine Meunier, Ruth Kearns and Uli Frauenfelder   609

Language-universal constraints on speech segmentation
*Dennis Norris, James M. McQueen, Anne Cutler, Sally Butterfield
and Ruth Kearns*   637

continued overleaf...

---

*This book is also a special issue of the journal *Language and Cognitive Processes*, and forms issues 5 & 6 of Volume 16 (2001). The page numbers are taken from the journal and so begin with p. 465.

Lipreading and the compensation for coarticulation mechanism
Jean Vroomen and Beatrice de Gelder 661

Short reports

Phoneme-like units and speech perception
Terrance M. Nearey 673

Mapping from acoustic signal to phonetic category:
Internal category structure, context effects and speeded
categorization
Joanne L. Miller 681

Why phonological constraints are so coarse-grained
Janet Pierrehumbert 691

Access to lexical representations: Cross-linguistic issues
William D. Marslen-Wilson 699

Some empirical tests of Merge's architecture
Arthur G. Samuel 709

The source of a lexical bias in the Verbal Transformation Effect
Mark A. Pitt and Lisa Shoaf 715

Phonological variation and its consequences for the word
recognition system
M. Gareth Gaskell 723

Taking the hit: Leaving some lexical competition to be
resolved post-lexically
*Ellen Gurman Bard, Catherine Sotillo, M. Louise Kelly
and Matthew P. Aylett* 731

Subject Index 738

LANGUAGE AND COGNITIVE PROCESSES, 2001, *16* (5/6), 465–468

Preface

The workshop Spoken Word Access Processes (SWAP) was held in Nijmegen during the last three days of May 2000. It was attended by 64 psycholinguists—graduate students, post-doctoral scientists and senior researchers—representing an estimated 13 nationalities and at least 9 native languages. This special issue of *Language and Cognitive Processes* contains a selection of papers based on presentations at that workshop. There were a total of 23 talks and 22 posters presented at SWAP, as listed in the Appendix below. The present selection represents the main themes that were addressed at the workshop. In the introductory article, we sketch those themes and draw links not only between the eight other articles and the eight short reports published here, but also between them and the other work presented at SWAP. The articles describe eight research projects on different issues in spoken word recognition; the short reports are brief descriptions of projects which are reported in more detail elsewhere.

SWAP was financially supported by the Max-Planck-Gesellschaft zur Förderung der Wissenschaften, and was an International Speech Communication Association (ISCA) Tutorial and Research Workshop. We would like to take this opportunity to record our thanks, to both the MPG and ISCA, for their support of SWAP. Our thanks also go to the workshop's scientific committee, and to Rian Zondervan, for her wonderful secretarial and administrative support. Finally, we would like to thank the reviewers of papers for this special issue for their wise and timely counsel, and especially Mike Tanenhaus, who acted as editor for the two papers in the issue which we co-authored.

James M. McQueen and Anne Cutler,
Max Planck Institute for Psycholinguistics,
Nijmegen, The Netherlands
March 2001

APPENDIX

Talks given at SWAP

Ellen G. Bard, Catherine Sotillo & Matthew P. Aylett (University of Edinburgh). Taking the hit: Why lexical and phonological processing should not make lexical access too easy

Alain Content, Nicolas Dumay & Uli H. Frauenfelder (Free University of Brussels & University of Geneva). The role of syllable structure in lexical segmentation: Helping listeners avoid mondegreens

Carol A. Fowler & Lawrence Brancazio (Haskins Laboratories & Northeastern University). Freedback in audiovisual speech perception

Uli H. Frauenfelder & Alain Content (University of Geneva & Free University of Brussels). Activation flow in models of spoken word recognition

Gareth Gaskell (University of York). A quick rum picks you up, but is it good for you? Sentence context effects in the identification of spoken words

Stephen D. Goldinger (Arizona State University). The role of perceptual episodes in lexical processing

John Kingston (University of Massachusetts, Amherst). Context effects on sensitivity and response bias

Paul A. Luce & Nathan R. Large (University at Buffalo). Do spoken words have attractors?

William D. Marslen-Wilson (MRC Cognition and Brain Sciences Unit). Organising principles in lexical access and representation? A view across languages

James M. McQueen, Anne Cutler & Dennis Norris (MPI for Psycholinguistics & MRC Cognition and Brain Sciences Unit). Why Merge really is autonomous and parsimonious

Joanne L. Miller (Northeastern University). Mapping from acoustic signal to phonetic category: Nature and role of internal category structure

Terrance M. Nearey (University of Alberta). Phoneme-like units and speech perception

Sieb Nooteboom, Esther Janse, Hugo Quené & Saskia te Riele (University of Utrecht). Multiple activation and early context effects

Dennis Norris, Anne Cutler, James M. McQueen, Sally Butterfield & Ruth Kearns (MRC Cognition and Brain Sciences Unit & MPI for Psycholinguistics). Language-universal constraints on the segmentation of English

Christophe Pallier (Laboratoire de Sciences Cognitives et Psycholinguistique CNRS). Word recognition: Do we need phonological representations?

Janet Pierrehumbert (Northwestern University). Why phonological constraints are so granular

Mark Pitt & Lisa Shoaf (Ohio State University). Beyond traditional measures of lexical influences on perception

Arthur G. Samuel (SUNY Stony Brook). Some empirical tests of Merge's architecture

Richard Shillcock (University of Edinburgh). Spoken word access: evidence from statistical analyses of the lexicon

Michael K. Tanenhaus, James S. Magnuson, Bob M. McMurray & Richard N. Aslin (University of Rochester). Does lexical knowledge mediate perceptual effects of compensatory co-articulation? Evidence from research with an artificial lexicon

Jean Vroomen & Beatrice de Gelder (Tilburg University). Lipreading and the compensation for coarticulation mechanism

Doug Whalen (Haskins Laboratories). Occam's razor is a double-edged sword: Reduced interaction is not necessarily reduce power

Pienie Zwitserlood & Else Coenen (University of Münster). Consequences of assimilation for word recognition and lexical representation

Posters presented at SWAP

Petra van Alphen (MPI for Psycholinguistics). Does subcategorical variation influence lexical access?

Shigeaki Amano & Tadahisa Kondo (NTT Communication Science Laboratories). Neighbourhood and cohort in lexical processing of Japanese spoken words.

Jens Bölte & Else Coenen (University of Münster). *Domato* primes paprika: Mismatching pseudowords activate semantic and phonological representations.

Sami Boudelaa & William Marslen-Wilson (MRC Cognition and Brain Sciences Unit). Non-concatenative morphemes in language processing: Evidence from Modern Standard Arabic *Dannie van den Brink, Colin Brown & Peter Hagoort* (MPI for Psycholinguistics).

Electrophysiological evidence of early contextual influences during spoken-word recognition: The N200

Nicole Cooper (MPI for Psycholinguistics). Native and non-native processing of lexical stress in English word recognition

Anne Cutler, Dennis Norris & James M. McQueen (MPI for Psycholinguistics & MRC Cognition and Brain Sciences Unit). Tracking TRACE's troubles

Delphine Dahan, James S. Magnuson, Michael K. Tanenhaus & Ellen M. Hogan (MPI for Psycholinguistics & University of Rochester). Tracking the time course of subcategorical mismatches on lexical access: Evidence for lexical competition

Matt H. Davis, William D. Marslen-Wilson & M. Gareth Gaskell (MRC Cognition and Brain Sciences Unit & University of York). Lexical segmentation and ambiguity: Experimental and computational investigations of the recognition of onset-embedded words

Nicholas Dumay, Uli H. Frauenfelder & Alain Content (Free University of Brussels & University of Geneva). Acoustic-phonetic cues and lexical competition in segmentation of continuous speech

Usha Goswami & Bruno De Cara (Institute of Child Health). Lexical representations and development: The emergence of rime processing

Sarah Hawkins & Noel Nguyen (University of Cambridge & University of Provence). Predicting syllable-coda voicing from the acoustic properties of syllable onsets

Cecilia Kirk (University of Massachusetts, Amherst). Syllabic cues to word segmentation

Arie van der Lugt (University of Exeter). The time-course of competition

Kerstin Mauth (MPI for Psycholinguistics). Does morphological information influence phonetic categorisation?

Fanny Meunier, William Marslen-Wilson & Mike Ford (MRC Cognition and Brain Sciences Unit). Suffixed word lexical representations in French

Agnieszka A. Reid & William D. Marslen-Wilson (MRC Cognition and Brain Sciences Unit). Complexity and alternation in the Polish mental lexicon

Jennifer M. Rodd, M. Gareth Gaskell & William D. Marslen-Wilson (MRC Cognition and Brain Sciences Unit & University of York). Effects of semantic ambiguity in spoken word recognition

Joan Sereno & Hugo Quené (University of Kansas & University of Utrecht). Facilitation and inhibition using a segmental phonetic priming paradigm

Rachel Smith & Sarah Hawkins (University of Cambridge). Allophonic influences on word-spotting experiments

Liang Tao (Ohio University). Prosody and word recognition in Beijing Mandarin: A case study

Andrea Weber (MPI for Psycholinguistics). The role of phonotactics in the segmentation of native and non-native continuous speech

LANGUAGE AND COGNITIVE PROCESSES, 2001, *16* (5/6), 469–490

Spoken word access processes: An introduction

James M. McQueen and Anne Cutler

Max Planck Institute for Psycholinguistics, Nijmegen, The Netherlands

We introduce the papers in this special issue by summarising the current major issues in spoken word recognition. We argue that a full understanding of the process of lexical access during speech comprehension will depend on resolving several key representational issues: what is the form of the representations used for lexical access; how is phonological information coded in the mental lexicon; and how is the morphological and semantic information about each word stored? We then discuss a number of distinct access processes: competition between lexical hypotheses; the computation of goodness-of-fit between the signal and stored lexical knowledge; segmentation of continuous speech; whether the lexicon influences prelexical processing through feedback; and the relationship of form-based processing to the processes responsible for deriving an interpretation of a complete utterance. We conclude that further progress may well be made by swapping ideas among the different sub-domains of the discipline.

The proportion of the world's population that is kept awake at night worrying about spoken word access processes is, undoubtedly, vanishingly small. After all, hardly anyone has even heard the phrase *Spoken word access processes*. Such things are hardly the stuff mobile-phone conversations are made on. And yet in another way, as we psycholinguists know, spoken word access processes are what those conversations depend on. An English listener chosen at random might not understand this phrase as a whole, but this would not be because of a failure to recognise the words themselves.

Spoken word recognition is remarkably robust and seemingly effortless. Chances are high that our native speaker of English would be able to recognise our four-word phrase with no difficulty, even if it were spoken over a mobile phone in a noisy station by someone whose voice he or she had never heard before, irrespective of how fast that talker spoke, and

---

Requests for reprints should be sent to James M. McQueen, Max Planck Institute for Psycholinguistics, Wundtlaan 1, 6525 XD Nijmegen, The Netherlands. Email: james.mcqueen@mpi.nl

---

http://www.tandf.co.uk/journals/pp/01690965.html   DOI: 10.1080/01690960143000209

irrespective of the sex or age of the talker. This is in spite of the fact that all of these factors can radically alter the acoustic characteristics of the phrase. The robustness and effortlessness of spoken word recognition make it something that listeners simply take for granted. They do not appreciate that there is a complex problem to be solved in speech recognition; it just happens. How often have spoken-word recognition researchers, in answer to polite questions about what it is they do, found themselves explaining not their research itself, but rather that there is in fact a domain of enquiry there to be studied? One of the problems here is the lack of a simple word in English to describe the act of recognising words in the spoken domain, like "to read" in the written domain. Curiously, other languages do have speech-specific listening words (like "verstaan" in Dutch and "kikitoru" in Japanese); anglophones appear particularly uninterested in speech recognition.

Spoken word access processes, therefore, are mental processes which listeners take for granted. They are not the processes by which a listener interprets the sequence of words in an utterance, but rather the processes by which that sequence of words is derived from the acoustic speech signal. They are the perceptual processes which take the sequence of buzzes, bursts, and chirps that make up the raw acoustic signal and convert them into a sequence of words. These word-sequences form our primary perceptual representation of spoken language and form the input to the interpretative processes by which we derive the meaning of utterances.

This volume contains articles and short reports based on presentations at the workshop Spoken Word Access Processes (SWAP), held in Nijmegen in May 2000. The papers cover the major issues that the field is currently concerned with, and thus, like the workshop, provide a snapshot of the state of the SWAP art. We summarise those issues here, as they relate to the papers in this volume, and to the other papers presented at the SWAP workshop (as listed in the Appendix to the Preface). We will refer to the authors of papers and short reports in the present issue using bold type, and to the others who presented at SWAP using italics.

Although the field is only just over a quarter of a century old, much has already been learned about spoken word recognition. As the present papers attest, however, much remains uncertain. Fortunately, as the papers also attest, the field is still very active. We hope that in another 25 years we will know yet more about spoken word access processes, even if the mobile-phone users of the 2020s continue to be blissfully ignorant of them.

THE SPOKEN WORD

What, then, are spoken words? What are the mental entities which we recognise when we listen to spoken language? Many answers to this question have been proposed, ranging from the claim that words in the mental lexicon are highly detailed episodic representations (i.e., each individual utterance of a word is stored in the form in which it is heard, coding, for example, information about the speaker that spoke it and the nature of any background noise) to the claim that the lexicon consists of highly abstract phonological representations (such as those in under-specification theory which code only the information necessary to specify the phonological form of a word). Three themes related to this issue were discussed at SWAP and are represented in this volume: the unit of perception, phonological representation, and semantic and morphological representation.

The unit of perception

The spoken word does not consist of easily identifiable and extractable subunits. While it is possible to describe a spoken word as a sequence of phonemes, or as a sequence of syllables, or as a complex bundle of acoustic-phonetic features, it is extremely hard to identify those units (of whatever grain size) in the acoustic speech signal. In particular, it is impossible to identify the exact temporal locations of the beginnings or ends of phonemes (or features, syllables or words). Since talkers coarticulate (the vocal-tract gestures for neighbouring sounds can be made simultaneously), the speech signal does not consist of a sequence of discrete units. One of the most venerable but still recurring issues in spoken word recognition, therefore, is whether there is an intermediate level of representation between the input and the mental lexicon, and, if so, what the "units of perception" at that level of processing are.

This issue is of course intimately related to the issue of the form that words take in the mental lexicon. Since these intermediate units form the lexical access code (the means by which the speech signal makes contact with the lexicon) then, on the simplest account, access and lexical representations should have the same units (e.g., phonemic access representations should map onto a phonemically structured lexicon). At the very least, there should be a straightforward mapping of prelexical representations onto lexical representations.

Nearey argues that phonemes play a central role in speech recognition. He presents simulations showing how the recognition of nonsense syllables can be very well predicted from the recognition of their component phonemes. He also argues that a model in which syllables are factored into their phonemes can account for the results of multidimensional phonetic categorisation experiments. **Miller** takes Nearey's line of argument further. She bases her argument on research examining variation in speaking rate. She has shown in earlier work that the processes which make adjustments for changes in speaking rate are mandatory (e.g., Miller & Dexter, 1988); listeners automatically adjust their criteria for interpreting durational cues to speech sounds depending on the speaking rate. One such cue is Voice Onset Time (VOT), in English stop consonants. A VOT which counts as a good /p/, for example, at one speaking rate, will be judged to be a poorer /p/ at a different speaking rate (Miller & Volaitis, 1989). In the present paper, Miller describes how changes in speaking rate and changes in lexical context have qualitatively different effects on category goodness judgements. A key underlying assumption, however, consistent with Nearey's arguments, is that there are prelexical representations which are essentially phonemic in nature. Category goodness judgements are therefore considered to be based on phonemic categories which are extracted prelexically, and which have internal structure.

On the basis of these two papers, it might therefore appear that there is now agreement not only that there are "units of perception", but also that they are phonemic. This, however, is definitely not the case. *Goldinger*, following up on his earlier research (e.g., Goldinger, 1996, 1998), argued at SWAP for the episodic view: that the lexicon consists of detailed episodic traces of individual words. Listeners certainly appear to have detailed memories of specific instances of words. Palmeri, Goldinger, and Pisoni (1993), for example, showed that listeners could recognise more rapidly that a word in a spoken list had already occurred in that list if the word was said by the same speaker earlier in the list than if it had been said by someone else. Goldinger showed, furthermore, that subjects appear to imitate words that they have previously heard, that is, their utterances of a particular word tend to be more like another token of that word (spoken by another speaker) after they have heard that token than before they have heard it. These results appear inconsistent with the view that the lexicon consists only of abstract phonological representations, which can only be accessed by abstract phonemic representations. *Hawkins and Nguyen*, in their SWAP poster, also argued against this strong abstractionist position. They showed that listeners' decisions about word-final stops are influenced by the acoustic-phonetic nature of the [l] at the onset of those words. These kinds of data suggest that coarticulation can create dependencies even between non-adjacent sounds in production. It would also be more consistent with a model in which lexical entries contain subtle acoustic-phonetic details rather than abstract strings of phonemes.

Dupoux, Pallier, Mehler, and Kakehi, on the other hand, argue for abstract intermediate representations. Results from an experiment on Japanese vowel epenthesis suggest that Japanese listeners use their knowledge about the phonological structure of Japanese to create an abstract lexical access code. They appear to create, for example, epenthetic vowels in locations where such vowels should appear in the speech signal (i.e., between consonants) even if there is no vocalic information actually present in the input. While Dupoux et al. are agnostic about the nature of prelexical representations (they could be phonemic, syllabic, or moraic), their data certainly challenge the view that there are no such representations.

It therefore seems that the most extreme positions in the debate about "units of perception" are no longer tenable. Those arguing for an episodic account of the lexicon, with no intermediate abstract phonological representations, need to address the data which demonstrate abstraction and normalisation. The reverse is of course equally true: those arguing for prelexical representations, be they phonemic or otherwise, need to confront the data showing that listeners are able to remember the fine detail associated with particular utterances of particular words. There is therefore considerable scope for the development of what one might call "hybrid models", that is, accounts of spoken word recognition with both episodic and abstractionist components.

One of the major problems with the old "units of perception" debate (are syllables, phonemes, features or something else the basic units?) was that the data simply did not distinguish clearly between these alternatives (see, e.g., McQueen & Cutler, 1997; Pisoni & Luce, 1987). As *Whalen* pointed out at SWAP, this remains a problem. Marslen-Wilson and Warren (1994), for example, made the case that acoustic-phonetic features are the basic lexical access units, but it has since been shown that their data can equally well be explained by a model with phonemic access representations (**Dahan, Magnuson, Tanenhaus, & Hogan**; McQueen, Norris, & Cutler, 1999; Norris, McQueen & Cutler, 2000). We hope that more progress may be made on this issue if more attention is devoted to the distinction between abstractionist and episodic accounts than to distinctions among different types of access units.

Phonological representation

Spoken words are highly variable. In normal speech, words rarely appear in their citation forms, that is, as they would do if spoken slowly and carefully in isolation. Some of this variation is due to factors which we have already mentioned; changes in the rate of speech of the talker, the talker's age, sex, dialect, and speaking style, as well as changes in the amount and nature of background noise, all influence the acoustic form of a spoken word. Though some of this variation is very unpredictable (the exact form of a novel talker's vocal tract; how carefully a talker will utter a particular word), some of it is more predictable (the spectral structure of a talker's vowels, indicating for example that she is female, can be used to predict the form of her vowels later in the utterance; faster speaking rate will tend to shorten all segments in an utterance). This kind of variation has in fact provided one of the primary motivations for a prelexical level of processing. Normalisation processes can act on the signal at this level of processing, to adjust for this variability and to generate an abstract code which can then be used for lexical access. Further research on the effects of fine-grained acoustic-phonetic detail due to this kind of variation on the lexical access process should lead to advances in our understanding of prelexical representations.

Another kind of variation, however, is very predictable. Changes in the surface form of spoken words can be predicted by phonological rules of assimilation, epenthesis, deletion, and resyllabification. Several presentations at SWAP addressed how this kind of variation is dealt with during spoken word recognition. How is the word *sweet*, for example, recognised when it is pronounced as [swik] in the phrase *sweet girl*? Answers to this question again have an intimate relationship with the issue of the phonological form of words in the mental lexicon. One proposal, for example, is that the lexicon consists of underspecified phonological representations (e.g., Lahiri & Marslen-Wilson, 1991). Since English words ending in coronal stops, like *sweet*, can undergo place assimilation, and take on the place of articulation of a following bilabial or velar consonant, their lexical representations can be considered to lack specification of the place of articulation of their final phonemes. Thus, when a listener hears [swik], for example, the final [k] will not mismatch with the lexical representation of *sweet*.

Coenen, Zwitserlood, and Bölte present evidence from German which challenges this view. They show that recognition of an assimilated form depends on the availability of an appropriate phonological context: the pattern of results for words in isolation was not the same as for words in sentence contexts. These results are consistent with similar findings in English (Gaskell & Marslen-Wilson, 1996, 1998; Marslen-Wilson, Nix, & Gaskell, 1995). Just as in phonology, where many theorists have moved away from underspecification theory (towards, e.g., Optimality Theory), so too are psycholinguists moving away from the view that the lexicon consists of underspecified representations. Results such as those of Coenen et al. suggest that, even if lexical representations are abstract, there need also to be what Gaskell and Marslen-Wilson (1996, 1998) have referred to as phonological inference processes: mechanisms which evaluate the surface form of words in the phonological context of their neighbouring words.

Pierrehumbert also discusses the phonological form of words in the mental lexicon, but from a rather different perspective. The question which she addresses concerns learning: how we come to master the phonological regularities of our native language. She shows that as vocabulary size increases, even though different listeners will have different words in their vocabularies, more complex phonological regularities can be inferred. If the recognition of words that have undergone assimilation (or had some other phonological process applied to them in production) requires inference processes, then these processes must themselves be acquired. Accounts of the acquisition of spoken language therefore need to explain not only how spoken forms are learned, and how those forms are linked to meanings, but also how phonological inferencing processes can be acquired through exposure to the very words which will later be recognised through the operation of those processes.

Semantic and morphological representation

The third issue concerning representation that was discussed at SWAP was the relationship between the phonological form of a word and the other information stored in the mental lexicon. How is the knowledge about the form of a word linked to its syntactic and semantic properties? *Shillcock* showed that there are small but striking relationships between form and meaning: similar sounding words tend to be similar in meaning. Phonetic symbolism of this type has implications for the structure of the lexicon and, Shillcock argued, may be the result of the brain's tendency to store information topographically. *Rodd, Gaskell and Marslen-Wilson's* poster focused more exclusively on the semantic level. They discussed how semantically ambiguous words are recognised. It appears that words with multiple meanings (e.g., *bark*) are recognised more slowly than unambiguous words, while those with multiple senses (e.g., *twist*) are recognised more rapidly. Rodd et al. argued that these results are consistent with models of the lexicon with distributed semantic representations: competition between multiple meanings delays recognition, while the additional information provided by words with multiple senses benefits recognition.

How might these semantic representations be linked to representations of word forms? One common assumption is that, intervening between sound and meaning representations, there are morphemic representations. Morphemes are, after all, the link between form and content. While most psycholinguists agree that there is a morphological level of representation (e.g., Marslen-Wilson, Tyler, Waksler & Older, 1994; Schreuder & Baayen, 1995; see McQueen & Cutler, 1998, for a review), there is considerable disagreement about exactly what kind of information is coded there. Are morphologically complex words stored as wholes, or in their component parts, and, if so, is this equally true for derived, inflected, and compounded words? **Marslen-Wilson** reviews recent cross-linguistic work on this issue. This kind of research was reported in several posters at SWAP: work on Arabic by *Boudelaa and Marslen-Wilson*, on French by *Meunier, Marslen-*

Wilson and Ford and on Polish by *Reid and Marslen-Wilson*. It appears that there are no language-universals here: the kind of morphological information that is stored in a given listener's mental lexicon seems to depend on the morphological structure of that listener's native language; some languages encourage a more strongly decompositional form of representation than others.

Cross-linguistic research has proved to be very valuable in developing our understanding of spoken word recognition, for example in the domain of speech segmentation (see, e.g., Cutler, Mehler, Norris & Segui, 1986; Otake, Hatano, Cutler & Mehler, 1993). Such comparisons can show which aspects of speech processing are shared by speakers of all languages, and which reflect adaptation to particular structures in the listener's native language. They can also show the limitations in theorising which may be imposed when most of the available data come from a very small number of languages. We therefore welcome and encourage more cross-linguistic work, not only in the domain of morphology, where it has again already proved to be very valuable, but also in other domains of SWAP.

ACCESS PROCESSES

Competition

How then are spoken words accessed and recognised? The field began to make serious progress on this aspect of the topic with the advent of computational models in the mid-1980s. There is now virtually unanimous agreement on the broad outline of the lexical access process. From an enormous amount of research we know that lexical access involves continuous activation of multiple candidate words, and that there is a process of competition between the activated candidates out of which the eventual winning words emerge (see, for example, Allopenna, Magnuson, & Tanenhaus, 1998; Cluff & Luce, 1990; Gow & Gordon, 1995; Marslen-Wilson, 1987, 1990; Marslen-Wilson, Moss, & Van Halen, 1996; McQueen, Norris, & Cutler, 1994; Norris, McQueen, & Cutler, 1995; Shillcock, 1990; Swinney, 1981; Tabossi, Burani, & Scott, 1995; Vroomen & de Gelder, 1995, 1997; Wallace, Stewart, & Malone, 1995; Wallace, Stewart, Sherman, & Mellor, 1995; Zwitserlood, 1989; Zwitserlood & Schriefers, 1995).

Evidence from phonological priming studies (Goldinger, Luce, & Pisoni, 1989; Goldinger, Luce, Pisoni, & Marcario, 1992; Monsell & Hirsh, 1998; Radeau, Morais, & Segui, 1995; Slowiaczek & Hamburger, 1992; and *Sereno & Quené*, at SWAP) also suggests that candidate words compete with one another during word recognition. *Amano and Kondo's* statistical analyses of the structure of the Japanese lexicon were inspired by the idea that multiple candidate words are activated when a spoken word is heard. *Goswami and De Cara* showed that the emergence of phonological awareness in children, specifically children's judgements about rhyme, is influenced by the number of words sharing the same rime. These results suggest yet again that spoken word recognition involves the activation of multiple candidate words.

Vitevitch and Luce (1998, 1999) have argued that the spoken word recognition system is sensitive to sound similarities between words at two distinct levels of processing. If many words share the same sequence of phonemes, that sequence will tend to occur often in speech. Vitevitch and Luce observed facilitatory effects due to the frequency of phoneme sequences, which they attributed to a sublexical level of processing, where common sequences of sounds are easier to process than rare sequences. This level of processing might be analogous to the prelexical level of processing discussed above – an intermediate level that acts as an interface between the acoustic-phonetic speech signal and the lexicon. Vitevitch and Luce also observed inhibitory effects of sound similarity and argued that they were due to competition between words at the lexical level. If a word has many lexical neighbours (i.e., similar sounding words), which are all activated when that word is heard, that word will be harder to recognise than a word in a sparse neighbourhood. **Luce and Large** provide further evidence for the simultaneous operation of sublexical facilitation and lexical competition during spoken word recognition.

Mismatch

Not all the details of the activation and competition process are agreed on, however. Many issues are still subject to research and debate, including: which information affects activation; whether some types of information are more strongly weighted than others; and exactly how the competition process is structured (e.g., does it involve lateral inhibition?). These issues received considerable attention at SWAP. Among the posters was work on the use of tone information in lexical access in Mandarin (*Tao*), and work on how both native and non-native listeners process lexical stress information while listening to English (*Cooper*). The question here is whether prosodic information is used to constrain lexical access. Answers to this question have clear implications not only for the form of lexical representations, but also for the form of prelexical representations. Purely phonemic access representations, for example, cannot code lexical stress information. The study of non-native speech processing is of course interesting in its own right. How do listeners recognise the words of a second language? Second language listeners certainly draw on access processes used for first language comprehension in recognising their second language (see Cutler, in press, for a review); but are they able to learn new procedures or to suppress inappropriate old procedures? Second-language research is, however, also relevant to models of native word recognition; the way listeners process their second languages is likely to be informative about how they process their first languages. As with other cross-linguistic work, second language research provides a means of examining to what extent access processes are language-universal, and to what extent they are tuned to the specific phonological properties of particular languages.

The poster by *Bölte and Coenen* examined segmental rather than suprasegmental constraints on lexical access. To what extent is a word activated when the input mismatches with that word by one phoneme? *Van der Lugt* examined whether mismatching information in a carrier word fragment would influence the lexical competition process, and hence the detection of a shorter word embedded in the carrier. The work by Bölte and Coenen and by van der Lugt follows in the tradition of work on segmental mismatch carried out by Connine and colleagues (e.g., Connine, Blasko, & Wang, 1994; Connine, Titone, Deelman, & Blasko, 1997). This kind of work has clear parallels with that done on assimilation. In the assimilation case, a phoneme is substituted which, though appropriate to the phonological environment, is inconsistent with the isolated, citation form of the word. In the other work on mismatch, however, the substituted phoneme is not licensed by the phonological environment. Although the system appears fairly intolerant of this kind of mismatching information, small amounts of mismatch do not necessarily block lexical access (Connine et al., 1994, 1997; Marslen-Wilson et al., 1996). The access system appears to be more tolerant, however, of the "mismatch" caused by assimilation or other phonological processes. In other words, the system seems to tolerate natural variation.

Frauenfelder, Scholten, and Content test the predictions that the TRACE model (McClelland & Elman, 1986) and the Shortlist model (Norris, 1994) make about the effects of mismatching segmental information on lexical activation. They present results from two phoneme monitoring experiments in which target phonemes appeared in real French words and in nonwords which had been constructed by changing one or more phonemes of French words. They manipulated the position of the target phoneme and, in the nonwords, the position of the phoneme(s) which mismatched with the original real word (e.g., the [f] in *focabulaire* and the [n] in *vocabulaine*, both based on *vocabulaire*, vocabulary). Frauenfelder et al. argue that their results challenge TRACE (where mismatching information does not actively count against the activation of candidate words), but are consistent with Shortlist (where bottom-up inhibition from mismatching phonemes can strongly deactivate candidate words). As this paper attests, the evaluation of computational implementations of models of spoken word recognition has become an important part of the field.

Subsegmental constraints on lexical access were also examined at SWAP. The poster by *van Alphen* showed that variation in the amount of prevoicing in Dutch voiced stops does not appear to influence the degree of activation of words containing those stops. In this particular case, then, variation in the signal does not seem to affect the outcome of the lexical access process. In their poster, however, *Davis, Marslen-Wilson, and Gaskell* argued that words embedded in other words, like *cap* in *captain*, are acoustically different from unembedded tokens of those words (i.e., when the talker actually intends *cap*), and that the lexical access system is sensitive to these differences.

Dahan et al. examine other subsegmental effects: the influence on lexical access of mismatch between place of articulation cues in vowels and place cues in following stops (e.g., in a token of *net*, made by splicing the [nɛ] from *neck*, with cues in the vowel signalling the upcoming velar [k], to a final alveolar [t] release burst). Using an eye-tracking paradigm (subjects were asked to look at a visual display and to follow instructions like "click on the net"), Dahan et al. found evidence that word activation is influenced by subsegmental mismatch and evidence of competition between activated candidate words. These results support those obtained with similar materials using gating, lexical decision, and phoneme decisions tasks (Marslen-Wilson & Warren, 1994; McQueen et al., 1999). Dahan et al. also simulate their data with the TRACE model. Their paper again demonstrates how important it is to evaluate how well computational models can account for a particular set of data. The interplay between data and modelling will, we hope, continue to drive research in spoken word recognition.

The eye-tracking paradigm holds considerable promise; it appears that subtler differences in lexical activation can be tracked (and with greater temporal resolution) with this paradigm than with more traditional reaction time paradigms. While the lexical access system may be sensitive to the subsegmental differences, however, it is also very robust. Thus the asymptotic state of the recognition system should be the same for different surface variants of the same underlying utterance (i.e., the same words will be recognised in spite of small variations in the surface forms). It is thus perhaps not surprising that subsegmental mismatch effects appear to be rather subtle. We feel that considerable work remains to be done to map out the effects of fine-grained phonetic information on the lexical access process, using eye-tracking and other paradigms. As we pointed out earlier, the speech signal contains finer quality information than can be captured by a phonemic transcription, both with respect to the information available at any one moment in time and with respect to how that information can change over a very fine time-scale. Attention to this kind of detail will be important for the development not only of accounts of prelexical representation but also of the lexical competition process.

Segmentation

Spoken words usually occur not by themselves but in the middle of a running stream of speech sounds. Coarticulation of speech sounds occurs not only within but between words. This means that, at least within phonological phrases, speech tends to be a continuous stream of sounds, rather than a discontinuous sequence of words. Speech certainly lacks the reliable and unambiguous marking of word boundaries which is provided by the white spaces between the words in this text. One of the essential components of the lexical access process is therefore segmentation: how are discrete words recovered from the speech stream? Several presentations at SWAP were devoted to this theme.

Content, Meunier, Kearns, and Frauenfelder examine segmentation in French. They challenge the old idea that word recognition in French is based on a syllabic classification of the speech stream (i.e., that the prelexical "unit of perception" is the syllable; Mehler, 1981; Mehler, Dommergues, Frauenfelder, & Segui, 1981). They argue instead that syllables provide cues for lexical segmentation, specifically, that syllable onsets indicate the likely locations of word boundaries. While the theory of segmentation based on syllabic classification necessarily makes a strong claim about the nature of prelexical representations, the theory proposed by Content et al. is neutral on this topic. No claim about the size of the units in the lexical access code needs to be made; all that is required is that the locations of syllable onsets can be extracted prelexically and then used to constrain lexical access.

The view proposed by Content et al. has close links with that discussed by **Norris, McQueen, Cutler, Butterfield, and Kearns**. On Norris et al.'s view, segmentation is achieved through lexical competition (i.e., as in both TRACE and Shortlist). The competition process is, however, enriched by a segmentation procedure, the Possible Word Constraint (PWC; Norris, McQueen, Cutler, & Butterfield, 1997). The PWC uses cues in the speech signal to the location of likely word boundaries (including, for example, syllable onset locations in French). The PWC also uses information about what speech material constitutes a plausible part of the ongoing lexical parse. A section of speech between a candidate word and the location of a likely word boundary must contain a vowel. If there is only consonantal material, then that candidate word is not likely to be part of the utterance and its activation is therefore reduced (thus, for example, *arm* in "sheep farm" is penalised because the [f] between the beginning of *arm* and the boundary between the [p] and the [f], in this case signalled by the phonotactics of English, is not a possible word). Note that the boundary cues listeners use are necessarily language-specific. The sequence [pf], for example, though impossible within an English syllable, is possible in German syllables. Norris et al. review evidence which suggests that the PWC itself is, however, a simple, language-universal constraint. Irrespective of the phonological constraints as to what constitutes a well-formed word in any particular language, the information that is used in on-line segmentation is simply whether the residue of speech between a candidate word and a likely word boundary contains a vowel.

Four posters at SWAP also addressed issues in segmentation. *Dumay, Frauenfelder and Content* presented further evidence on French segmentation, arguing that in addition to the cues provided by syllable onsets, lexical competition has an important role to play. Dumay et al. also argued, along with *Smith and Hawkins*, that fine differences in the available acoustic-phonetic information have consequences for segmentation: some boundaries may be marked more clearly than others. In Smith and Hawkins' case, these acoustic differences were due to allophonic variation (differences between the syllable-onset and syllable-coda allophones of English consonants). *Kirk* had a similar point to make about English listeners' use of allophonic variation in segmentation. She also argued that constraints from phonological grammar (e.g., the tendency to maximise the number of consonants in a syllable onset, or the tendency for stressed syllables to attract consonants) can also influence how continuous speech is segmented. *Weber* showed that German listeners use their knowledge of both German phonotactics and English phonotactics in the segmentation of English speech. These findings are consistent with other demonstrations of the use of phonotactics in segmentation (Van der Lugt, in press; McQueen, 1998; Yip, 2000). Weber's results also show how the procedures that are adopted when learning to segment and recognise one's native language are recruited in segmenting a second language.

There is therefore now a relatively long list of cues which listeners appear to use for segmentation and which vary among languages, including phonotactics, allophonics, other acoustic-phonetic cues, silence, and metrical cues based on the input language's rhythmic structure. An important issue which remains to be addressed is the relative ranking of these cues: do some cues carry more weight in segmentation than others? Another issue for future research links work on segmentation to work on mismatching information in lexical access. To what extent do cues in the speech signal have their effect by directly influencing the degree of activation of lexical representations, and to what extent do they provide boundary markers, by which a segmentation procedure like the PWC can then, indirectly, influence lexical activation?

Feedback?

Despite the agreement that has been achieved on the sort of architecture needed to model access processes, there is one giant issue of disagreement still remaining, namely whether the flow of information within the spoken-word recognition system is unidirectional or bidirectional. Is there feedback from the lexicon to the prelexical level, such that lexical knowledge can influence the earlier stages in the lexical access process? There was extensive discussion of this issue at the SWAP workshop. Indeed, one of the motivations for the workshop was to continue the discussion of this issue as centered round the Merge model (Norris et al., 2000), in which there is no feedback. Many of those present at SWAP had contributed commentaries on the *Behavioral and Brain Sciences* target article, and many had attended a stimulating discussion on the topic at the fall 1999 ASA meeting in Columbus, Ohio. SWAP was thus round three in this debate.

One important result to come out of the meeting was that it appeared that a consensus had been reached on what counts as a necessary test of feedback. Experimental demonstrations of lexical involvement in phonemic decision-making can be explained either as a result of feedback from the lexicon to prelexical phonemic representations, the activation of which then determine the decisions (as in TRACE), or as a result of feedforward connections from the lexicon to a level of processing where explicit phonemic decisions are made (as in Merge). What is needed to distinguish between these accounts is therefore an unambiguous measure of prelexical processing. We can then ask whether the lexicon influences prelexical processing (as a feedback model would predict) or not (as a model without feedback would predict). One such measure of prelexical processing is the demonstration that the perceptual system appears to adjust for coarticulation between neighbouring consonants. Specifically, identification of stop consonants varies depending on the nature of preceding fricatives (Mann & Repp, 1981) or liquids (Mann, 1980). Most psycholinguists are agreed that this compensation for coarticulation process has a prelexical locus. Although some have argued that the effect is due to general, low-level acoustic contrast effects (Lotto & Kluender, 1998; Lotto, Kluender & Holt, 1997), recent research suggests that it reflects speech-specific processes (Fowler, Brown, & Mann, 2000).

Elman and McClelland (1988), in a well-known paper, appeared to demonstrate lexical involvement in fricative-stop compensation for coarticulation, as predicted by TRACE. Pitt and McQueen (1998), however, have shown that this effect was likely to be due to transitional probability differences (between the vowels and fricatives in the different lexical contexts). They also demonstrated a dissociation between lexical involvement in decisions about the fricative sounds and, simultaneously, no lexical involvement in compensation for coarticulation. This dissociation is predicted by Merge, but not by TRACE.

Given the importance of compensation for coarticulation to the feedback debate, it perhaps comes as no surprise that five talks at SWAP were on this topic. Three of these presentations described the beginnings of ongoing research projects. *Fowler and Brancazio* proposed an ingenious test of the Merge model, where lexical information is provided by visual (lip-read) speech. Does this visual information also influence compensation for coarticulation? *Tanenhaus, Magnuson, McMurray and Aslin* proposed another ingenious test, this time using an artificial language-learning paradigm to manipulate "lexical status" and transitional probabilities in nonsense contexts, and then to measure, using the eye-tracking paradigm, whether these contexts influence compensation for coarticulation. *Kingston* sought to examine the effect of compensation for coarticulation on both stop identification and stop discrimination. The important issue here is whether the contexts (in Kingston's case, the liquids [l] and [r]) influence perceptual sensitivity.

Vroomen and de Gelder, like Fowler and Brancazio, examine the influence of visual speech on fricative-stop compensation for coarticulation. They found, in a parallel to Pitt and McQueen (1998), a dissociation: listeners used lipread information in identifying fricatives, but did not appear to use this information to identify the following stops. In contrast to the recent results of Fowler et al. (2000), lipread information did not appear to modulate the compensation for coarticulation mechanism. While this particular contradiction remains to be resolved, it seems clear that the study of the integration of auditory and visual speech cues can be valuable not only in the feedback debate, but perhaps also in other domains of spoken word recognition. For example, do visual cues to speech sounds carry as much weight as auditory cues in the activation of lexical hypotheses?

Samuel also examines lexical involvement in compensation for coarticulation. He describes recent results, which, like those of Elman and McClelland (1988), appear to show an influence of lexical context (in fricative-final words) on the identification of following stops. Unlike Elman and McClelland's materials, however, the new materials are controlled for the transitional probabilities between the word-final fricatives and the preceding vowels. These results, always assuming that they do not, like those of Elman and McClelland, prove to be open to an explanation which does not require lexical feedback, appear to challenge Merge's assumption that there is no feedback from the lexicon to prelexical levels.

Another potential measure of prelexical processing, and thus a possible tool for testing claims about feedback, is the selective adaptation effect. When listeners hear multiple tokens of a speech sound, and are then required to label a continuum of sounds between the adaptor phoneme and another phoneme, they tend to label ambiguous sounds less often as the adaptor than as the other phoneme (Eimas & Corbit, 1973). Samuel (1997) has demonstrated lexical influences on selective adaptation, using words with noise-replaced phonemes as adaptors, and **Samuel** describes similar effects using words with ambiguous phonemes as adaptors. He argues that this is further evidence for feedback. As we have discussed elsewhere (Norris et al., 2000), however, we are not yet convinced that the locus of the adaptation effect with noise-replaced phonemes is purely prelexical. The same argument applies to adaptation with ambiguous phonemes. Selective adaptation may thus not provide a critical test of feedback.

One other paper also discussed lexical effects and the feedback issue. **Pitt and Shoaf** describe the Verbal Transformation Effect (VTE): when listeners hear the same word repeated very many times at a rapid rate, the word tends to be perceived as other words. They report lexical effects in the VTE, and examine their cause. These lexical effects could perhaps be used to evaluate whether there is feedback in spoken word recognition. This issue is certainly not settled, so new approaches to the problem are certainly to be welcomed. As we argued in Norris et al. (2000), feedback is unnecessary since it cannot benefit word recognition. Since feedback is useless for word recognition, convincing evidence is required to show that it does in fact exist in the human speech recognition system. We were delighted to see so many people at SWAP taking up this challenge.

In addition to these developments, further progress may be made by considering the feedback issue in the context of the other issues discussed here. For example, consider the fact that the argument for feedback depends on the assumption that there are phonemic prelexical representations, from which explicit phonemic decisions are made. In a radically episodic model, for example, with no prelexical level of representation, or in a model where the prelexical representations are featural, there are no phoneme units that lexical activation could be fed back to. If phoneme representations have to be constructed in the context of such models to explain lexical effects on phonemic decision-making, then those representations are, by definition, not part of the lexical access system, and any flow of information to those representations therefore cannot entail feedback. More generally, the feedback question hinges on assumptions about a hierarchy of representations including, minimally, prelexical and lexical levels. In the context of a highly distributed model, with no discrete representations of word forms or of sublexical units, for example, it becomes hard to define what would or would not constitute lexical involvement in prelexical processing, and feedback might not be a relevant concept. Claims about information flow and claims about representations are thus interdependent.

Higher-level processes

A major challenge facing the field is the unification of work on lexical semantics with work on lexical form. How, if at all, does the retrieval of a word's meaning impinge upon recognition of its form? Word meanings are usually considered to be involved at the level of processing where an interpretation of an utterance is achieved, that is, at a later stage of processing than that at which a parse of the lexical forms of an utterance is constructed. This is therefore another question about feedback, but now at the interface between interpretative and lexical-form processing rather than the interface between lexical-form and prelexical processing. Several presentations addressed this issue at SWAP, in a number of different ways.

Gaskell asks whether sentential context can influence the identification of potentially assimilated forms of words. For example, the [rʌm] in [... rʌmpɪks ...] could either be the word *rum* or an assimilated token of the word *run*. Gaskell shows that *run* is activated by this input, but only in the context of a preceding sentence about running. *Nooteboom, Janse, Quené and te Riele*, in a rhyme detection experiment, showed that sentence context can have a very rapid effect on the activation of words. Words rhyming with a prespecified cue word were detected faster when they were predictable from the sentence context. *Van den Brink, Brown and Hagoort*, using an Event-Related Potential (ERP) measure, also demonstrated rapid use of sentential context during spoken word recognition. ERP waveforms diverged 150 ms after word onset for words in congruent versus incongruent contexts. *Mauth* showed that Dutch listeners in a phonetic categorisation task tend to interpret an ambiguous word-final sound on a [xat]-[xak] continuum as [t], thus forming the inflected Dutch verb *gaat* (goes), rather than the nonword *gaak*. But again this effect was only observed in a sentence context.

Bard, Sotillo, Kelly, and Aylett, finally, review evidence suggesting that word recognition requires the use, not only of acoustic-phonetic and lexical information, but also discourse information. They argue that there is so much variability in casual continuous speech, caused by phenomena such as deaccenting, vowel reduction, consonant deletion, and assimilation, that there is no simple way to predict or constrain these phonological changes. They therefore suggest that one way listeners deal with this variability is that they use their knowledge about the ongoing discourse to resolve the ambiguities in the signal.

One could interpret all of these results as evidence of feedback from interpretative levels of processing to the level of word-form processing. Sentential context could thus exert a direct effect on the activation of lexical candidates. But there is an alternative explanation, akin to that offered by the Merge model to account for lexical context effects on phonemic processing. This is that sentence context has its influence by feeding information forward to a level of perceptual decision-making, rather than back to the representations of word-forms initially activated by the speech signal. This is not a new idea. Indeed, several authors have argued that sentence context does not influence the process of speech encoding, but instead influences perceptual decision-making (Van Alphen & McQueen, in press; Connine, 1987; Samuel, 1981). A common view is that sentential context can influence lexical selection (the choice from a set of activated candidate words) but not which words are activated (which is determined by the signal alone; see, e.g., Marslen-Wilson, 1987; Zwitserlood, 1989). But it remains unclear whether feedback is required to explain effects of context on lexical selection. Feedback is involved only if the context modulates the activation of word-form representations. If instead context influences some other representation of that word, such as its morphemic representation, or has its influence only on perceptual decisions, or if one considers that lexical selection occurs at the same level of processing as the construction of the interpretation of the utterance, then there is no need to postulate feedback to explain sentence context effects. What might be very useful in this debate would be an experiment analogous to those on compensation for coarticulation—that is, an experiment which examined whether sentence context influences a process which is an integral part of the process of word-form activation.

CONCLUSIONS

One of the benefits of a workshop conference is that presenters are encouraged (if not forced by persistent questioners) to re-evaluate their work in the context of other presentations. While written research papers do of course discuss new empirical results in the context of the relevant literature, what counts as relevant enough to be included in a particular article will in part be determined by space limitations. A workshop like SWAP thus provides a potentially much broader challenge than that thrown up by the requirement to write a well-integrated research article. Not many articles on mismatching information in lexical access, for example, will discuss the representation of morphologically complex words. And yet this kind of comparison of seemingly rather disparate issues raises important questions. What, for example, is accessed when a mispronounced word is heard? If both a representation of the word's phonological form and a representation of its morphological structure are activated, is the activation of both representations modulated by the mismatching information? Does the activation of the morphemic representation depend upon some criterial level of activation of the phonological representation?

We have therefore attempted in this review to draw attention to the connections between different issues in spoken word recognition. Assumptions that are taken for granted in one domain may well be those that are directly tested in another. This of course makes good sense, since meaningful experimental questions can only be asked by carving up the topic into smaller parts. But a look at the connections between sub-topics may well reveal new research questions, or new ways of looking at old questions. There are many more links to be drawn than we could discuss here; we encourage those reading the papers in this special issue to continue to draw them.

REFERENCES

Allopenna, P.D., Magnuson, J.S., & Tanenhaus, M.K. (1998). Tracking the time course of spoken word recognition using eye movements: Evidence for continuous mapping models. *Journal of Memory and Language, 38*, 419–439.

Cluff, M.S., & Luce, P.A. (1990). Similarity neighborhoods of spoken two-syllable words: Retroactive effects on multiple activation. *Journal of Experimental Psychology: Human Perception and Performance, 16*, 551–563.

Connine, C.M. (1987). Constraints on interactive processes in auditory word recognition: The role of sentence context. *Journal of Memory and Language, 26*, 527–538.

Connine, C.M., Blasko, D.G., & Wang, J. (1994). Vertical similarity in spoken word recognition: Multiple lexical activation, individual differences, and the role of sentence context. *Perception and Psychophysics, 56*, 624–636.

Connine, C.M., Titone, D., Deelman, T., & Blasko, D. (1997). Similarity mapping in spoken word recognition. *Journal of Memory and Language, 37*, 463–480.

Cutler, A. (in press). Listening to a second language through the ears of a first. *Interpreting.*

Cutler, A., Mehler, J., Norris, D., & Segui, J. (1986). The syllable's differing role in the segmentation of French and English. *Journal of Memory and Language, 25*, 385–400.

Eimas, P.D., & Corbit, J.D. (1973). Selective adaptation of linguistic feature detectors. *Cognitive Psychology, 4*, 99–109.

Elman, J.L., & McClelland, J.L. (1988). Cognitive penetration of the mechanisms of perception: Compensation for coarticulation of lexically restored phonemes. *Journal of Memory and Language, 27*, 143–165.

Fowler, C.A., Brown, J.M., & Mann, V.A. (2000). Contrast effects do not underlie effects of preceding liquids on stop-consonant identification by humans. *Journal of Experimental Psychology: Human Perception and Performance, 26*, 877–888.

Gaskell, G., & Marslen-Wilson, W.D. (1996). Phonological variation and inference in lexical access. *Journal of Experimental Psychology: Human Perception and Performance, 22*, 144–158.

Gaskell, M.G., & Marslen-Wilson, W.D. (1998). Mechanisms of phonological inference in speech perception. *Journal of Experimental Psychology: Human Perception and Performance, 24*, 380–396.

Goldinger, S.D. (1996). Words and voices: Episodic traces in spoken word identification and recognition memory. *Journal of Experimental Psychology: Learning, Memory, and Cognition, 22*, 1166–1183.

Goldinger, S.D. (1998). Echoes of echoes?: An episodic theory of lexical access. *Psychological Review, 105*, 251–279.

Goldinger, S.D., Luce, P.A., & Pisoni, D.B. (1989). Priming lexical neighbors of spoken words: Effects of competition and inhibition. *Journal of Memory and Language, 28*, 501–518.

Goldinger, S.D., Luce, P.A., Pisoni, D.B., & Marcario, J.K. (1992). Form-based priming in spoken word recognition: The roles of competition and bias. *Journal of Experimental Psychology: Learning, Memory, and Cognition, 18*, 1211–1238.

Gow, D.W., & Gordon, P.C. (1995). Lexical and prelexical influences on word segmentation: evidence from priming. *Journal of Experimental Psychology: Human Perception and Performance, 21*, 344–359.

Lahiri, A., & Marslen-Wilson, W. (1991). The mental representation of lexical form: A phonological approach to the recognition lexicon. *Cognition, 38*, 245–294.

Lotto, A., & Kluender, K. (1998). General contrast effects in speech perception: Effect of preceding liquid on stop consonant identification. *Perception and Psychophysics, 60*, 602–619.

Lotto, A., Kluender, K., & Holt, L. (1997). Perceptual compensation for coarticulation by Japanese quail (*coturnix coturnix japonica*). *Journal of the Acoustical Society of America, 102*, 1134–1140.

Mann, V.A. (1980). Influence of preceding liquid on stop-consonant perception. *Perception and Psychophysics, 28*, 407–412.

Mann, V.A., & Repp, B.H. (1981). Influence of preceding fricative on stop consonant perception. *Journal of the Acoustical Society of America, 69*, 548–558.

Marslen-Wilson, W.D. (1987). Functional parallelism in spoken word-recognition. *Cognition, 25*, 71–102.

Marslen-Wilson, W.D. (1990). Activation, competition, and frequency in lexical access. In G.T.M. Altmann (Ed.), *Cognitive models of speech processing: Psycholinguistic and computational perspectives* (pp. 148–172). Cambridge, MA: MIT Press.

Marslen-Wilson, W., Moss, H.E., & Van Halen, S. (1996). Perceptual distance and competition in lexical access. *Journal of Experimental Psychology: Human Perception and Performance, 22*, 1376–1392.

Marslen-Wilson, W., Nix, A., & Gaskell, G. (1995). Phonological variation in lexical access: Abstractness, inference and English place assimilation. *Language and Cognitive Processes, 10*, 285–308.

Marslen-Wilson, W., Tyler, L.K., Waksler, R., & Older, L. (1994). Morphology and meaning in the English mental lexicon. *Psychological Review, 101*, 3–33.

Marslen-Wilson, W., & Warren, P. (1994). Levels of perceptual representation and process in lexical access: words, phonemes, and features. *Psychological Review, 101*, 653–675.

McClelland, J.L., & Elman, J.L. (1986). The TRACE model of speech perception. *Cognitive Psychology, 18*, 1–86.

McQueen, J.M. (1998). Segmentation of continuous speech using phonotactics. *Journal of Memory and Language, 39*, 21–46.

McQueen, J.M., & Cutler, A. (1997). Cognitive processes in speech perception. In W.J. Hardcastle & J. Laver (Eds.), *The handbook of phonetic sciences* (pp. 566–585). Oxford: Blackwell.

McQueen, J.M., & Cutler, A. (1998). Morphology in word recognition. In A. Spencer & A.M. Zwicky (Eds.), *The handbook of morphology* (pp. 406–427). Oxford: Blackwell.

McQueen, J.M., Norris, D., & Cutler, A. (1994). Competition in spoken word recognition: Spotting words in other words. *Journal of Experimental Psychology: Learning, Memory and Cognition, 20*, 621–638.

McQueen, J.M., Norris, D., & Cutler, A. (1999). Lexical influence in phonetic decision making: Evidence from subcategorical mismatches. *Journal of Experimental Psychology: Human Perception and Performance, 25*, 1363–1389.

Mehler, J. (1981). The role of syllables in speech processing: Infant and adult data. *Philosophical Transactions of the Royal Society, Series B, 295*, 333–352.

Mehler, J., Dommergues, J.-Y., Frauenfelder, U.H., & Segui, J. (1981). The syllable's role in speech segmentation. *Journal of Verbal Learning and Verbal Behavior, 20*, 298–305.

Miller, J.L., & Dexter, E.R. (1988). Effects of speaking rate and lexical status on phonetic perception. *Journal of Experimental Psychology: Human Perception and Performance, 14*, 369–378.

Miller, J.L., & Volaitis, L.E. (1989). Effect of speaking rate on the perceptual structure of a phonetic category. *Perception and Psychophysics, 46*, 505–512.

Monsell, S., & Hirsh, K.W. (1998). Competitor priming in spoken word recognition. *Journal of Experimental Psychology: Learning, Memory, and Cognition, 24*, 1495–1520.

Norris, D.G. (1994). Shortlist: A connectionist model of continuous speech recognition. *Cognition, 52*, 189–234.

Norris, D., McQueen, J.M., & Cutler, A. (1995). Competition and segmentation in spoken word recognition. *Journal of Experimental Psychology: Learning, Memory, and Cognition, 21*, 1209–1228.

Norris, D., McQueen, J.M., & Cutler, A. (2000). Merging information in speech recognition: Feedback is never necessary. *Behavioral and Brain Sciences, 23*, 299–325.

Norris, D., McQueen, J.M., Cutler, A., & Butterfield, S. (1997) The possible-word constraint in the segmentation of continuous speech. *Cognitive Psychology, 34*, 191–243.

Otake, T., Hatano, G., Cutler, A., & Mehler, J. (1993). Mora or syllable? Speech segmentation in Japanese. *Journal of Memory and Language, 32*, 258–278.

Palmeri, T.J., Goldinger, S.D., & Pisoni, D.B. (1993). Episodic encoding of voice attributes and recognition memory for spoken words. *Journal of Experimental Psychology: Learning, Memory, and Cognition, 19*, 309–328.

Pisoni, D.B., & Luce, P.A. (1987). Acoustic-phonetic representations in word recognition. *Cognition, 25*, 21–52.

Pitt, M.A., & McQueen, J.M. (1998). Is compensation for coarticulation mediated by the lexicon? *Journal of Memory and Language, 39*, 347–370.

Radeau, M., Morais, J., & Segui, J. (1995). Phonological priming between monosyllabic spoken words. *Journal of Experimental Psychology: Human Perception and Performance, 21*, 1297–1311.

Samuel, A.G. (1981). Phonemic restoration: Insights from a new methodology. *Journal of Experimental Psychology: General, 110*, 474–494.

Samuel, A.G. (1997) Lexical activation produces potent phonemic percepts. *Cognitive Psychology, 32*, 97–127.

Schreuder, R., & Baayen, R.H. (1995). Modeling morphological processing. In L.B. Feldman (Ed.), *Morphological aspects of language processing* (pp. 131–154). Hillsdale, NJ: Lawrence Erlbaum Associates Inc.

Shillcock, R. C. (1990). Lexical hypotheses in continuous speech. In G.T.M. Altmann (Ed.), *Cognitive models of speech processing: Psycholinguistic and computational perspectives* (pp. 24–49). Cambridge, MA: MIT Press.

Slowiaczek, L.M., & Hamburger, M.B. (1992). Prelexical facilitation and lexical interference in auditory word recognition. *Journal of Experimental Psychology: Learning, Memory, and Cognition, 18*, 1239–1250.

Swinney, D.A. (1981). Lexical processing during sentence comprehension: Effects of higher order constraints and implications for representation. In T. Myers, J. Laver, & J. Anderson (Eds.), *The cognitive representation of speech* (pp. 201–209). Amsterdam: North-Holland.

Tabossi, P., Burani, C., & Scott, D. (1995). Word identification in fluent speech. *Journal of Memory and Language, 34*, 440–467.

Van Alphen, P., & McQueen, J.M. (in press). The time-limited influence of sentential context on function word identification. *Journal of Experimental Psychology: Human Perception and Performance, 27.*

Van der Lugt, A. (in press). The use of sequential probabilities in the segmentation of speech. *Perception and Psychophysics.*

Vitevitch, M.S., & Luce, P.A. (1998). When words compete: Levels of processing in spoken word recognition. *Psychological Science, 9,* 325–329.

Vitevitch, M.S., & Luce, P.A. (1999). Probabilistic phonotactics and neighborhood activation in spoken word recognition. *Journal of Memory and Language, 40,* 374–408.

Vroomen, J., & de Gelder, B. (1995). Metrical segmentation and lexical inhibition in spoken word recognition. *Journal of Experimental Psychology: Human Perception and Performance, 21,* 98–108.

Vroomen, J., & de Gelder, B. (1997). Activation of embedded words in spoken word recognition. *Journal of Experimental Psychology: Human Perception and Performance, 23,* 710–720.

Wallace, W.P., Stewart, M.T., & Malone, C.P. (1995). Recognition memory errors produced by implicit activation of word candidates during the processing of spoken words. *Journal of Memory and Language, 34,* 417–439.

Wallace, W.P., Stewart, M. T., Sherman, H.L., & Mellor, M. (1995). False positives in recognition memory produced by cohort activation. *Cognition, 55,* 85–113.

Yip, M.C.W. (2000). Recognition of spoken words in continuous speech: Effects of transitional probability. In B. Yuan, T. Huang, & X. Tang (Eds.), *Proceedings of ICSLP 2000,* Vol. 3 (pp. 758–761). Beijing: China Military Friendship Publish.

Zwitserlood, P. (1989). The locus of the effects of sentential-semantic context in spoken-word processing. *Cognition, 32,* 25–64.

Zwitserlood, P., & Schriefers, H. (1995). Effects of sensory information and processing time in spoken-word recognition. *Language and Cognitive Processes, 10,* 121–136.

LANGUAGE AND COGNITIVE PROCESSES, 2001, *16* (5/6), 491–505

New evidence for prelexical phonological processing in word recognition

Emmanuel Dupoux and Christophe Pallier

Laboratoire de Sciences Cognitives et Psycholinguistique, CNRS-EHESS, Paris, France

Kazuhiko Kakehi

Graduate School of Human Informatics, Nagoya University, Japan

Jacques Mehler

International School for Advanced Studies, Trieste, Italy

When presented with stimuli that contain illegal consonant clusters, Japanese listeners tend to hear an illusory vowel that makes their perception conform to the phonotactics of their language. In a previous paper, we suggested that this effect arises from language-specific prelexical processes. The present paper assesses the alternative hypothesis that this illusion is due to a "top-down" lexical effect. We manipulate the lexical neighbourhood of nonwords that contain illegal consonant clusters and show that perception of the illusory vowel is not due to lexical influences. This demonstrates that phonotactic knowledge influences speech processing at an early stage.

Most models of spoken word recognition postulate that the acoustic signal is transformed into a prelexical representation, typically a string of phonemes, and that this representation is used to access the lexicon. Such models have to spell out how the acoustic signal is transformed into a prelexical representation and whether this representation is enhanced by one's lexical knowledge. Many studies have established that the mapping

Requests for reprints should be addressed to Emmanuel Dupoux, LSCP, 54 bd Raspail, 75006 Paris, France Email: dupoux@lscp.ehess.fr

We thank Nicolas Bernard and Takao Fushimi for their help in preparing the stimuli and running the experiment. We also thank Sharon Peperkamp and two anonymous reviewers for very useful comments on a previous version of this manuscript. Part of this work was presented at Eurospeech '99 (Dupoux, Fushimi, Kakehi, & Mehler, 1999).

http://www.tandf.co.uk/journals/pp/01690965.html   DOI: 10.1080/01690960143000191

between the signal and the prelexical representation is not simple. In their famous "Perception of the Speech Code" paper, Liberman, Cooper, Shankweiler, and Studdert-Kennedy (1967) stressed the complexity of the relationships between the acoustic signal and the phonetic message: neighbour phones interact so much that a single acoustic stretch is often ambiguous and requires a larger context to be interpretable (see, for example, Mann & Repp, 1981; Miller & Liberman, 1979; Whalen, 1989). Their proposed solution was that listeners use their knowledge of how speech sounds are produced to decode the speech signal (for example, to compensate for coarticulation). A second source of information is lexical knowledge. Indeed, numerous studies have demonstrated lexical influences on phoneme identification (Frauenfelder, Segui & Dijkstra, 1990; Ganong, 1980; Samuel, 1981a, 1987). The phenomenon of phonemic restoration attests that lexical knowledge can produce the perception of a phoneme that is not present in the signal (even if acoustics play an important role in the phenomenon; cf. Samuel 1981b). A third source of information that can be used by the speech perception apparatus is phonotactic knowledge. There exists some empirical evidence that listeners tend to assimilate illegal sequences of phonemes to legal ones (Hallé, Segui, Frauenfelder, & Meunier, 1998; Massaro & Cohen, 1983). Thus, French listeners tend to hear the sequence /dl/, which is illegal in French, as /gl/, which is legal (Hallé et al. 1998).

Among these three sources of information, the influence of phonotactics is the least well established. Both the Massaro and Cohen (1983) and the Hallé et al. (1998) studies used stimuli in only one language. Therefore, it is possible that the observed effects were due to universal effects of compensation for coarticulation: it could be that /dl/ is universally harder to perceive than /gl/. A more convincing demonstration of phonotactic effects must involve a cross-linguistic manipulation. A second difficulty is the potential confound between phonotactic and lexical information. It can be argued that nonwords containing illegal sequences of phonemes typically have fewer lexical neighbours than legal nonwords. As a matter of fact, McClelland and Elman (1986) interpreted the phonotactic effects of Massaro and Cohen as the result of top-down influences from the lexicon (a "lexical conspiracy" effect). They reported on unpublished data where an apparent phonotactic effect (the preference for /dw/ over /bw/ in nonwords with an ambiguous initial phoneme) was reversed in the presence of a strong lexical candidate: "?wacelet", yielded the perception of "bwacelet" (from *bracelet*) instead of "dwacelet" (despite the illegality of the /bw/ cluster). The authors argued that the usual preference of /dw/ over /bw/ is due to the presence of /dw/ words (and no /bw/ words) in the lexicon. They simulated these data, as well as Massaro and Cohen's (1983) "phonotactic" result, using the TRACE model, which has top-down connections from the lexicon to the prelexical level, but no phonotactic knowledge (but see Pitt & McQueen, 1998 for arguments against this interpretation).

In this paper, we wish to examine the relative role of phonotactics and lexical knowledge in prelexical processing by building on an effect which has been well documented cross-linguistically: the perception of illusory vowels in Japanese. Dupoux, Kakehi, Hirose, Pallier, & Mehler (1999) have demonstrated that Japanese listeners, but not French listeners, perceive an /u/ vowel between consonants forming illegal clusters in Japanese (e.g., between /b/ and /z/).[1] These data show that the perceptual system of Japanese listeners inserts an illusory vowel between adjacent consonants in order to conform to the expected pattern in this language. We called this phenomenon "vowel epenthesis". It suggests that the role of phonotactics is so important as to produce the illusion of a segment which is not actually present in the signal.

Though Dupoux et al. (1999) attributed this effect to phonotactic knowledge, it cannot be excluded, a priori, that the illusion results from top-down lexical influences. One may imagine that many Japanese words contain sequences $/C_1uC_2/$ in which C_1C_2 represent consonant clusters present in the nonword stimuli used in the experiment. It could then be argued that the activations of such lexical items conspire to produce the perception of /u/. Thus, the potential existence of real Japanese words, phonetic neighbours of the nonword stimuli, may have induced participants to report a vowel that is not present in the signal. Some may find excessive the proposal that lexical effects can be so strong as to blindly insert a vowel that is not present in the signal. However, as we noted above, there are well documented demonstrations that the lexicon can fill in missing speech sounds, at least when the underlying signal is degraded or ambiguous (Samuel, 1981a; Warren, 1984). In the present case, the signal is clear, but it contains sequences of phonemes that are illegal for Japanese speakers. The existence of an influence of lexical knowledge in such a situation is an open question.

This paper aims at determining the source of the vowel epenthesis effect in Japanese. We try to determine whether the illusory vowel is inserted during the first stage of speech processing, under the influence of phonotactic constraints, or whether it comes from the participants' lexical knowledge. To this aim, we created nonwords containing illegal consonant clusters in Japanese. These items produce only one lexical neighbour when a vowel is inserted between the consonants. Specifically, for some items,

---

[1] In Japanese, the syllabic types are restricted to C(y)V, V, and C(y)VN. As a result, the only legal consonant clusters are of the nasal plus consonant type.

the lexicon encourages the insertion of the vowel /u/ (like in *sokdo* → *sokudo,* speed). In other items, the lexicon calls for the insertion of a vowel other than /u/ to generate a word (like *mikdo* → *mikado,* emperor). How do Japanese listeners perceive these illegal nonwords? If perceptual processes insert the vowel /u/ within the /kd/ cluster irrespective of the lexical status of the outcome, then the listeners should report hearing an /u/ inside both /sokdo/ and /mikdo/. If, in contrast, their perception is influenced by the nearest real Japanese word, we expect them to report an /u/ and an /a/ respectively.

EXPERIMENT 1

Stimuli with a CVCCV pattern were selected such that there is only one possible vowel that can be inserted in the consonant cluster to produce a real Japanese word. The stimuli were then split into two sets, according to the vowel that yields a Japanese word. In the u-Set, the vowel that produced a word was /u/, like in *sokdo→sokudo.* In the non-u-Set, the vowel was /a/, /e/, /i/ or /o/, like in *mikdo→mikado.* Participants were tested on two tasks, transcription and lexical decision. In the transcription task, participants were presented with stimuli and asked to transcribe them into the Roman alphabet. In the lexical decision task, participants decided whether the items were words in Japanese or not. If epenthesis is lexically driven, one expects a strong effect of lexical neighbourhood on the perception of the items containing a consonant cluster. In particular, items in the u-Set (e.g., *sokdo)* should be perceived with an epenthetic /u/, and items in the non-u-Set (e.g., *mikdo*) should be perceived with a vowel other than /u/ since that is the only way to obtain a Japanese word. In other words, items in both sets should behave similarly in the lexical decision experiment, since all items can produce Japanese words once the appropriate vowel is inserted. In contrast, if vowel epenthesis arises before lexical access, both *sokdo* and *mikdo* items should produce the perception of an illusory /u/, and consequently, only *sokdo* will be processed as a Japanese word. That is, while *sokdo* becomes *sokudo* (a word in Japanese) after /u/ epenthesis, *mikdo* becomes *miku̲do* (a nonword in Japanese). In order to assess the performance on the test items, we included control words like *sokudo* and *mikado* and nonwords like *sokado* and *mikudo* in the lists.

Method

Materials.   Two sets of 19 triplets were constructed. The first set was called the u-Set and contained triplets with the following structure: illegal nonword, word, legal nonword. The first item was a (C)VCCV disyllable containing an illegal consonant cluster in Japanese (e.g., *sokdo*). The other two items had identical segments as the first except for the insertion of a vowel between the middle consonants. The second item of the triplet was a Japanese word obtained by the insertion of an /u/ (e.g., *sokudo*). The third item was a nonword obtained by the insertion of one of the following three vowels: /a/, /e/, /i/ or /o/ (e.g., *sokado*). The second set (the non-u-Set) was similar in all respects to the u-Set, except that the vowels that yielded a word and a nonword, respectively, were swapped around. That is, the illegal nonword *mikdo* yielded the word *mikado* through the insertion of an /a/ and yielded the nonword *mikudo* through the insertion of an /u/. In all cases, there was only one possible way to make a word in Japanese through the insertion of a vowel in the consonant cluster of the first element of a triplet. The items are listed in the Appendix. An additional list of 78 filler items was also constructed, consisting of half words, half legal nonwords.

The stimuli were recorded by a female native speaker of Japanese, trained in phonetics, who had been instructed to produce the cluster stimuli without any intervening vowel. All stimuli were checked and when a few glottal pulses appeared between the consonants, they were deleted by digital editing.

Procedure.   In the phonetic transcription task, all the items from the 38 triplets were presented through headphones in a different pseudo-random order for each participant. Participants were instructed to type the transcription of the items in the Roman alphabet on a computer keyboard. In the lexical decision task, the same items, with the filler items, were presented through headphones using the EXPE software (Pallier, Dupoux, & Jeannin, 1997). Lists were presented in a different pseudo-random order for each participant. Participants were instructed to classify the stimuli into real Japanese words versus non-existent words as fast as they could. If no response was given within 4 s after the presentation of an item, the next stimulus was presented. Participants were given a practice session of 10 trials with feedback, followed by the main experiment during which no feedback was given.

Participants.   Fourteen native speakers of Japanese were tested on the lexical decision experiment. Seven of them also performed the phonetic transcription task (after completing the lexical decision task). They were all Japanese volunteers recruited in Paris.

Results and discussion

In this experiment, four triplets in the u-Set and three in the non-u-Set had to be removed because of more than 50% transcription errors or more than 40% lexical decision errors on the words or nonwords. Most of these errors occurred on /h/-initial words, whose first segment was misperceived as /f/ or /r/, or deleted.[2] This left 15 triplets in the u-Set and 16 triplets in the non-u-Set. No participant was rejected.

First, the phonetic transcription results for the consonant cluster items were analysed separately for items in the u-Set and items in the non-u-Set. Seventy-nine per cent of the transcriptions of the consonant cluster items in the u-Set contained an epenthetic /u/ inserted between the consonants. Only 1% of the responses contained a different vowel (/i/ instead of /u/ in one item). The remaining 20% of the transcriptions reproduced the consonant cluster. In the non-u-Set, 75% of the transcriptions contained an epenthetic /u/, 1% are cases of consonant deletion (/juSi/ instead of /jurSi/), and 24% reproduced the consonant cluster. The difference in /u/ transcription between the two items sets was not significant ($\chi^2(1) =$ 0.10, $p > .10$).

Second, the lexical decision data were analysed in terms of per cent 'word' responses. The data are displayed in Table 1. As one can see, words were labelled as words in 94% of the cases, and nonwords in only 7% of the cases. The results of the cluster items depended on set type. Seventy-one per cent of the cluster items in the u-Set are labelled as words, a score significantly different from chance ($p < .007$). Planned contrasts showed that this score differed significantly from the score obtained with control non-words ($F_1(1,13) = 222, p < .001; F_2(1,14) = 120, p < .001$) and control words ($F_1(1,13) = 23, p < .001; F_2(1,14) = 8, p < .02$). In contrast, the cluster items in the non-u-Set were classified as words in only 8% of the trials, a score significantly below chance ($p < .001$). This score was significantly different from the score with the control words ($F_1(1,13) =$

TABLE 1
Per cent "word" response to cluster and control items in Experiment 1

	Nonwords	Words	Clusters
u-Set			
Per cent "word" response	2.8%	91.0%	71.4%
Example	*sokado*	*sokudo*	*sokdo*
non-u-Set			
Per cent "word" response	10.3%	96.9%	8.0%
Example	*mikudo*	*mikado*	*mikdo*

---

[2] The phoneme /h/ has different allophones depending on the following context, including bilabial and palatal fricatives as well as the glottal [h]. The bilabial is usually transcribed with an "f" in the Roman alphabet. We nevertheless only accepted transcriptions of /h/-initial words with "h" as correct.

$868, p < .001; F_2(1, 15) = 1329, p < .001$), but did not differ from the score with the control nonwords (both $Fs < 1$).

Third, we analysed the RTs for responses falling into the 'predicted' category. For items in the u-Set the predicted category was "Word" for both the Japanese words and for illegal cluster items. For the non-u-Set items the predicted category was "NonWord" for Japanese nonwords and for illegal cluster items. The reaction times are shown in Table 2. An ANOVA revealed that the control words yielded significantly faster latencies than control nonwords ($F_1(1, 13) = 28, p < .001; F_2(1, 30) = 49, p < .001$). Cluster items in the u-Set tended to yield faster RTs than control nonwords ($F_1(1, 13) = 3.3, .05 < p < .1; F_2(1, 14) = 4.5, p = .053$), but did not differ significantly from control words (both $Fs < 1$). In contrast, cluster items in the non-u-Set yielded slower RTs than the control words ($F_1(1, 13) = 23, p < .001; F_2(1, 15) = 62, p < .001$), but did not differ significantly from the control nonwords ($F_1(1, 13) = 2.9, p > .1; F_2(1, 15) = 3.3, .05 < p < .1$). Thus, the latencies to respond to cluster items depended on the items in the lexical category to which they are assimilated.

The overall pattern of results for this experiment was straightforward. The transcription task yielded similar rates of /u/ insertion irrespective of the presence or absence of a neighbouring lexical item with that particular vowel. We found no insertion of a vowel other than /u/ (except for one participant who reported an /i/ in "namda" producing the Japanese word "namida"; this amounts to 1% of the responses). Thus, globally, the presence of biasing lexical neighbours did not influence transcriptions. The same conclusion arose from the analysis of the lexical decision data. Participants consistently classified cluster items as if they had inserted an /u/ prior to lexical access.

The reported results could be attributable to the fact that the stimuli were recorded by a native Japanese speaker. Even though the speaker was trained in phonetics, at times she could not avoid inserting short vowels between the cluster consonants. Her speech was digitally edited to remove pitch pulses corresponding to an inter-consonantal vowel. However, it could be that traces of coarticulation remained in the adjacent consonant allowing Japanese participants to reconstruct the underlying vowel. To

TABLE 2

Reaction times (ms), standard error, and per cent error to cluster and control items in Experiment 1

| | Nonwords | | | Words | | | Clusters | | |
	RT	SE	Err	RT	SE	Err	RT	SE	Err
u-Set	1223	33	2.8%	1046	33	9.0%	1093	77	28.6%
non-u-Set	1315	68	10.2%	933	31	3.1%	1234	61	8.0%

control for this possibility, in the next experiment, we used a speaker whose maternal language allows consonant clusters.

EXPERIMENT 2

In order to remove the possibility that the effects obtained in the previous experiment are due to potential traces of /u/ produced by the Japanese speaker, the stimuli were recorded anew, but this time they were spoken by a native speaker of French. He was instructed to imitate words and non-words produced by a Japanese speaker, and produced the cluster stimuli without any intervening vocalic element. If the effects obtained in the previous experiment were due to coarticulation, much less vowel epenthesis should occur in the new experiment. If, in contrast, the results were due to true phonologically driven phoneme restoration, the same results as in Experiment 1 should be found.

Method

The method was identical to the one employed in Experiment 1.

Materials. The same sets of u- and non-u-triplets were used as in the previous experiments. The stimuli were recorded by a native speaker of French who imitated a native speaker of Japanese as follows: The Japanese speaker first read a given triplet, and the French speaker repeated, trying to imitate the segmental and suprasegmental features of Japanese except in the cluster condition, where the consonant cluster was pronounced as such. Each triplet was recorded three times, and the best tokens were selected by a French and Japanese listener. The stimuli were then digitally recorded (16 kHz).

Procedure. The procedures for the phonetic transcription task and lexical decision task were the same as in the previous experiment.

Participants. Fifteen native speakers of Japanese, recruited in Paris, participated in the lexical decision experiment. Seven of them also performed the phonetic transcription task.

Results and discussion

Overall, five triplets in the non-u-Set and five triplets in the u-Set were removed because the words or nonwords yielded more than 40% errors or were incorrectly transcribed by more than half of the participants. This left 14 triplets in the u-Set and 14 triplets in the non-u-Set. Two participants who made more than 50% errors on the nonwords (both for distractors and test items) were removed from subsequent analysis.

First, the phonetic transcription results for the consonant cluster items were analysed separately for items in the u-Set and items in the non-u-Set. In the u-Set, 65% of the transcriptions of the consonant cluster items contained an epenthetic /u/ inserted between the consonants. Only 1% of the responses contained a different vowel (/o/ instead of /u/ in one item), and in 3%, the second consonant was deleted. The remaining 30% of the transcriptions reproduced the consonant cluster. In the non-u-Set, 59% of the transcriptions contained an epenthetic /u/, 9% a different vowel (the vowel /i/), and 31% reproduced the consonant cluster response. The /i/ response arose in two items: *rekSi* and *rikSi*. It is interesting to note that the /i/ responses turns these two items into real Japanese words (*rekiSi* and *rikiSi*, respectively). Note also that in these items, 21% of the responses were still /u/ insertions. The difference in /u/ insertion rates between the u-Set and the non-u-Set did not reach significance ($\chi^2(1) = 0.52, p > .10$).

Second, the lexical decision data were analysed in terms of per cent 'word' response. The data are displayed in Table 3. As one can see, words were labelled as words (93% of the cases), and nonwords were not (8% of the cases). The results of the cluster items depended on the type of set. An average 70% of the cluster items in the u-Set were labelled as words, a score significantly different from 50% ($p < .007$). Planned contrasts showed that this score was significantly different from the score with the control nonwords ($F_1(1, 12) = 103, p < .001; F_2(1, 13) = 108, p < .001$) and with the control words ($F_1(1, 12) = 12, p < .003; F_2(1, 13) = 13, p < .001$). In contrast, the cluster items in the non-u-Set were classified as words in only 19% on average (significantly below 50%, $p < .001$). This score was significantly different from the score with the control words ($F_1(1, 12) = 341, p < .001; F_2(1, 13) = 109, p < .001$), and from the control non-words although the difference was significant only for the participants analysis ($F_1(1, 12) = 11.7, p < .005; F_2(1, 13) = 1.7, p > .1$).

TABLE 3
Per cent "word" response to cluster and control items in Experiment 2

	Nonwords	Words	Clusters
u-Set			
Percent "word" response	6.0%	91.8%	70.4%
Example	*sokado*	*sokudo*	*sokdo*
non-u-Set			
Per cent "word" response	10.4%	96.1%	18.7%
Example	*mikudo*	*mikado*	*mikdo*

Third, we analysed the RTs for the responses in the dominant category, that is, responses as 'word' for cluster items in the u-Set and responses as 'non-word' for items in the non-u-Set. These responses are shown in Table 4, together with the RTs for the control words and nonwords. An ANOVA revealed that the control words yielded significantly faster latencies than control nonwords ($F_1(1, 12) = 16$, $p < .002$; $F_2(1, 13) = 91$, $p < .001$). Cluster items in the u-Set did not differ significantly from control words (both $Fs < 1$), but yielded significantly faster RTs than the control nonwords in the participants' analysis ($F_1(1, 12) = 4.7$, $p < .05$; $F_2(1, 13) = 2.7$, $p > .1$). In contrast, cluster items in the non-u-Set yielded slower RTs than the control words ($F_1(1, 12) = 28.0$, $p < .001$; $F_2(1, 13) = 56.5$, $p < .001$), but did not differ significantly from the control nonwords ($F_1(1, 12) = 1.9$, $p > .1$; $F_2(1, 13) = 3.0$, $p > .1$). In other words, the latencies to respond to cluster items were again similar to the latencies for the items in the lexical category to which they are assimilated.

In the above analysis of the transcription task, we found that the stimuli recorded by the French speaker produced 10% more cluster responses than in the previous experiment ($p < .001$). This suggests that the /u/ epenthesis effect can be enhanced when coarticulation cues remain in the adjacent consonants. The overall /u/ response rate was still very high (62%), however, a rate quite similar to that reported in Dupoux et al. (1999). In addition, two items in the non-u-Set yielded identification of /i/ instead of /u/ (namely, rekSi and rikSi). A post hoc analysis showed that the lexical decision responses for these two items were 77% and 54% "word" responses, respectively, whereas all the other items in the non-u-Set yielded a majority of nonword responses. Could it be that these two items reflect a lexical influence on the epenthesis effect? If so, the insertion of /i/ is due to the presence of the Japanese words rekiSi and rikiSi. However, none of the other items in the non-u-Set behaved similarly. Despite the existence of lexical items with non-u vowels between the medial consonant, all the other items elicited the perception of an /u/ and a nonword response. An alternative interpretation for rekSi and rikSi is that there are cases in Japanese of /i/ epenthesis. Shinohara (1997) discussed some of these cases, and while she argued that /i/ epenthesis may not be a

TABLE 4
Reaction times (ms), standard error, and percent error to cluster and control items in Experiment 2

| | Nonwords | | | Words | | | Clusters | | |
	RT	SE	Err	RT	SE	Err	RT	SE	Err
u-Set	1231	78	6.0%	1055	40	8.2%	1084	37	29.6%
non-u-Set	1241	64	10.4%	949	34	3.8%	1323	86	18.7%

productive phenomenon, it is worthwhile noting that the majority of the existing cases of loan words with /i/ insertion arise in the context of voiceless stop-fricative clusters (i.e., *textile* → /teki*sutairo*/), hence the same context as in *rikSi*. Interestingly, there were five items in the non-u-Set where the insertion of /i/ should have yielded a word. None of these items had a voiceless stop-fricative cluster, and none of them gave rise to the perception of an /i/. This suggests that the insertion of /i/ in *rekSi* and *rikSi* may also have a prelexical origin. Further research should uncover whether these cases are bona fide prelexical epenthesis effects or lexical influences.

GENERAL DISCUSSION

We created Japanese nonwords that contained illegal consonant clusters, and manipulated their lexical neighbourhood. The stimuli were either digitally edited utterances produced by a native Japanese talker (Experiment 1), or natural utterances produced by a native speaker of a language that allows consonant clusters (Experiment 2). In both cases, and irrespective of the lexical status of the perceptual outcome, Japanese listeners reported hearing a vowel /u/ between the consonants. For example, they transcribe *sokdo* as 'sokudo' (a real Japanese word), and *mikdo* as 'mikudo' (a nonword), taking no account of the existence of a lexical neighbour with a different vowel (*mikado*). In a speeded lexical decision task, participants classified the stimuli like *sokdo* as real words, and the stimuli like *mikdo* as nonwords. Moreover, lexical decision times with the stimuli containing the illegal consonant cluster were as fast as with the stimuli containing a vowel /u/.

These results allow us to reject a purely lexical account of vowel epenthesis, and support the interpretation of epenthesis as a prelexical process. Interestingly enough, our data do not reveal any influence of lexical information at all. Lexical influences should have produced more epenthesis in items from the u-Set than in items from the non-u-Set, but this was not the case: the rates of /u/ epenthesis were not greater in items with /u/ neighbours (*sokdo*) than in items with non-/u/ neighbours (*mikdo*).

This interpretation, however, is made more complex because of *high vowel devoicing* in Japanese. In several dialects, high vowels (i.e., /i/ and /u/) are often devoiced between voiceless obstruents, or utterance finally after voiceless obstruents. Several factors seem to influence the likelihood of devoicing: speech rate, pitch accent placement, consonant type (stop versus fricative), as well as sociological effects (see Kondo, 1997; Varden 1998). Similarly, the precise phonetic implementation of devoicing seems to be non-homogeneous, ranging from something close to a whispered vowel (with formant structure), to fricative noise (without formant structure), going even to pure deletion (Tsuchida, 1997; Varden 1998). Even though there is this variability, Japanese listeners may encounter words like *sokudo* in normal speech in phonetic forms that are similar to /sokdo/. Could it be that this phenomenon accounts for our results?

Two arguments can be offered to counter this view. First, a post-hoc analysis revealed that the eight items containing voiceless obstruent clusters did not yield more epenthesis of /u/ than the other items (Experiment 1: 78% vs. 76%, respectively, $p > .10$; Experiment 2: 65% vs. 61%, $p > .10$). Second, the vowel /i/ devoices as readily as the vowel /u/. Nevertheless, /i/ epenthesis is quite infrequent, both in our experimental results and in the pattern of foreign word borrowings (see for instance Shinohara, 1997). If high vowel devoicing were the sole basis for the vowel epenthesis effect in perception, we should have found equal amounts of /u/ and /i/ epenthesis.

Nevertheless, let us assume, counterfactually, that high vowel devoicing applies only to /u/ and within all the consonant clusters used in our material. One may then suppose that items in the u-set (like *sokudo*) have two possible phonetic forms (e.g., /sokdo/ and /sokudo/) stored in the mental lexicon of Japanese listeners. It is certainly not the case, however, that /mikdo/ is stored as a variant *mikado* (because /a/ does not devoice). The lexical feedback hypothesis, therefore, cannot explain the results of the transcription task where participants transcribed /mikdo/ as *mikudo* as readily as they transcribed /sokdo/ as *sokudo*. In brief, the existence of vowel devoicing in Japanese does not alter our conclusion that it is the phonological context, not the lexical context, that triggers the illusory perception of /u/.

It turns out that the transcription task provides a critical piece of evidence against lexical involvement. This task could be criticised as being rather off-line and metalinguistic; without denying that, we note that Dupoux et al. (1999) found very similar results with off-line transcription and more on-line tasks such as speeded ABX discrimination. Furthermore, Dehaene-Lambertz, Dupoux & Gout (2000), using evoked potentials in an oddball paradigm, found that Japanese participants showed no mismatch negativity response (MMN) to a change from *ebzo* to *ebuzo*, whereas French participants show an early MMN response to the same change (140–280 ms after the offset of /b/). This further supports our hypothesis that phonotactic constraints modulate the brain response at a very early processing stage, prior to lexical access.

Overall, our results suggest that models of speech perception must take phonotactic information into consideration. Questions still remain about what the mechanisms could be. We can foresee two alternative accounts. The first account postulates a rule-based process that inspects the phonetic representation of utterances (Church, 1987; Frazier, 1987) and inserts a vowel whenever there is an illegal sequence of consonants (as in (1)). The rules would look like those typically proposed in phonological accounts of loan word adaptations.

$$\emptyset \rightarrow [u] \ / \ C\_C \tag{1}$$

A problem with this account is that there is no independent evidence for this rule in the phonology of standard Japanese. It is thus not clear how it would be acquired by children given that they are not presented with pairs of foreign words together with their Japanese adaptations.

The second account postulates a pattern matching process that assimilates foreign sounds to the phonetically closest prototypes of the native language. It is similar to the Perceptual Assimilation Model (Best, 1994; see also Takagi & Mann, 1994), with the important modification that whole syllables rather than individual segments are used as prototypes. Phonetic pattern matching explains why /u/ is used as an epenthetic vowel, instead of /i/ or /a/. /u/ tends to be the shortest vowel (Beckman, 1982) and the one with the most formant variability (Keating & Huffman, 1984). Hence, /ku/ is the closest syllabic prototype that matches the segment /k/ in /mikdo/. Of course, cross-linguistic research is needed to further work out and test these alternative accounts and also to understand how and when phonotactic constraints are acquired by young infants.

REFERENCES

Beckman, M. (1982). Segment duration and the "mora" in Japanese. *Phonetica, 39*, 113–135.

Best, C.T. (1994). The emergence of native-language phonological influence in infants: A perceptual assimilation model. In J. Goodman & H. Nusbaum (Eds.), *The development of speech perception: The transition from speech sounds to spoken words* (pp. 167–224). Cambridge, MA: MIT Press.

Church, K.W. (1987). Phonological parsing and lexical retrieval. *Cognition, 25*, 53–69.

Dehaene-Lambertz, G., Dupoux, E., & Gout, A. (2000). Electrophysiological correlates of phonological processing: a cross-linguistic study. *Journal of Cognitive Neuroscience, 12*, 635–647.

Dupoux, E., Fushimi, T., Kakehi, K., & Mehler, J. (1999). Prelexical locus of an illusory vowel effect in Japanese. *Proceedings of Eurospeech '99, 7th European Conference on Speech Communication and Technology.*

Dupoux, E., Kakehi, K., Hirose, Y., Pallier, C., & Mehler, J. (1999). Epenthetic vowels in Japanese: A perceptual illusion? *Journal of Experimental Psychology: Human Perception and Performance. 25*, 1568–1578.

Frauenfelder, U.H., Segui, J., & Dijkstra, T. (1990). Lexical effects in phonemic processing: Facilitatory or inhibitory? *Journal of Experimental Psychology: Human Perception and Performance, 16*, 77–91.

Frazier, L. (1987). Structure in auditory word recognition. *Cognition, 25*, 157–187.

Ganong, W.F. (1980). Phonetic categorisation in auditory word perception. *Journal of Experimental Psychology: Human Perception and Performance, 6*, 110–125.

Hallé, P., Segui, J., Frauenfelder, U., & Meunier, C. (1998). Processing of illegal consonant clusters: a case of perceptual assimilation? *Journal of Experimental Psychology: Human Perception and Performance, 24*, 592–608.

Keating, P.A., & Huffman, M.K. (1984). Vowel variation in Japanese. *Phonetica, 41*, 191–207.

Kondo, M. (1997). *Mechanisms of vowel devoicing in Japanese.* Ph.D. dissertation, University of Edinburgh.

Liberman, A.M., Cooper, F.S., Shankweiler, D.P., & Studdert-Kennedy, M. (1967). Perception of the speech code. *Psychological Review, 74*, 431–461.

Mann, V.A., & Repp, B.H. (1980). Influence of vocalic context on perception of the /S/-/s/ distinction. *Perception and Psychophysics, 28*, 213–228.

Massaro, D.W., & Cohen, M.M. (1983). Phonological constraints in speech perception. *Perception and Psychophysics, 34*, 338–348.

McClelland, J.L., & Elman, J.L. (1986). The TRACE model of speech perception. *Cognitive Psychology, 18*, 1–86.

Miller, J.L., & Liberman, A.M. (1979). Some effects of later-occurring information on the perception of stop consonants and semivowels. *Perception and Psychophysics, 25*, 457–465.

Pallier, C., Dupoux, E., & Jeannin, X. (1997). Expe: An expandable programming language for on-line psychological experiments. *Behavior Research, Methods, Instruments and Computers, 29*, 322–327.

Pitt, M.A., & McQueen, J.M. (1998). Is compensation for coarticulation mediated by the lexicon? *Journal of Memory and Language, 39*, 347–370.

Samuel, A.G. (1981a). Phonemic restoration: Insights from a new methodology. *Journal of Experimental Psychology: General, 110*, 474–494.

Samuel, A.G. (1981b). The role of bottom-up confirmation in the phonemic restoration illusion. *Journal of Experimental Psychology: Human Perception and Performance, 7*, 1131–1142.

Samuel, A.G. (1987). Lexical uniqueness effects on phonemic restoration. *Journal of Memory and Language, 26*, 36–56.

Shinohara, S. (1997). *Analyse phonologique de l'adaptation japonaise de mots étrangers.* Unpublished doctoral dissertation, Université de la Sorbonne Nouvelle.

Takagi, N., & Mann, V. (1994). A perceptual basis for the systematic phonological correspondences between Japanese loan words and their English source words. *Journal of Phonetics, 22*, 343–336.

Tsuchida, A. (1997). *The phonetics and phonology of Japanese vowel devoicing.* Ph.D. dissertation. Cornell University.

Varden, J.K. (1998). *On high vowel devoicing in standard modern Japanese: implications for current phonological theory.* Unpublished Ph.D. dissertation. University of Washington.

Warren, R.M. (1984). Perceptual restoration of obliterated sounds. *Psychological Bulletin, 96*, 371–383.

Whalen, D.H. (1989). Vowel and consonant judgements are not independent when cued by the same information. *Perception and Psychophysics, 46*, 284–292.

APPENDIX

Items in the u-Set

bakro-bakuro-bakaro,
huksi-hukusi-hukisi,
kokdo-kokudo-kokado,
kokti-kokuti-kokiti,
samsa-samusa-samosa,
tuksi-tukusi-tukesi,
yursi-yurusi-yurisi

harka-haruka-haraka,
hikme-hikume-hikime,
kokmu-kokumu-kokamu,
komgi-komugi-komigi,
sokdo-sokudo-sokido,
yakba-yakuba-yakaba,

hirma-hiruma-hiroma,
kaksa-kakusa-kakasa,
kokso-kokuso-kokaso,
magro-maguro-magaro,
soksi-sokusi-sokasi,
yakza-yakuza-yakaza,

Items in the non-u-Set

arsi-arasi-arusi,
kikme-kikime-kikume,
namda-namida-namuda,
reksi-rekisi-rekusi,
sekri-sekiri-sekuri,
taksa-takasa-takusa,
waksa-wakasa-wakusa

hiktu-hiketu-hikutu,
kormo-koromo-korumo,
nikbi-nikibi-nikubi,
riksi-rikisi-rikusi,
sikti-sikiti-sikuti,
tegru-tegaru-teguru,

huksa-hukasa-hukusa,
mikdo-mikado-mikudo,
omsa-omosa-omusa,
sakba-sakaba-sakuba,
takra-takara-takura,
wakme-wakame-wakume,

LANGUAGE AND COGNITIVE PROCESSES, 2001, *16* (5/6), 507–534

Subcategorical mismatches and the time course of lexical access: Evidence for lexical competition

Delphine Dahan

Max Planck Institute for Psycholinguistics, Nijmegen, The Netherlands

James S. Magnuson, Michael K. Tanenhaus, and Ellen M. Hogan

University of Rochester, NY, USA

Participants' eye movements were monitored as they followed spoken instructions to click on a pictured object with a computer mouse (e.g., "click on the net"). Participants were slower to fixate the target picture when the onset of the target word came from a competitor word (e.g., *ne(ck)t*) than from a nonword (e.g., *ne(p)t*), as predicted by models of spoken-word recognition that incorporate lexical competition. This was found whether the picture of the competitor word (e.g., the picture of a neck) was present on the display or not. Simulations with the TRACE model captured the major trends of fixations to the target and its competitor over time. We argue that eye movements provide a fine-grained measure of lexical activation over time, and thus reveal effects of lexical competition that are masked by response measures such as lexical decisions.

It is now generally accepted that as listeners attend to a spoken word, they simultaneously entertain multiple lexical candidates, which compete for recognition (see Frauenfelder & Floccia, 1998, for a review). However, the mechanism by which competition among active candidates is realised and resolved remains controversial. In some localist connectionist models, such as TRACE (McClelland & Elman, 1986) and Shortlist (Norris, 1994), word candidates compete with each other via inhibitory lateral connections. Thus, the activation of a lexical candidate at a given point in time in the

Requests for reprints should be addressed to Delphine Dahan, Max Planck Institute for Psycholinguistics, Postbus 310, 6500 AH Nijmegen, The Netherlands.
E-mail: delphine.dahan@mpi.nl

This work was supported by an NSF grant SBR-9729095 to M.K. Tanenhaus and R.N. Aslin, and by an NSF GRF to J.S. Magnuson.

http://www.tandf.co.uk/journals/pp/01690965.html   DOI: 10.1080/01690960143000074

recognition process is determined both by its fit with the input and by the activation of other candidates. In contrast, the Cohort model (Marslen-Wilson, 1987, 1990) does not assume lateral inhibition. The activation of a lexical candidate is affected only by its goodness of fit with the input and not by the activation levels of competitors; lexical competition takes place only at the decision stage of recognition. More recently, Gaskell and Marslen-Wilson (1997, 1999) have proposed a distributed model in which word recognition is viewed as the activation of a set of features that encode information about the form and meaning of this word. Because the same set of features encodes patterns associated with all the words, the pattern of activation that is generated by the network as partial input is processed is a blend of the patterns associated with each lexical candidate that is consistent with that input. Given larger numbers of candidates consistent with a partial input, the distributed pattern generated by the network will become more and more distant from the pattern associated with the target word. This, in effect, is a form of lexical competition, best described in terms of interference between fully distributed patterns of lexical representation.

Marslen-Wilson and Warren (1994) presented evidence that, they argued, was inconsistent with competition operating via lateral inhibition. They created cross-spliced word sequences whose initial portion had been excised from another token of the same word (e.g., *jo*(b) + (jo)*b*, W1W1 sequence), from another existing word (e.g., *jo*(g) + (jo)*b*, W2W1 sequence), or from a nonword (e.g., *jo*(d) + (jo)*b*, N3W1 sequence). For the W2W1 (*jo(g)b*) and N3W1 (*jo(d)b*) sequences, formant transitions in the vowel provided misleading information about the place of articulation of the following consonant. Thus, these stimuli contained *subcategorical* phonetic mismatches (Streeter & Nigro, 1979; Whalen, 1984, 1991). They reasoned that if lexical candidates inhibit one another as predicted by TRACE, lexical decisions to words with subcategorical mismatches cross-spliced from words should be slower than lexical decisions to the words cross-spliced from nonwords. In TRACE, for W2W1 sequences, the initially activated competitor W2 (e.g., *jog*) inhibits the target W1 (e.g., *job*); in N3W1 sequences, this inhibition is substantially weaker because the nonword N3 (e.g., *jod*) only weakly supports both W2 and W1. Inhibition modifies the activation of words throughout processing. Thus, the degree to which the competitor W2 is activated affects the activation of the target W1 throughout the recognition process. Simulations with TRACE confirmed these predictions. The response probability for the target W1, calculated with a form of Luce's (1959) choice rule (roughly, a transformation of the activation of the target divided by the sum of all the other words' transformed activation), was substantially lower in W2W1 than in N3W1.

However, Marslen-Wilson and Warren (1994) found that the mean lexical-decision latencies to the W2W1 and N3W1 sequences did not differ from one another, whereas both were significantly longer than responses to the W1W1 sequences. This result was subsequently replicated by McQueen, Norris, and Cutler (1999). Marslen-Wilson and Warren argued that the absence of a difference between the W2W1 and N3W1 conditions provided strong evidence against models that incorporate lexical competition via lateral inhibition throughout the activation process.

More recently, Norris, McQueen, and Cutler (2000) have simulated the pattern of lexical decisions for stimuli with subcategorical mismatches using a small competition-activation model with lateral inhibition between active lexical candidates (the Merge model). They conducted simulations in which the word level was allowed to cycle through 15 iterations on each time slice, followed by a reset of lexical-activation levels, before the next slice was processed. Despite early and substantial differences in the activation of W1 given W2W1 and N3W1 (with W1's activation initially significantly depressed in the former case), the competition between W2 and W1 in W2W1 was resolved very quickly (in terms of input slices) in this network. Norris et al. showed that, with an appropriate decision threshold, lexical competition would be resolved before lexical decisions are initiated, yielding the observed latency pattern (W1W1 < N3W1 ≈ W2W1). They argued that TRACE's failure in the Marslen-Wilson and Warren simulations was not due to lateral inhibition, but rather to lexical competition being resolved too slowly in TRACE. These conflicting simulations illustrate how difficult it is to distinguish among competing models without detailed information about the time course of activation of lexical competitors. The different patterns of activation predicted by models with and without lateral inhibition might occur too early in processing to be detected using lexical decisions.

Recently, a growing number of researchers, building upon work by Cooper (1974) and Tanenhaus, Spivey-Knowlton, Eberhard, and Sedivy (1995), have begun to use eye movements to explore questions about the time course of spoken-language comprehension, including the time course of spoken-word recognition in continuous speech. For example, Allopenna, Magnuson, and Tanenhaus (1998) had participants follow spoken instructions to pick up and move pictures using a computer mouse. On critical trials, participants saw displays containing items with similar names (e.g., *beaker, beetle,* and *speaker,* as well as an unrelated item). The probability of fixating each object as the target word unfolded over time was hypothesised to be closely linked to the activation of the lexical representation of this object (i.e., its name), under the assumption that the activation of the name of a picture influences the probability that a participant shifts attention to that picture and makes a saccadic eye movement to fixate it. The minimum latency to plan and launch a saccade is estimated to be between 150 and 180 ms in simple tasks (e.g., Fischer, 1992; Saslow, 1967), whereas intersaccadic intervals in tasks such as visual search fall in the range of 200 to 300 ms (e.g., Viviani, 1990). Allopenna et al. found that the proportion of fixations to referents and competitors began to increase 200 to 300 ms after word onset, demonstrating that eye movements were sensitive to changes in lexical activation within the first 100 ms of the spoken word. Moreover, the probability of fixating each item over time as the target word was heard mapped closely onto predicted response probabilities from the TRACE model. Dahan, Magnuson, and Tanenhaus (2001) provided further support for the linking hypothesis between lexical activation and fixations in a set of experiments examining the time course of frequency effects on lexical activation. In conjunction with simulations using TRACE, these data provided strong support for models in which frequency has continuous, immediate effects on activation.

The Allopenna et al. and Dahan et al. studies demonstrate that the eye-tracking paradigm can provide detailed time-course information about lexical activation in continuous speech. It can provide a measure of competitors' activation over time when these competitors, along with the target, are visually displayed. Moreover, it can capture subtle time-course effects such as effects of frequency. Furthermore, the task (i.e., identifying the referent picture) requires participants to map the target word's auditory form onto semantic and visual information: This ensures that the task is specifically tapping into the process of word recognition. Thus, the paradigm appears well suited to measuring the target's activation over time in the three cross-splicing conditions studied by Marslen-Wilson and Warren (1994).

The present study had two goals. First, we used the eye-tracking paradigm to track the time course of lexical activation and hence to examine the time course of lexical competition. Eye movements to the picture associated with the target W1 were monitored in all three cross-splicing conditions, with the picture associated with the competitor W2 absent from the display (Experiment 1) or present (Experiment 2). Results from both experiments provided clear evidence for lexical competition. Second, we evaluated whether fixation patterns mapped onto predictions generated by TRACE.

EXPERIMENT 1

The goal of this experiment was to track the time course of lexical activation for cross-spliced target words. We monitored participants' eye movements to pictured objects as they heard a referent's name in each of three splicing conditions: W1W1, W2W1, and N3W1. We hypothesised that the latency with which participants would make an eye movement to fixate the target picture (associated with W1) would reflect the target W1's lexical activation. In order to minimise the proportion of trials where participants were already fixating the target picture at the onset of the target word, participants were first instructed to point with the mouse cursor to one of the displayed distractor pictures (e.g., "Point to the bass"). As soon as the mouse cursor reached the picture, the critical instruction containing the target word was played (e.g., "now the net"). The purpose of this procedure was to draw participants' attention toward the distractor picture, thus away from the target picture, just before the target word was heard.

Method

Participants.   Thirty students at the University of Rochester partici-pated in this experiment and were paid $7.50. All were native speakers of English.

Materials.   Fifteen triplets composed of two real words and a nonword were selected (e.g., *net, neck, *nep*). These items are listed in Appendix A. All the items were monosyllabic and ended with a stop consonant (labial /b/ or /p/, coronal /d/ or /t/, or velar /g/ or /k/). Within the triplet, one word was assigned the role of target (W1), and the other, the role of competitor (W2). The nonwords (N3) were constructed by changing the place of articulation of W2's final consonant. A number of constraints applied in the selection of these triplets. The primary constraint was that, by changing the place of articulation of the final stop consonant of a word, both a word and a nonword were generated. For the purposes of Experiment 1, the targets, and, for Experiment 2, both the targets and competitors, had to be picturable nouns (e.g., *net, neck*). The final constraint imposed on the nonwords was that they not correspond to the initial sequence of many real words, to minimise lexical activation that the nonword sequence could generate (e.g., the triplet *bat/back/*bap* was excluded because *bap* corresponds to the initial sequence of many words, such as *baptism* and *baptise*). To reach a reasonable number of experimental triplets, we had to relax these criteria for some items. In particular, we used the sequences *tat* and *hark* as nonwords, even though they are words but of extremely rare use. If participants were to treat them as words, this would cause the W2W1 and N3W1 conditions to become more similar, and hence go against our hypothesis that performance in these conditions should differ. Moreover, some nonword sequences matched the beginning of some other words, but only rare words (e.g., *nep* matches *Neptune* and *nepotism*).

Finally, the voicing feature of the stop consonant was kept constant for all three items for seven triplets (e.g., *net*, *neck*, **nep*), while the voicing feature of the target differed from that of the competitor and the nonword for the other eight triplets (e.g., *pit*, *pig*, **pib*). Because the crucial comparison was between the W2W1 and N3W1 conditions, both W2 and N3 shared the same voicing. As the results will show, these two sets of triplets yielded similar patterns of results.

In order to generate cross-spliced stimuli, each item of the 15 triplets was recorded by a male native speaker of American English in a sound-proof room, sampling at 22050 Hz with 16-bit resolution. Each item was embedded in the sentence used as the critical instruction in the experiment (e.g., "now the net/neck/*nep"). Each sentence was then edited. The final stop consonants of the W1 items were spliced onto the initial portion (up to the end of the vowel) of another token of W1 (e.g., *now the ne*(t) + *t*), or of a token of W2 (e.g., *now the ne*(ck) + *t*), or of a token of N3 (e.g., *now the ne*(p) + *t*). This procedure generated three versions for each of the 15 experimental target words. On average, the duration of the *now the* part of the instruction was 461 ms for the W1W1 stimuli, 468 ms for the W2W1 stimuli, and 452 ms for the N3W1 stimuli; the duration of the target word up to the end of the vowel (i.e., before the splicing point) was 376 ms, 378 ms, and 383 ms for the W1W1, W2W1, and N3W1 stimuli, respectively. The average duration of the last consonant was 206 ms.[1]

---

[1] To test that coarticulatory cues in W2W1 sequences were not stronger than those in N3W1 sequences, we conducted a forced-choice phonetic decision experiment (see McQueen et al., 1999, Experiment 6). Listeners heard only the vowels excised from the 45 experimental items (e.g., [ɛ] from *net*, *neck*, and **nep*), and had to indicate, for each vowel, what the following segment had been by choosing among two response alternatives. The vowel plus the correct following consonant formed an existing word in 11 items (5 for W1, 2 for W2, and 4 for N3). McQueen et al. controlled for possible lexical biases in the consonant choice by having both consonant alternatives (the target and the distractor) forming either a word or a nonword. However, this procedure had the disadvantage of including consonant distractors that were never targets on other trials. We neutralised lexical bias by equating the number of (correct and incorrect) lexical alternatives between the W2 and N3 items. Only stop consonants were used as response alternatives, and six different pairings were used, with the following frequency: K-P (14), K-T (7), T-P (7), B-G (10), B-D (5), D-T (2). Each of the 45 vowels was presented three times; the 135 trials were presented in random order. Twelve participants were tested. On average, the percentage of correct responses was 78%, 69%, and 71%, for W1, W2, and N3 items, respectively, and did not vary significantly ($F_1(2,22) = 3.09$, $F_2(2,28) = 1.08$). Crucially, W2 items did not yield more correct responses than N3 items ($F_1(1,11) = 0.43$; $F_2(1,14) = 0.09$), indicating that coarticulatory cues to the following consonant in the vowel were equally strong in both sets of items. Any difference in performance when the items are fully presented cannot be attributed to differences in amount of coarticulatory information in the W2W1 and N3W1 sequences.

For each of the 15 experimental target words, three distractor words were selected. They were all picturable monosyllabic words. One of them began with the same consonant as the target word (e.g., for the target word *net*, the distractor was *nurse*). This was done to prevent participants from identifying the target picture on the basis of the initial consonant alone, before hearing the crucial subcategorical mismatch carried by the vowel. The other two distractor words were selected so that their names were phonologically highly dissimilar from the target. Items used in the experimental trials are listed in Appendix B.

In addition to the 15 experimental trials, 15 filler trials were constructed. For each trial, four picturable monosyllabic words were selected. For ten fillers, two picture names overlapped at onset (e.g., *bed* and *bell*) and neither of them was the target. This aspect of the fillers was especially designed for Experiment 2, where both W1 and W2 were visually present in the display, to prevent participants from developing expectations that pictures with phonologically similar names were likely to be targets. For the five other fillers, the four pictures' names were phonologically dissimilar. For eight of the 15 fillers, the trial structure was identical to that of the experimental trials: Participants were first instructed to point to a picture, then to another picture (e.g., "Point to the star. Now the goat. Click on it and put it below the diamond."). For seven of the fillers, participants were instructed to click on the picture they initially pointed to (e.g., "Point to the frog. Click on it and put it above the triangle.").

The spoken instructions for the filler trials were recorded by the same speaker as those for the experimental trials, during the same session. Subcategorical mismatches on ten instructions of the filler trials were created to prevent critical trials from being identified as those with cross-spliced stimuli (e.g., the onset and nucleus of the target word *cup* was cross-spliced with the final consonant of its counterpart *cut*).

The 120 pictures ([15 experimental + 15 filler] trials × 4 pictures) were all black and white line-drawings. They were selected from the Snodgrass and Vanderwart (1980) and the Cycowicz, Friedman, Rothstein, and Snodgrass (1997) picture sets, as well as from children's picture dictionaries and a commercially available clip-art database.

Procedure.   Prior to the eye-tracking experiment itself, participants were first exposed to each of the 120 pictures and familiarised with each intended name. This pre-exposure ensured that each picture was clearly identified and labelled as intended. Each picture was presented on a computer screen along with its printed name. Participants were free to inspect the picture as long as necessary, and moved to the next picture by pressing the keyboard's space bar.

The eye-tracking part of the study immediately followed. Participants were seated at a comfortable distance from the computer screen. Eye gaze was monitored using an Applied Scientific Laboratories head-mounted eye-tracker (model E 5000). A scene camera was aligned with the participant's line of sight. A calibration procedure allowed software to superimpose crosshairs showing the point of gaze on a HI-8 video tape record of the scene camera. The scene camera sampled at a rate of 30 frames per second, and each frame was stamped with a time code. Auditory stimuli were played to the participant through headphones and simultaneously to the HI-8 VCR, providing an audio record of each trial.

The structure of each trial was as follows: First, a 5 × 5 grid with a centred cross appeared on the screen, and participants were told to click on the cross. This allowed the experimenter to check that calibration accuracy was acceptable, as participants briefly fixated the cross before clicking on it. Then four line-drawings and four coloured geometric shapes appeared on specific cells of the grid. As the pictures appeared on the screen, the first spoken instruction started, asking participants to point to one of the distractor pictures using the computer-mouse cursor (e.g., "Point to the bass"). As soon as the cursor reached the distractor picture, the second and critical instruction was played, instructing participants to point to the target picture (e.g., "now the net"). Participants were then told to move the target picture above or below one of the geometric shapes (e.g., "Click on it and put it above the circle"). Once this was accomplished, the next trial began. On some filler trials, participants were instructed to click on and move the first picture they pointed to (e.g., "Point to the key. Click on it, and put it below the square"). This was intended to ensure that people directed their attention to the first picture. The positions of the geometric shapes were fixed from one trial to the other. The position of each picture was randomised for each participant and each trial. Five fillers were presented at the beginning of the session, to familiarise participants with the task.

Three lists were constructed by varying which of the three versions of each target word was presented (W1W1, W2W1, or N3W1). Within each list, five critical items were assigned to each condition. Ten participants were randomly assigned to each list. For each list, three random orders were created; approximately the same number of participants were assigned to each random order.

The data were collected from the videotape records using an editing VCR with frame-by-frame controls and synchronised video and audio channels. Coders used the crosshairs generated by the eye tracker to establish, for each experimental trial, which of the four pictures or the cross was fixated at each time frame (see Dahan, Swingley, Tanenhaus, & Magnuson [2000], for full details on the coding procedure).

Results

Analysis of latency. We measured, for each participant and each trial, the latency (from target onset) with which the participants fixated the target picture immediately before clicking on it with the mouse. This mouse-cursor movement was taken as an indication that participants had recognised the target word. Despite our efforts to draw participants' attention away from the target picture, participants fixated this picture at target onset on 18.1% of the trials (the non-mentioned distractor pictures were fixated on 17% of the trials). However, on most such trials, participants fixated another picture before returning to the target; on only a few trials did they keep fixating the target (21 out of 450, 4.7%). These trials were excluded from subsequent analyses. For seven participants, one additional trial was missing because of technical failures.

Table 1 presents the mean latency for each splicing condition, as a function of the voicing status within the triplet (same voicing, as in *net/neck/*nep*, or different voicing, as in *pit/pig/*pib*). The mean latency to fixate the target picture was 638 ms in W1W1, 851 ms in W2W1, and 673 ms in N3W1. A two-way ANOVA (splicing condition × voicing status) revealed a significant effect of splicing condition ($F_1(2, 58) = 13.7, p < .001, MSE = 57092.5; F_2(2, 26) = 12.5, p < .001, MSE = 14154.3$), no effect of voicing, and no interaction with splicing condition. Newman–Keuls tests indicated that the latency was significantly slower in W2W1 than in the W1W1 and N3W1 conditions, with no significant difference between W1W1 and N3W1 (with $\alpha = .05$). The mean latency in W1W1 is similar to that found for non-cross-spliced targets of similar lexical frequency (Dahan et al., 2001).[2]

The latency analysis revealed a significant difference between W2W1 and N3W1, as well as between W1W1 and W2W1. By contrast, N3W1 and W1W1 did not differ significantly, although latencies were numerically slower in N3W1. Participants were slower at recognising the target word and identifying the referent picture when mismatching coarticulatory information in the target word's vowel matched a real word (as in the W2W1 sequences) than when this coarticulatory information did not match an existing word (as in the N3W1 sequences). Very little effect of

---

[2] Additional analyses were conducted after excluding trials for which the latency was less than 200 ms or more than 1500 ms. Fixations occurring before 200 ms were likely to have been programmed before the onset of the target word, and not resulting from processing the target word. Trials where participants took more than 1500 ms to fixate the target were treated as outliers. In total, 38 out of the 422 remaining trials were excluded (9.0%, 11, 11, and 16 in W1W1, W2W1, and N3W1, respectively). Analyses yielded the same pattern of results as found in the full data set.

TABLE 1

Experiment 1. Mean latency (in ms) and standard errors (between parentheses) for each splicing condition as a function of the voicing status within the triplet (same-voice vs. different-voice)

	Same-voice		Different-voice	
	Example	Latency	Example	Latency
W1W1	ne(t)t	639 (44)	pi(t)t	636 (40)
W2W1	ne(ck)t	834 (39)	pi(g)t	867 (59)
N3W1	ne(p)t	712 (51)	pi(b)t	634 (57)

mismatching information was observed when the coarticulatory information did not match an existing word.

Analysis of fixations over time. We computed the proportions (across participants) of fixations to the target picture over time, for each of the three splicing conditions. For each participant and each trial, we established which of the four pictures or the cross was fixated at each time frame, beginning at the onset of the target word. The proportion of fixations to each picture at each time frame was then computed for each participant, and these proportions were averaged across participants. Figure 1 presents the proportions of fixations to the target picture over time for each splicing condition. Fixations between conditions were comparable until about 600 ms after target onset, where the fixations in W2W1 started diverging from those in W1W1 and N3W1. Recall that the duration of the pre-splice fragment was about 400 ms, with coarticulatory cues being presumably strongest in the late portion of the vowel. Given a 200-ms delay to program and launch an eye movement, fixations occurring around 600 ms are likely to result from the processing of the coarticulatory information. When this information matched an existing word, as in W2W1, fixations to the target were considerably delayed; when this information did not match a word, as in N3W1, no such delay was observed. Difference in fixations between W2W1 and N3W1 extended until about 1200 ms after target onset. A two-way ANOVA (splicing condition × voicing status) on mean fixation proportions over a time window extending from 600 to 1200 ms after target onset revealed a significant effect of splicing condition ($F_1(2, 58) = 12.55, p < .0001, MSE = 0.0376; F_2(2, 26) = 15.06, p < .0001, MSE = 0.008$), no main effect of voicing, and no interaction with splicing condition. Planned comparisons revealed a significant difference in target fixations over the 600- to 1200-ms window between the N3W1 and W2W1 conditions ($t_1(29) = 3.63, p < .005, t_2(14) = 3.33, p < .01$) and between the W1W1 and W2W1 conditions

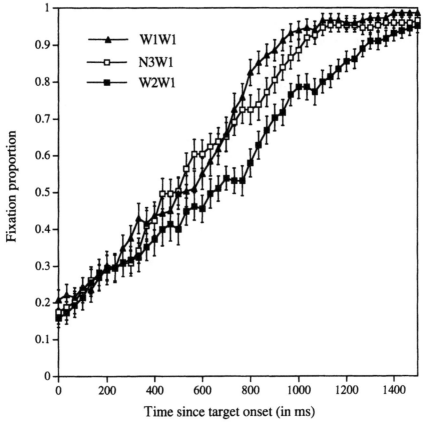

Figure 1. Experiment 1: Proportion of fixations to the target picture (W1) over time for each splicing condition (W1W1 [filled triangles], W2W1 [filled squares], N3W1 [empty squares]). Bars indicate standard errors.

$(t_1(29) = 5.56, p < .0001, t_2(14) = 5.42, p < .0001)$, but no significant difference between the W1W1 and N3W1 conditions.

The fixation analysis revealed a competition effect extending roughly from 600 to 1200 ms after target onset. Given that the mean duration of the target word was 585 ms and even after adding a 200 ms delay for programming an eye movement, this suggests that the competition between W2 and W1 may persist for several hundred ms after the disambiguating information is encountered. However, it is possible that the eye-movement data exaggerate how long it takes for lexical competition to resolve because on some trials, participants made multiple eye movements before fixating the target, and each new fixation involved some motor delay. In order to eliminate effects due to multiple fixations, we conducted a subanalysis that included only those trials on which participants made a single fixation from the onset of the target word, and in which that fixation was to the target. (That fixation always began from any picture except the target picture.) This analysis included 23.5% of the trials. Figure 2 presents fixation proportions to the target picture over time in each splicing condition. As is apparent from the figure, evidence of lexical competition (i.e., difference between the W2W1 and N3W1 conditions) extended until about 1000 ms after target-word onset. Recall that, on the main analysis, competition effects were observed as early as 200 ms after the offset of the pre-splice portion (at 600 ms, with a mean pre-splice portion of 380 ms), confirming that 200 ms is a reasonable estimate of the delay for observing effects of processing and integrating the spoken input in the eye-tracking task. Moreover, the post-splice consonant was 206 ms long on average. If lexical competition were to resolve as soon as disambiguating information

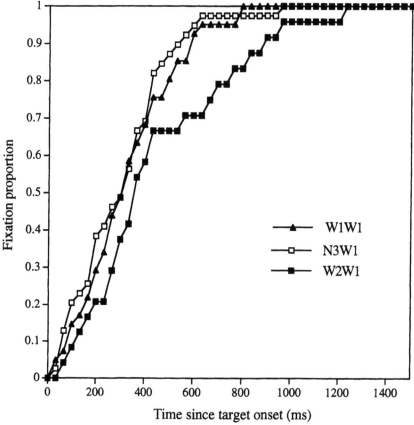

Figure 2. Experiment 1: Proportion of fixations to the target picture (W1) over time for each splicing condition (W1W1 [filled triangles], W2W1 [filled squares], N3W1 [empty squares]) on single-fixation trials (see text).

has been heard and processed, evidence for such resolution would be expected around 800 ms after target onset. Although this analysis should be interpreted with caution (no statistical analyses were conducted, due to the small number of data points per subject), it suggests that lexical competition continues for several hundred ms beyond the point where the disambiguating information has been processed.

Discussion

The latency with which participants fixated the target picture was slower when mismatching information in the target word matched a competitor word than when it did not. The latency analysis showed a small (nonsignificant) difference between the W1W1 and N3W1 conditions, whereas the difference between the W1W1 and W2W1 conditions was substantial. This suggests that lexical access is much more disrupted when mismatching coarticulatory information matches a word than when it does not. Eye movements to the target picture thus confirm the general prediction made by models that assume lexical competition throughout the recognition process. Early in the W2W1 sequence, the competitor W2 becomes highly active and competes with the target W1. The recognition of the target word is thus delayed. In contrast, early in the N3W1 sequence, W2 is only weakly active, so its activation has a much smaller effect on the recognition of W1. The eye-movement analyses capture the time-course aspect of the competition effect: Fixations to the target picture in the W2W1 and N3W1 conditions remain fairly similar up to 600 ms after target onset; at this point, the proportion of target fixations in W2W1 is delayed compared to the other conditions, as a result of the strong activation of the competitor (W2).

EXPERIMENT 2

Experiment 1 demonstrated that the recognition of the target word is more delayed when it contains mismatching coarticulatory information that matches an existing competitor word than when the mismatching information does not favour a potential lexical competitor. Experiment 2 was designed to assess more directly the competitor's activation by measuring fixations to this competitor over time in each of the splicing conditions. Furthermore, fixations to the target and its competitor over time provide the basis for a direct comparison between these fixation patterns and the activation patterns generated by a model that incorporates lexical competition. In order to obtain time-course data on the activation of both the target and the competitor in each of the splicing conditions, we presented the competitor picture along with the target picture and two distractors.

Method

Participants. Thirty students at the University of Rochester participated in the experiment and were paid $7.50. All were native speakers of
English. None of them had participated in Experiment 1.

Materials. The materials were identical to those used in Experiment 1,
with the exception of the displayed pictures. Here, the competitor picture
was displayed along with the target picture and two unrelated distractors
(e.g., the picture of a net, a neck, a bass, and a deer). The list of the pictures
is presented in Appendix B.

Procedure. The procedure was identical to that used in Experiment 1.
Three lists were constructed, by varying which of the three versions of each
experimental target word was presented (W1W1, W2W1, or N3W1).
Within each list, five critical items were assigned to each condition. Ten
participants were randomly assigned to each list. For each list, three
random orders were created; approximately the same number of
participants were assigned to each random order.

Results and discussion

Because of technical failures, five trials were missing; in addition, for nine
trials (2%), participants erroneously clicked on the competitor picture.
These trials were excluded from the analyses. Figure 3 presents the fixation
proportions to the target W1 (upper panel) and its competitor W2 (lower
panel), for each splicing condition. Fixations to the target over time
indicated a fast rise in W1W1, separating from the other conditions shortly
after 600 ms; the target fixations rose more slowly in N3W1, and slowest in
W2W1. Fixations to the competitor W2 revealed a complementary picture.
The competitor picture was fixated most in W2W1, where coarticulatory
information in the vowel matches the competitor's name, intermediate in
N3W1, where coarticulatory information weakly matches both W1 and
W2, and least in W1W1, where coarticulatory information favours W1. In
the latter condition, fixations to target and competitor increased in parallel
until shortly after 600 ms, where competitor fixations began to decrease,
and target fixations, to increase. Fixations at this point thus reflect the use
of coarticulatory information in the vowel supporting the target over the
competitor.

We computed the mean proportion of fixations to the target and
competitor for each splicing condition over the 600- to 1200-ms time
window. On average, the target was fixated most given W1W1,
substantially less given N3W1, and least given W2W1 (70%, 49%, and
42%, respectively); a complementary pattern was observed for the

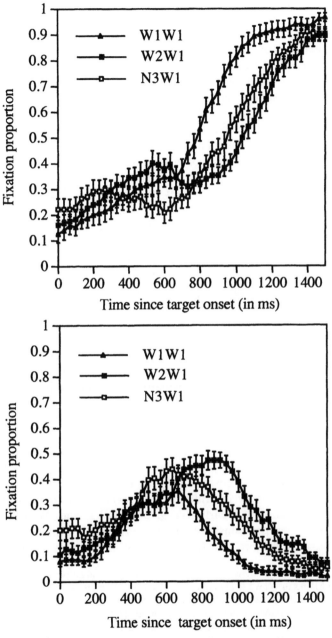

Figure 3. Experiment 2: Proportion of fixations to the target picture (W1) (upper panel) and the competitor picture (W2) (lower panel) over time, for each splicing condition (W1W1 [filled triangles], W2W1 [filled squares], N3W1 [empty squares]). Bars indicate standard errors.

competitor (15%, 29%, and 39%, respectively). A three-way ANOVA (picture [target or competitor] × splicing condition × voicing status) revealed a main effect of picture ($F_1(1, 28) = 56.6$, $p < .0001$, $MSE = .0612$; $F_2(1, 13) = 16.93$, $p < .001$, $MSE = .0607$) and a significant interaction between splicing condition and picture ($F_1(2, 56) = 26.65$, $p < .0001$, $MSE = .0603$; $F_2(2, 26) = 23.26$, $p < .0001$, $MSE = .0159$), reflecting the complementary pattern found for the target and competitor fixations across the splicing conditions. (The data from one subject were excluded from the subject analyses because of missing data causing empty cells.) No other main effect or interaction reached significance. A similar pattern of results (although marginally significant by items) was found when the analysis was restricted to the two crucial conditions (W2W1 and N3W1) and averaged across voicing status. There was a main effect of picture ($F_1(1, 29) = 28.86$, $p < .0001$, $MSE = .0320$; $F_2(1, 14) = 3.3$, $p = .09$, $MSE = .0467$) and an interaction between picture and splicing condition ($F_1(1, 29) = 5.32$, $p < .05$, $MSE = .0225$; $F_2(1, 14) = 2.8$, $p = .12$, $MSE = .0275$). Pairwise comparisons revealed a significant difference between W2W1 and N3W1 only on competitor fixations ($t_1(29) = 2.52$, $p < .05$, $t_2(14) = 1.99$, $p = .06$).[3]

Fixations to both the target and the competitor pictures over time revealed differences between the splicing conditions. Given W1W1, the target (W1) and its competitor (W2) were both equally activated until the sensory input, presumably the coarticulatory information in the vowel, favoured W1 over W2. While the input was consistent with both W1 and W2, these items were equally likely to be fixated. This is consistent with "cohort" effects previously demonstrated with the eye-tracking paradigm (Allopenna et al., 1998; Dahan et al., 2000; Tanenhaus et al., 1995). When coarticulatory information was encountered in the vowel given W1W1 or W2W1, fixations to the mismatching item decreased. Participants' sensitivity to coarticulatory information was revealed by the contrastive patterns for W1 and W2 early on given W1W1 and W2W1. Eye movements thus capture sensitivity to fine-grained information in the sensory input. Furthermore, the lesser decrease in fixations to W1 given

---

[3] We also conducted an analysis on the latency in fixating the target picture. On average, the latency was 819 ms in W1W1 (standard error = 33 ms), 1110 ms in W2W1 (standard error = 42 ms), and 1052 ms in N3W1 (standard error = 43 ms). A two-way (splicing condition × voicing status) ANOVA showed a main effect of condition ($F_1(2,56) = 14.9$, $p < .0001$, $MSE = 91887$; $F_2(2,26) = 17.27$, $p < .0001$, $MSE = 17379$), with no main effect of voicing and no interaction. Pairwise comparisons revealed significant differences between W1W1 and both W2W1 and N3W1, but not between W2W1 and N3W1. Note that both mean latencies and variability were noticeably greater than in Experiment 1, certainly due to the eye movements made to the competitor picture before fixating the target picture. Nevertheless, there was a trend toward slower latencies in fixating the target picture in W2W1 than in N3W1, confirmed in the fixation-proportion analysis.

N3W1 compared to W2W1 revealed lexical competition. The effect of mismatch was substantially less when the mismatching information did not favour any lexical alternative.

SIMULATIONS OF THE EYE-MOVEMENT DATA WITH THE TRACE MODEL

In order to test whether the eye-movement data are consistent with predictions from a model that incorporates lexical competition via lateral inhibition, we simulated the fixations to the target and competitor by transforming activation generated by TRACE into fixation probabilities. We used the publicly available TRACE implementation (*ftp://ftp.crl.ucsd.edu/pub/neuralnets*) with the standard parameter set reported in McClelland and Elman (1986).[4] The lexicon was augmented to 257 words to include the closest possible transcriptions of our stimuli given TRACE's limited phoneme set. The transcriptions of our stimuli are presented in Appendix A.

TRACE provides a coarse approximation of coarticulation by spreading features from a segment forward and backward six slices, such that each segment spans 11 cycles. Segments overlap because adjacent phoneme centres are six cycles apart. Features spread with a triangular function, such that they peak at each phoneme centre, and decrease gradually forward and backward from the peak. In our simulations, words were preceded by 6 cycles of silence; thus, the onset of each word was at cycle 7, with phoneme centres at cycle 12, 18, and 24. In order to generate W2W1 and N3W1 cross-spliced inputs, the cross-splicing point was chosen to follow the time slice immediately preceding the centre of the last consonant. Input stimuli were presented to TRACE, one at a time. All lexical items were allowed to compete.

Figure 4 shows the raw TRACE activation over time for W1 and W2 nodes as W1W1, W2W1, and N3W1 inputs were presented, averaged over the 15 items (upper panel). These activation patterns were converted into predicted fixation probabilities over time using a variant of the Luce choice rule applied to the four visually present alternatives, i.e., W1, W2, and two phonologically unrelated distractors (for a more detailed explanation of the issues involved in mapping activation onto fixation proportions, see Allopenna et al., 1998; Dahan et al., 2001; Magnuson, Tanenhaus, Aslin, & Dahan, submitted). Fixation probabilities are shown in the lower panel of Figure 4. The fixation probability for W1 rises fastest given W1W1,

---

[4] The default parameter set in the distribution version differs from that reported by McClelland and Elman (1986). In the original paper, all features were set to spread forward and backward six slices, whereas in the distribution code, different features spread different numbers of slices.

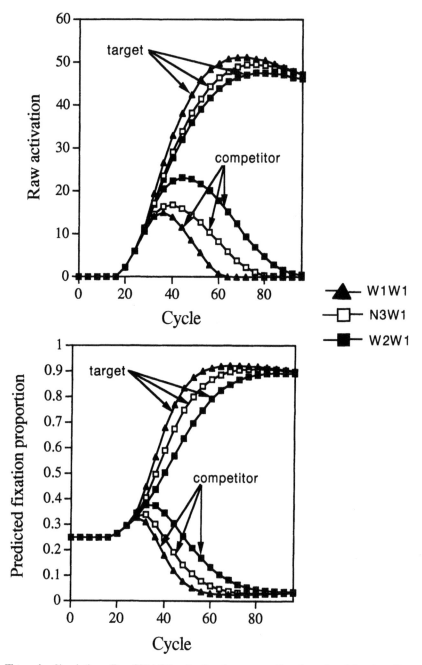

Figure 4. Simulations: Raw TRACE activation (upper panel) and predicted fixations (lower panel) for the target (W1) and the competitor (W2), over cycles, for each splicing condition (W1W1 [filled triangles], W2W1 [filled squares], N3W1 [empty squares]).

somewhat slower given N3W1, and slowest given W2W1. Note that W1 fixations reach a high probability in all conditions, even when the input in the vowel favours its competitor W2, as in W2W1 sequences. Activation levels are thus modulated by information occurring later in the input, counteracting earlier information. The model predicts more fixations to W2 given W2W1, less given N3W1, and the least given W1W1. The predicted fixations closely mirror the human data shown in Figure 3.

These simulations diverge from the TRACE simulations reported by Marslen-Wilson and Warren (1994) in important ways. Their simulations did predict a lower probability of recognising the target (W1) given W2W1 than given N3W1 or W1W1, in agreement with our human data and simulations. However, the probability of recognising W1 given W2W1 was only temporarily delayed in our simulations, while it remained very low even after 80 cycles in Marslen-Wilson and Warren's. Furthermore, they simulated lexical activation to cross-spliced nonword sequences (W2N1, e.g., *smo(g)b*), and found that the probability of recognising W2 given W2N1 reached roughly the same level as the probability of recognising W1 given W1W1 (see their Figures 12 and 13). Translated into lexical-decision judgements, these probabilities predict high error rates in lexical decisions given W2N1, because the nonword sequences W2N1 receive as much "word" support as the word sequences (W1W1 or N3W1). However, lexical decisions to the nonword sequences W2N1 had a very low error rate, both in the Marslen-Wilson and Warren (1994) and the McQueen et al. (1999) studies. Marslen-Wilson and Warren attributed the discrepancies between the human data and their simulations to TRACE's architecture (in particular, the presence of lateral inhibition between word nodes and absence of bottom-up inhibition). Because our simulations of the same conditions did not show the patterns reported by Marslen-Wilson and Warren, this suggests that these patterns resulted more from parameter and/or stimulus choices than from the principles underlying TRACE's architecture.[5]

---

[5] We have not been able to uncover the source of the discrepancies between our simulations and those reported by Marslen-Wilson and Warren (1994). However, it is clear that the pattern we report represents typical TRACE behaviour. It holds for splicing at multiple locations and three different parameter sets (those reported in McClelland & Elman [1986], the default parameter settings in the Unix distribution of the TRACE simulator, and the parameters described by Frauenfelder and Peeters [1998]). Similar results hold across different variants of the Luce choice rule with a range of values for the *k* parameter (see Magnuson, Dahan, and Tanenhaus, 2001, for details), different sets of stimuli (the CVC analogs to our stimuli, every possible stimulus set in the lexicon used by Marslen-Wilson and Warren, and the specific set of five triplets used by Marslen-Wilson and Warren [league/lead/ *leab, pug/pub/*pud, slab/slag/*slad, stab/stag/*stad, and shrub/shrug/*shrud; Warren, personal communication]), and two different implementations of TRACE (the Unix

(*continued overleaf*)

In summary, our TRACE simulations mirror the eye-movement data, with delayed fixation probabilities over time for the target (W1) in W2W1 compared to N3W1, caused by a high fixation probability for W2.

GENERAL DISCUSSION

The present study examined lexical competition when mismatching coarticulatory cues in a vowel (i.e., inconsistent with the actual identity of the following consonant) match another existing word and when these cues do not match an existing word. Earlier studies (Marslen-Wilson & Warren, 1994; McQueen et al., 1999) collected lexical-decision latencies to cross-spliced word sequences containing mismatching coarticulatory cues and found no effect of the lexical status of the conflicting cues. Marslen-Wilson and Warren (1994) interpreted this result as evidence against lateral inhibition between activated word units, as instantiated in the TRACE and Shortlist models. However, Norris et al. (2000) showed that the absence of a lexical effect between W2W1 and N3W1 is compatible with a model incorporating lateral inhibition if lexical competition is resolved before lexical-decision responses are generated. On their account, such lexical competition takes place but is resolved before activation reaches a sufficient threshold to generate a lexical decision.

The present eye-movement data showed that the recognition of W1 is delayed given W2W1, compared to N3W1, demonstrating clear lexical competition between the competitor (W2) and the target (W1), regardless of whether W2 was visually present or not. Using the linking hypothesis developed by Allopenna et al. (1998) and Dahan et al. (2001), we showed that lexical activation generated from TRACE mirror the eye-movement data quite closely. Predicted fixations to the competitor W2 reach a higher level and fixations to the target W1 are more delayed in W2W1 than in N3W1. Importantly, the subcategorical mismatch affects activation only *temporarily*. The target's activation reached the same maximum value in all splicing conditions, suggesting that the target will always be ultimately recognised. This contrasts with the simulations reported in Marslen-Wilson

---

implementation, and the Macintosh implementation, "MacTRACE", provided to us by Paul Warren). Although we obtained stronger competition effects given W2W1 for some items than for others (e.g., longer words, especially the CCVCs used by Marslen-Wilson and Warren), the patterns more closely resembled the results shown in Figure 4 than the pattern reported by Marslen-Wilson and Warren. In short, we were unable to replicate the pattern reported in Marslen-Wilson and Warren (1994) with any combination of these variables. Thus, it seems safe to conclude that whereas some combination of stimuli and parameters may result in simulations with the pattern presented in Marslen-Wilson and Warren (1994), the simulations that we report in this article are more representative of the results that arise from the TRACE architecture.

and Warren (1994), where the ultimate response probabilities favoured the pre-splice portion of the input (e.g., W2's activation given W2N1 was at least as high as W1's activation given W1W1), leading researchers to incriminate various aspects of TRACE's architecture, such as lateral inhibition and lack of bottom-up mismatch (Marslen-Wilson & Warren, 1994) or lack of "optimisation" at every input slice (Cutler, Norris, & McQueen, 2000; Norris et al., 2000). Although the source of the discrepancies between the present simulations and those reported by Marslen-Wilson and Warren remains unclear, the present results indicate that Marslen-Wilson and Warren's simulations cannot be considered decisive evidence against the architectural assumptions of TRACE (see discussion in footnote 5).

Both the eye-movement data and the TRACE simulations showed an effect of the lexical status of the pre-splice portion of the sequence. Target recognition, as assessed by fixations, was more delayed when the pre-splice portion of the sequence came from another word (as in W2W1) than when it did not (as in N3W1). However, lexical-decision studies (Marslen-Wilson & Warren, 1994; McQueen et al., 1999) showed no difference in response latencies between these conditions. Why do lexical-decision latencies fail to show a difference between the W2W1 and N3W1 conditions, while we find such a strong difference in the eye-movement data? McQueen et al. (1999) argued that the lexical-decision data show no difference between the W2W1 and N3W1 conditions because the lexical competition between W2 and W1 is quickly resolved and W1 dominates the activation pattern, "leaving no trace of that competition process in the [lexical-decision] responses made to the cross-spliced words" (page 1385). According to Norris and colleagues (Cutler et al., 2000; Norris et al., 2000), the dynamics of word-node activation in Merge (i.e., optimisation by letting the network cycle 15 times and resetting word nodes at each time slice) are required to account for the lexical-decision data. In their simulations, the competition between W2 and W1 is resolved by the end of the final consonant of the cross-spliced stimuli and W1's activation reaches a response threshold with the same delay in the W2W1 and N3W1 conditions. However, our eye-movement data, and in particular the subanalysis conducted on Experiment 1 (see Figure 2), suggest that effects of lexical competition in cross-spliced stimuli extend well beyond the target-word offset, that is, until after processing of the post-splice consonant is likely to have completed. Even when considering only single-fixation trials, the delay with which participants fixated the target picture was longer when the pre-splice portion of the target word matched a competing word than when it did not, and this effect extended about 200 ms after the post-splice consonant had been heard and processed. Thus, effects of competition can be observable for some time after sufficient input to resolve ambiguity has been heard and processed. This apparently delayed resolution of lexical competition, with respect to the time course with which spoken input becomes available, seems more compatible with a model like TRACE, where a word's activation at any particular point in time depends on both its activation at the previous time step and the current input, resulting in gradual increases and decreases of word activation, than with a model like Merge (or Shortlist), where multiple activation cycles and a reset of word nodes result in an optimal interpretation of the input at each time slice. Further evidence suggesting that the impact of speech information on the state of the lexical system is not immediate is provided by Zwitserlood and Schriefers (1995).

If competition effects do extend several hundred ms after disambiguating information has been heard, why aren't these effects reflected in lexical-decision latencies? A possible explanation for the absence of competition effects in the lexical-decision responses, as suggested by Norris and colleagues, is that participants responded after lexical competition had resolved. Mean reaction times in the McQueen et al. study were about 470 ms after target offset in the W2W1 and N3W1 conditions. If processing and motor-response delays in lexical decisions can be as short as 200 ms, responses could have been generated after full competition resolution. Note that on this account, there is no need to assume optimisation in competition resolution. However, this apparent lack of sensitivity of the lexical-decision task to lexical competition is at odds with other evidence that lexical-decision responses to a target word are influenced by the activation of its competitors. For instance, Luce and Pisoni (1998) showed that lexical-decision latencies to words in high-density neighbourhoods (i.e., words with many phonologically similar competitors) are slower than latencies to words in low-density neighborhoods. Why would response latencies to cross-spliced words, for which the initial activation of the pre-splice competitors is certainly very high, fail to show a competition effect? If anything, one would expect to see an especially strong competition effect with such stimuli.

As an alternative account for the absence of lexical-competition effects in the lexical-decision data, we propose that lexical-competition effects are masked in the mean lexical-decision latencies because the activation of competitors as well as targets influences lexical-decision responses. The lexical-decision task does not require correct identification of the intended target. Participants may also respond 'yes' in response to the high activation of a competitor item. More specifically, some 'yes' responses to W2W1 sequences would be triggered by W2's early strong activation, while the impact of competitors' activation would be small on responses to N3W1 sequences. The mean lexical-decision latency in the W2W1 condition would thus include a range of latencies, from early responses to the initial activation to W2 to late responses to W1, delayed by lexical competition. In contrast, the mean lexical-decision latency in the N3W1 condition would include responses triggered by W1 activation, moderately slowed down by the presence of a subcategorical mismatch.

As a first step in evaluating this hypothesis, we tested whether the variability in lexical-decision latencies to W2W1 sequences was greater than the variability in latencies to N3W1 sequences, as our account of the lexical-decision data implies.[6] We analysed the lexical-decision latencies from McQueen et al. (1999, Experiment 3), using standard deviation as a simple index of variability.[7] Following McQueen et al., reaction times slower than 1500 ms after sequence offset were excluded, but missing data points, due to outlying RTs or to errors, were not replaced. Latency standard deviations per participant and per condition were then computed and submitted to a one-way ANOVA. Mean standard deviations were 162 ms, 201 ms, and 168 ms for W1W1, W2W1, and N3W1 conditions, respectively, with a significant effect of conditions ($F(2, 88) = 11.85, p < .0001, MSE = 1700.8$). Newman–Keuls tests indicated that the standard deviation was greater in the W2W1 condition than in the N3W1 condition (with $\alpha = .05$).

The higher latency variability in W2W1 than in N3W1, despite equivalent means, suggests that the responses generated in these conditions may come from different underlying patterns of lexical activation. In order to provide further support for our account of the lexical-decision data, we developed a simple model to simulate these data under the assumption that a "yes" response is generated probabilistically when either the target (W1) or the competitor (W2) reaches threshold. (The activation of other words in the lexicon remains low and could have only negligible impact.) We conducted separate simulations using the eye-movement data collected in Experiment 2 and TRACE-activation data. Each simulation was run 1000 times for each of the 15 experimental items, across a range of response thresholds.[8] These simulations showed that

---

[6] It might seem that a stronger test of our hypothesis would be to test whether the distribution of lexical-decision responses in W2W1 differs from the response distribution in N3W1, and in particular, whether it fits a mixture of the two distributions generated by W2 and W1 activation (this mixture need not result in a bimodal distribution, in contrast with what Norris et al. [2000, p. 356] have argued). However, because the W2W1 and N3W1 distributions are very similar when the data from all the subjects are combined, and the number of data points per subject per condition is very small, explicit tests of the hypothesis are difficult.

[7] We are grateful to James McQueen, Dennis Norris, and Anne Cutler for providing their raw data.

[8] Space constraints preclude extensive details on the algorithm used in the simulations but a fuller report can be obtained from the authors.

predicted lexical-decision means given W2W1 and N3W1 were roughly identical and higher than for W1W1 across a range of thresholds before diverging, whether computed from fixation proportions from Experiment 2 or from TRACE activation. These simulations demonstrate that identical lexical-decision means can be obtained from different underlying W1 and W2 activation patterns in the W2W1 and N3W1 conditions, if one assumes that "yes" responses can be triggered by the activation of either the target W1 or its close competitor W2.

It is important to note that our lexical-decision simulations do not provide a comprehensive account of the McQueen et al. (1999) and Marslen-Wilson and Warren (1994) data. In particular, the simulation incorrectly predicts a higher error rate for the nonword sequence W2N1 (e.g., *smo(g)b*) than for the sequence N3N1 (e.g., *smo(d)b*) because early activation of W2 would trigger some "yes" responses. The human data showed low and equivalent error rates for both conditions. However, a closer look at the error rates reveals a complex pattern. Error rates were substantially higher in W2W1 and N3W1 than in all the other conditions, in both Marslen-Wilson and Warren (1994) and McQueen et al. (1999). This suggests a bias for the listeners to respond "no" to stimuli containing mismatching coarticulatory cues. Neither our lexical-decision simulation nor Norris et al.'s model accounts for these high error rates. A complete simulation of the lexical-decision data, accounting for both response latencies and error rates, will require a more complex decision mechanism than a simple threshold. The decision rule adopted by participants in these studies may well have been affected by the unusual nature of the stimuli, which contained a large proportion of cross-spliced sequences.

Regardless of how the lexical-decision data are interpreted, simulations of lexical activation of cross-spliced sequences with subcategorical mismatches all assume that, at some point during the recognition process, the recognition of the target W1 is more impaired given W2W1 than N3W1. The lexical-competition effect is apparent both in the TRACE simulations presented here and in Merge's activation levels in Norris et al. (2000), where word nodes in these localist connectionist models directly compete via lateral inhibition. These models are thus consistent with our eye-movement data. As shown in its simulations of the Marslen-Wilson and Warren data, the distributed model of speech perception (Gaskell & Marslen-Wilson, 1997, Figure 3) also predicts lexical-competition effects during the recognition of the target W1, although they are predicted to be small and transient. Our eye-movement data are also potentially consistent with the Cohort model (Marslen-Wilson, 1987) if one assumes that eye movements do not reflect lexical-activation levels per se, but are generated probabilistically from a *continuously* operating decision mechanism. A decision rule would continuously evaluate a candidate's activation proportionally to its competitors' activation. This would predict delayed target recognition in W2W1, because the most active competitor (W2) would be more active in W2W1 than in N3W1 (assuming other competitors were equally active). However, our eye-movement data rule out a model where lexical competition takes place at a late decision stage of recognition, because lexical-competition effects were observed well before the end of the cross-spliced stimuli.

We conclude by highlighting the critical implications of the current work. First, our results provide clear evidence for lexical competition. Second, because most current models incorporate some form of lexical competition, distinguishing among competing models will require detailed information about the time course of lexical activation, including how quickly competition is resolved, and an explicit hypothesis linking behavioural data to underlying processes. Our results demonstrate that the eye-tracking paradigm meets these criteria when coupled with simulations from an explicit model. Finally, the present study provides information about the time course of lexical competition that may provide important constraints on models of spoken word recognition.

REFERENCES

Allopenna, P.D., Magnuson, J.S., & Tanenhaus, M.K. (1998). Tracking the time course of spoken word recognition using eye movements: evidence for continuous mapping models. *Journal of Memory and Language, 38*, 419–439.

Cooper, R.M. (1974). The control of eye fixation by the meaning of spoken language. A new methodology for the real-time investigation of speech perception, memory, and language processing. *Cognitive Psychology, 6*, 84–107.

Cutler, A., Norris, D., & McQueen, J. (2000). Tracking TRACE's troubles. In A. Cutler, J. M. McQueen, & R. Zondervan (Eds.), *Proceedings of the Workshop on Spoken Word Access Processes* (pp. 63–66). Nijmegen: Max Planck Institute for Psycholinguistics.

Cycowicz, Y.M., Friedman, D., Rothstein, M., & Snodgrass, J.G. (1997). Picture naming by young children: Norms for name agreement, familiarity, and visual complexity. *Journal of Experimental Child Psychology, 65*, 171–237.

Dahan, D., Magnuson, J.S., & Tanenhaus, M.K. (2001). Time course of frequency effects in spoken-word recognition: evidence from eye movements. *Cognitive Psychology, 42*, 317–367.

Dahan, D., Swingley, D., Tanenhaus, M.K., & Magnuson, J.S. (2000). Linguistic gender and spoken-word recognition in French. *Journal of Memory and Language, 42*, 465–480.

Fischer, B. (1992). Saccadic reaction time: Implications for reading, dyslexia and visual cognition. In K. Rayner (Ed.), *Eye Movements and Visual Cognition: Scene Perception and Reading* (pp. 31–45). New York: Springer-Verlag.

Frauenfelder, U.H., & Floccia, C. (1998). The recognition of spoken words. In A.D. Friederici (Ed.), *Language comprehension: a biological perspective* (pp. 1–40). Berlin: Springer.

Frauenfelder, U.H. & Peeters, G. (1998). Simulating the time course of spoken word recognition: an analysis of lexical competition in TRACE. In J. Grainger and A.M. Jacobs (Eds.), *Localist connectionist approaches to human cognition* (pp. 101–146). Mahwah, NJ: Lawrence Erlbaum Associates Inc.

Gaskell, M.G., & Marslen-Wilson, W.D. (1997). Integrating form and meaning: a distributed model of speech perception. *Language and Cognitive Processes, 12,* 613–656.

Gaskell, M.G., & Marslen-Wilson, W.D. (1999). Ambiguity, competition, and blending in spoken word recognition. *Cognitive Science, 23,* 439–462.

Luce, P.A., & Pisoni, D.B. (1998). Recognizing spoken words: The Neighborhood Activation Model. *Ear and Hearing, 19,* 1–36.

Luce, R.D. (1959). *Individual choice behavior.* New York: Wiley.

Magnuson, J.S., Dahan, D., & Tanenhaus, M.K. (2001). On the interpretation of computational models: The case of TRACE. In J.S. Magnuson & K.M. Crosswhite (Eds.), *University of Rochester Working Papers in the Language Sciences, 2*(1), 71–91.

Magnuson, J.S., Tanenhaus, M.K., Aslin, R.N., & Dahan, D. (submitted). The time course of spoken word recognition in an artificial lexicon.

Marslen-Wilson, W. (1987). Functional parallelism in spoken word-recognition. *Cognition, 25,* 71–102.

Marslen-Wilson, W. (1990). Activation, competition, and frequency in lexical access. In G.T.M. Altmann (Ed.), *Cognitive models of speech processing. Psycholinguistic and computational perspectives* (pp. 148–172). Hove, UK: Lawrence Erlbaum Associates Ltd.

Marslen-Wilson, W., & Warren P. (1994). Levels of perceptual representation and process in lexical access. *Psychological Review, 101,* 653–675.

McClelland, J.L., & Elman, J.L. (1986). The TRACE model of speech perception. *Cognitive Psychology, 18,* 1–86.

McQueen, J.M., Norris, D., & Cutler, A. (1999). Lexical influence in phonetic decision making: evidence from subcategorical mismatches. *Journal of Experimental Psychology: Human Perception and Performance, 25,* 1363–1389.

Norris, D. (1994). Shortlist: a connectionist model of continuous speech recognition. *Cognition, 52,* 189-234.

Norris, D., McQueen, J.M., & Cutler, A. (2000). Merging information in speech recognition: feedback is never necessary. *Behavioral and Brain Sciences, 23,* 299–325.

Saslow, M.G. (1967). Latency for saccadic eye movement. *Journal of the Optical Society of America, 57,* 1030–1033.

Snodgrass, J.G., & Vanderwart, M. (1980). A standardized set of 260 pictures: Norms for name agreement, image agreement, familiarity, and visual complexity. *Journal of Experimental Psychology: Human Learning and Memory, 6,* 174–215.

Streeter, L.A., & Nigro, G.N. (1979). The role of medial consonant transitions in word perception. *Journal of Acoustical Society of America, 65,* 1533–1541.

Tanenhaus, M.K., Spivey-Knowlton, M.J., Eberhard, K.M., & Sedivy, J.C. (1995). Integration of visual and linguistic information in spoken language comprehension. *Science, 268,* 1632–1634.

Viviani, P. (1990). Eye movements in visual search: Cognitive, perceptual, and motor control aspects. In E. Kowler (Ed.), *Eye movements and their role in visual and cognitive processes* (pp. 353–393). Amsterdam: Elsevier.

Whalen, D.H. (1991). Subcategorical phonetic mismatches and lexical access. *Perception and Psychophysics, 50,* 351–360.

Whalen, D.H. (1984). Subcategorical phonetic mismatches slow phonetic judgments. *Perception & Psychophysics, 35,* 49–64.

Zwitserlood, P., & Schriefers, H. (1995). Effects of sensory information and processing time in spoken-word recognition. *Language and Cognitive Processes, 10,* 121–136.

APPENDIX A

Same voicing

Target W1	Word Competitor W2	Nonword Competitor N3
net (*git*)	neck (*gik*)	*nep (*gip*)
tap (*tap*)	tack (*tak*)	tat (*tat*)
bud (*bud*)	bug (*bug*)	*bub (*bub*)
butt (*b^t*)	buck (*b^k*)	*bup (*b^p*)
carp (*kup*)	cart (*kut*)	*cark (*kuk*)
fort (*srt*)	fork (*srk*)	*forp (*srp*)
harp (*lrp*)	heart (*lrt*)	hark (*lrk*)

Different voicing

Target W1	Word Competitor W2	Nonword Competitor N3
cat (*kat*)	cab (*kab*)	*cag (*kag*)
bat (*bat*)	bag (*bag*)	*bab (*bab*)
road (*rid*)	rope (*rip*)	*roke (*rik*)
pit (*pit*)	pig (*pig*)	*pib (*pib*)
hood (*sud*)	hook (*suk*)	*hoop (*sup*)
knot (*gut*)	knob (*gub*)	*knog (*gug*)
beak (*bik*)	bead (*bid*)	*beab (*bib*)
rod (*rud*)	rock (*ruk*)	*rop (*rup*)

Note: * indicates a sequence that is not a real word in American English. The transcriptions adopted in the TRACE simulations (given the lack of some phonemes) are indicated in parentheses.

APPENDIX B

Experimental Trials

Distractor 1	Target W1	Distractor 2 / Competitor W2	Distractor 3
bass	net	nurse / neck	deer
skunk	tap	trunk / tack	peas
fox	bud	bow / bug	eye
clams	butt	bride / buck	ghost
swing	carp	comb / cart	moon
light	fort	flag / fork	hat
desk	harp	house / heart	claw
vase	cat	crown / cab	tree
pen	bat	bone / bag	stool
knee	road	rug / rope	glass
ark	pit	pot / pig	flute
eggs	hood	hose / hook	brush
mouse	knot	knight / knob	beer
saw	beak	bench / beads	thumb
bear	rod	rake / rocks	fries

Note: Distractor 1 corresponds to the target picture from the initial "point to" instruction. Distractor 2 was displayed only in Experiment 1; the Competitor W2, only in Experiment 2.

LANGUAGE AND COGNITIVE PROCESSES, 2001, *16* (5/6), 535–564

Variation and assimilation in German: Consequences for lexical access and representation

Else Coenen, Pienie Zwitserlood, and Jens Bölte

University of Münster, Germany

The consequences of surface variation in speech on lexical access have recently received considerable attention. The lexical system is intolerant to mismatch between input and lexical representation, but an exception is phonologically regular variation. One example is assimilation of consonants that adopt the place of articulation of adjacent consonants in fast speech. Data are presented from crossmodal form priming experiments in German on regressive and progressive assimilation at word boundaries. The results show that some, but not all forms of lawful variation are tolerated by the lexical system. The consequences of these findings for psycholinguistic and linguistic models, some of which incorporate explanations for regular variation, are discussed.

To understand spoken language, listeners have to map the speech input onto lexical representations that specify the sound structure of words. This process is usually very fast and efficient, even though words can be pronounced differently in fluent speech than when carefully uttered in isolation. Not all deviations from correct pronunciation are tolerated. In recent years, evidence has accumulated that mismatch between input and lexical representation can pose problems for word recognition (Connine, Blasko, & Titone, 1993; Connine, Titone, Deelman, & Blasko, 1997; Marslen-Wilson, 1993; Marlsen-Wilson & Gaskell, 1992; Marslen-Wilson & Zwitserlood, 1989). Mispronounced words (e.g., *noney*) failed to effectively activate the form representations of the intended real word

Requests for reprints should be sent to Pienie Zwitserlood, Psychologisches Institut II, Fliednerstraße 21, 48149 Münster, Germany. Email: zwitser@psy.uni-muenster.de

We are very grateful to Ricarda Petzmeyer, who prepared and ran Experiment 2 in partial fulfilment of her Masters thesis (Petzmeyer, 2000). We thank Heidi Gumnior for lending us her voice. We gratefully acknowledge the valuable comments by Hugo Quene and Gareth Gaskell on an earlier version of this paper. The data of Experiment 1 were presented at the 41. Tagung experimentell arbeitender Psychologen, Leipzig, 1999 and the Regionalkolloquium, Braunschweig, 1999.

http://www.tandf.co.uk/journals/pp/01690965.html   DOI: 10.1080/0169096014300155

(e.g., HONEY) or a semantic associate of that word (e.g., BEE). Minimal mismatch, in terms of phonological features, does not completely preclude lexical access (Bölte & Coenen, 2001; Connine et al., 1993). All these experiments used prime stimuli presented in isolation, and did not distinguish between naturally occurring, regular variations and accidental mispronunciations.

A frequent type of regular variation is assimilation. In connected speech, speech segments can assimilate to adjacent segments, such that *hot bath* can be produced as [a]*hopbath*.[1] Stated in terms of phonological features, the segment [t] can lose its own (coronal) place of articulation and adopt the (labial) place of the following segment [b]. Three issues are important here. First, assimilation is context-dependent, that is, it only occurs in the presence of an adjacent segment that triggers—or licenses, in speech perception terms—the change. Thus, *hot* will only be pronounced as *hop* when followed by a word starting with a labial (e.g., *bath)*, not when followed by words whose first segments have another place of articulation (e.g., *gruel)*. Second, not all features can undergo assimilation. To stay with our example of place assimilation: Coronal segments (e.g., [t], [d], [n]) can legally change to labial ([p], [b], [m]) or velar ([k], [g], [ng]). However, labial or velar segments never adopt a coronal place of articulation (Kohler, 1995). We will thus label such changes illegal. Third, assimilation is often not complete. Complete assimilation with a change in phoneme status ([t] → [p]) does indeed occur, but often changes are graded, with traces of the original place of articulation present in the signal (Gow, 2000; Nolan, 1992).

Assimilation, as a phenomenon in speech production, has important implications for speech perception and word recognition. Perception models which incorporate a more or less abstract specification of the sound structure of words have to deal with deviations between the input and lexical specifications. A theoretically relevant issue concerns the legality of such deviations. Whereas legal and naturally occurring changes should be tolerated by such models, this must not be so for other deviations.

To add to a growing body of evidence, we investigated regular variation in German, typically present in fast and informal speech, comparing regular variation to other deviations that do not occur naturally. A range of factors relevant to assimilation was investigated within the same study. First, we contrasted legal changes such as coronal-to-labial (as in [a]*hopbath)* with illegal changes, such as labial-to-coronal (as in *totdrawer* for top drawer). Second, we investigated the context-dependency of assimilation, by contrasting contextually appropriate and inappropriate changes

---

[1] In the examples, legal and contextually appropriate assimilation will be marked by an [a]. All other changed words were pseudowords.

(ᵃ*hopbath* vs. *hopgruel*). Third, we studied the directionality of the assimilation, by comparing the frequent case of regressive assimilation (ᵃ*hopbath*) with progressive cases (ᵃ*hotnug* for hot mug), which are not very common in German (Kohler, 1995). We tested assimilation in its extreme form, that is, the assimilated items were spoken such that a change of phoneme status occurred.[2]

There are a number of theoretical approaches to account for assimilation, both from linguistic and psycholinguistic perspectives, which we briefly discuss. The first proposal comes from phonology and holds that not all phonological features of segments are specified in the underlying structure. For example, radical underspecification theory states that features which are redundant, predictable and unmarked, are not specified (Archangeli, 1988; Kiparsky, 1985; Pulleyblank, 1988).[3] Since the feature [coronal] can assimilate to labial or velar, it is assumed to be unmarked and not specified. Thus, a coronal segment such as [t] is not specified for its place of articulation, while a labial segment such as [p] is fully specified. Although discussed controversially in linguistics (McCarthy & Taub, 1992; Steriade, 1995), underspecification is an elegant way to cope with legal variation in the speech input. Assuming a close correspondence between underlying phonological structure and word form representations in the mental lexicon, assimilated cases present no mismatch between surface speech information and lexical representations, if the latter are under-specified (Lahiri & Marslen-Wilson, 1991). Note that with underspecified representations, the contextual appropriateness of an assimilation should not play a major role.

Important to other linguistic approaches is the graded nature of assimilation. The basic units in models from articulatory phonology are not features but gestures, that is, abstract characterisations of articulatory events, that have their complement in perception (Browman & Goldstein, 1992). Assimilation is explained in terms of such gestures, which, each having an intrinsic time duration, can overlap in time.[4] In cases of temporal overlap, some gestures can dominate others. Moreover, combinations of gestures, so called gestural scores, do not code all vocal tract information at all points in time and are thus in some sense underspecified. Byrd (1992) demonstrated that the asymmetry between legal (e.g., ᵃ*hopbath*) and illegal (e.g., *totdrawer*) changes can be accounted for by the gestural model.

---

[2] Whereas it is easy to produce a complete change of phoneme status with nasals, it is less easy with plosives, because the consonantal release is normally not complete. We used plosives in only 4 out of 18 sets in the critical condition of regressive place assimilation, to which this argument applies.

[3] In the following, we refer to radical underspecification by "underspecification".

[4] A similar proposal, in featural terms, is made by Gow (2000), who explains partial assimilation as the simultaneous presence of two features.

Some psycholinguistic models also allow for a less than perfect match between input and representation. For the TRACE model of spoken word recognition (McClelland & Elman, 1986), with its featural, phonemic, and lexical levels, and with bi-directional and excitatory connections between layers, assimilation does not pose severe problems. An input such as /greem/ will activate word nodes (e.g., *green, grief, gleam, cream*), even if there is no perfect match. Mismatch has no direct negative consequences for word units, although recognition might be delayed. One exception in TRACE is when another word form represents a closer match to the input. When a word such as *gun* is assimilated to /gum/ (as in [a]*gumpowder)*, the existing word node *gum* provides a closer match to the input than the assimilated word (see Gaskell, this issue; Gow, 2000; Koster, 1987). In that case, competition between word nodes will delay or even prevent recognition. Importantly, since TRACE was not designed to differentiate between fortuitous mispronunciations and lawful variation, it does not predict any differences between legal and illegal deviations. Moreover, the context which licenses variation (e.g., the [p] in *powder*) should be irrelevant.

The first psycholinguistic model to incorporate underspecification was the Cohort model (Marslen-Wilson, 1993). It is as intolerant to mismatch between input and lexical representation as earlier versions of the model (Marslen-Wilson, 1987), but this intolerance does not apply in all cases. Based on data from Bengali and English (Lahiri & Marslen-Wilson, 1991), an underspecification view of the mental lexicon was adopted, such that legal variations due to coarticulation or assimilation no longer constitute a mismatch at the lexical level. Phonological context was not taken into account at this stage.

Phonological context does play a role in a recent (distributed) connectionist instantiation of the Cohort model (Gaskell, Hare, & Marslen-Wilson, 1995; Gaskell & Marslen-Wilson, 1997, 1998, 1999). The most prominent properties of the model are a direct and simultaneous mapping of the featural input onto semantic and phonological output representations at the lexical layer. To allow for a broader time scope, a set of hidden units is linked in a recurrent way to the state of hidden units at previous time-steps. This allows for an evaluation of featural context, and thus of contextual appropriateness.

EXPERIMENTS ON ASSIMILATION

Whereas there is a long research tradition into effects of coarticulation on speech perception (e.g., Howell, 1983; Mann & Repp, 1980; Martin & Bunnell, 1982; Meyer & Gordon, 1985), few studies have investigated the type of variation we are interested in here. Koster (1987), for Dutch, showed that legal place assimilation is not without costs. Detection of [n] was faster in unchanged *eten brood* (eat bread) than in assimilated [a]*etem brood* cases. In contrast, Otake, Yoneyama, Cutler, and van der Lugt (1996) reported no such effects for the detection of assimilated moraic nasals in Japanese. Interestingly, Weber (2001) found facilitation of detection times for consonants following obligatory place assimilation in German (e.g., detection of [p] after /femp/) compared to violations of assimilation (e.g., /fenp/). These studies focused more on the mapping of assimilated sounds onto abstract prelexical representations (segments, morae) than on lexical representation.

Gaskell, Marslen-Wilson and colleagues (Gaskell & Marslen-Wilson, 1996, 1998, 1999; Marslen-Wilson, Nix, & Gaskell, 1995) investigated unassimilated and assimilated words such as *late* and [a]*lake*, embedded in a sentence context (*They thought the late/lake cruise ...*). With assimilated words cut off before consonantal release, a forced choice test revealed good discrimination, but a gating task showed a clear asymmetry (Marslen-Wilson et al., 1995). Non-coronal items were interpreted as potentially coronal, but not vice versa. This is in line with underspecification. Surprisingly, a crossmodal form priming experiment, with assimilated primes presented in isolation (e.g., [a]*heap* or [a]*heak* as primes for the possible underlying word form HEAT), showed interference rather than facilitation. Marslen-Wilson et al. concluded that the presence of context might be crucial for effects in on-line tasks.

In follow-up studies (Gaskell & Marslen-Wilson, 1996, 1998) with changed and unchanged words embedded in sentences, place assimilation of coronal segments was contextually viable if the following segment licensed the change (e.g., *Sandra will only eat* [a]*leam bacon*). The same change was unviable if followed by a velar context (e.g., *leam gammon*). With the context following the prime cut off (e.g., *Sandra will only eat lean/*[a]*leam*, target LEAN), assimilated tokens primed as strongly as unchanged words. This stands in stark contrast to the results for words presented in isolation (Marslen-Wilson et al., 1995). So, either the presence of a consonantal release matters, or changed items are interpreted as assimilated when a prosodic context is present. Moreover, as underspecification would have it, access to lexical representations on the basis of assimilated tokens is possible even without a licensing context. When a licensing context was present (e.g., *bacon*), assimilated words primed as strongly as unchanged words. But effects were severely reduced for assimilated words in unviable context (e.g., *gammon*). This is not easily reconciled with underspecification in the lexicon. If the place value of coronals is unspecified, context should not matter. More in line with underspecification, Lahiri (1995), with German materials in an auditory-auditory form priming experiment, found no significant difference between changed words (ªweim, from *wein*, wine) as a function of the viability of the following context. So, available data on the importance of a licensing context provide support in favour of and against underspecification.

EXPERIMENTAL CONSIDERATIONS

In the present study, we manipulated contextual viability or appropriateness, the legality of the change and the direction of assimilation within the same experiment, which constitutes an improvement on the methodology of earlier studies. Assimilation was always complete, resulting in a change in phoneme status (see note 2). We tested assimilated items in context (Experiment 1) and in isolation (Experiment 2). Our experiments expanded on the conditions under which assimilation has been investigated so far.

Contextual viability or licensing.   As in most of the above experiments, we presented unchanged and changed words, in viable and unviable contexts. A context was viable when a segment in the context word contained the feature that triggered the change in the segment involved in assimilation. An example is *wort* (word) changed to ªworp before *mal* (just), with [m] containing the feature [labial]. The change was unviable when the context segment was incongruent with the change, as in *worp* before *kurz* (briefly), with [k] containing the feature [velar]). Unlike the cases used by Marslen-Wilson et al. (1995), assimilation never resulted in identical segments in assimilated and context words.

Type of assimilation.   So far, only assimilation of place of articulation was discussed. We tested two types of assimilation: Assimilation of place of articulation, and of voice. In place assimilation, a coronal feature can be realised as labial or velar, if an adjacent segment contains the labial or velar feature. Similarly, a voiced consonant can lose the feature [voiced] in the context of a segment which is voiceless (see below).

Direction of assimilation.   We also varied the direction of assimilation, which can be regressive or progressive. So far, only regressive assimilation has been investigated, with a context segment triggering a featural change in the preceding segment. In progressive assimilation a featural change is triggered in a following segment (e.g., ªhemp for *hemt*, shirt or ªlebmde for *lebnde*, living). As the examples show, progressive place assimilation is attested word-internally in German, not across word boundaries (Kohler, 1995). Our experiments were designed to test the general idea of underspecification, as well as assumptions about a special status of word-onsets in word recognition (Marslen-Wilson & Zwitserlood, 1989). We therefore tested progressive place assimilation across word boundaries, as in bring [a]*kulpen* for bring *tulpen* (bring tulips). If [coronal] is generally not specified in the language, similar effects might be observed for progressive as for regressive or word-internal assimilation. Voice assimilation could only be tested progressively. In German, the rule of syllable-final devoicing devoices all voiced segments in coda position. So, loss of voice is obligatorily here, independent of the featural specification of the following segment.

Legality of change.   We tested phonologically legal and illegal cases, as did Lahiri (1995). As mentioned earlier, we consider assimilation that is attested in the language to be the legal case. Legal place assimilation involved changes from a coronal to a velar or labial place of articulation. Illegal changes are from a velar or labial to a coronal place of articulation, which are not attested in German (Kohler, 1995).

For voice assimilation, [voiced] was assumed to be unspecified, while [unvoiced] is specified. Thus, changing a voiced segment into an unvoiced one would constitute the legal assimilation, while transforming a voiceless into a voiced segment constitutes the illegal case. Where "legality" captures established phonological facts for place assimilation, the situation is far less clear for voice (cf. Kenstowicz, 1994). The rigorous application of syllable-final devoicing in German renders it likely that [voiced] is the unspecified case. Moreover, Kohler (1995) reports progressive and regressive assimilation of voice in German. All cases concern loss of voice in licensing contexts (which are abundant in a related language such as Dutch): [a]*hat [s]elbst* for *hat [z]elbst* or [a]*deutpar* for *deutbar*. Although loss of voice is reported to be complete, phonetically, the segment remains weak (i.e., lenis). Given the somewhat unclear status of the [voiced] feature and of the facts in the language, we should treat legality of change with caution in voice assimilation.

Predictions

The theories and models summarised above make the following predictions. If assimilation is treated just as any other noise in the signal, as in TRACE, none of the manipulations should make a difference. Illegal and legal changes should be treated alike, and context should be irrelevant. For underspecification, legality of the change should matter, but context should not. If particular features are not specified in the lexicon, a "loss" of such features due to assimilation should clearly be tolerated, independently of context. Theoretically, the directionality of assimilation should not matter either. Finally, contextual appropriateness of the change is important for the distributed instantiation of the Cohort model.

EXPERIMENT 1: CROSSMODAL FORM PRIMING IN SENTENCE CONTEXT

We investigated assimilation of adjacent segments in sentential context by means of a crossmodal identical form priming paradigm. As in the experiments by Gaskell and Marslen-Wilson (1996, 1998), assimilated and unchanged words were embedded in sentences, and the targets for the lexical decision task were the visually presented unchanged words. Materials for the experiment were pretested for discriminability of changed and unchanged words.

Method

Participants.   Ninety-six native speakers of German were tested in the main experiment, twenty in the pretest. They were mainly students of Münster University, participating for course credits.

Materials.   Six different material groups were constructed, one for each combination of the factors Type of Assimilation (regressive and progressive place, and progressive voice) and Legality (legal vs. illegal change). A sample set of materials is given in Appendix A. There were 18 targets within each of these material groups. Six primes, embedded in a sentence context, were constructed for each target. Primes were either unchanged (*wort*) or changed (*worp*). Changed and unchanged primes were followed by words that either licensed the change ([a]*worp mal*, viable context) or not (*worp kurz*, unviable context). The two baseline conditions contained unchanged (e.g., *blatt*, sheet) and changed (e.g., *blapp*) control words, which were unrelated to the targets of crossmodal priming but shared the critical segment. Changed control words always appeared in an unviable context. Thus, we had a two (unchanged × changed) by three (viable, unviable, control) within design for each of the six material groups.

Prime words were presented in sentential context. The first context sentence was a lead-in, the second sentence contained the critical prime word. Within each material group, test and control primes were matched for frequency and number of syllables. Changed and unchanged segments were all plosives ([p], [b], [t], [d], [k], [g]) or nasals ([m], [n], [ng]). Prime words were nouns or adjectives, with one or two syllables. They were never separated from the critical context word by a prosodic boundary, because assimilation usually does not cross such boundaries (Holst & Nolan, 1996). Although the speaker read the material with normal and fluent speaking rate, care was taken that the change was always complete, that is, a different segment was spoken in assimilated and unchanged conditions. In no case did the changed segment result in a real word: All changed words were pseudowords.

The complete material set was spoken by a female speaker onto DAT tape. Materials were digitised at 22.05 kHz with 16 bit resolution and stored on hard disk. All speech editing was done under visual and auditory control, using the CSRE 4.5 Software package.

Pretest

A pretest was carried out to check whether the critical items were unambiguously perceived as unchanged or changed. For this test, the lead-in sentence as well as all of the critical sentence following the context word were cut out (e.g., *kannst du das wort mal/[a]worp mal*). Four conditions were pretested: the test and control words of each item set in their unchanged (e.g., *wort, blatt*) and changed (e.g., *worp, blapp*) variants. Control items were presented in their control sentence, test items in the viable context only. Given the naturalness of the (complete) assimilation, items were probably produced with greater articulatory ease in the viable context. Thus, this constitutes a conservative test for the perceptibility of the change, since it could more readily be missed.

We included additional pseudoword pairs to control for a potential lexical bias effect (Ganong, 1980; Samuel, 1996). These pseudowords were derived from the test stimuli, with the same changed or unchanged segment and the same context segment (e.g., *blatt—blapp → gratt–grapp*). So, within each item set there was a 2 × 3 design with Change (unchanged/changed) and Item type (test item, control item, pseudoword). The 648 partial sentences were divided over two lists, so that the unchanged and changed version of each item appeared on separate lists.

Participants performed a binary forced-choice task, with written versions of the changed and unchanged stimuli as the two alternative answers. They also had to indicate the confidence in their response on a five point scale (1: not at all confident, 5: very confident). Each trial consisted of a warning tone, followed by the sentence fragment with critical and context word.

Participants produced 96.9% correct responses on average (see Table 1 for error percentages as a function of conditions). The mean confidence rating was 4.6. There were hardly any errors in the voice assimilation condition (0.5%). More errors were made for place assimilation (4.4%). Here, changed items attracted more errors than unchanged ones. This effect concerned words and pseudowords equally. Thus, there was no bias towards making a word response.

We used the following criteria to decide which of the material sets could be included in the analyses of the main experiment. When at least half of the responses in one of the four conditions were erroneous, the complete item set was excluded from the analyses. This concerned six item sets (out of 18) for regressive place assimilation, phonologically legal, and two item

TABLE 1
Pretest 1: Error percentages as a function of conditions

| Direction and type | Context | Legality of assimilation | | | |
| | | Phonologically legal | | Phonologically illegal | |
		Unchanged	Changed	Unchanged	Changed
Regressive	Viable	6.7	16.7	3.9	11.7
place	Control	0.6	17.2	0.6	8.9
Progressive	Viable	1.1	0.0	0.6	0.6
place	Control	0.6	0.6	0.0	0.6
Progressive	Viable	0.0	1.1	0.0	0.0
place	Control	0.6	1.1	1.1	1.7

sets for regressive place assimilation, phonologically illegal. After exclusion of these items the overall mean error rate was reduced to 1.7%.

Main experiment

Design. All materials, with lead-in sentences and complete second sentences of all conditions, were tested with crossmodal priming. An item set consisted of a visually presented target, which was combined with six primes, embedded in sentences. The factors Change (changed vs. unchanged word) and Context (viable, unviable, control) were within-material factors. Type of Assimilation (regressive place, progressive place, progressive voice) and Legality (legal vs. illegal change) were varied between item sets. All 18 item sets in each of the six material groups were used.

Materials were rotated across six lists, with a different sentence of each item set on each list. Of the 108 sentences per list, two thirds had related prime target pairs, one third had unrelated pairs (control condition). To counterbalance this difference, 36 unrelated fillers were added. The resulting 144 sentences all had real word targets, so that another 144 sentences with pseudoword targets were constructed, with a similar combination of conditions as the experimental material. As for word targets, half of the pseudoword targets were preceded by form-related primes (e.g., *rast* (rest) *rask*), the other half by unrelated primes. Each list of 288 sentences was randomised and recorded in ascending and descending order, to avoid position effects. An additional 24 practice sentences preceded the experimental items.

Procedure. Up to three participants were tested simultaneously. The material was presented in three blocks, with breaks in between. Each trial started with a short warning tone. After 350 ms, the sentence pair was presented via headphones. At the acoustic offset of the prime which was embedded in the second sentence, the visual target was presented for 350 ms on a monitor (Sony Multiscan 100sf) in front of each participant. Participants had to press a yes button if the target was a word and a no button if it was not. Word responses were given with the dominant hand. Reaction time was measured from target onset, for 1500 ms. After 1750 ms the next trial started. A test session lasted about 45 min.

Results

Three of the ninety-six participants, from three different lists, were excluded because of high error rates. Errors, as well as the eight item sets with poor performance in the pretest, were excluded from data analyses. So were reaction times above 1500 ms. The overall error rate for the remaining participants and items was 5.8%. Table 2 displays the mean reaction times and error rates for each material set, as a function of conditions.

Separate ANOVAs, with subjects (F_1) and items (F_2) as random factor, were calculated for each of the six material groups, because each group had different targets. Because targets were counterbalanced over lists, we included List as an additional factor in the F_1 analyses to remove some of the variability that results from different participants seeing the same target under different priming conditions (Pollatsek & Well, 1995). This was not done for the F_2 analyses, because the number of items was unbalanced after removal of sets that showed poor performance in the

TABLE 2

Experiment 1: Mean RTs in ms and error percentages (in parentheses) as a function of conditions

| | | Legality of assimilation | | | |
| | | Phonologically legal | | Phonologically illegal | |
Direction and type	Context	Unchanged	Changed	Unchanged	Changed
Regressive place	Viable	593 (1.1)	608 (3.2)	638 (2.0)	671 (9.2)
	Unviable	587 (1.1)	640 (1.6)	632 (2.8)	680 (9.3)
	Control	684 (7.5)	669 (2.7)	718 (14.6)	701 (11.6)
Progressive place	Viable	614 (2.9)	671 (7.2)	619 (3.6)	693 (5.4)
	Unviable	632 (4.7)	676 (9.3)	640 (1.4)	682 (5.4)
	Control	701 (7.2)	690 (8.2)	718 (10.0)	707 (7.9)
Progressive voice	Viable	615 (2.2)	648 (5.0)	646 (2.2)	691 (6.8)
	Unviable	608 (2.2)	669 (5.0)	620 (4.3)	695 (5.4)
	Control	689 (6.8)	684 (2.2)	719 (12.9)	698 (9.0)

pretest. Values for the factor List will not be reported, nor will F values
< 1.

Because we were interested in differences in lexical activation
depending on Context, Legality and Change, we used priming effects as
a measure of lexical activation. Priming effects were computed by
subtracting the means in test conditions from the means in corresponding
control conditions, within each factor level. These means had been derived
by either averaging over items (F_1) or participants (F_2), in each condition.[5]
The factors in each of the six ANOVAs with priming effects as the
dependent measure were Change (unchanged vs. changed), Context
(viable vs. unviable) and List (1–6), for the subjects analyses. The
reliability of priming effects was tested against zero; all statistical
information concerning these t-tests is provided in Appendix B. Results
will be reported separately for each material group, starting with
phonologically legal regressive place assimilation. Figure 1 presents
priming effects for each material group as function of conditions.

Regressive place assimilation, phonologically legal.   There was a main
effect for Change (*wort*, unchanged vs. *worp*, changed), $F_1(1, 84) = 7.986$,
$p = .006$, which just failed significance by items: $F_2(1, 11) = 4.409, p = .06$.
Overall, effects were larger for unchanged (*wort*: 94 ms) than for changed
words (*worp*: 45 ms). The main effect of Context just failed significance for
$F_1(1, 84) = 3.411, p = .068$ and was not significant by items (F < 1). A
significant interaction further qualified the main effect(s): $F_1(1, 84) =$
$4.665, p = .034$, and $F_2(1, 11) = 4.938, p = .048$. As expected, Context was
irrelevant for unchanged items (*wort mal* vs. *wort kurz*), with almost equal
and highly significant effects in viable (*wort mal*: 91 ms) and unviable
contexts (*wort kurz*: 97 ms; see Appendix B). Consequently, the
interaction was due to a difference between assimilated items. Although
both showed reliable facilitation ([a]*worp mal*: 61 ms in viable context, *worp
kurz*: 29 ms in unviable context), the effect was twice as large when a viable
context licensed the change, $t_1(90) = 2.381, p = .019, t_2(11) = 2.028, p =$
.068 (note that power is reduced by loss of items). The error data showed
no speed-accuracy trade-off effects, because there were more errors in
changed (2.4%) than in unchanged (1.1%) conditions (leaving out baseline
data).

The larger effect in viable contexts demonstrates that the presence of a
licensing segment does influence the success of the mapping between input

---

[5] In ANOVAs on means with the baseline included, significant main effects and
interactions were obtained for each material group. The ANOVAs without baselines showed
the same pattern of significance for main effects and interactions in the same item groups as
the analyses on difference scores.

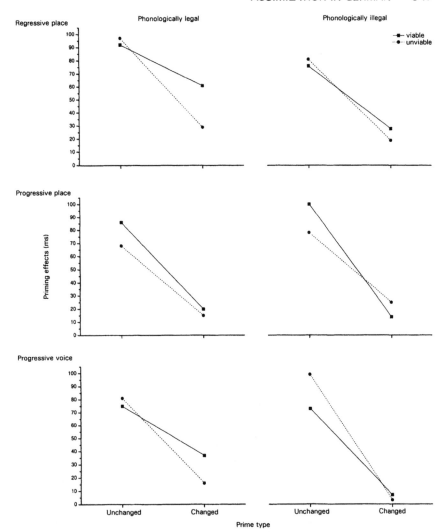

Figure 1. Experiment 1: priming effects in six material groups, as a function of Context and Change.

and lexical representation. This was not expected by underspecification, for which context should not matter. Another question is whether assimilated words in viable contexts were as effective as unchanged words. In a direct comparison of means, Gaskell & Marslen-Wilson (1996) found no difference. We find a small one: mean RT was 593 ms for unchanged (*wort*) and 608 for changed words (*worp*: $t_1(90) = 1.145$, $p = .255$; $t_2(11) < 1$). Another way of looking at this issue is by comparing effect sizes. Numerically, the effect is 30 ms larger for unchanged than for assimilated words. However, this difference also failed significance: $t_1(89) = 1.595, p = .114$; $t_2(11) = 1.169, p = .267$. We will come back to this question.

Taken together, the results support a speech recognition system that analyses deviations in connection with phonological context. When assimilation is licensed by a following segment, lexical access is only mildly affected (*wort mal*: 91 ms vs. ᵃ*worp mal*: 61 ms). The same change in unviable context leads to a strong decrease in priming, relative to the unchanged condition (*wort kurz*: 97 ms vs. *worp kurz*: 29 ms).

The next section investigates whether such minimal changes have to meet the rules of assimilation in speech production. Are changes in place of assimilation restricted to [coronal] or is a comparable minimal deviation in other place features equally tolerated in word recognition?

Regressive place assimilation, phonologically illegal. The main effect for Change was significant for $F_1(1, 84) = 15.785, p < .001$ and $F_2(1, 15) = 5.448, p = .034$. Illegally changed words (*run*: 26 ms) reduced the priming effect to approximately one third, compared to unchanged words (*rum*: 83 ms). The main effect for Context was not significant (both $F < 1$), nor was the interaction: $F_1(1, 84) = 1.250, p = .267$; $F_2(1, 15) = 1.267, p = .278$. Whereas there was clear facilitation for unchanged primes (*rum*: 83 ms), priming for illegally changed items (*run*: 26 ms) was only reliable by participants (see Appendix B). In accordance to the reaction time data, far more errors occurred in the changed (9.3%) than in the unchanged condition (2.4%).

Clearly, the results for illegal regressive assimilation are different from those for legal assimilation. When changes are illegal, it does not matter whether the phonological context is congruent with the change. This is in accordance with underspecification theory, since the changed features are regarded as specified. The—not completely reliable—overall priming effect for illegally changed words was comparable to the effect for legal assimilation in unviable contexts (26 and 29 ms, see above). Facilitation and effect trends in such conditions can be attributed to general form overlap between primes and targets. It seems that the mismatching segment merely reduced the priming effect instead of inhibiting lexical access.

In the next section we turn to changes at word onset. The beginnings of words are supposed to be even more intolerant of deviations (Marslen-Wilson & Zwitserlood, 1989), but legality of word-onset deviations has not yet been investigated.

Progressive place assimilation, phonologically legal. Effects for this material group were very similar to the preceding group. The main effect of Change was significant, with $F_1(1, 87) = 18.889, p < .001$; $F_2(1, 17) =$

8.660, $p = .009$. Unchanged words (*not*: 78 ms) facilitated reactions to targets four times as much as changed items (*mot*: 17 ms). The effect of Context failed significance: $F_1(1, 87) = 1.999$, $p = .161$; $F_2(1, 17) = 2.492$, $p = .133$. The interaction was also not significant (both F < 1). There were twice as many errors in the changed (8.3%) than in the unchanged condition (3.8%).

In contrast to unchanged words (*not*: 78 ms), changed items (*mot*: 17 ms) did not produce reliable facilitation (see Appendix B). The results differ considerably from those for legal regressive place assimilation. Apparently, small changes at word onset prevent reliable access to lexical representations, independent of phonological context. One has to keep in mind that progressive place assimilation does sometimes occur, but hardly ever at word onset, as was tested here. As such, the data are in agreement with the facts of speech production. They also support evidence from the comprehension domain for a privileged status of word onsets (Marslen-Wilson, 1993; Marslen-Wilson & Zwitserlood, 1989).

The data are not so easily reconciled with underspecification, given that a feature such as [coronal] is unspecified. This exact same feature that can be assimilated without much costs in the regressive situation cannot be changed in the progressive situation. Although underspecification theory explains assimilation phenomena as they naturally occur in speech production, and although place assimilation is rarely found at word onset, the theory has to provide ways to account for the fact that assimilation at word onset is treated as a mispronunciation by the listener.

Progressive place assimilation, phonologically illegal. The factor Change was significant, with $F_1(1, 86) = 21.846$, $p < .001$, $F_2(1, 17) = 11.728$, $p = .003$. Unchanged items (*mehl*: 89 ms) primed more than four times as much as illegally changed items (*nehl*: 20 ms). There was no effect of Context (both F < 1). The interaction of Change and Context was significant for $F_1(1, 86) = 4.242$, $p = .042$ but not for $F_2(1\ 17) = 2.486$, $p = .133$.

The interaction shows a cross-over pattern. On the one side, there is an unexpected difference in effect size for unchanged words in viable (*tat mehl*: 99 ms) and unviable contexts (*gab mehl*: 78 ms), as was the case for legal progressive place assimilation. It is again unclear what the nature of this difference is, which failed significance for $t_1(91) = 1.858$, $p = .066$ and $t_2(17) = 1.390$, $p = .183$. On the other side, there is a 11 ms difference in the opposite direction between changed items (viable, *tat nehl*: 14 ms; unviable, *gab nehl*: 25 ms), which was far from being significant (both $t < 1$). As to the individual priming effects, the 14 ms effect was not significant, while the 25 ms effect was reliable (see Appendix B). As in the other material groups, the changed conditions had about twice as many errors as the unchanged conditions (5.4% vs. 2.5%). In sum, the results are quite similar to those of phonologically legal progressive place assimilation. Changed items show small effects and context has no systematic influence. We will now turn to legal voice assimilation, which, under particular circumstances, does occur (Kohler, 1995).

Voice assimilation, phonologically legal. The main effect of Change was significant, with $F_1(1, 87) = 13.748, p < .001; F_2(1, 17) = 11.028, p = .004$. Effects were three times as large for unchanged words (*brei*: 78 ms) than for legally changed words (*prei*: 26 ms). Context was not significant, $F_1(1, 87) = 1.058, p = .306, F_2 < 1$. The interaction of Context with Change reached significance for $F_1(1, 87) = 4.223, p = .043$ but failed significance by items: $F_2(1, 17) = 2.182, p = .158$. Again, the changed words resulted in more errors than unchanged words (5.0% vs. 2.2%).

An inspection of the interaction shows that context had no effect for unchanged words (*auf brei*: 74 vs. *um brei*: 81 ms), but facilitation for changed words was modulated by context. While the effect of 36 ms for assimilated words in viable contexts (*auf prei*) was significant, the 15 ms effect for the same words in unviable contexts was not (*um prei*; see Appendix B). The 21 ms difference between assimilated words in viable and unviable context was significant for $t_1(92) = 2.094, p = .039$, but $t_2(17) = 1.265, p = .223$. Assimilated words (*prei*) produced less facilitation than unchanged ones (*brei*) in all contexts. This was obviously true in unviable context (*um brei*: 81 vs. *um prei*: 15 ms: $t_1(92) = 3.701, p < .001; t_2(17) = 3.414, p = .003$) but also in viable context (*auf brei*: 74 vs. [a]*auf prei*: 36 ms: $t_1(92) = 2.331, p = .022; t_2(17) = 2.485, p = .024$). Unlike for legal regressive place, a direct comparison of means also showed a significant difference between unchanged words (*auf brei*: 615 ms) and legally assimilated words in viable contexts ([a]*auf prei*: 648 ms): $t_1(92) = 3.146, p = .002; t_2(17) = 2.556, p = .020$.

Again, as with regressive place assimilation, we found evidence for lexical activation by legally assimilated words, this time with a *preceding* context licensing a change at word onset ([a]*auf prei*). But here, the same change in unviable contexts (*um prei*) prevents such activation. Effects are smaller than for regressive place assimilation, and a clear difference is found here between facilitation due to unchanged (*brei*) and changed words (*prei*). Thus, although licensed assimilation allows for access to the lexical representation, there is a penalty for the less than perfect fit. If the feature [voiced] were unspecified, such a difference should not have emerged.

Voice assimilation, phonologically illegal. The main effect of Change was significant, $F_1(1, 87) = 30.072, p < .001; F_2(1, 17) = 17.097, p = .002$.

The overall 86 ms facilitation effect for unchanged primes (*toast*) was reduced to mere 5 ms for illegally changed primes (*doast*). There was no effect of Context: $F_1(1, 87) = 1.532, p = .219, F_2 < 1$. The interaction of Change with Context was significant by participants, with $F_1(1,87) = 4.154$, $p = .045$, not for items $F_2 < 1$. Changed conditions attracted more errors than the unchanged (6.1% vs. 3.3%).

Priming in both unchanged conditions was significant, but again, there was a 26 ms difference between viable (*am toast*: 73 ms) and unviable (*auf toast*: 99 ms) contexts, although context is a dummy variable here. Illegally changed items clearly produced no priming in either context (viable: *am doast*: 7 ms; unviable: *auf doast*: 3 ms: see Appendix B).

Discussion

As expected, there were large crossmodal identical priming effects in all material groups. But only two out of six material sets showed clear facilitation for changed words: regressive coronal assimilation ([a]*worp mal*) and progressive voice assimilation ([a]*auf prei*), when legal and in viable context. Small effects or trends were found in other conditions, as was the case with illegal regressive (*run trug*) and progressive place (*tat nehl*) assimilation. We attribute such residual priming effects to overlap between spoken input and targets. Similar effects are reported in the literature, also with primes and targets that mismatch in one feature only (Bölte, 1997; Bölte & Coenen, 2001; Connine et al., 1993; Zwitserlood, 1996, for an overview). In one case, reliable facilitation was found for legal changes in the absence of a licensing context. This was for regressive place assimilation, although the size of the effect was half of the facilitation obtained in the presence of a viable context.

First and foremost, our results are in agreement with the phonetic facts of German, and with their frequency of occurrence in connected speech. Deviations that typically occur in speech production, such as regressive place assimilation, clearly activated the appropriate lexical representation. This is also the best documented case of assimilation in German, as in other languages (Kohler, 1995; Paradis & Prunet, 1991). Regressive place assimilation revealed larger effects than progressive voice. Deviations are comparably small, but progressive voice assimilation is less frequent.

But even assimilation that does occur in the language seems not to be completely without costs. Numerically and sometimes statistically, there was less priming for assimilated than for unchanged words. This stands in apparent contrast to results by Gaskell and Marslen-Wilson (1996), who found no difference between unchanged and assimilated words. As pointed out earlier, they only compared means, we compared means and effect sizes. Importantly, what is shared between English and German is a tolerance of the word recognition system for regular variation: Lexical access is not blocked when presented with a "mismatching" feature, provided that the context segment shares this feature.

No such effect is found for the progressive case of coronal place assimilation. As we argued, this agrees fully with the facts for German, but it presents a challenge for the application of underspecification theory to the speech perception domain. Whatever rule prevents segments that are unspecified for [coronal] to surface in an assimilated way at word onset, it cannot be a general rule, blocking all variation at word onset. For we did find effects at word onset, for legal progressive voice assimilation. Before evaluating the consequences of the results for the predictions that were formulated before Experiment 1, we present data from an experiment with words presented out of context.

EXPERIMENT 2: CROSSMODAL FORM PRIMING IN ISOLATION

Experiment 2 investigated the material from Experiment 1, this time presented in isolation. According to a strict view of underspecification, it should not matter whether context is present or not, but for some accounts, context is important (Gaskell & Marslen-Wilson, 1996; Gow, 2000). The empirical evidence is less clear cut. On the one hand, both Gaskell & Marslen-Wilson (1996) and Gow (2000) found significant priming with assimilated tokens when the critical post-assimilation context was removed (e.g., *Sandra will only eat lean/*[a]leam*). Of course the presence of sentence context might have cued participants to the possibility of assimilated words. On the other hand, no facilitation was found for assimilated items presented in isolation (Marslen-Wilson et al., 1995), even when the release of the critical consonantal burst was cut off. Our Experiment 2 served to ascertain whether assimilation in German requires context to be tolerated in speech recognition. As in Experiment 1, there was a complete change in phoneme status between unchanged and changed words.

It turned out to be impossible to create intelligible items by cutting out critical words from their sentence contexts. Thus, a new recording was made. We are aware of differences between words spoken in context and in isolation, such that data from Experiment 1 and 2 should only be compared with necessary caution. A forced-choice phonetic decision pretest was carried out to assess the discriminability of the stimuli, this time in the absence of a context word.

Pretest

The design was the same as in the first pretest, except that no pseudoword pairs were included. Changed and unchanged test and control words of all material groups were tested. In the absence of context, direction of assimilation rather refers to position of the deviation (word onset/offset). A total of 432 stimuli, presented in isolation, were tested. The hard- and software and the procedure were the same as with Experiment 1. Twenty native German speakers participated for course credits.

There were 96.2% correct responses on average (see Table 3 for error rates as a function of conditions). The mean confidence rating was 4.8. As in the first pretest, the complete set of responses for a particular item was excluded from further analysis when 50% or more wrong answers occurred in one of the conditions. This applied to seven item sets for regressive place assimilation, phonologically legal and one set for the illegal condition. As in Experiment 1, items in legal, regressive place assimilation were discriminated worst.

Main experiment: Method

Participants. Sixty-one native speakers of German were tested, mainly students of Münster University, participating for course credits. None had taken part in the pretests or in Experiment 1.

Design, Materials, and Procedure. All primes of Experiment 1 were spoken in isolation, by a female native speaker. Digitising and speech editing were similar to Experiment 1. Context, of course, was not a factor. Again, the six material groups were analysed separately, with a 2 × 2 design with Change and Test/Control (related prime vs. unrelated baseline). Items were rotated across four test versions to avoid repetition of targets. Spoken primes (e.g., *wort, worp, blatt,* or *blapp*) were presented in isolation, immediately followed by a visual target (e.g., WORT), displayed

TABLE 3
Pretest 2: Error percentages as a function of conditions

Direction and type	Context	Legality of assimilation			
		Phonologically legal		*Phonologically illegal*	
		Unchanged	*Changed*	*Unchanged*	*Changed*
Regressive place	Viable	0.0	20.0	8.3	0.6
	Control	2.1	15.0	5.6	4.5
Progressive place	Viable	5.0	1.9	1.6	1.2
	Control	0.0	4.5	3.0	1.9
Progressive voice	Viable	0.0	1.8	0.0	1.3
	Control	1.1	0.6	0.6	0.6

TABLE 4
Experiment 2: Mean RTs in ms and error percentages (in parentheses) as a function of conditions

| Direction and type | Context | Legality of assimilation | | | |
| | | Phonologically legal | | Phonologically illegal | |
		Unchanged	Changed	Unchanged	Changed
Regressive place	Viable	527 (4.9)	628 (7.4)	537 (1.9)	664 (12.6)
	Control	619 (6.2)	619 (4.3)	673 (5.8)	666 (9.7)
Progressive place	Viable	544 (1.9)	639 (9.4)	546 (1.6)	633 (5.6)
	Control	648 (8.3)	636 (9.0)	636 (6.8)	630 (4.8)
Progressive voice	Viable	519 (1.9)	599 (4.5)	534 (3.2)	618 (8.0)
	Control	614 (4.5)	616 (3.7)	671 (8.8)	650 (7.6)

for 350 ms. Each list contained 108 experimental trials and 108 spoken fillers with pseudoword targets, half of which were form-related to their primes. In addition, there were 40 warm up trials. The procedure was the same as in Experiment 1, except that there was no break. The experiment lasted about 20 minutes.

Results

Data from two participants and three item sets were excluded from analyses because of high error rates, and from one item set because of technical problems. In addition, only item sets that performed satisfactorily in the pretest were included. Incorrect answers and reaction times above 1500 ms were discarded. As in Experiment 1, List was included as a factor in the subject analyses (Pollatsek & Well, 1995). The overall mean error rate was 5.9%. Mean reaction times and error rates for all material groups and conditions are shown in Table 4. For information on t-tests for priming effects see Appendix C.

Regressive place assimilation, phonologically legal. The effect of Test/Control was significant for $F_1(1, 53) = 20.785$, $p < .001$, but not for $F_2(1, 10) = 1.236$, $p = .292$.[6] The main effect for Change was significant with $F_1(1, 53) = 32.473$, $p < .001$, and marginal for $F_2(1, 10) = 4.207$, $p = .067$. The interaction was also significant: $F_1(1, 53) = 22.391$, $p < .001$; $F_2(1, 10) = 4.974$, $p = .050$. There were no effects on errors. The interaction shows that while unchanged items (*wort*) showed a sound priming effect of 92 ms,

---

[6] Only 11 of 18 item sets were tested in this material group, which reduced power in the analysis.

changed items did not prime the related target at all (*worp* −9 ms; see Appendix C). Clearly, legally changed words did not activate the lexical representation when presented in isolation. This holds here for the most typical case of assimilation in German: regressive place assimilation. This result contrasts with what was found in Experiment 1, with items embedded in sentential context.

Regressive place assimilation, phonologically illegal. Test/Control was significant, with $F_1(1, 54) = 42.600, p < .001; F_2(1, 13) = 19.684, p < .001$. So were Change ($F_1(1, 54) = 30.235, F_2(1, 13) = 19.189$, both $p < .001$) and the interaction, $F_1(1, 54) = 45.522, F_2(1, 13) = 48.979$, with both $p < .001$. There were more errors in changed (11.2%) than in unchanged (3.9%) conditions. Again, there was clear identical crossmodal priming (*rum*: 136 ms), but no priming for the changed items (*run*: 2 ms).

Progressive place assimilation, phonologically legal. Both main effects and the interaction were significant. The results for Test/Control were $F_1(1, 54) = 56.513, p < .001; F_2(1, 17) = 9.264, p = .007$, for Change $F_1(1, 54) = 39.978, p < .001; F_2(1, 17) = 11.969, p = .007$, and for the interaction $F_1(1, 54) = 44.996; F_2(1, 17) = 21.112$, both $p < .001$. The accuracy data showed that identical primes produced less errors (1.9%) than the other three conditions (8.9%). Identical primes (*not*) facilitated responses (104 ms), changed words (*mot*) did not (−3 ms).

Progressive place assimilation, phonologically illegal. As before, both main effects and the interaction were significant: Test/Control: $F_1(1, 54) = 49.785, p < .001; F_2(1, 16) = 5.655, p = .030$; Change: $F_1(1, 54) = 31.298, p < .001; F_2(1, 16) = 14.179, p = .002$; for the interaction: $F_1(1, 54)$ was 38.000, $p < .001$; $F_2(1, 16)$ was 12.192, $p = .003$. Identical test primes (1.6%) produced less errors than the other three conditions (5.7%). As with all other material groups, reliable facilitation was found for unchanged (*mehl*: 90 ms), not for changed words (*nehl*: −3 ms).

Progressive voice assimilation, phonologically legal. There were again significant main effects; for Test/Control: $F_1(1, 54) = 39.584$ and $F_2(1, 17) = 21.060$, both with $p < .001$, for Change: $F_1(1, 54) = 22.615, F_2(1, 17) = 18.397$, both with $p < .001$. The interaction was significant with $F_1(1, 54) = 22.712, p < .001, F_2(1, 17) = 12.301, p = .003$. There were no effects on errors. The priming effect for unchanged words, e.g., *brei*: 95 ms, decreased to 17 ms for changed items (*prei*). The effect for changed items failed significance (see Appendix C). The 78 ms difference between unchanged (*brei*) and changed (*prei*) test conditions was reliable, for $t_1(58) = 5.622$

and $t_2(17) = 6.249$, both $p < .001$. Thus, again, the only significant effect was for identical primes.

Progressive voice assimilation, phonologically illegal.   Main effects and interaction were significant, Test/Control with $F_1(1, 54) = 108.823$, $F_2(1, 16) = 72.687$, $p < .001$, Change with $F_1(1, 54) = 17.366$, $p <; F_2(1, 16) = 6.293$, $p = .023$. The values for the interaction were $F_1(1, 54) = 49.174$, $F_2(1, 16) = 31.247$, both $F < .001$. The error data showed that identical test primes (3.2%) produced less errors than the other conditions (8.1%). Again, a highly significant crossmodal identity effect was found in this material group (*toast*: 137 ms). The effect for changed items (*doast*) amounted to 32 ms and also reached significance (see Appendix C). This is the only condition in which changed items produced reliable priming. Nevertheless, the effect is only one-quarter of the size of the identity priming effect. This difference in effect size was significant: $t_1(58) = 6.852$, $t_2(16) = 5.590$, both $p < .001$.

Discussion

When changed words are presented in isolation, there are—with one exception, to which we will return—no effects on reactions to visual target words with which these changed words share a large amount of overlap. The data are compatible with Marslen-Wilson et al. (1995), who also obtained null effects for items presented in isolation. We found no systematic differences between legal and illegal changes, whereas in Experiment 1, we did. In Experiment 1, we obtained robust facilitation of legally assimilated words when the preceding or following segment licensed the assimilation. Although it is hard to directly compare results obtained with different speech tokens, we have no reason to believe that the changed words spoken in isolation were in any crucial aspect different from the ones spoken in sentence contexts. In both cases, consonants were completely changed. The release of plosive consonants at word offset was of course clearer in isolation than in context. However, only 4 out of 18 sets in legal regressive place assimilation had plosive consonants. Thus, the difference in the pattern of results is most probably due to the presence or absence of context.

The only exception to an overall null result for changed words was illegal voice assimilation at word onset. This finding is difficult to understand, since there were no priming effects for this condition in Experiment 1. One potential explanation is in terms of German dialects. It is the case that voicing of unvoiced consonants (e.g., *papa* spoken as /baba/) is the standard pronunciation in the dialects of Cologne, Obersachsen, and Schwaben. Speakers of these dialects voice consonants at syllable and word onset. They do it all the time, independently of context. German listeners have to set their parameters to such variants whenever they encounter these dialects. Given that dialectal speech is abundant in popular TV series, it is most likely that our student population was familiar with these dialects.

It is possible that participants in Experiment 2, after hearing a couple of voiced consonants at word onset which are not voiced in standard German, set the parameter to "voice at syllable onset". Why then did this not happen in Experiment 1? Participants in Experiment 1 listened to many sentences, with many correct, non-voiced, pronunciations of voiceless consonants at syllable onset. They had no reason to infer that a dialectal variant was spoken and thus would not have changed parameters. Interestingly, there are no dialects of German in which changes in place of articulation are produced as a rule. Of course, such explanations are highly speculative, and more research is needed to investigate this issue.

The results of this experiment, as well as the data from the pretest, nevertheless show that listeners have no problem in discriminating featural deviations. Apparently, such deviations block access to the lexical representation when context is absent. In particular, there are no hints in any of the legal conditions that the assimilated feature is interpreted towards the unassimilated case. This is bad news for strict views of underspecification.

GENERAL DISCUSSION AND CONCLUSIONS

What the combined data from both experiments first and foremost show is that context is necessary to gain access to lexical representations by means of input which deviates from perfect pronunciation. Changed words presented in isolation essentially show no priming. But even when presented in sentences, changed words activate the lexicon under very restricted circumstances only. The lexical system is intolerant to changes that are illegal, that do not occur in the language (see also Weber, 2001, for a special status of such changes). Although the one-feature difference between spoken input and target word constitutes an almost perfect match, there is, at maximum, weak and mostly unreliable facilitation. This is different for changes that are actually produced in the language, due to assimilation processes. These show clear effects, but only when licensed by a feature in a preceding or following segment. This pattern of effects is clearly problematic for models such as TRACE (McClelland & Elman, 1986). All changes were equally small, and all resulted in pseudowords which should not have been harmful in terms of lexical competition. TRACE thus wrongly predicts that the effects of changed consonants should have been equivalent across all conditions.

The gestural model, which elegantly deals with partial assimilation, could explain our data from Experiment 1 if residual traces of the original gesture were present in the signal. In fact, Nolan (1992) showed that such traces can be utilised by listeners even when these traces are not detectable with electropalatography. Although we tried hard to produce a complete segment change, we have no way of knowing whether such traces were present in our segments. Given the close correspondence between articulation and perception in this model, it could explain our findings even in the absence of acoustic traces.

How does underspecification fare in the light of our results? The theory correctly predicts no effects when changes are phonologically illegal. But other aspects are problematic for underspecification. Firstly, under-specified representations should not bother with context to license a change in surface form. But we clearly find that a licensing context is a prerequisite. Second, how would underspecification handle our results for assimilation of voice? One could argue for [voiced] as the unspecified feature, allowing voiced segments to be devoiced. But it remains unclear how underspecification could handle the quantitative differences between regressive place and progressive voice assimilation. Also somewhat problematic for this theory are the null effects for legal progressive place assimilation in viable context. It is not easy to think of rules which would block place assimilation at word onset, while allowing it elsewhere. As argued earlier, such rules cannot generally apply to word onsets, because we find effects for voice at this position.

So, underspecification alone cannot explain the results. Additional mechanisms have to be operative. There are two proposals in the literature: inference and anticipation. Gaskell and Marslen-Wilson (1996) assumed a process of phonological inference that evaluates the contextual appropriateness of assimilations. Lahiri (1995) argues against such an inference process. Based on data from an experiment on German, she proposed a combination of underspecifed lexical representations with an anticipation mechanism. In her unviable contexts, assimilated words led to longer latencies than unchanged words. This she interprets as an anticipation effect. The presence of a change creates the expectancy that a segment with particular features (e.g., labial or velar) should come next. This anticipation is not satisfied in unviable contexts. Such an anticipation explanation was also provided by Otake et al. (1996), for Japanese, by Lahiri and Marslen-Wilson (1991), for nasalised vowels in English, and by Gow (2000), for cases of assimilation in which the original place feature is not completely neutralised. Our data are hard to reconcile with Lahiris underspecification-cum-anticipation view. First, it predicts no difference between unchanged and legally changed words in viable contexts. But we do find such differences. Moreover, the view predicts slower responses in our changed (*blapp kurz*) than in our unchanged (*blatt mal*) control conditions, because a labial is anticipated in the former (all changed control conditions had unviable context segments). The fact that changed control conditions consistently produce faster latencies than unchanged conditions lends no support to the anticipation view.[7]

What about the inference view? The inference process evaluates whether all requirements are met to license the change (Gaskell & Marslen-Wilson, 1998, 1999). If changes are legal and contextually appropriate, lexical representations can be accessed. This is supported by the strong context effects in our data. Second, as argued by Lahiri (1995), inference should take time, because assimilated words always have to be evaluated against the context. As a consequence, reactions should be slower with assimilated than with unchanged words, even when the change is licensed. This argument was originally held against the inference account, because Gaskell and Marslen-Wilson (1996) found no costs for assimilation in viable contexts. We do: depending on whether means or effects are compared, the costs range from 15 to 30 ms. Clearly, the inference view can accommodate these findings quite well.

All this leaves us with one issue unresolved. None of the accounts can readily capture the most eye-catching aspect of our data: the fact that they clearly mirror what speakers of German actually do. Assimilated words gain access to the listeners' lexical representations to the extent that speakers produce them. So, production constrains comprehension, in that listeners are intolerant to illegal changes that are never produced. Variation that is pervasive in fast speech, such as regressive place assimilation, produces the best results. Less frequent variation, such as progressive voice, has less of an effect on the perception side. The position of changed segments matters. If we test for the place assimilation at word onset, where speakers do not produce it, we find no effects. It would be interesting to see how learning models such as the one proposed by Gaskell and Marslen-Wilson (1995) behave when frequency facts are taken into account. In the light of our data, we genuinely believe that the production-comprehension correspondence should be taken seriously if we want to understand how the mapping of speech input onto the lexicon is accomplished. After all, most listeners also speak.

---

[7] We are grateful to Gareth Gaskell for pointing out this effect in our data.

REFERENCES

Archangeli, D. (1988). Aspects of underspecification theory. *Phonology, 5*, 183–207.

Bölte, J. (1997). *The role of mismatching information in spoken word recognition*. Hamburg: Kovač.

Bölte, J., & Coenen, E. (2001). *Phonological information is not mapped onto semantic information in a one to one manner?* Manuscript submitted for publication.

Browman, C.P., & Goldstein, L. (1992). Articulatory phonology: An overview. *Phonetica, 49*, 155–180.

Byrd, D. (1992). Perception of assimilation in consonant clusters: A gestural model. *Phonetica, 49*, 1–24.

Connine, C.M., Blasko, D.G., & Titone, D. (1993). Do the beginnings of spoken words have a special status in auditory word recognition? *Journal of Memory and Language, 32*, 193–210.

Connine, C.M., Titone, D., Deelman, T., & Blasko, D. (1997). Similarity mapping in spoken word recognition. *Journal of Memory and Language, 37*, 463–480.

Ganong, W.F. (1980). Phonetic categorisation in auditory word perception. *Journal of Experimental Psychology: Human Perception and Performance, 6*, 110–125.

Gaskell, M.G. (this issue). Phonological variation and its consequences for the word recognition system. *Language and Cognitive Processes, 16*, 723–729.

Gaskell, M.G., Hare, M., & Marslen-Wilson, W.D. (1995). A connectionist model of phonological representation in speech perception. *Cognitive Science, 19*, 407–439.

Gaskell, M.G., & Marslen-Wilson, W.D. (1996). Phonological variation and inference in lexical access. *Journal of Experimental Psychology: Human Perception and Performance, 22*, 144–158.

Gaskell, M.G., & Marslen-Wilson, W.D. (1997). Integrating form and meaning: A distributed model of speech perception. *Language and Cognitive Processes, 12*, 613–656.

Gaskell, M.G., & Marslen-Wilson, W.D. (1998). Mechanisms of phonological inference in speech perception. *Journal of Experimental Psychology: Human Perception and Performance, 24*, 380–396.

Gaskell, M.G., & Marslen-Wilson, W.D. (1999). Ambiguity, competition, and blending in spoken word recognition. *Cognitive Science, 23*, 439–462.

Gow, D.W. jr. (2000). Assimilation, ambiguity, and the feature parsing problem. *Proceedings of the Sixth International Conference of Speech and Language Processing,* Beijing; Vol. 2, 535–538.

Holst, T., & Nolan, F. (1996). Modelling [s] to [ʃ] accommodation. *Journal of Phonetics, 24*, 113–137.

Howell, P. (1983). The effect of delaying auditory feedback of selected components of the speech signal. *Perception and Psychophysics, 34*, 387–396.

Kenstowicz, M. (1994). *Phonology in generative grammar.* Cambridge, MA: Blackwell Press.

Kiparsky, P. (1985). Some consequences of lexical phonology. *Phonology, 2*, 85–138.

Kohler, K. J. (1995). *Einführung in die Phonetik des Deutschen.* Berlin: Erich Schmitz.

Koster, C. J. (1987). *Word recognition in foreign and native language.* Dordrecht, The Netherlands: Foris.

Lahiri, A. (1995). Undoing place assimilation. *Paper presented at the 129th Meeting of the Acoustical Society of America,* Washington, D.C.

Lahiri, A., & Marslen-Wilson, W.D. (1991). The mental representation of lexical form: A phonological approach to the recognition lexicon. *Cognition, 38*, 245–294.

Mann, V.A., & Repp, B.H. (1980). Influence of preceding fricative on stop consonant perception. *Journal of the Acoustical Society of America, 69*, 548–558.

Marslen-Wilson, W.D. (1987). Functional parallelism in spoken word-recognition. *Cognition*, *25*, 71–102.

Marslen-Wilson, W.D. (1993). Issues of process and representation in lexical access. In G.T.M. Altmann & R. Shillcock (Eds.), *Cognitive models of speech processing: The Second Sperlonga Meeting* (pp. 187–210). Hove, UK: Lawrence Erlbaum Associates Ltd.

Marslen-Wilson, W.D., & Gaskell, G (1992). Match and mismatch in lexical access [Abstract]. *International Journal of Psychology*, *27*, 61.

Marslen-Wilson, W.D., Nix, A., & Gaskell, G. (1995). Phonological variation in lexical access: Abstractness, inference and English place assimilation. *Language and Cognitive Processes*, *10*, 285–308.

Marslen-Wilson, W.D., & Zwitserlood, P. (1989). Accessing spoken words: The importance of word onsets. *Journal of Experimental Psychology: Human Perception and Performance*, *15*, 576–585.

Martin, J.G., & Bunnell, H.T. (1982). Perception of anticipatory coarticulation effects in vowel—stop consonant—vowel sequences. *Journal of Experimental Psychology: Human Perception and Performance*, *8*, 473–488.

McCarthy, J., & Taub, A. (1992). Review of Paradis and Prunet 1991. *Phonology*, *9*, 363–370.

McClelland, J.L., & Elman, J.L. (1986). The TRACE model of speech perception. *Cognitive Psychology*, *18*, 1–86.

Meyer, D.E., & Gordon, P.C. (1985). Speech production: Motor programming of phonetic features. *Journal of Memory and Language*, *24*, 3–26.

Nolan, F. (1992). The descriptive role of segments: Evidence from assimilation. In G.J. Docherty and D.R. Ladd (Eds.), *Papers in laboratory phonology II: Gesture, segment, prosody* (pp. 261–280), Cambridge: Cambridge University Press.

Otake, T., Yoneyama, K., Cutler, A., & van der Lugt, A. (1996). The representation of Japanese moraic nasals. *Journal of the Acoustical Society of America*, *100*, 3831–3842.

Paradis, C., & Prunet, J.-F. (1991). *Phonetics and phonology. The special status of coronals: Internal and external evidence.* San Diego, CA: Academic Press.

Petzmeyer, R. (2000). *Phonologische Primingeffekte unter Berücksichtigung von Assimila-tions-prozessen. Eine empirische Untersuchung zur Worterkennung.* Unpublished Masters thesis, University of Münster, Germany.

Pollatsek, A., & Well, A.D. (1995). On the use of counterbalanced designs in cognitive research: A suggestion for a better and more powerful analysis. *Journal of Experimental Psychology: Learning, Memory, and Cognition*, *21*, 785–794.

Pulleyblank, D. (1988). Vocalic underspecification in Yoruba. *Linguistic Inquiry*, *19*, 233–270.

Samuel, A. (1996). Phoneme restoration. *Language and Cognitive Processes*, *11*, 647–653.

Steriade, D. (1995). Underspecification and markedness. In J.A. Goldsmith (Ed.), *The handbook of phonological theory* (pp. 114–175). Cambridge, MA: Blackwell.

Weber, A. (2001). Help or hindrance: How violation of different assimilation rules affects spoken-language processing. *Language and Speech*, *44*, 95–118.

Zwitserlood, P. (1996). Form priming. *Language and Cognitive Processes*, *11*, 589–596.

APPENDIX A

Examples of primes as a function of conditions

Direction and type	Context	Legality of assimilation			
		Phonologically legal		Phonologically illegal	
		Unchanged	*Changed*	*Unchanged*	*Changed*
Regressive place	Viable	WOR*T* mal	WOR*P* mal	RU*M* trug	RU*N* trug
	Unviable	WOR*T* kurz	WOR*P* kurz	RU*M* brauchten	RU*N* brauchten
	Control	BLA*TT* mal	BLA*PP* kurz	LEI*M* brauchten	LEI*N* brauchten
Progressive place	Viable	hab *N*OT	hab *M*OT	tat *M*EHL	tat *N*EHL
	Unviable	fing *N*OT	fing *M*OT	gab *M*EHL	gab *N*EHL
	Control	mach *N*EST	mach *M*EST	trug *M*ÜLL	trug *N*ÜLL
Progressive voice	Viable	auf *B*REI	auf *P*REI	am *T*OAST	am *D*OAST
	Unviable	um *B*REI	um *P*REI	auf *T*OAST	auf *D*OAST
	Control	am *B*AUCH	am *P*AUCH	auf *T*RATSCH	auf *D*RATSCH

Note: Critical phonemes are in italics, primes in capital letters. An example of a complete sentence pair: "Das habe ich immer noch nicht verstanden. Kannst du das *Wort mal* deutlicher aussprechen?" (Literal: "I still didn't get it. Can you the *word just* better articulate?")

APPENDIX B

Experiment 1 t-test values for Subject and Item analyses for priming effects as a function of conditions

Legality of assimilation

Direction and type	Context	Analysis	Phonologically legal — Unchanged	Phonologically legal — Changed	Phonologically illegal — Unchanged	Phonologically illegal — Changed
Regressive place	Viable	Subject	$t(91) = 6.663$, $p < .001$	$t(90) = 4.144$, $p < .001$	$t(90) = 6.226$, $p < .001$	$t(91) = 1.955$, $p = .027$
		Item	$t(11) = 4.755$, $p < .001$	$t(11) = 2.875$, $p = .008$	$t(15) = 4.764$, $p < .001$	$t(15) = 1.244$, $p = .117$
	Unviable	Subject	$t(91) = 6.642$, $p < .001$	$t(92) = 2.007$, $p = .024$		
		Item	$t(11) = 5.128$, $p < .001$	$t(11) = 1.872$, $p = .044$		
Progressive place	Viable	Subject	$t(92) = 7.773$, $p < .001$	$t(92) = 1.374$, $p = .087$	$t(91) = 7.842$, $p < .001$	$t(92) = 1.201$, $p = .117$
		Item	$t(17) = 4.452$, $p < .001$	$t(17) = .824$, $p = .211$	$t(17) = 8.762$, $p < .001$	$t(17) = .860$, $p = .201$
	Unviable	Subject			$t(91) = 5.505$, $p < .001$	$t(92) = 2.047$, $p = .022$
		Item			$t(17) = 3.999$, $p < .001$	$t(17) = 1.842$, $p = .042$
Progressive voice	Viable	Subject	$t(92) = 5.917$, $p < .001$	$t(92) = 3.150$, $p = .001$	$t(92) = 6.129$, $p < .001$	$t(92) = .596$, $p = .277$
		Item	$t(17) = 5.695$, $p < .001$	$t(17) = 2.657$, $p = .009$	$t(17) = 5.405$, $p < .001$	$t(17) = .232$, $p = .410$
	Unviable	Subject	$t(92) = 6.495$, $p < .001$	$t(92) = 1.141$, $p = .129$	$t(92) = 8.262$, $p < .001$	$t(92) = .211$, $p = .417$
		Item	$t(17) = 4.885$, $p < .001$	$t(17) = .901$, $p = .190$	$t(17) = 4.951$, $p < .001$	$t(17) = .435$, $p = .335$

Note: All tests were one-sided. The t-tests for the means progressive place, phonologically legal and regressive place, phonologically illegal were collapsed over levels of the factor Context (viable/unviable) because there was no significant interaction.

APPENDIX C

Experiment 2 *t*-test values for Subject and Item analyses for priming effects experimental vs. control

Direction and type	Analysis	Legality of assimilation			
		Phonologically legal		*Phonologically illegal*	
		Unchanged	Changed	Unchanged	Changed
Regressive place	Subject	$t(58) = 6.412$ $p < .001$	$t(57) = .470$ $p = .320$	$t(58) = 8.422$ $p < .001$	$t(58) = .175$ $p = .431$
	Item	$t(10) = 1.642$ $p = .066$	$t(10) = 1.719$ $p = .058$	$t(13) = 7.132$ $p < .001$	$t(13) = .330$ $p = .374$
Progressive place	Subject	$t(58) = 9.110$ $p < .001$	$t(58) = .243$ $p = .405$	$t(58) = 8.846$ $p < .001$	$t(58) = .267$ $p = .395$
	Item	$t(17) = 4.567$ $p < .001$	$t(17) = .768$ $p = .227$	$t(16) = 3.347$ $p = .002$	$t(16) = .161$ $p = .437$
Progressive voice	Subject	$t(58) = 8.907$ $p < .001$	$t(58) = 1.285$ $p = .102$	$t(58) = 13.068$ $p < .001$	$t(58) = 2.769$ $p = .004$
	Item	$t(17) = 5.328$ $p < .001$	$t(17) = 1.034$ $p = .158$	$t(16) = 9.589$ $p < .001$	$t(16) = 2.277$ $p = .019$

Note: All tests were one-sided.

LANGUAGE AND COGNITIVE PROCESSES, 2001, *16* (5/6), 565–581

Phonotactics, density, and entropy in spoken word recognition

Paul A. Luce and Nathan R. Large

University at Buffalo, Amherst, NY, USA

Previous research has demonstrated that increases in phonotactic probability facilitate spoken word processing, whereas increased competition among lexical representations is often associated with slower and less accurate recognition. We examined the combined effects of probabilistic phonotactics and lexical competition by generating words and nonwords that varied *orthogonally* on phonotactics and similarity neighbourhood density. The results from a speeded same-different task revealed simultaneous *facilitative* effects of phonotactics and *inhibitory* effects of lexical competition for real word stimuli. However, the nonword stimuli produced an apparently anomalous pattern of results. In a subsequent experiment, we identified the source of this anomaly by estimating behaviourally the specific lexical competitors activated by our nonwords. Our results suggest that, under specific circumstances, neighbourhood density and probabilistic phonotactics may combine to produce non-additive or synergistic effects of lexical competition on processing times.

Increased frequency of the components of spoken stimuli facilitates processing (Pitt & Samuel, 1995; Vitevitch & Luce, 1999). At the same time, competition among lexical representations inhibits processing (Luce, Goldinger, Auer, & Vitevitch, 2000; Luce & Pisoni, 1998; Vitevitch & Luce, 1999). Both of these effects are predicted by any of a class of activation-competition models, including Shortlist (Norris, 1994), TRACE (McClelland & Elman, 1986), PARSYN (Luce et al., 2000), and

Requests for reprints should be addressed to P. Luce or N. Large, Language Perception Laboratory, Department of Psychology, University at Buffalo, Buffalo, NY, 14260, USA. Email: luce@acsu.buffalo.edu or large@acsu.buffalo.edu

This research was supported by grant number 1 R01 DC 026580 from the National Institute on Deafness and Other Communication Disorders, National Institutes of Health and by a National Science Foundation Graduate Fellowship.

http://www.tandf.co.uk/journals/pp/01690965.html   DOI: 10.1080/01690960143000137

ARTPHONE (Grossberg, Boardman, & Cohen, 1997). In particular, each of these models predicts that sublexical frequency effects—or effects of *probabilistic phonotactics*—are as much a part of the recognition process as the well-documented effects of lexical competition.

Empirical support for the distinction between sublexical and lexical effects in spoken word recognition comes, in part, from a number of studies conducted by Vitevitch and Luce (1998, 1999; see also Pitt & Samuel, 1995), who investigated processing of words and nonwords that varied in probabilistic phonotactics (defined as the positional frequencies of segments and biphones) and neighbourhood density (a measure of lexical competition; see Luce & Pisoni, 1998). Specifically, they examined stimuli falling into one of four conditions: (1) High density-high phonotactic probability words, (2) low density-low phonotactic probability words, (3) high density-high phonotactic probability nonwords, and (4) low density-low phonotactic probability nonwords. Note that for both the words and nonwords, neighbourhood density and probabilistic phonotactics *covaried*, reflecting the strong positive correlation in the language between number of overlapping words and segmental frequency. Typically, as the number of overlapping words increases, the frequencies of the segments comprising the overlapping words also increase.

When *words* were presented in auditory naming and same-different matching tasks, *inhibitory* effects of neighbourhood density were observed: High probability-density words were responded to more slowly than low probability-density words. However, for *nonwords*, a *facilitative* effect of probabilistic phonotactics was obtained: High probability-density nonwords were responded to more quickly than low probability-density nonwords. These results are consistent with the hypothesis that effects of similarity neighbourhood density are inhibitory and have a lexical focus whereas effects of probabilistic phonotactics are facilitative and have a sublexical focus.

To garner further evidence for the operation of two levels of representation and processing, Vitevitch and Luce attempted to (1) bias the processing of nonwords toward the lexical level and (2) bias the processing of words toward the sublexical level. If effects of similarity neighbourhood density and probabilistic phonotactics have loci at different levels of processing, encouraging processing of nonwords at a lexical level should reveal effects of neighbourhood competition. To this end, Vitevitch and Luce (1999) presented words and nonwords that varied on phonotactic probability and density in an auditory lexical decision task. This task necessitates activation of lexical items in memory to categorise the stimulus successfully, even when the stimulus is a nonword. That is, to make a lexical decision on both words and (phonotactically legal) nonwords, one must activate representations at a lexical level. Thus,

Vitevitch and Luce predicted that the same nonwords that previously showed facilitative effects of probabilistic phonotactics in the naming and same-different tasks would show neighbourhood density effects in auditory lexical decision. Their predictions were confirmed: Words and nonwords with high probability phonotactics and neighbourhood density were responded to more slowly than words and nonwords with low probability phonotactics and neighbourhood density.

Vitevitch and Luce (1999) also attempted to determine if the effects of neighbourhood density that are so pervasive for words could be modified by focusing participants' processing on a sublexical level. They again presented words and nonwords that covaried on phonotactic probability and neighborhood density in a same-different task. In the previous experiment using this task, Vitevitch and Luce presented the words and nonwords blocked. That is, participants heard a list containing only words or a list containing only nonwords. They reasoned that if the presentation of words and nonwords was mixed, participants would focus their processing on the sublexical level, which is common to *all* of the stimuli. Although they did not predict that words would actually show a reversal of the density effect in favour of probabilistic phonotactics (owing to the overwhelming dominance of the lexical level in normal spoken language processing), they nonetheless predicted an attenuation of the effect of similarity neighbourhood competition. Again, the predictions were confirmed: High phonotactic probability nonwords were responded to faster than low phonotactic probability nonwords. However, the effects of similarity neighbourhood competition previously observed for these word stimuli were now considerably attenuated, resulting in no significant effect of neighborhood density for the words.

Despite the previous demonstrations of differential effects of lexical competition and sublexical frequency, to date there has been no definitive demonstration of *simultaneous* inhibitory effects of lexical competition and facilitative effects of probabilistic phonotactics for real words. Given the crucial role phonotactics may play in distinguishing between autonomous and interactive models (Norris, McQueen, & Cutler, 2000), an important step in determining the loci of effects of sublexical phonotactics and lexical competition is to demonstrate their combined effects on real word processing within a given task environment. In our own previous work (Vitevitch & Luce, 1999), we speculated that unpacking the two effects by orthogonally combining neighbourhood density and probabilistic phono-tactics might be impossible, given the high correlation between the two variables. This speculation proved to be unfounded.

We examined the combined effects of lexicality, similarity neighbour-hood density, and probabilistic phonotactics on processing times for carefully matched sets of spoken words and nonwords. In the course of our investigation, we not only confirmed and extended previous findings, we uncovered an effect that can not be predicted by a *simple* combination of activation and competition at sublexical and lexical levels of representation.

EXPERIMENT 1

Method

Participants. Forty-five English-speaking adult participants were recruited from the University at Buffalo community. All participants reported no history of a speech or hearing disorder.

Materials. Forty-five consonant-vowel-consonant stimuli were selected for each of eight conditions (see Appendix 1). The conditions were created by orthogonally combining two levels of (1) lexicality (word and nonword), (2) log-frequency-weighted similarity neighbourhood density (high and low), and (3) phonotactic probability (high and low). Log-frequency-weighted similarity neighbourhoods were computed by comparing a given phonemic transcription (constituting the stimulus) to all other transcriptions in an on-line version of Webster's Pocket Dictionary (Luce & Pisoni, 1998), a 20,000 word on-line lexicon containing computer-readable phonemic transcriptions and frequency counts based on Kucera and Francis (1967). A neighbour was defined as any transcription that could be converted to the transcription of the stimulus by a one phoneme substitution, deletion, or addition in any position. The log frequencies of the neighbours were then summed for each word and nonword, rendering frequency-weighted neighbourhood density (FWND) measures.

Two measures were used to determine phonotactic probability: (1) positional segment frequency (how often a particular segment occurs in a position in a word) and (2) positional biphone frequency (segment-to-segment co-occurrence probability). These metrics were also computed based on Webster's Pocket Dictionary.

All conditions were matched across shared levels of a given variable (e.g., all high phonotactic probability conditions had approximately equal mean probabilities). In addition, all four word conditions were matched on log frequency and all eight word and nonword conditions were matched on stimulus duration. Omnibus F tests and pairwise comparisons resulted in no significant differences among matched conditions (all $ps > .05$). Stimulus statistics are shown in Table 1.

In addition to the manipulated variables (neighbourhood density and phonotactic probability), five other statistics were computed for the word and nonword stimuli: unweighted neighbourhood density, average neighbourhood frequency (log), isolation point (see Marslen-Wilson &

TABLE 1
Stimulus statistics

Lexicality	Condition*	Average log frequency	Average FWND**	Average product of phoneme probabilities	Average product of biphone probabilities	Average duration (msc)
Words	HD-HP	2.4	47	1.3×10^{-4}	1.6×10^{-5}	505
	HD-LP	2.2	46	0.4×10^{-4}	0.4×10^{-5}	529
	LD-HP	2.2	27	1.4×10^{-4}	1.5×10^{-5}	495
	LD-LP	2.3	28	0.2×10^{-4}	0.4×10^{-5}	505
Nonwords	HD-HP	-	46	1.4×10^{-4}	1.4×10^{-5}	506
	HD-LP	-	43	0.5×10^{-4}	0.6×10^{-5}	502
	LD-HP	-	27	1.6×10^{-4}	2.0×10^{-5}	493
	LD-LP	-	26	0.4×10^{-4}	0.4×10^{-5}	505

Lexicality	Condition*	Average density (unweighted)	Average NHF*** (log)	Average isolation point (phonemes)	Average cohort size	Average cohort frequency (log)
Words	HD-HP	20	2.4	3.0	624	3.0
	HD-LP	19	2.4	3.0	496	2.9
	LD-HP	12	2.2	3.0	624	3.0
	LD-LP	12	2.3	3.0	523	2.9
Nonwords	HD-HP	20	2.3	2.6	650	3.0
	HD-LP	18	2.4	2.2	460	2.8
	LD-HP	12	2.2	2.5	608	3.0
	LD-LP	12	2.2	2.3	524	2.9

* H, high; L, low; D, density; P, phonotactics.
** Frequency-weighted (log base 10) neighbourhood density.
***Neighbourhood frequency.

Welsh, 1978), average cohort size, and average cohort frequency (log). "Isolation point" refers to the point at which each word or nonword stimulus diverges from all possible words in the lexicon, yielding either a single possible word (uniqueness point), or no possible words (nonword point; see Marslen-Wilson 1980), respectively. All five statistics were computed using Webster's Pocket Dictionary. The values for these statistics as a function of condition are shown in the lower panel of Table 1.

Unweighted density and average neighbourhood frequency were computed to ensure that conditions high in FWND have *both* high density *and* high neighbourhood frequency, and that low FWND conditions have low density and neighbourhood frequency. Inspection of the values for unweighted density reveals that the high FWND conditions have more neighbours, irrespective of frequency, than the low FWND conditions

$(F(1, 352) = 510.50, p < .05)$. In addition, high FWND conditions have, on the average, higher frequency neighbours than low FWND conditions $(F(1, 352) = 34.70, p < .05)$. Most important, however, none of the word or nonword conditions are anomalous in terms of unweighted density or average neighborhood frequency.

Cohort statistics were computed to ensure that any observed effects could not be attributed exclusively to variations in cohort structure. Analysis of isolation points as a function of condition revealed significant effects of lexicality and phonotactics: Words have later isolation points than nonwords $(F(1, 352) = 309.18, p < .05)$ and stimuli with high phonotactic probabilies have later isolation points than stimuli with low phonotactic probabilities $(F(1, 352) = 17.27, p < .05)$. (The latter effect was due entirely to the nonwords.) Note that the covariation of phonotactic probability and isolation point works against our hypothesis regarding the effects of phonotactics: Later isolation points should be associated with *slower* reaction times (e.g., Marslen-Wilson & Welsh, 1978), whereas higher phonotactic probability should be associated with *faster* processing.

Analyses of average cohort size and frequency revealed that stimuli with high probability phonotactic patterns had larger cohorts with more frequent members $(F(1, 352) = 19.47, p < .05$ and $F(1, 352) = 29.80, p < .05)$. Both effects reflect the positive correlation in the language between number of overlapping words and segmental frequency, and both effects should militate against predicted effects of phonotactic probability. However, once again, none of the conditions for either the words or nonwords prove anomalous according to any of the cohort measures.

The word and nonword stimuli were recorded by a trained speech scientist, low-pass filtered at 10 kHz, and digitised at a sampling rate of 20 kHz using a 16-bit analog-to-digital converter. All words were edited into individual files and stored on computer disk.

Procedure.   The stimuli were presented to participants for speeded same-different judgements, with time to respond *same* constituting the primary dependent variable. *Different* trials constituted fillers and were not analysed. Reaction times in this task have previously proven sensitive to the variables under scrutiny (Vitevitch & Luce, 1999).

Each participant was seated at a testing station equipped with a pair of headphones and a response box. Presentation of stimuli and response collection was controlled by computer. Participants were presented with two spoken stimuli at a comfortable listening level and were instructed to respond *same* or *different* as quickly and as accurately as possible by pressing appropriately labelled buttons. *Same* responses were made with the dominant hand. The inter-stimulus interval was 50 ms. Reaction times were measured from the onset of the second stimulus in the pair to the button press response. If the maximum reaction time (3 s) expired, the computer automatically recorded an incorrect response and presented the next trial. The words and nonwords were presented to separate groups of participants. Twenty participants were presented with the words and 25 with the nonwords. Half of the trials consisted of two identical stimuli (constituting *same* trials) and half of the trials consisted of different stimuli. No participant heard a given stimulus on more than one trial. All different trials consisted of filler items matched to the targets in terms of phonotactics and frequency (for words).

Prior to the experimental trials, each participant received 12 practice trials. These trials were used to familiarise the participants with the task and were not included in the final data analysis.

Results and discussion

The mean reaction times in ms for correct *same* responses are shown in Figure 1. Two (Density) $\times$ 2 (Phonotactic Probability) ANOVAs for words and nonwords were performed for participants (F_1) and items (F_2). Responses resulting from reaction times less than 200 ms and greater than 1200 ms were scored as incorrect. Five words and four nonwords were excluded because they failed to reached a predetermined level of accuracy or produced mean reaction times 2.5 standard deviations above the mean for all items in a given condition. Unless otherwise noted, all significant effects had p values of .05 or less. Accuracy was above 94% for all conditions and produced no significant results.

High density words ($\overline{X} = 708$) were responded to more slowly than low density words ($\overline{X} = 688$; $F_1(1, 19) = 21.32$ and $F_2(1, 171) = 6.09$). High probability words ($\overline{X} = 689$) were responded to more quickly than low probability words ($\overline{X} = 707$; $F_1(1, 19) = 6.68$ and $F_2(1, 171) = 4.17$). The interaction between density and phonotactic probability was not significant ($F_1(1, 19) = 3.92$ and $F_2(1, 171) = 2.40$).

For nonwords, the effect of density was significant by participants ($F_1(1, 24) = 4.827$) but not items ($F_2(1, 172) = 1.34$). The effect of phonotactic probability was not significant (both Fs < 1), nor was the interaction of density and phonotactic probability significant ($F_1(1, 24) = 2.27$ and $F_2(1, 172) = 1.06$).

The results for the *words* reveal simultaneous inhibitory effects of neighbourhood density and facilitative effects of probabilistic phonotactics, demonstrating that—for words—sublexical effects of component probability have effects above and beyond those of lexical density. These data are most consistent with recognition models positing the operation of distinct sublexical and lexical units (such as Shortlist, TRACE, ARTPHONE, or PARSYN).

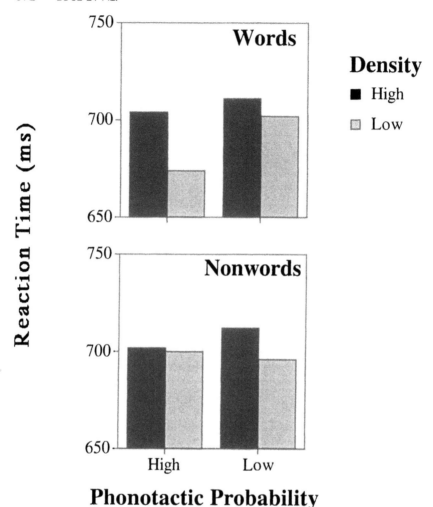

Figure 1. Same-Different reaction times (ms) for words and nonwords as a function of density (dark vs. light bars) and phonotactic probability (*x* axis).

On the other hand, the *nonwords* failed to show reliable effects of either density or phonotactic probability, in contrast to previous findings demonstrating effects for nonwords of both probabilistic phonotactics (in same-different matching) and neighbourhood density (in lexical decision; Vitevitch & Luce, 1999). Comparison of reaction times for words and nonwords, shown in Figure 2, suggests that the failure to observe the predicted data pattern for the nonwords may lie in *one* anomalous condition. In three of the four density-probability conditions, reaction times were virtually identical for words and nonwords: (1) high density-

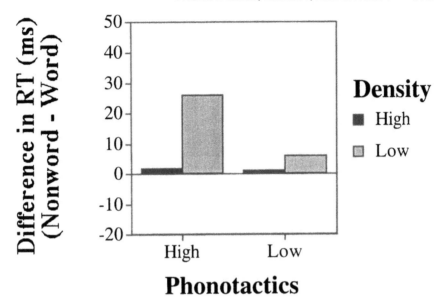

Figure 2.   Mean differences in reaction time between words and nonwords as a function of density (dark vs. light bars) and phonotactic probability (*x* axis).

high probability (Δ reaction time = 2 ms, both *F*s < 1), (2) high density-low probability (Δ reaction time = 1 ms, both *F*s < 1), and (3) low density-low probability (Δ reaction time = 6 ms, both *F*s < 1). However, a marked difference between words and nonwords was obtained for the low density-high probability condition: Nonwords in this condition were responded to 26 ms slower than words ($F_1(1, 43) = 13.23$ and $F_2(1, 88) = 4.37$). We speculate that if nonwords in the low density-high probability condition had behaved as expected, we would have observed the predicted pattern of phonotactic facilitation and neighbourhood competition.

One possible reason for the observed nonword data pattern is that neighbourhood density and phonotactic probability do not always combine in a simple additive, linear fashion. Some current connectionist models suggest that spoken word recognition is the result of complex interactions among representations of various sizes or at multiple levels (McClelland & Elman, 1986; Norris, 1994; Vitevitch & Luce, 1999). Such processing interactions may produce effects that are not predicted by statistics that independently estimate lexical and sublexical activation and competition (i.e., neighbourhood density and probabilistic phonotactics). For example, the potentially anomalous result for the low density-high probability condition may have resulted from an underestimation of the degree of lexical competition. Lessened intralexical inhibition due to the relatively lower number of competing neighbours in low density neighbourhoods, coupled with heightened activation of the neighbours based on their higher phonotactic probabilities, may have produced particularly severe competitive environments for these nonwords. Moreover, the lack of a single lexical representation consistent with the input may have further exaggerated the effects of lexical competition, given that no dominant representation would gain an immediate foothold and suppress activation of its competitors. Thus, the combined effects of (1) a low density neighbourhood, (2) high probability sublexical representations, and (3) the lack of a single lexical representation providing an exact match to the input may have combined to produce a particularly problematic processing environment.

To determine if our statistical measures of neighbourhood density and sublexical probability had indeed underestimated lexical competition for the nonwords in the low density-high probability condition (as suggested by the comparison of the word and nonword data), we conducted a second experiment in which we estimated the degree of lexical activation evoked by our nonwords somewhat more directly than relying on inferences based on corpus searches. Specifically, we asked participants to generate *similar sounding* words (or lexical neighbours) to each of the nonwords used in Experiment 1 (see Greenberg & Jenkins, 1964; Cutler, Sebastián-Gallés, Soler-Vilageliu, & van Ooijen, 2000). We then computed a measure of *entropy* over the word responses to index the number of different lexical items activated by a given nonword. Increases in entropy reflect increases in the number of different words to which a nonword is similar (as measured by this neighbour generation task). Once again, the resulting measure of entropy provides a *behavioural*, rather than purely *statistical*, estimate of lexical competition that may reflect processing interactions inadequately captured by our independent measures of neighbourhood density and phonotactic probability. After collecting the entropy values for the nonwords, we reanalysed the reaction times for the nonwords in Experiment 1 as a function of entropy.

EXPERIMENT 2

Method

Participants. Twenty-one English-speaking adult participants were recruited from the University at Buffalo community. All participants reported no history of a speech or hearing disorder.

Materials. The stimuli consisted of the nonwords used in Experiment 1.

Procedure. Each participant was seated at a testing station equipped with a pair of headphones with an attached microphone. Presentation of stimuli and response collection was controlled by computer. Participants were presented a spoken nonword at a comfortable listening level and were instructed to say aloud, as quickly as possible, a real word that sounded like the nonword stimulus. Responses were recorded on audiotape for later analysis.

Prior to the experiment proper, participants read examples of stimuli ("meech") and a few possible appropriate responses ("each", "me", "beach", "breach", or "beseech"), and responded to 10 spoken nonwords as practice trials.

Results and discussion

Ninety per cent of the obtained responses were real words. Mean reaction time to produce these responses was 1749 ms. Table 2 shows the most common word responses as a function of phonemic overlap with the target nonword. Seventy-one per cent of the responses involved one-segment substitutions, suggesting that our neighbourhood metric (based, in part, on phoneme substitutions) should have been capable of capturing at least gross differences in neighbourhood density for spoken nonwords, a prediction not supported by the results of Experiment 1.

As an additional index of lexical activation, entropy values were computed for each nonword based on the word responses. High entropy values indicate that a nonword evoked many different word responses; low entropy values are associated with nonwords that produced a small number of different word responses.

TABLE 2

Percentages of word responses to nonwords in the neighbour generation task as a function of segmental overlap.

Example target nonword: /fin/		
Example word response	*Change*	*Percentage of word responses**
feet	Final consonant	34%
mean	Initial consonant	27%
phone	Vowel	10%
foam	Vowel + final consonant	8%
meat	Initial and final consonant	7%
bin	Initial Consonant + Vowel	3%

* The 11% of responses not shown in this table consisted of a diverse set of categories (additions of single segments, additions of syllables, etc.), none of which individually accounted for more than 3% of the total responses.

Each nonword stimulus was designated as belonging to high or low entropy categories based on a median split of the rank-ordered entropy values. The nonwords were then assigned to one of eight conditions, produced by combining two levels of entropy, density, and phonotactic probability. In order to match the resulting cells on stimulus duration and lexical statistics, we deleted 26 stimuli, leaving 83 high and 71 low entropy nonwords. The numbers of stimuli per cell (and examples) for the high entropy items were: High density-high phonotactics, $N = 25$ (/b æ b/); high density-low phonotactics, $N = 15$ (/fut/); low density-high phonotactics, $n = 20$ (/bɪv/); and low density-low phonotactics, $N = 23$ (/s æ θ/). The numbers of stimuli per cell (and examples) for the low entropy items were: High density-high phonotactics, $N = 16$ (/f i n/); high density-low phonotactics, $N = 25$ (/m ɔ t/); low density-high phonotactics, $N = 10$ (/h ɑ m/); and low density-low phonotactics, $N = 20$ (/ʃ u l/). Omnibus F tests and pairwise comparisons resulted in no significant differences among matched conditions on frequency-weighted neighbourhood density, probabilistic phonotactics, or stimulus duration (all Fs < 1.0).

We ran participant and item ANOVAs on the high and low entropy nonwords as a function of density and probabilistic phonotactics. The results of this post-hoc analysis of the nonword reaction times obtained in Experiment 1 are shown in Figure 3.

For the low entropy nonwords, a marginal effect of density was obtained by participants ($F_1(1, 24) = 3.85$, $p = .06$) but not items ($F_2(1, 67) = 2.1$). High phonotactic probability nonwords ($\overline{X} = 682$) were responded to more quickly than low phonotactic probability nonwords ($\overline{X} = 702$; $F_1(1, 24) = 6.12$ and $F_2(1, 67) = 4.39$). The interaction of density and phonotactic probability was not significant ($F_1(1, 24) = 1.53$ and $F_2 < 1$).

For the high entropy nonwords, no significant effects of density (both Fs < 1) or phonotactic probability ($F_1(1, 24) = 2.00$ and $F_2(1, 79) = 1.13$) were obtained. The interaction of density and phonotactics was significant by participants ($F_1(1, 24) = 4.46$) but not items ($F_1(1, 79) = 1.79$).

Partitioning the nonword stimuli from Experiment 1 according to the entropy values obtained in Experiment 2 reveals that low entropy nonwords exhibit the expected facilitative effect of phonotactic probability. There was also a trend toward an inhibitory effect of neighbourhood density. (The reduced statistical power of this post-hoc analysis may have made this somewhat weaker effect for nonwords more difficult to detect.) On the other hand, high entropy nonwords exhibited no significant effects of either variable. These results suggest that neighbourhood density and phonotactic probability are—at least for nonwords—mediated by the strength of activation of specific similar representations.

Comparison of reaction times across entropy condition (high vs. low), shown in Figure 4, reveals that three of the four conditions exhibited

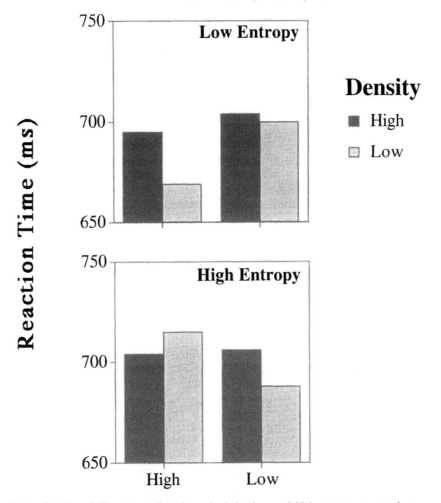

Figure 3. Same-Different reaction times (ms) for low and high entropy nonwords as a function of density (dark vs. light bars) and phonotactic probability (x axis).

virtually no differences as a function of entropy: (1) high density-high probability (Δ reaction time = 9 ms, both Fs <1), (2) high density-low probability (Δ reaction time = 2 ms, both Fs <1), and (3) low density-low probability (Δ reaction time = 12 ms, $F_1(1,24) = 1.33$ and F_2 <1). However, a marked difference between high and low entropy was obtained for the low density-high probability condition. In particular, high entropy nonwords in this condition were responded to 46 ms slower than low entropy nonwords ($F_1(1,24) = 18.64$ and $F_2(1,29) = 7.12$).

In summary, the results of the entropy analysis strongly suggest that our original statistical measures of neighbourhood density and phonotactic

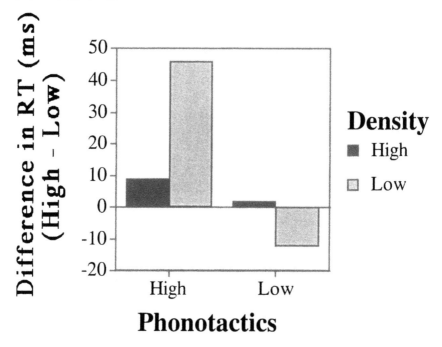

Figure 4. Mean differences in reaction time between high and low entropy stimuli as a function of density (dark vs. light bars) and phonotactic probability (*x* axis).

probability failed to predict the degree of lexical competition for certain of the nonwords in the low density-high probability condition. When only low entropy nonwords in all conditions were examined, a data pattern emerged that was virtually identical to that observed for words in Experiment 1. However, consistent with the hypothesis that certain of the nonwords in the low density-high probability conditions were succumbing to increased lexical competition, high entropy nonwords in this condition were responded to significantly more slowly than low entropy nonwords.

GENERAL DISCUSSION

Our original intent was to unconfound similarity neighbourhood density and phonotactic probability in an attempt to demonstrate their simultaneous effects on processing. Indeed, we were successful at demonstrating *both* facilitative effects of phonotactic probability and inhibitory effects of lexical competition for *words*. Thus, although lexical competition may typically dominate processing for real words (Vitevitch & Luce, 1999), phonotactic probability also has demonstrable and predictable effects on processing speed.

Our efforts at demonstrating effects of density and phonotactic probability for nonwords did not (at least at first) meet with comparable success. When we examined nonwords that were closely matched to real words on density and phonotactics, no reliable effects of either variable were observed. Comparison of the word and nonword data revealed a correspondence between processing times in all experimental conditions except one: Nonwords in the low density-high probability condition produced longer-than-expected reaction times.

Subsequent analyses of the nonword data revealed that effects of lexical competition appear to have been underestimated for a portion of the nonwords in the low density-high probability condition. When lexical competition was assessed behaviourally using the neighbour generation task, those nonwords having the fewest neighbours (low entropy items) behaved as predicted. However, our post-hoc analysis revealed that high entropy nonwords in the low density-high probability condition—that is, those nonwords that evoked multiple word responses—were processed more slowly than predicted based on our *statistical* measures of neighbourhood density and phonotactic probability. Thus, our measure of entropy identified a set of nonwords in the low density-high probability condition that apparently produce stronger lexical competition than predicted by our statistical measures.

Why, then, did our statistical measures of lexical competition and phonotactic probability accurately predict performance in all but one of our eight original conditions? We propose that lexical competitors, whose strengths are determined by the synergistic effects of sublexical activation and lexical competition, may exert influences on processing above and beyond the simple combined, additive effects of sublexical probability and neighbourhood density. Recall that the low density-high probability condition, which exhibited the greatest difference as a function of lexicality (Experiment 1) and entropy (Experiment 2), contains those nonwords having few lexical neighbours but highly probable sublexical components. In this unusual situation, in which the normal positive correlation of density and phonotactic probability is broken, processing interactions between lexical and sublexical representations may give rise to heightened effects of lexical competition not predicted by our standard measures of density or probabilistic phonotactics.

In particular, we propose that nonwords high in entropy in the low density-high probability condition strongly activate a handful of lexical items whose attraction to or support by the input pattern is particularly high and whose competition is severe. In short, low lexical density and high sublexical probability appear to combine synergistically to make these particular nonwords vulnerable to specific, highly similar competing lexical items. Work is currently underway to determine the precise circumstances under which low density-high probability stimuli give rise to the high entropy situations identified by our neighbour generation task. Nonetheless, the current results point to the need to consider the effects of lexical and sublexical statistics in the context of potentially complex processing interactions.

In short, our principal claim is that a simple combination of effects of lexical competition and phonotactic probability may fail to capture nonlinear combinations of the effects of activation and competition at lexical and sublexical levels of representation for nonwords. We speculate that similar results may be obtained for real words that lack strong activation of form-based lexical representations (e.g., low frequency words). Nonetheless, we believe that the present results support the previously hypothesised roles of lexical and sublexical representations in spoken word recognition, while at the same time suggesting a complex interplay of density and probabilistic phonotactics.

REFERENCES

Cutler, A., Sebastián-Gallés, N., Soler-Vilageliu, O., & van Ooijen, B. (2000). Constraints of vowels and consonants on lexical selection: Cross-linguistic comparisons. *Memory and Cognition, 28*, 746-755.

Greenberg, J.H., & Jenkins, J.J. (1964). Studies in the psychological correlates of the sound system of American English. *Word, 20*, 157–177.

Grossberg, S., Boardman, I., & Cohen, M. (1997) Neural dynamics of variable-rate speech categorization. *Journal of Experimental Psychology: Human Perception and Performance, 23*, 483–503.

Kucera, H., & Francis, W.N. (1967). *Computational analysis of present-day American English.* Providence, RI: Brown University Press.

Luce, P.A., Goldinger, S.D., Auer, E.T., & Vitevitch, M.S. (2000). Phonetic priming, neighborhood activation, and PARSYN. *Perception and Psychophysics, 62*, 615–625.

Luce, P.A., & Pisoni, D.B. (1998). Recognizing spoken words: The neighborhood activation model. *Ear and Hearing, 19*, 1–36.

Marslen-Wilson, W.D. (1980). Speech understanding as a psychological process. In J.C. Simon (ed.), *Spoken language generation and understanding.* Dordrecht: Reidel.

Marslen-Wilson, W.D., & Welsh, A. (1978). Processing interactions and lexical access during word recognition in continuous speech. *Cognitive Psychology, 10*, 29–63.

McClelland, J.L., & Elman, J.L. (1986). The TRACE model of speech perception. *Cognitive Psychology, 18*, 1–86.

Norris, D.G. (1994). Shortlist: A connectionist model of continuous speech recognition. *Cognition, 52*, 189–234.

Norris, D.G., McQueen, J.M., & Cutler, A. (2000). Merging information in speech recognition: Feedback is never necessary. *Behavioral and Brain Sciences, 23*, 299–325.

Pitt, M.A., & Samuel, A.G. (1995). Lexical and sublexical feedback in auditory word recognition. *Cognitive Psychology, 29*, 149–188.

Vitevitch, M.S., & Luce, P.A. (1998). When words compete: Levels of processing in spoken word recognition. *Psychological Science, 9*, 325–329.

Vitevitch, M.S., & Luce, P.A. (1999). Probabilistic phonotactics and neighborhood activation in spoken word recognition. *Journal of Memory and Language, 40*, 374–408.

APPENDIX

Word and nonword stimuli in each of the density-probability conditions*

Word Stimuli				Nonword Stimuli			
High-High	High-Low	Low-High	Low-Low	High-High	High-Low	Low-High	Low-Low
bol	bæθ	bab	bɛg	bem	bʊd	bɑɪm	bep
but	bɔt	bam	bʊk	bæb	bʌtʃ	bɪv	dædʒ
dem	dʌg	bɪb	dɪʃ	dek	ded	bæv	dætʃ
dæd	dum	bim	fez	dɪz	fɑɪd	dab	dʊs
dʌd	fek	dak	fɪʃ	dod	fedʒ	dap	fɛg
faɪl	fem	dal	fʊl	dʌs	fut	dɛp	fɪdʒ
fɛd	fɔt	dɛf	fʊt	dʌt	ged	dɪv	fɔs
fɛl	gen	dɔn	gis	fɪd	ges	dæl	gɑɪs
fel	get	dos	gɔn	fɪk	hɑɪm	fɑɪk	hɪð
fæd	hid	fɪg	hɑʊl	fin	hed	fam	hɪʒ
fon	hip	fok	hɛdʒ	fɪp	hem	fɛp	hɔn
ful	hɪtʃ	fom	hæf	fɪs	hɪg	fim	hʌp
fʌn	lem	fɜ'n	hop	fʌt	hik	fæp	hus
gɪr	lod	fʌs	hup	gɑɪn	him	fæv	kitʃ
gor	læg	gɛs	kev	gɛr	lep	fos	log
hel	lʌk	gæs	lɛg	hɑɪn	lɪg	gɪs	lʊn
hʌl	mez	hɑɪr	lob	hɪv	lim	ham	lov
hʌm	mit	hem	læf	hæb	lʌd	hɪb	lɜ's
kad	mɔl	hen	lɔn	kæŋ	mɑʊn	hos	mɑɪv
kip	nɑɪt	hom	lus	koz	mɑʊt	hʌs	mɑʊl
kom	nit	hɜ's	mɛʃ	lad	mep	kob	mɪʃ
lɑɪs	nʌt	kan	mætʃ	lar	mev	lam	miv
lɪd	pitʃ	kɪs	mud	lot	mip	lan	mæŋ
lɪp	piz	lɪm	nis	lʌs	mɔt	lɛp	mum
lɪt	rɑɪd	lɪv	nʌl	mɛd	nek	læl	nɑɪr
mek	red	lɜ'n	nun	mok	nes	lær	num
min	redʒ	lʌl	pɑʊt	mʌn	nik	mim	patʃ
mæd	rez	mab	pev	nar	pʊk	mæb	pʌz
mun	rif	map	pæθ	pɛd	rɔl	mæv	rɑɪb
nɑɪn	rɪŋ	mɪθ	pʊl	pem	ʃar	mom	rɪʃ
non	sedʒ	mʌd	rɑɪp	pæz	ʃes	nɪm	roʃ
nʌn	ʃek	nak	rɪdʒ	pʌm	ʃet	nɪs	ruk
par	ʃer	nɛk	ræθ	rem	ʃɪk	næs	rʌz
ped	ʃɪk	pam	rotʃ	rɛt	siθ	pab	ʃɪm
pen	ʃit	pɛk	rʌg	ræb	sitʃ	pɪm	sæθ
pik	ʃæk	pop	ʃɑɪn	rok	ʃok	pæv	ʃom
pæd	sʌŋ	pɜ's	sef	rʌd	ted	pɜ'd	ʃɜ'n
rot	tɑɪd	rek	ʃɛf	ʃæn	tip	ral	sudʒ
ʃɪn	tal	rɪb	ʃɪp	sɜ'd	tʃek	rɪv	ʃul
sis	tem	sɑɑr	ʃon	sɜ'k	tʃel	ræv	tædʒ
sɔt	tʃɪr	tap	tep	sʌg	tʃet	sʌv	tʃɪm
tɑɪl	tʃit	tɪp	tɔt	tɑɪs	tʃʌn	tɪd	tʃin
tel	tʃor	tæb	tʃɛk	ten	tud	tæv	tʃæs
tol	tum	tær	tʃɪl	tʌl	tup	tos	tʃɔs
tʃɪn	vel	væn	tʃok	vɪl	vet	væs	vit

*High-High refers to high density-high probability, High-Low refers to high density-low probability, etc.

LANGUAGE AND COGNITIVE PROCESSES, 2001, *16* (5/6), 583–607

Bottom-up inhibition in lexical selection: Phonological mismatch effects in spoken word recognition

Uli H. Frauenfelder

Laboratoire de Psycholinguistique Expérimentale,
University of Geneva, Switzerland

Mark Scholten

Laboratoire de Psycholinguistique Expérimentale,
University of Geneva, Switzerland

Alain Content

Laboratoire de Psychologie Expérimentale,
Free University Brussels, Belgium

Two phoneme monitoring experiments are reported that examine the amount of lexical activation produced by words containing initial, medial, or final mispronunciations. Experiment 1 showed that minimal (one distinctive feature) mismatches in the initial phoneme produced lexical activation relative to a baseline control nonword, but only when the target phoneme was situated at word offset and not word-internally. This finding suggests that considerable bottom-up support is required to override the inhibitory influence of the initial mismatching phonological information. Experiment 2 revealed no lexical activation after a medial mismatch, a finding that is

Requests for reprints should be addressed to Uli Frauenfelder, Laboratoire de Psycholinguistique Expérimentale, FPSE, Bd du Pont-d'Arve 40, CH-1205 Genève, Suisse. E-mail: Ulrich.Frauenfelder@pse.unige.ch

This research was supported by grants from the Fonds National Suisse de la Recherche Scientifique (FNS 1114-0395.93, 1113-049698.96 and 1114-059532.99). Thanks go to Cindy Connine, Nicolas Dumay, and Mark Pitt for their helpful comments on an earlier version. A preliminary report was presented at the 36th Annual meeting of the Psychonomics Society (Los Angeles, 1995). These experiments were also included in Mark Scholten's master thesis at the University of Nijmegen.

http://www.tandf.co.uk/journals/pp/01690965.html   DOI: 10.1080/01690960143000146

consistent with bottom-up inhibition, but inconsistent with models assuming only lateral inhibition. Taken together these findings provide evidence for a selection process which includes bottom-up inhibition as a major component.

Current models generally agree that spoken word recognition involves the activation of a set of lexical candidates and the selection of the target word from this activated set. By all accounts, the amount of activation received by any given word unit—target or competitor—depends upon this unit's fit with the sensory input. This fit reflects the quality and the quantity of the match between the sensory input and the lexical form representation. Models differ, however, in their assumptions about the exact mechanisms underlying the selection process by which the words mismatching the input are eliminated from the candidate set and the correct word is identified.

Two distinct mechanisms of lexical selection have generally been proposed: bottom-up inhibition and lateral inhibition. First, lexical selection can be achieved by means of bottom-up inhibition, like in the original Cohort model (Marslen-Wilson & Welsh, 1978). Under the strongest assumptions, when mismatching sensory information is received, it immediately and completely deactivates the inappropriate lexical units. More recent versions of the COHORT model (Marslen-Wilson, 1987) as well as other models like SHORTLIST (Norris, 1994) have allowed for graded activation that depends upon phonological distance and thus assigned a weaker deactivating influence to mismatching information. Second, lexical selection can take place through lateral inhibition. According to TRACE (McClelland & Elman, 1986), lateral inhibition between lexical competitors allows the best-fitting and most activated candidates, and in particular, the target, to inhibit and deactivate the weaker ones. Finally, bottom-up inhibition and lateral inhibition are not mutually incompatible and can be combined in the same model, as is the case for SHORTLIST.

As a first step in defining empirical tests that evaluate these two mechanisms of lexical selection, it is necessary to identify the main factors that they assume to determine lexical excitation and inhibition. The factor that is most relevant for both mechanisms is the goodness of fit (both in quality and quantity) between the input representation and that of the target lexical representation. The better the fit between these two representations, the greater the activation of the target. Similarly, of course, the poorer the fit, the less activation or—in terms of bottom-up inhibition—the more deactivated the lexical item is. This factor is decisive for determining lexical activation in models assuming bottom-up activation and inhibition.

The second relevant factor concerns the goodness of fit between the input and the representations of the lexical competitors. In models with lateral inhibition, the closer and longer the fit is with lexical competitors, the more the target receives inhibitory influences. In contrast, in models assuming only bottom-up inhibition, this factor should not play a role. These two factors, input to target match and input to competitor match have been termed horizontal and vertical similarity, respectively, by Connine (1994). The present study aims to analyse the mechanisms that underlie the effect of horizontal similarity upon lexical activation.

One common experimental means of testing the contribution of these factors to lexical selection is to introduce mismatches or mispronunciations into the sensory input and to determine the amount of resulting or remaining lexical activation. More specifically, it is useful to vary the degree and position of this mismatching information, since the two selection mechanisms make some different predictions about how vertical and horizontal similarity affect lexical activation. By manipulating the degree of mismatch, it is possible to evaluate the tolerance of the processing system to distortion and to determine whether the system allows graded activation or not. By manipulating the position of the mismatch in the mispronounced word, it is possible to evaluate the importance of competitors in determining the target's activation level. Indeed, when mismatches arrive late in the stimulus, and when there are no more activated competitors, the two mechanisms are differentially relevant. Bottom-up inhibition deactivates the target, whereas lateral inhibition no longer has any impact upon target activation since it cannot operate in the absence of activated competitors. As we will see, models based upon bottom-up inhibition or on lateral inhibition make different predictions.

Spoken word recognition models clearly vary in how well they tolerate initial phonological mismatches in the sensory input. They can range from extreme intolerance and total lexical deactivation by any mismatch in the speech input via bottom-up inhibition, like in the original CoHORT model, to relative tolerance and graded activation, like in SHORTLIST and TRACE. The precise predictions of TRACE and SHORTLIST with respect to the effect of initial mismatches upon lexical activation are not well established. It was originally claimed (Elman & McClelland, 1988) that TRACE deals with minor initial mismatches efficiently and easily recognises distorted inputs (e.g., "barty" as "party"). However, detailed simulations with TRACE (Frauenfelder & Content, 2000) have shown that when presented with nonword inputs that differ from words in a single distinctive feature in their initial phoneme, TRACE generally fails to recognise the mispronounced words. Unfortunately, no analogous simulations exist with SHORTLIST, in part, due to the fact that the model's front end does not take into phonological distance into account. Thus it is difficult to predict the behaviour of SHORTLIST precisely. Most likely, however, the differences in the predictions for initial mismatches of the two models are more quantitative than qualitative in nature and depend more upon details of implementation than upon fundamental architectural choices.

The experimental literature on the activation of words by inputs mispronounced in their initial phoneme is somewhat contradictory and not yet conclusive. The pattern of results obtained depends upon various factors, including the experimental paradigm used, the type of lexical activation tested (e.g., semantic vs. phonological), the competitor environment and length of the mispronounced word, and the degree of the mismatch. Many studies have focused on the semantic activation produced by initially mismatching inputs using some version of the semantic priming paradigm, either cross-modal or intra-modal (Connine, Blasko, & Titone, 1993; Marslen-Wilson, Moss, & van Halen, 1996; Marslen-Wilson & Zwitserlood, 1989). In these studies, participants made lexical decisions upon either visually or auditorily presented target words that were preceded immediately by a mispronounced semantically related word. Globally, significant priming effects were obtained when the nonword prime was phonologically close to the target word (one distinctive feature difference) and had no other rhyming competitors, suggesting that the factors identified above (match to target and match to competitors) are important.

Other studies have evaluated the effect of initial mismatch upon phonological rather than semantic activation. Connine, Titone, Deelman, & Blasko (1997) used the generalised phoneme monitoring task (Frauenfelder & Segui, 1989) to examine the amount of activation produced by nonwords which varied in their degree of initial mismatch from a target word. The phoneme targets were located in item-final position. The results of these experiments showed a graded effect with decreasing detection latencies for nonwords that were phonologically more similar to words. Interestingly, even the nonwords that deviated from the intended word by several (at least five) distinctive features produced some lexical activation with respect to the unrelated nonword control. It appears that experimental measures of the activation of phonological representations are more sensitive than those of the activation of semantic representations and thus may provide a better basis for testing the proposed selection mechanisms.

The predictions of models based upon bottom-up and lateral inhibition about the impact of later arriving phonological mismatches are more differentiated than those for initial position. For a model like TRACE based upon lateral inhibition, a late phonological mismatch in the input will have little or no effect upon the activation level of the target. Indeed, once the target word has reached a certain level of activation and has no more active lexical competitors that can be reinforced by the mispronounced input, its activation level will be affected minimally by the distortion.

Differences in the activation curves of a target word by an accurate and a mispronounced input are attributable to the fact that the mismatching phoneme provides somewhat less bottom-up support for the target than the appropriate phoneme. In contrast, for models with bottom-up inhibition, the situation is quite different. Late phonological mismatches can deactivate the target word which can only regain in activation strength if there is sufficient subsequent matching input after the mismatch.

Relatively few studies provide information about the deactivation of already activated words by later arriving phonological mismatches. As mentioned above, such studies can, in principle, offer a clean test for bottom-up inhibition that neutralises the influence of lexical competition. Some early research (Zwitserlood, 1989) with the cross-modal semantic priming paradigm has examined the effect of sensory information (/e/) that matches the target (/kapIte/ from kapitein), but mismatches its activated competitor (/kapita:/ from kapitaal, capital). The results showed that activated competitors were immediately deactivated when mismatching information was received. Unfortunately, it is impossible in this study to determine whether it was the mismatching input that eliminated this competitor through bottom-up inhibition or whether the matching target had received sufficient activation from the additional input to inhibit this mismatching competitor. In another cross-modal semantic priming experiment, Connine, Blasko, and Titone (1993) compared the priming effects for initial and medial mismatches in two- or three-syllable words. They obtained effects of similar magnitude for both positions and concluded that initial information is not more heavily weighted or crucial for accessing spoken words.

The present study used the generalised phoneme monitoring task to tap into lexical activation and examine the effect of initial and late mismatches. The way in which detection latencies reflect lexical processing and activation has been a subject of debate in the psycholinguistic literature. Proponents of autonomous models such as Race (Cutler & Norris, 1979) originally argued that the lexical effect observed was the result of an output from the lexical module. Any facilitatory effect of the lexicon required prior recognition of the word, and thus the task was assumed not to be sensitive to early pre-recognition lexical activation. In contrast, TRACE includes top-down connections between lexical and phoneme units so that as lexical units gain in activation, they return some of this activation to the phoneme level. Hence phoneme detection latencies are taken to be an early and relatively direct indicator of lexical activation.

One empirical approach taken to test these models is to determine the locus of the lexical effect and to observe its evolution across different target positions. Frauenfelder, Segui, and Dijkstra (1990) found that the effect emerged relatively late, only when the phoneme target was located after the UP. They argued that such late lexical effects, presumably appearing after word recognition, were more consistent with autonomous models. Subsequently, Pitt and Samuel (1995) conducted a similar study in which lexical effects appeared even for targets located before the UP, and they interpreted their findings as supporting interactive models.

More recently, however, Norris, McQueen, and Cutler (2000) have proposed an autonomous model, Merge, in which the lexicon can contribute to the phoneme detection response without assuming an interaction between lexical and phoneme levels of processing. According to this model lexical activation can influence phoneme detection responses relatively early, that is, before word recognition. It now appears then that even autonomous models do not require word recognition for lexical effects to appear. Despite the important remaining theoretical differences between autonomous and interactive processing models, both accounts are in agreement that the differences in phoneme monitoring latencies can be assumed to reflect lexical activation.

In the two phoneme monitoring experiments presented here, we introduce phonological mismatches into words in different positions. We also vary the position of the target to be detected in word and nonword carriers to track the evolution of phonological activation across time. More specifically, Experiment 1 investigates the effect of minimal initial mismatches upon phonological activation for two target positions: late in the items and at item offset. Experiment 2 evaluates the effect of medial phonological mismatches upon phonological activation and tests for bottom-up inhibition under conditions in which the contribution of lateral inhibition is reduced or even eliminated. Deactivation of the target-bearing word by the presence of a medial mismatch would constitute evidence for bottom-up inhibition and would thus argue against models like TRACE that base lexical selection only on lateral inhibition.

EXPERIMENT 1

This experiment tests for lexical activation in initial mismatch conditions by comparing phoneme detection latencies to targets in two positions in words and matched nonwords of two types. The first type, the baseline nonword, has no resemblance to any word and therefore should produce no lexical activation, whereas the second type, the close nonword, is derived from a word by changing a single distinctive feature in the initial phoneme. The difference in detection latencies to the phoneme targets in words and matched baseline nonwords, the so-called lexical effect, represents full lexical activation, whereas the difference between the close nonword and the baseline nonword reflects the partial activation of the word by the close nonword. The position of the target was also manipulated, being either just after the uniqueness point (UP) or at word offset. The UP is defined as that point in a word where the word diverges phonologically from all other words in the lexicon. This manipulation was included to determine whether the lexical effect increases as the target arrives later and more bottom-up support for the target-bearing word has been received.

Method

Participants.   Forty-six students of the University of Geneva, all native speakers of French without known hearing deficits, voluntarily participated in the experiment as part of their curriculum. Participants were assigned randomly to each of the four experimental lists.

Materials.   Forty-eight polysyllabic French words were selected from the French lexical database, BRULEX (Content, Mousty, & Radeau, 1990) according to two criteria. First, these words had a frequency of at least 100 per 100 million and were thus familiar to the participants. Second, these words contained two different target consonants in their final portion; one just after their UP and one at their offset. Each consonant target never occurred elsewhere in the same item to avoid multiple targets. The targets were liquids (31), stops (31), fricatives (17), and nasals (17).

On the basis of these words, 48 triplets of experimental stimuli were defined: the original words, Close nonwords, and Baseline nonwords. The two types of nonword stimuli were constructed by modifying the original words. Close nonwords were made by changing the first phoneme of the original word by one (and in four cases, two) distinctive features. The resulting nonword point (NWP) of these items was located approximately at the same position as the UP of the original word. Baseline nonwords were constructed by replacing several (at least three) initial phonemes of the original word by other phonemes of the same major phonetic class (a consonant was replaced by another consonant and the same for vowels), thereby retaining the CV structure of the original word. Since only the beginnings of the original words were modified in all nonword items, the local environment of the targets remained identical across the three item types. In this fashion, any detection latency difference between members of a triplet could not be attributed to the local phonological environment of the target (transitional probabilities, syllable frequencies, etc.). An example of an experimental triplet is shown in Table 1 and the lexical and temporal properties of the full stimulus set are given in Table 2. In summary, the test stimuli can be characterised in terms of three main factors: activation type (full vs. partial), position (first vs. second) and

TABLE 1

Examples of stimuli, mean RTs in ms and percentage correct responses for the different experimental conditions in Experiment 1 (target phonemes in bold and mismatching phonemes underlined)

| | | Lexicality | |
| | | *Baseline* | *Word/Close* |
Target position	*Activation condition*	*Nonword*	*Nonword*
First	Full	satobyl**ɛʀ** 461.3 (94.6)	vokabyl**ɛʀ** 412.9 (95.5)
	Partial	satobyl**ɛʀ** 459.0 (95.3)	fokabyl**ɛʀ** 460.0 (93.8)
Second	Full	satobyl**ɛʀ** 405.2 (96.4)	vokabyl**ɛʀ** 309.3 (97.8)
	Partial	satobyl**ɛʀ** 403.6 (94.2)	fokabyl**ɛʀ** 364.3 (93.1)

lexicality (Baseline nonword vs. Word or Close nonword). The Appendix lists the experimental stimuli and targets.

In addition to the 48 triplets of test items, 216 fillers (words and nonwords) were also created to include items without targets and to vary further the target position. There were 48 words and 96 nonwords without targets. In addition, 48 words and 24 nonwords were also included with targets in early word positions (word onset, first and second consonant positions after word onset) to prevent participants from expecting target phonemes towards the end of the item. All fillers were similar to the test items in their global phonological make-up and syllable structure.

Four experimental lists which each contained a subset of the test items were created. Each list contained two members of an experimental triplet: the baseline nonword and either the matching word or the close nonword. This latin-square design made it possible to avoid any priming effects that

TABLE 2

Lexical (uniqueness point and nonword point and cohort size) and durational properties (and their SD) of the stimuli used in Experiment 1

	UP/NWP *(No. of* *phonemes)*	*Cohort* *size* *(No. of words)*	*Distance from* *onset to* *target 1 in ms*	*Distance from* *onset to* *target 2 in ms*
Words	4.48 (0.77)	10.88 (11.69)	531.4 (111.6)	881.4 (146.5)
Close nonwords	3.92 (0.94)	16.04 (25.88)	556.9 (124.5)	907.0 (167.2)
Baseline nonwords	4.21 (0.74)	15.79 (22.88)	587.2 (145.6)	940.3 (180.0)

might have arisen in presenting an original word and its derived close nonword to the same participant. The test items were assigned to the four experimental lists so that each list contained an equal number of items (12) from each condition. In addition, the groups of 12 stimuli were divided such that they varied in the nature of the target phoneme (e.g., stops, liquids, etc.). The resulting 336 stimuli were arranged in four pseudo-randomised blocks of 84 items. The word or the close nonword items were assigned to blocks such that they were separated from their corresponding baseline nonword by at least one block. These blocks were presented in the same order to all participant groups.

Procedure and apparatus.   The stimuli were recorded on DAT-tapes by a native speaker of French and then transferred to the hard disk of a computer at a sampling rate of 16 KHz. The experimental lists that were created by adding target specifications and warning beeps were then re-recorded on DAT tapes. Response times were recorded by an AST 4/25 SL laptop running the NESU (Nijmegen Experimental Set-Up) software package, developed at the Max-Planck Institute (Nijmegen, the Nether-lands).

Participants were tested individually or in groups of two or three. They first heard the target specification (the consonant target produced in its default syllable context and a name beginning with the target—e.g., "/l/ as in Lara"). Then they received a short warning tone followed by a pause of 50 ms and finally the test (or filler) item. Participants had 2500 ms from item onset to respond. A 2 s pause preceded the next trial. Between each block of 84 items there was a short break of approximately 3 min. Participants received written instructions and then performed 20 warm-up trials. They were instructed to push on the response button with the index finger of their dominant hand as quickly as possible when they heard the target phoneme.

Results

Reaction times (RTs) were measured from the onset of the target phoneme, which was determined both auditorily and visually using a waveform editor. Response times faster than 100 ms or slower than 1000 ms were discarded from the analysis. No participants were excluded from the analysis; all had an error rate of less than 15%. Mean RTs and mean per cent correct (PC) scores were calculated separately for each subject and item. Overall mean RTs and PC scores for the main experimental conditions are given in Table 1. The close match between the two corresponding RT means in the baseline nonword conditions indicates that they provide a highly stable measure for evaluating the lexical effect.

Three-way ANOVAs were performed on the PC and RT data with the factors, activation, position, and lexicality. No main effects were fully significant in the error analyses, but the interaction between activation and position was marginally significant [$F_1(1, 45) = 6.22, p < .02$]. All three factors, however, showed highly significant main effects in RTs both by-subject and by-item: activation [$F_1(1, 45) = 25.66, p < .0001$]; [$F_2(1, 47) = 15.97, p < .001$], position [$F_1(1, 45) = 132.55, p < .0001$]; [$F_2(1, 47) = 59.75, p < .001$], and lexicality [$F_1(1, 45) = 92.82, p < .0001$]; [$F_2(1, 47) = 46.38, p < .001$].

More importantly, two significant interactions were also found: lexicality and position [$F_1(1, 45) = 38.05, p < .001; F_2(1, 47) = 12.77, p < .001$] and activation and lexicality [$F_1(1, 45) = 39.86, p < .001; F_2(1, 47) = 41.66, p < .001$]. The other interactions, including the triple interaction were not significant ($F < 1$).

The two significant interactions have a coherent interpretation. The interaction between lexicality and position clearly shows that lexical activation increased as the listener received more sensory input. The interaction between lexicality and activation shows that there is a greater lexical effect for words than for the close nonwords. Globally, the word condition showed a 72 ms effect, whereas the close nonword condition produced only a 20 ms advantage.

Figure 1 shows RT differences that correspond to the lexical effect for full and partial activation conditions in the two target positions. Specific comparisons in the full activation condition showed a significant effect for both target positions: position 1 [$F_1(1, 45) = 23.47, p < .001; F_2(1, 47) = 28.78, p < .001$] and position 2 [$F_1(1, 45) = 92.06, p < .001; F_2(1, 47) = 111.12, p < .001$]. In contrast, for the partial activation condition, the lexical effect was significant for position 2 [$F_1(1, 45) = 15.49, p < .001; F_2(1, 47) = 17.69, p < .001$], but not for position 1 (both Fs < 1).

Discussion

This first experiment measured monitoring latencies to phoneme targets in two different positions to track lexical activation across time. It compared the size of the lexical effect produced in the full and partial activation conditions. As expected, robust lexical effects were found for both target positions in the full activation condition. Moreover, the lexical effect increased as the target arrived later in the item. In contrast, a significant lexical effect for stimuli containing a minimal initial mismatch was only obtained when the target was located in final position of the target-bearing item. When the target phoneme occupied the earlier position, just after the UP, no lexical effect was found for close nonwords.

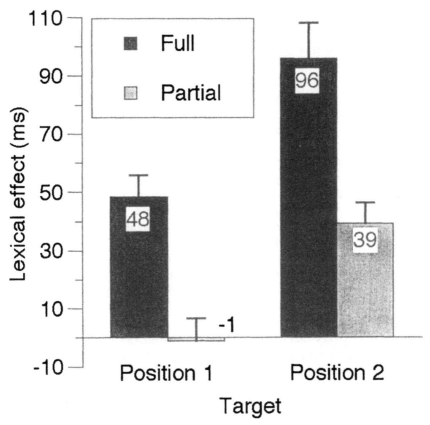

Figure 1.   RT differences and error bars for the Full activation (words) and Partial activation (close nonwords) conditions relative to the Baseline nonwords for the two target positions in Experiment 1.

Two observations can be made about the results for the full activation condition. First, our finding of an increasing lexical effect with later target positions in this condition replicates a well-established result in the literature (Frauenfelder et al., 1990; Marslen-Wilson, 1984; Pitt & Samuel, 1995). As more bottom-up input supporting the target bearing word arrives, even after the uniqueness point, the target's activation level continues to increase. Second, the decrease in the detection latencies observed in the baseline nonword condition for the final target position might appear to be somewhat surprising. One might expect that since the lexicon does not contribute to the detection responses for these items, the latencies should be constant across target position. However, it is important to note that the two target positions are not identical from a bottom-up perspective. In particular, there is no following acoustic information to mask the target in item final position, and therefore the detection process is quicker. This finding of faster RTs to item final targets is, in fact, rather consistently observed (Frauenfelder et al., 1990; Pitt & Samuel, 1995).

For the partial activation condition, the demonstration of a lexical effect for the close nonwords in the second position condition is important. First, this result replicates, with a larger variety of targets, the findings of Connine et al. (1997) and produces an effect that is approximately equivalent in size (40–50 ms) to the one they observed for the final position of trisyllabic items used in their Experiment 1. We found no lexical effect for the earlier target position. This suggests that insufficient bottom-up evidence had accumulated by the time this target arrived to override the inhibitory effect of the initial mismatching phoneme.

The present findings provide further evidence against models like the original COHORT model, which are totally intolerant of phonological mismatches. Indeed, in such models any initial mismatch—even minimal—is sufficient to prevent the intended word from becoming activated and to exclude it from the competitor set. These findings, however, are also consistent with an alternative account which attributes the lexical effect obtained for the partial activation condition in final position to a late second-pass recovery mechanism (Marslen-Wilson, 1993). One diagnostic that has been proposed to distinguish second-pass from more perceptual first-pass accounts is the range of the observed RTs. The detection latencies that we observed were rapid (less than 450 ms) and fall well below the 700 ms cut-off proposed for perceptual accounts by Connine et al. (1997), making a post-perceptual explanation somewhat unlikely. In other experimental paradigms like mispronunciation detection in which participants are required to determine under time pressure whether experimental items are mispronounced or not, the RTs are considerably longer than those obtained here, suggesting a possible post-perceptual locus. However, it is important to remain cautious, since as pointed out by Connine et al. (1997), speed-based criteria for distinguishing these two types of explanations must be made more explicit to be useful. Finally, it should also be noted that the speed of any second-pass response most likely depends upon the amount of lexical activation that has been produced by the nonword input. In this sense, the RT difference observed may well reflect the amount of initial lexical activation, even if the response is based upon a second-pass strategy.

Regarding the predictions of computational models for initial mismatches, we have already pointed out that the simulation results for SHORTLIST and TRACE are not well established. Unlike what is commonly assumed, our simulations (Frauenfelder & Content, 2000) showed that TRACE's recognition performance was globally quite poor for stimuli with small initial phonological mismatches. Indeed, when an activation level of 0.50 was taken arbitrarily to represent the recognition threshold, few words (22%) were recognised. These mispronounced words were nonetheless somewhat activated since their activation level rose above their resting threshold. The question remains of how to relate such simulated activation to that measured in experiments. Given that the predictions of the models are not clearly differentiated and depend upon internal factors like the parameter settings and external factors like the stimulus set, the present data do not discriminate between the two competing models.

As mentioned in the Introduction, TRACE and SHORTLIST diverge much more clearly in their predictions for medial mismatches than for initial mismatches. For SHORTLIST, the presence of word-internal mismatching information in the signal produces bottom-up inhibition that strongly deactivates the lexical target. In contrast, since the target word no longer has any lexical competitors when the mismatching information is received, TRACE predicts no difference between the activation curves for word and nonword conditions due to lateral inhibition. The predictions of the two models were confirmed by pilot simulations (Frauenfelder & Content, 2000). The activation curves produced by SHORTLIST decreased dramatically at the moment when the mismatching phoneme is received and remained only weakly activated for the remaining input. It is important to note that unlike the quantitative differences in models' predictions for Experiment 1, the predictions here are qualitatively different and result from explicit architectural choices on activation flow.

EXPERIMENT 2

This experiment tested for the existence of bottom-up inhibition by introducing mismatching information medially or finally into the same words as were used in Experiment 1. The location of the target phoneme with respect to the mismatching phoneme was varied: either the target preceded ("preceding mismatch" condition) or the target followed ("following mismatch" condition) the mismatching information. In both conditions, one of the phonemes that served as a target in Experiment 1 retained that role (/l/ or /r/ in vocabulaire) and the other was replaced by an inappropriate phoneme (/r/ to /z/ or /l/ to /n/ giving "vocabulaise" or "vocabunaire"), which differed from the original one by several distinctive features.

As in the previous experiment, the size of the lexical effect in the partial activation condition was compared with that in the full activation condition using a matched baseline nonword. The "following mismatch" condition provides a test of bottom-up inhibition accounts which predict a strong decrease in the lexical effect for the partial activation condition. The "preceding mismatch" condition should give some information about the temporal resolution of the phoneme monitoring task. If the phoneme monitoring response is immediate and rapid, we expect no interference by later arriving mismatch information. Consequently, lexical effects of equal size in the full and partial conditions are expected, if the detection latencies directly reflect lexical activation at the moment that the target comes in.

Method

Participants. Forty students of the University of Geneva, all native speakers of French, without known hearing deficits, voluntarily partici-pated in the experiment as part of their curriculum. Participants were assigned randomly to one of the four experimental lists.

Materials. The same 48 original test words from Experiment 1 were used to construct the nonword stimuli of this experiment. The relevant experimental comparisons, target preceding mismatch and target following mismatch with their full activation controls, are illustrated in Table 3 and a description of the lexical and temporal properties of the nonword stimuli used are given in Table 4.

In the first set of comparisons, the target preceded the mismatching phoneme. The target was the same as that used for position 1 in Experiment 1 and a mismatching phoneme differing in two or three phonological features was substituted for the phoneme that served as the target in position 2. The same phoneme substitution was also performed in the baseline nonwords of Experiment 1 to create matching baseline

TABLE 3

Examples of stimuli, mean RTs in ms and percentage correct responses for the different experimental conditions in Experiment 2 (target phonemes in bold and mismatching phonemes underlined)

| Target position | Activation condition | Lexicality | |
		Baseline Nonword	Word/mismatch Nonword
Preceding mismatch	Full	satobyl**ɛʀ** 465.4 (94.8)	vokabyl**ɛʀ** 410.5 (96.3)
	Partial	satobyl*ɛz* 474.3 (94.6)	vokabyl*ɛz* 440.5 (94.8)
Following mismatch	Full	satobyl**ɛʀ** 394.6 (96.7)	vokabyl**ɛʀ** 328.7 (96.7)
	Partial	satobyn*ɛʀ* 428.9 (96.3)	vokabyn*ɛʀ* 423.6 (95.8)

TABLE 4
Lexical (uniqueness point and nonword point) and durational properties (and their SD)
of the stimuli used in Experiment 2

Target position	Nonword	*NWP* *(No. of phonemes)*	*Distance to target* *in ms*
Preceding mismatch	Mismatch	(7.75) (0.89)	527.9 (108.2)
	Baseline	4.21 (0.74)	578.9 (137.5)
Following mismatch	Mismatch	(5.63) (0.89)	916.1 (165.4)
	Baseline	4.21 (0.74)	962.0 (185.8)

nonwords. Similarly, for the experimental comparison in which the target followed the mismatch, the targets corresponded to the position 2 targets of Experiment 1 and a mismatching phoneme was substituted for the phoneme that served as the target in position 1.

The choice of the substituted phoneme depended upon its phonological distance (2 to 3 distinctive features) from the original phoneme as well as upon the frequency of the resulting item-final syllable. Thus, the average frequency of the final syllable of the mismatch conditions (e.g., /lɛz/) approximated that of the full activation condition (e.g., /lɛr/) as closely as possible. This control was included in order to eliminate possible syllable frequency effects upon detection latencies. However, the critical comparisons for estimating the lexical effect in the full and partial conditions were based on the same target-bearing syllable (e.g. /lɛz/ in vocabulaize and satodulaize). All other aspects of materials, including the fillers and foils as well as the preparation of the four experimental lists were identical to those in Experiment 1. The Appendix lists the experimental stimuli and targets.

Procedure.   All procedural aspects were the same as in Experiment 1.

Results

Mean RTs were computed from target phoneme onset for each subject and each experimental item. RTs below 100 or above 1000 ms were eliminated from the analysis. The mean RTs and percent correct (PC) scores for all conditions are shown in Table 3.

Target preceding mismatch.   A two-way ANOVA was conducted using the RT data with lexicality and activation as the main factors. This analysis yielded main effects of activation [$F_1(1, 39) = 11.25, p < .001; F_2 (1, 47) = 4.64, p < .001$] and lexicality [$F_1(1, 39) = 45.91, p < .001; F_2(1, 47) = 20.36, p < .001$]. The interaction between these two factors was only significant by item [$F_1(1, 39) = 2.3, p < .14; F_2(1, 47) = 5.44, p < .05$]. Specific comparisons in the full activation condition showed a significant lexical effect [$F_1(1, 39) = 31.35, p < .001; F_2(1, 47) = 51.48, p < .001$]. For the partial activation condition, the lexical effect was also significant, although numerically reduced as shown in Figure 2 [$F_1(1, 45) = 11.93, p < .05; F_2(1, 47) = 15.03, p < .05$]. The fact that the interaction was significant in the item and not the subject analyses suggests the need to conduct more detailed analyses of the inter-individual variation. This analysis is presented in the discussion of Experiment 2. There were no significant differences in an ANOVA on PC scores.

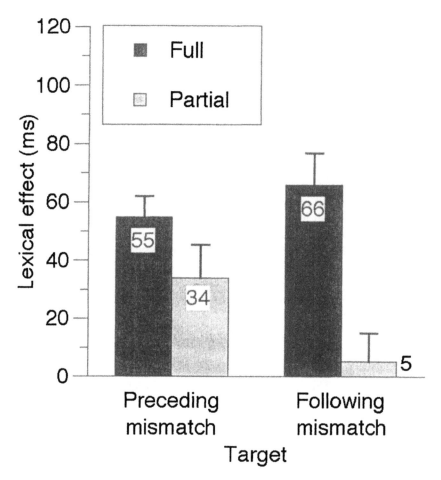

Figure 2. RT differences and error bars for the Full activation (words) and Partial activation (mismatching nonwords) conditions relative to the Baseline nonwords for the two target positions in Experiment 2.

Target following mismatch.   A two-way ANOVA was conducted on the RT data with lexicality and activation as the main factors. This analysis yielded main effects both by-subject and by-item for activation [$F_1(1, 39) = 83.75, p < .001; F_2 (1, 47) = 36.41, p < .001$] and lexicality [$F_1(1, 39) = 25.50, p < .001; F_2(1, 47) = 11.98, p < .001$]. The interaction between these two factors was also significant [$F_1(1, 39) = 16.22, p < .001; F_2(1, 47) = 7.01, p < .01$]. There were no significant differences in an ANOVA on PC scores ($Fs < 1$). As illustrated in Figure 2, a highly significant difference was obtained for the full activation condition as confirmed by the local comparisons [$F_1(1, 39) = 38.39, p < .0001; F_2(1, 47) = 17.39, p < .0001$], but no lexical effect was found in the partial activation condition [both $Fs < 1$].

Discussion

This experiment has examined the impact of mismatching information located either medially or finally. The position of the target was varied with respect to the position of these mismatches. In what follows, we will first discuss the critical condition in which the target follows the phonological mismatch. We looked for a deleterious influence of this mispronunciation on lexical activation and indeed, the results showed no lexical effect, that is, no significant difference between mismatching nonwords and baseline nonwords. Since a clear lexical effect was obtained in the corresponding full activation condition in this experiment as well as in Experiment 1, we can be certain that the target-bearing word is clearly activated at the moment that the mismatching phoneme arrives. Consequently, the absence of a lexical effect in the partial activation condition suggests that the activated word has been deactivated by this mismatching information via bottom-up inhibition.

An alternative explanation for the absence of RT differences in this partial activation condition appeals to the attentional consequences of the mismatch on the detection process, what we will term a "surprise effect". Here, the phonological mismatch surprises participants and hence delays their responses to targets which arrive immediately after this mismatch. Although it is difficult to choose between this surprise account and the bottom-up inhibition explanation (or the combination of both) on the basis of the data presented here, they make different predictions concerning the size and direction of the lexical effect in the partial activation condition, and its relation to the size of this effect in the full activation condition.

First, according to a bottom-up inhibition account, detection performance should never be slower for the mismatch items than for their baseline nonword control. Inhibition can only reduce or eliminate the lexical effect, but not reverse it. In contrast, according to a surprise effect explanation, the disruptive influence of the mismatch can, in principle, produce slower RTs in the mismatch condition relative to the baseline condition, overriding any lexical facilitation produced by the initial part of the mismatching stimuli. Thus, the absence of a reversed lexical effect in the overall RT pattern provides no support for the surprise explanation.

A more subtle way to distinguish between the two accounts refers to the correlations between the lexical effects in the full and partial activation conditions. According to the bottom-up inhibition account, highly activated words which receive some bottom-up inhibition still retain a relatively high level of activation. Hence, there should be a positive correlation between the lexical effects in the full and partial activation conditions. In contrast, for the surprise account, the larger the lexical activation, the more likely the participants are to have anticipated the word and to be negatively affected by violations of their expectations. Thus, a negative correlation should be found between the lexical effects for the full and partial conditions. Globally, the observed correlation was non-significant and close to zero ($r = -.065$, ns), thus providing no support for either account.

In a further analysis we examined this correlation for two subgroups of subjects which were defined on the basis of the speed of their bottom-up processing using the mean RTs for baseline nonwords. We expected that this variable would be related to the amount of attention devoted to the speech input. These attentional differences might condition the presence of a surprise effect: the more closely the participant pays attention to the input, the more likely an unexpected mismatch will be noticed and create a surprise. We thus defined two subgroups based on a median-split on the average response latencies across all nonword baseline conditions.

Figure 3 (right panel) presents the scatterplot showing the relation between the lexical effects in the full and partial conditions for the two groups. For the fast group, the resulting correlation ($r = -.324$, $p = .17$) was negative, although not significant. The lexical effect in the full activation condition was 67 ms ($SD = 56$; 282 and 349 ms, respectively, for the words and baseline nonwords). In the partial activation condition a negative -16 ms trend in the opposite direction was observed ($SD = 71$; 396 and 380 ms, for the mismatch and baseline nonwords). This suggests that among the rapid participants, those showing the largest lexical effect in the full activation condition were most detrimentally affected by the mismatch in the partial activation condition. The finding of a negative lexicality effect together with a negative correlation may be consistent with a surprise effect explanation. However, as can be seen from the figure, the negative slope and mean effect are essentially due to three participants. When these participants were eliminated, the mean effect was 8 ms. ($SD = 40$) and the correlation was clearly non-significant ($r = -.15$, $p > .50$).

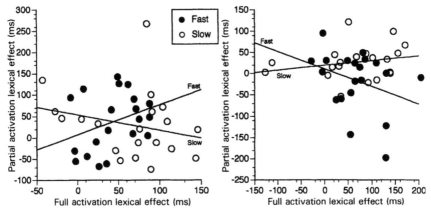

Figure 3. Scattergram for fast and slow participants of lexical effects in the full vs. partial activation condition for the target preceding the mismatch (left panel) and the target following the mismatch (right panel) conditions.

For the slow group, the relation was positive ($r = .236, p = .32$), and the mean lexical effects in the full and partial activation condition were 65 ms ($SD = 81$; 375 and 440 ms) and 27 ms ($SD = 41$; 451 and 478 ms). The slow participants who showed the largest lexical effect in the full activation condition also showed the most residual activation for the partial condition. The decrease in the lexical effect from the full to the partial activation condition together with the positive correlation is consistent with a bottom-up inhibition account. Taken together, the results for the preceding mismatch condition suggest that the surprise effect exists, but is limited to fast participants. Given the pattern obtained for the slow group, the most parsimonious interpretation is that bottom-up inhibition plays a role in both groups, but is modulated by a surprise effect for the fast group.

For the condition in which the target preceded the mismatching information (Figure 3, left panel), a significant but reduced lexical effect was found for the partial activation condition. However since this reduction was not significant in the subject analysis, we conducted a more detailed analysis of the inter-individual variation. We predicted that the faster group would be less sensitive to the later arriving mismatch information than the slower group which should be slowed down by the mismatch either due to bottom-up inhibition or to a surprise effect. The analyses confirmed these predictions. Fast participants showed no difference in the size of the lexical effect for the full (group mean 44 ms, $SD = 32$; 363 vs. 407 ms) and partial activation (group mean 38 ms, $SD = 68$; 385 vs. 423 ms) conditions and the correlation was positive ($r = .331$, $p = .16$). It is interesting to note that the interval that separates the onset of the target from the onset on the mismatching phoneme is around 400 ms.

In sum, fast participants launched their detection response before the mismatch information was received so that no reduction in the lexical effect was observed.

In contrast, for the slower participants the lexical effect showed a marked decrease from the full activation (group mean 66 ms, $SD = 54$; 458 vs. 524 ms) to the partial activation condition (30 ms, $SD = 78$; 496 vs. 526 ms) and the correlation was not significant ($r = -.246$, $p = .30$). These results suggest that for the slow participants the mismatch information still arrives in time to have a negative impact on detection performance.

Returning to the condition of central interest, the following mismatch condition, we have found some evidence that medial mismatch has a major disruptive influence upon the detection of later arriving phonemes. In light of the predictions made by the TRACE and SHORTLIST simulations, the absence of a lexical effect for the words containing medial mismatching information supports SHORTLIST over TRACE. Indeed, whereas TRACE predicts little or no effect of the mismatch, SHORTLIST predicts the observed deactivating effect of the mismatch information.

GENERAL DISCUSSION

Two main issues have been addressed here: The extent to which initial mismatching information prevents later-arriving matching information from activating a target word and the extent to which later-arriving mismatching information reduces the activation produced by earlier matching information. The first experiment revealed some lexical activation despite the presence of an initial mismatch, but only after considerable bottom-up matching information was accumulated. Thus a lexical effect was observed only for item-final targets but not for item-medial ones. The second experiment showed that a phonological mismatch coming late in a stimulus item has a strong negative impact upon lexical activation, in effect, eliminating any trace of a lexical effect in the detection latencies.

This study has used the phoneme monitoring task to tap into the activation of phonological representations in the lexicon produced by mispronounced tokens of these words. An important methodological issue that still remains to be addressed involves comparing the measures of lexical activation based on phonological and semantic representations as they are generated by phoneme monitoring and cross-modal semantic priming, respectively. This analysis is all the more urgent given the lack of convergence in the findings obtained with these tasks. Indeed, we have a somewhat contradictory situation in which the phoneme monitoring task appears to provide a more sensitive measure of lexical activation, for example, revealing lexical activation by initial phonological mismatches for which no activation was observed with the semantic priming paradigm. In contrast, the reverse seems to be the case for the later arriving mismatches. Our phoneme monitoring findings show no trace of lexical activation for these mismatches, whereas cross-modal priming experiments (Connine et al., 1993) have measured priming effects that are significant and similar in magnitude to those for initial mismatches.

In the absence of more systematic comparisons between these tasks, however, we can only propose a number of task properties which need to be taken into account to clarify this paradoxical situation. First, the present findings suggest that the behaviour observed in the phoneme monitoring task is rapid and closely time-locked to the signal. Indeed, the results from the "preceding mismatch" condition in the second experiment show that rapid participants respond before the mismatch information arrives and thus are not affected by it. In contrast, the participants who respond only 100 ms more slowly on average, but who have processed the mismatching information, are strongly affected. This reveals the sensitivity of the phoneme monitoring response to on-going lexical activation. Unfortunately, however, despite having an experimental tool with considerable temporal sensitivity, the researcher generally cannot be certain of what stage of processing is actually being tapped into. In the first experiment, the temporal interval separating the mismatching initial phoneme and the phoneme target (approximately 500 ms) is sufficiently great that many different processing steps could have taken place, including perhaps second pass processing. This suggests that measuring rapid RTs is a necessary, but not sufficient condition for testing perceptual processing. The temporal distance between the onset of the process of interest and of response generating the dependent variable is also crucial. In the present context, then, this means that the phonological mismatch and the target should be put in close temporal proximity.

However, the second experiment, in particular, the "preceding mismatch" condition, points to a possible limitation of this approach since it may introduce contaminating attentional effects. Participants detecting phonemes must focus their attention on the phonemic level, the same level as that of the phonological mismatch. Moreover, since the target and mismatch are in close temporal proximity, attentional and not only perceptual consequences of the mispronunciation may be measured as interference or surprise effects. Although our results provide only limited support for the role of attentional factors, this possibility should be examined more systematically.

Semantic priming obviously requires that activation reach the semantic level presumably via a series of processing steps. In most current conceptions of lexical processing, the activation of semantic information follows phonological activation, and so the amount of excitation reaching the semantic level may be less. This may explain the greater sensitivity of phonologically based measures. However, a comparison of semantic and phonological priming at different SOAs is needed to test this explanation and to obtain more detailed information on the relative time-course of semantic and phonological activation. With respect to measuring the deactivating effects of medial phonological mismatches, it is less clear that cross-modal semantic priming is an appropriate tool. In the framework that we have adopted, bottom-up inhibition depends upon the phonological match between the signal and the target lexical form representation. Although the link between phonological and semantic activation is not well understood, there is no reason to believe that even an extremely abrupt decrease of activation at the phonological level should immediately erase all activation at the semantic level.

One of the basic goals in the study of spoken word recognition is characterising the nature of the information flow which allows lexical selection and recognition. We have identified two possible component mechanisms of lexical selection, one based on bottom-up inhibition and the other on lateral inhibition. Our experimental results have focused on the former and indicate that spoken word recognition models need to include some form of bottom-up inhibition. The presence of a medial mismatch completely eliminated the lexical effect, a result which can be accounted well for in terms of a bottom-up inhibition mechanism. However, more precise analyses of the lexical effect in the full and partial conditions do not rule out the contribution of a "surprise effect" to the disappearance of the lexical effect. The results from the first experiment point to the importance of bottom-up match that may compensate for the initial mismatch. A large number of matching phonemes (at least six that on average separate the mismatching initial phoneme and the item final target) is required to overcome the initial mismatch and permit lexical activation. Findings such as these should contribute to the setting in computational models of parameters related to the connection strengths of bottom-inhibition and activation, and perhaps lateral inhibition.

The present experiments have not included a test of lateral inhibition. However, other studies have shown that lateral inhibition plays a role in lexical activation and processing. Priming studies by Goldinger, Luce, and Pisoni (1989) and Goldinger, Luce, Pisoni, and Marcario (1992) show that the recognition of a word is slower when it is preceded by a phonologically similar word than by a dissimilar word. This inhibition is most likely attributable to competition between the prime and target. More direct evidence for competition effects has been provided in a word spotting experiment (McQueen, Norris, & Cutler, 1994). Here, the recognition of a non-initial embedded word (e.g., *mess*) was delayed by its overlapping competitor (e.g., *domestic*). The longer spotting latencies for the words embedded in word fragments suggest not only that words with different alignments (carrier and embedded words) are activated simultaneously, but also that the longer carrier word competes with and inhibits the embedded word.

Putting these findings supporting lateral inhibition together with our results in favour of bottom-up inhibition, we arrive at a picture of the selection process that is based on a combination of both types of activation flow—as in SHORTLIST. Clearly, it will be important in future studies to determine the relative importance of these two components in the lexical selection process. More detailed simulations with improved computational implementations of TRACE and SHORTLIST, in particular, with more complete front-ends, are vital for producing the appropriate simulation data. Such research would help clarify the rather vague predictions made about lexical activation for initially mispronounced words. Additional experimental data on the temporal evolution of lexical activation are also needed. The present monitoring results constitute a first step in understanding this temporal evolution, with two measures of lexical activation for the same word. Unfortunately, however, they are insufficient to identify the complete activation function, and thus more continuous measures, probably with another experimental technique, are needed.

In sum, the present findings provide some further constraints upon the architecture of localist models of spoken word recognition. They point to an important distinction between quantitative and qualitative differences in the predictions of computational models. The former, like those concerning the effect of initial mismatches, depend upon parameter setting and implementational details whereas the latter, related to the effects of medial mismatches, reflect fundamental choices in the models' architecture. With respect to the latter, these cast some doubt on models like TRACE that rely exclusively on lateral inhibition. Such models cannot account for the strong deactivation by medial mismatches. Future research efforts must attempt to characterise the delicate balance between bottom-up activation, bottom-up inhibition, and lateral inhibition.

REFERENCES

Connine, C.M. (1994). Vertical and horizontal similarity in spoken word recognition. In C. Clifton, Jr., L. Frazier, & K. Rayner (Eds.), *Perspectives on sentence processing*. Hillsdale, NJ: Lawrence Erlbaum Associates Inc.

Connine, C.M., Blasko, D.M., & Titone, D.A. (1993). Do the beginnings of words have a special status in auditory word recognition? *Journal of Memory and Language, 32*, 193–210.

Connine, C.M., Titone, D.A., Deelman, T., & Blasko, D. (1997). Similarity mapping in spoken word recognition. *Journal of Memory and Language, 37*, 463–480.

Content, A., Mousty, P., & Radeau, M. (1990). Brulex: une base de données lexicales informatisée pour le français écrit et parlé. *L'Année Psychologique, 90*, 551–566.

Cutler, A., & Norris, D. (1979). Monitoring sentence comprehension. In W.E. Cooper & E.C.T. Walker (Eds.), *Sentence processing: Psycholinguistic studies presented to Merrill Garrett.* Hillsdale, NJ: Lawrence Erlbaum Associates Inc.

Elman, J.L., & McClelland, J.M. (1988). Cognitive penetration of the mechanisms of perception: Compensation for coarticulation of lexically restored phonemes. *Journal of Memory and Language, 27,* 143–165.

Frauenfelder, U.H., & Content, A. (2000). Activation Flow in Models of Spoken Word Recognition. In A. Cutler, J.M. McQueen & R. Zondervan (Eds.), *Proceedings of the Workshop on Spoken Word Access Processes* (pp. 79–82). Nijmegen, The Netherlands: Max-Planck Institute for Psycholinguistics.

Frauenfelder, U.H., & Segui, J. (1989). Phoneme monitoring and lexical processing: Evidence for associative context effects. *Memory and Cognition, 17,* 134–140.

Frauenfelder, U.H., Segui, J., & Dijkstra, T. (1990). Lexical effects in phoneme processing: Facilitatory or inhibitory? *Journal of Experimental Psychology: Human Perception & Performance, 16,* 77–91.

Goldinger, S.D., Luce, P.A., & Pisoni, (1989). Priming lexical neighbors of spoken words: Effects of competition and inhibition. *Journal of Memory and Language, 28,* 501–518.

Goldinger, S.D., Luce, P.A., Pisoni, D.B., & Marcario, J.K. (1992). Form-based priming in spoken word recognition: The roles of competition and bias. *Journal of Experimental Psychology: Learning, Memory and Cognition, 18,* 1211–1238.

Marslen-Wilson, W.D. (1984). Function and process in spoken word recognition. In H. Bouma, & D.G. Bouwhuis (Eds.), *Attention and Performance X: Control of language processes.* Hove, UK: Lawrence Erlbaum Associates Ltd.

Marslen-Wilson, W.D. (1987). Functional parallelism in spoken word recognition. *Cognition, 25,* 71–102.

Marslen-Wilson, W.D. (1993). Issues of process and representation in spoken language understanding. In G. Altmann, & R. Shillcock (Eds.), *Cognitive models of speech processing.* Hove, UK: Lawrence Erlbaum Associates Ltd.

Marslen-Wilson, W.D., Moss, H.E., & van Halen, S. (1996). Perceptual distance and competition in lexical access. *Journal of Experimental Psychology: Human Perception and Performance, 22,* 1376–1392.

Marslen-Wilson, W.D., & Welsh, A. (1978). Processing interactions and lexical access during word-recognition in continuous speech. *Cognitive Psychology, 10,* 29–63.

Marslen-Wilson, W., & Zwitserlood, P. (1989). Accessing spoken words: On the importance of word onsets. *Journal of Experimental Psychology: Human Perception and Performance, 15,* 576–585.

McClelland, J.M., & Elman, J.L. (1986). The TRACE model of speech perception. *Cognitive Psychology, 18,* 1–86.

McQueen, J.M., Norris, D., & Cutler, A. (1994). Competition in spoken word recognition: Spotting words in other words. *Journal of Experimental Psychology: Learning, Memory and Cognition, 20,* 621–638.

Norris, D. (1994). SHORTLIST: A connectionist model of continuous speech recognition. *Cognition, 52,* 189–234.

Norris, D., McQueen, J.M., & Cutler, A. (2000). Merging information in speech recognition: Feedback is never necessary. *Behavioral and Brain Sciences, 23,* 299–370.

Pitt, M. A., & Samuel, A.G. (1995). Lexical and sublexical feedback in auditory word recognition. *Cognitive Psychology, 29,* 149–188.

Zwitserlood, P. (1989). The locus of the effects of sentential-semantic context in spoken-word processing. *Cognition, 32,* 25–64.

APPENDIX

Experimental stimuli (targets in bold) for Experiments 1 and 2

Experiments 1 and 2		Experiment 1		Experiment 2		
Word	Baseline nonword	Close Nonword	Mismatching nonword	Baseline nonword	Mismatching nonword	Baseline nonword
majuscule	somiscule	najuscule	majuscutte	somiscutte	majusrule	somisrule
crocodile	spamodile	trocodile	crocodise	spamodise	crocochile	spamochile
géranium	dolanium	cheranium	géraniutte	dolaniutte	gérasium	dolassium
baïonnette	chuïonette	païonnette	baïonème	chuïonème	baïoRette	chuïoRette
labyrinthe	numorinthe	nabyrinthe	labyring	numoring	labysinthe	numosinthe
dictionnaire	fulkionaire	tictionnaire	dictionaime	fulkionaime	dictiojairre	fulkiojaire
vocabulaire	satodulaire	focabulaire	vocabulaine	satodulaine	vocabunaire	satodunaire
mademoiselle	birgoiselle	nademoiselle	mademoisette	birgoisette	mademoimelle	birgoimelle
albinos	oclinos	èlbinos	albinol	oclinol	albivos	oclivos
gladiateur	flodiateur	cladiateur	gladiateup	flodiateup	gladiameur	flodiameur
marmelade	sègmelade	narmelade	marmelaf	sègmelaf	marmesade	sègmesade
référendum	sircilendum	léférendum	référenduk	sircilenduk	référenfum	sircilenfum
légionnaire	gafionnaire	dégionnaire	légionnaitte	gafionnaitte	légiolaire	gafiolaire
hiéroglyphe	bétoglyphe	wéroglyphe	hiéroglyn	bétoglyn	hiéroslyphe	bétoslyphe
sanatorium	dénotorium	fanatorium	sanatoriuge	dénotoriuge	sanatosium	dénotosium
basilique	fuchilique	dasilique	basilin	fuchilinne	basinique	fuchinique
tabernacle	vosarnacle	dabernacle	tabernafle	vosarnafle	tabersacle	vosarsacle
écrevisse	aplevisse	icrevisse	écrevinne	aplevinne	écretisse	apletisse
alligator	obéfator	èlligator	alligatonne	obéfatonne	allimator	obéfajor
algorithme	ignorithm	èlgorithme	algorivme	ignorivm	algosithme	ignosithm
hippopotame	alérotame	éppopotame	hippopotase	alérotase	hippoporame	alléRoRame
davantage	rifantage	bavantage	davantam	rifantame	davanmage	rifanmage
cellophane	lapophane	chélophan	cellophase	lapophase	cellobane	lapobane
dinosaure	makosaure	tinosaure	dinozauffe	makosauffe	dinopaure	makopaure
camembert	lainembert	tamembert	camembef	lainembef	camemsert	lainemsert
missionnaire	sédionnaire	bissionnaire	missionnaitte	sédionnaitte	missiojaire	sédiojaire
aborigène	iménigene	èborigène	aborigève	iménigève	aboritènc	iménitène
noctambule	fasmambule	moctambule	noctambuse	fasmambuse	noctamsule	fasmamsule
lunatique	raisatique	runatique	lunative	raisative	lunarique	raisarique
sagittaire	vubittaire	chagittaire	sagittainne	vubitainne	sagigaire	vubigaire
hirondelle	afondelle	urondelle	hirondesse	afonchere	hironchelle	afonchesse
fontanelle	buranelle	sontanelle	fontanesse	buranesse	fontavelle	buravelle
fiduciaire	bélysiaire	viduciaire	fiduciainne	bélysiainne	fiduniaire	bélyniaire
auparavant	usaravant	ouparavant	auparatant	usaratant	aupatavant	usatavant
subjonctif	gasponctif	chubjonctif	subjonctil	gasponctil	subjoncmif	gasponcmif
mucosité	ralosité	nucosité	mucosiné	ralosiné	mucopité	ralopité
béchamel	fèsamel	péchamel	béchamette	fèsamette	béchavel	fésavel
hélicoptère	augusoptère	ilicoptère	hélicoptènne	augusoptènne	hélicopmère	augusopmère
somnifère	balsifère	chomnifère	somnifèque	baslzifèque	somnilère	balzilère
culinaire	sakinaire	pulinaire	culinaisse	sakinaisse	culicaire	sakicaire
chrysanthème	blésanthème	prysanthème	chrysanthèque	bésanthèque	chrysanvème	blésanvème
sédentaire	lèkantaire	fédentaire	sédentainne	lékantainne	sédengaire	lèkangaire
testicule	faussemicule	desticule	testicune	faussemicune	testivule	faussemivule
génocide	limucide	chénocide	génocif	limucif	génolide	limulide
congélateur	mandolateur	pongélateur	congélateuf	mandolateuf	congélagneur	mâdolagneur
farandole	soufandole	varandole	farandomme	soufandomme	faranchole	soufanchole
bastingage	rablingage	pastingage	bastinganne	rablinganne	bastinfage	rablinfage
lapalissade	minolissade	rapalissade	lapalissaffe	minolissaffe	lapalimade	minolimade

LANGUAGE AND COGNITIVE PROCESSES, 2001, *16* (5/6), 609–636

Sequence detection in pseudowords in French: Where is the syllable effect?

Alain Content

Laboratoire de Psychologie Expérimentale, Free University Brussels, Belgium

Christine Meunier

CNRS and Laboratoire Parole et langage, University of Provence, Aix-en-Provence, France

Ruth K. Kearns

MRC Cognition and Brain Sciences Unit, Cambridge, UK

Uli H. Frauenfelder

Laboratoire de Psycholinguistique Expérimentale, University of Geneva, Switzerland

In two experiments, French speakers detected cv or cvc sequences at the beginning of disyllabic pseudowords varying in syllable structure and pivotal consonant. Overall, both studies failed to replicate the crossover interaction that has been previously observed in French by Mehler, Dommergues, Frauenfelder and Seguí (1981). In both experiments, latencies were shorter to cv than to cvc targets and this effect of target length was generally smaller for cvc•cv than for cv•cv carriers. However, a clear crossover interaction was observed for liquid pivotal consonants under target-blocking conditions,

Alain Content, Laboratoire de Psychologie Expérimentale, ULB-LAPSE CP191, Avenue F.D. Roosevelt, 50, B-1050 Bruxelles Belgium. E-mail: acontent@ulb.ac.be

The present research was supported by grants from the FNRS, Switzerland (1114-039553.93, 1113-049698.96 and 1114-059532.99) and from the Direction générale de la Recherche scientifique – Communauté française de Belgique (A.R.C. 96/01-203). Preliminary reports were presented at the second AMLAP Meeting (Torino, 1996), and at the 1997 Eurospeech Conference. Ruth Kearns is now with Procter and Gamble Technical Centres Ltd. Thanks go to Christophe Pallier for comments on a previous version and to Nicolas Dumay for his help in the final stages of manuscript preparation.

http://www.tandf.co.uk/journals/pp/01690965.html   DOI: 10.1080/01690960143000083

and especially for slow participants. A third experiment collected phoneme-gating data on the same pseudowords to obtain estimates of the duration of the initial phonemes. Regression analyses showed that phoneme duration accounted for a large proportion of the variance for cvc target detection, suggesting that participants were reacting rather directly to phonemic throughput. These findings argue against the hypothesis of an early syllabic classification mechanism in the perception of speech.

How acoustic-phonetic information is mapped onto lexical representations constitutes a central issue in the study of speech perception and spoken word recognition. Various kinds of linguistic units, ranging from phonetic features to syllables, have been proposed to mediate the mapping process. Among these units, researchers have long considered the syllable as an obvious choice. Indeed, since the syllable constitutes the domain of most coarticulation phenomena, it appears to provide a natural way of dealing with the problem of variability in the signal.

One influential source of evidence favouring the hypothesis that syllable units are instrumental in speech processing comes from studies using the sequence detection task (see Frauenfelder & Kearns, 1996). In the original study (Mehler, Dommergues, Frauenfelder, & Seguí, 1981), French subjects detected Consonant-Vowel (cv) or Consonant-Vowel-Consonant (cvc) targets in spoken target-bearing carrier words whose initial syllable was either cv or cvc. For instance, PA and PAL were detected in words like PA•LACE and PAL•MIER.[1] Detection latencies were shorter when the target exactly matched the first syllable of the carrier word, with responses to PA faster in PA•LACE than PAL•MIER, and responses to PAL faster in PAL•MIER than in PA•LACE. This crossover interaction between target type (cv versus cvc) and word type (cv words vs. cvc words) has been called the *syllable effect*.

One feature that makes this study particularly attractive is that its design inherently controls for potential artifacts related to target and carrier properties. Indeed, *exactly the same* targets and *exactly the same* stimuli were used in the syllabic match (cv in cv•cv words, cvc in cvc•cv words) and syllabic mismatch conditions (cv in cvc•cv words and cvc in cv•cv words). What remained unclear however from this seminal experiment was whether the syllable effect is driven by acoustic-phonetic matching information or involves language-specific perceptual mechanisms.

A later follow-up study provided an elegant demonstration of language specificity. Cutler and colleagues (Cutler, Mehler, Norris, & Seguí, 1986) constructed an English version of the original experiment. They tested British subjects with the new English and original French materials, as well as a group of French listeners with the English stimuli. No syllable effect

---

[1] The "•" symbol denotes a syllable boundary.

was obtained for native English speakers, either with English or with French stimuli. By contrast, French listeners produced a significant syllable effect in English, with a RT pattern rather similar to that of the original experiment. Thus, the presence of the syllable effect is a function of listeners' characteristics: It occurs for French listeners whatever the language, and it does not occur for English listeners.

The differences in the behaviour of French and English listeners were attributed by Cutler et al. (1986) to the phonological and rhythmic characteristics of the two languages. The absence of a syllable effect in English was attributed to its greater diversity in syllable structures and to the existence of cases in which one consonant simultaneously belongs to two adjacent syllables. The ambiguity caused by such ambisyllabic consonants and the complexity due to the rich inventory of syllable types in English were taken to make syllabic segmentation more difficult, thereby preventing English listeners from acquiring and using a syllabic segmentation routine.

Cutler et al.'s (1986) account predicts a syllable advantage in any language characterised by clear and regular syllable structure. Hence several follow-up studies have been performed in various Romance languages, using the same type of procedure as in the Mehler/Cutler studies. The results lead to a rather more complex picture than initially proposed. Sebastián-Gallés, Dupoux, Seguí, and Mehler (1992) assessed the syllable effect in Spanish as well as in Catalan. They found a syllable effect in Catalan, but only for a subset of words in which the critical sequence was unstressed. No effect was found for words bearing first-syllable stress. For Spanish, the syllable effect was only observed when a secondary task was imposed on participants so that reaction times were about 200 ms longer than in the standard conditions. Bradley, Sánchez-Casas, and Garciá-Albea (1993) also reported a syllable effect for Spanish. While these authors did not impose a secondary task on their subjects, they introduced catch trials so that the average RTs from their Spanish sample were also rather long, in the same range as in Sebastián-Gallés et al.'s (1992) last experiment.

Finally, in a recent study, Tabossi, Collina, Mazzetti, and Zoppello (2000) assessed the syllable effect in Italian and found a pattern similar to that obtained by Sebastián-Gallés with Spanish listeners. The results showed only a main effect of target length, with CVC targets slower than CV targets. No catch trials were used, and the RTs were in the 400 ms range, as in Mehler et al. (1981) and Sebastián-Gallés et al.'s (1992) standard experiments. As for Spanish, despite the regular syllable structure of Italian, no evidence of a syllabic processing routine was obtained.

To account for their findings, Sebastián-Gallés and colleagues (1992) relied on a proposal previously put forward by Dupoux (1989). He proposed a dual coding framework in which listeners can respond using either a subsyllabic or a syllabic perceptual representation. Dupoux reanalysed the original data from Mehler et al.'s (1981) study as a function of participants' overall reaction times and found that the characteristic crossover interaction was only significant for slow participants. He suggested that subjects could make a detection response by matching the target to either a subsyllabic or a syllabic representation of the carrier, and that the latter was only used in slow conditions. Sebastián-Gallés et al. (1992) interpreted their findings in the same framework. In their view, a syllabic representation is extracted from the signal, but subjects do not necessarily exploit it in performing the task, because they can also base their match decision on a phonemic code. Although the precise conditions that control the use of either strategy are not spelled out in any detail, the general idea is the following: The syllable effect is most likely to emerge either when acoustic-phonetic transparency is low, so that the extraction of segmental/subsyllabic representations is relatively hard, or when task demands induce participants to respond more slowly. The concept of acoustic-phonetic transparency encompasses a variety of factors which may affect phonetic perception, such as the amount of coarticulation between adjacent segments, the stress level of the sequence, or the size of the relevant phonemic inventory to which the acoustic input has to be matched.

In sum, recent investigations of the syllable effect in various Romance languages have considerably complicated the picture, and have led researchers to specify a number of boundary conditions for the emergence of the effect. Paradoxically, it is not totally clear that the account proposed by Sebastián-Gallés and colleagues predicts the initial finding in French. Based on the features discussed by Sebastián-Gallés et al. (1992) to compare phonetic transparency across languages, it is not clear whether French should be classified as a low or a high transparency language. On the one hand, French has more vowel categories than Catalan or Spanish, a factor deemed to decrease phonetic transparency. On the other hand, stress is not contrastive and there is no vowel reduction in French. Whatever the most appropriate analysis, given that the syllable effect does not occur systematically for all conditions in any Romance language, it seems important to replicate it in French. This was the first aim of the present study.

A second general issue concerns the explanation of the phenomenon. Mehler et al. (1981) assumed a perceptual interpretation of the effect. They concluded that the speech stream is perceptually segmented and classified into syllabic units at an early processing stage. According to that interpretation, the syllable effect is explained by assuming that detection latencies depend upon the goodness of the match between a syllabified representation of the carrier word and the target. Thus, in the case of cv•cv carriers, cv detection is rapid because the target directly matches the syllabic representation. In contrast, the detection of the cvc target takes more time because it requires the extraction of the initial consonant from the second syllable and its combination with the first syllable. For the cvc•cv words, the output of the syllabic process corresponds exactly to the cvc target, whereas the syllable must be decomposed into its segmental constituents in order to extract the cv target.

A slightly different type of explanation, previously suggested by Rietveld and Frauenfelder (1987), can however be envisaged. It supposes that the mental representation of the speech signal is richly specified and includes allophonic and subphonetic detail. This subphonetic explanation also assumes that detection times reflect the goodness of match between the perceptual information extracted from the carrier and the mental representation of the target, but it does not appeal to the hypothesis of syllabic segmentation and classification. In this view, the advantage of cv•cv words over cvc•cv words in cv detection results from the fact that at a fine-grained level of representation, the initial cv sequence of cv•cv words more closely matches the target than that of cvc•cv words. These phonetic differences might be a consequence of the organisation of speech segments in larger units such as syllables at the level of *production*. The essential point is that this view does not require that the higher-order—syllabic—structure be captured in perceptual representations.

One way to distinguish between these two explanations is to test the generality of the syllable effect across various stimulus conditions. In this regard, it is worth noting that most of the studies cited above used a very limited item set (but see Bradley et al., 1993 for an exception), presumably because they closely followed the methodology of the original study. In Mehler et al.'s (1981) experiment, only five pairs of words were used. All started with a plosive, followed by the same vowel (/a/), and either /l/ or /R/ as pivotal consonant.

Clearly, one unresolved issue is whether the syllable effect generalises to a more varied stimulus range. In view of the two explanations discussed above, this becomes important since the syllable processing routine should apply universally, whatever the specific phonetic properties of the stimuli. Thus, the latter hypothesis would predict that the syllable effect emerges whatever the nature of the pivotal consonant. Conversely, if the effect is driven by listeners' sensitivity to allophonic cues that permit the discrimination of cv and cvc syllables, one would expect the effect to vary as a function of the salience of syllabicity cues.

Hence, the second aim of the present research was to assess the syllable effect across the major classes of pivotal consonants, and to examine the relationships between the obtained RT patterns and the acoustic-phonetic properties of stimuli. An additional motivation was to assess the syllable effect on pseudoword carriers. Although the syllable effect has generally been thought to arise during prelexical stages of processing (Bradley et al., 1993; Dupoux, 1993; Seguí, Frauenfelder, & Mehler, 1981; but see McQueen, 1998 and Zwitserlood, Schriefers, Lahiri, & van Donselaar, 1993), none of the published studies in French has directly tested the target/carrier crossover interaction with pseudowords. In addition to avoiding the risk of lexical contamination, the use of pseudowords made it easier to devise experimental stimuli, given our aim to vary the pivotal consonants.

EXPERIMENT 1

Experiment 1 aimed at examining the presence of a syllable effect with pseudowords, with varied pivotal consonants. Because the design of the experiment entailed a large number of trials per participant, we did not use the standard monitoring procedure. Rather, the presentation of the target was followed after a short delay by a target-bearing stimulus, to which a key-press response was required, or by a filler in the no-go trials.

An additional aim was to assess the influence of catch trials on performance. In the absence of catch trials, participants have the opportunity to bypass the sequence detection instructions, and to respond on the basis of a partial match (Bradley et al., 1993; Norris & Cutler, 1988). The presence of catch trials in which the stimulus begins with the same phonemes as the target (e.g., CAR in CALBOR) should discourage such a strategy. Furthermore, according to Sebastián-Gallés et al. (1992) and Dupoux (1993), the syllable effect is more likely to emerge when participants are forced to slow down their detection responses, and it is known (Mills, 1980; Norris & Cutler, 1988) that the inclusion of foils slows down performance. The same experimental trials were used in a Foil and a No-foil condition, by replacing one half of the no-go fillers by catch trials. We expected to observe an enhanced syllable effect in the Foil condition.

Method

Participants.   Thirty-nine participants were tested in the Foil Condition and twenty-nine were tested in the No-foil Condition. In this and the following experiments, all participants were native speakers of French (Swiss dialect) and ranged between 19 and 40 years in age. No participant reported any hearing deficit. All were naive regarding the aims of the experiment and no participant was tested twice in different experiments. Most of them were psychology students at the University of Geneva and participated for course credit. A few were assistants from the Department who participated voluntarily.

Stimuli.   For the target-bearing trials, pairs of disyllabic pseudowords were constructed (see Appendix). Both members of a pair shared the same initial CVC sequence but varied in syllabic structure. In each pair, one pseudoword had a singleton pivotal consonant and the other pseudoword included a cluster of two successive consonants. The targets were the initial CV and CVC fragments of the carriers. As far as possible, we avoided using targets that correspond to familiar words in French. This was difficult for the CV targets, since nearly all possible CV strings in French are words, but most of the CVC targets were either non-words or infrequent words.

Three sets of carriers, each including eight pairs, used either liquids, fricatives (/ʃ/ and /f/), or stops (/p/ and /k/) as pivotal consonants. In these, the consonant clusters selected were never tautosyllabic (and never occurred at the onset of real French words), so that the syllabic structure of carriers with clusters was CVC•CV. Each set comprised two pairs of pseudowords with each of the four vowels /a/, /i/, /u/, /y/ in the first syllable.

A fourth set was included for exploratory purposes and will not be considered further in the present paper. It was devised to assess whether the RT effects are sensitive to syllabification preferences. It used either clusters with /s/ followed by a stop, which are ambiguous as regards syllabification preferences (•ST vs. S•T; Treiman, Gross, & Cwikiel-Glavin, 1992), or clusters starting in /f/ followed by a liquid, which are generally considered tautosyllabic.

For the no-go trials, 32 pairs of pseudowords were constructed. As for the target-bearing trials, the two members of each pair had the same initial CVC sequence. One pseudoword had a simple pivotal consonant and the other included a cluster. The pivotal consonant was approximately equally distributed among stops, liquids and fricatives, and about one quarter of the clusters used were tautosyllabic (e.g., /fl/) or ambiguous (/st/). The targets were the same as for the target-present trials. Each pair of pseudowords was randomly assigned one pair of targets, with the provision that there was no single phoneme match between the targets and the initial part of the pseudowords.

In addition, 128 catch trials (for the Foil Condition) and 128 filler trials (for the No-Foil Condition) were constructed, again based on the same set of 32 CV and 32 CVC targets. Two foils, one of CV•CV and one of CVC•CV structure, were constructed for each target. For the CV targets, the two foils diverged from the corresponding target by the first vowel. For the CVC targets, the foils shared the initial consonant and vowel with the corresponding target and differed on the second consonant. For the No-Foil condition, the foil carriers were replaced by another set of pseudowords matched in syllable structure and such that there was no phoneme overlap between targets and carriers.

Finally, an additional set of 26 trials, half with cv and half with cvc targets, was constructed for practice. It included 10 target-present trials, 6 target-absent trials and 10 Foil or Filler trials. The carriers and targets were read by two different native speakers of French (male, Belgian accent, for the carriers; female, Parisian accent, for the targets).

Procedure.   Each trial began with the auditory presentation of the target. After a 500 ms delay, a short warning signal was presented, followed after 150 ms by the carrier. Participants were tested individually in a sound-attenuated booth. Stimuli were presented through Sennheiser headphones. Participants were required to press a key as rapidly as possible if the target was present at the beginning of the carrier. Each participant received all carriers twice, once with the cv target and once with the cvc target. Stimulus presentation and RT collection was controlled by the PsyScope software (Cohen, MacWhinney, Flatt, & Provost, 1993), with a CMU button box.

The experiment included two blocks separated by a short break. The 192 carriers appeared in both blocks with alternate targets, so that cv and cvc targets were equally distributed within each block. The order of trials within blocks was fixed and pseudo-randomised with the constraint that matched targets would not appear in immediate succession, and the order of the two blocks was counterbalanced across participants.

Results

Performance was more accurate in the No-foil than in the Foil condition. There were 5.2% of misses in the Foil Condition, and 1.9% in the No-foil Condition. Particularly with the foils, participants sometimes produced false alarms (5.8% for the foils and 0.1% for the target-absent fillers, in the Foil condition; 1.1% in the No-Foil condition). Although the overall level of accuracy was high, a few participants in the Foil condition showed rates of misses or false alarms in the range of 10%.

The mean detection times for each subject and for each item were computed. Because of the evidence of a relation between the syllable effect and overall RT (Dupoux, 1993), no cutoff procedure was applied.[2] We restricted the latency analyses to the participants who reached a threshold of 95% correct responses altogether (target-bearing trials, foils, and fillers), thus eliminating eight participants in the Foil condition.

---

[2] We verified that the application of a 1000 ms cutoff did not change the statistical outcomes.

Mean RTS were submitted to four-way analyses of variance, including pivotal consonant set (Liquids, Stops, and Fricatives), carrier structure (cv•cv vs. cvc•cv), target type (cv vs. cvc) and condition (Foils vs. No-foils). The mean latencies for each set and condition are displayed in Figure 1.

Participants were faster in the No-foil than in the Foil condition [404 vs. 508 ms; $F_1(1, 58) = 86.57, p < .0001; F_2(1, 42) = 498.07, p < .0001$]. The

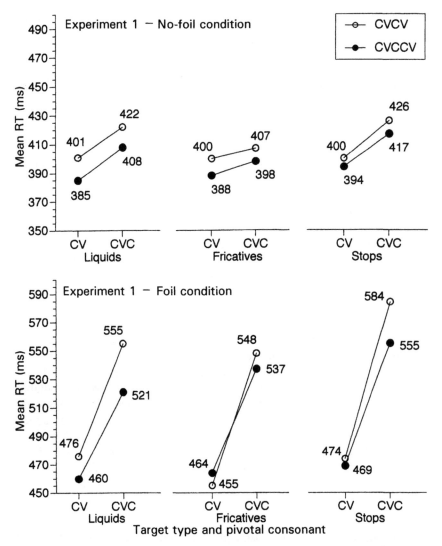

Figure 1. Mean latencies to CV and CVC targets for CVCV and CVCCV carrier pseudowords, in the No-foil (upper panel) and Foil (lower panel) condition of Experiment 1.

Target × Carrier interaction was significant in the subject analysis $[F_1(1, 58) = 3.94, p = .05; F_2 < 1]$, although the pattern did not correspond to the expected crossover interaction. The Target effect was highly significant, due to a large cv advantage $[F_1(1, 58) = 280.11, p < .0001; F_2(1, 42) = 119.74, p < .0001]$. The cvc•cv carriers produced slightly faster latencies, and the Carrier effect was significant by subject $[F_1(1, 58) = 35.07, p < .0001; F_2(1, 42) < 1]$. The Target effect interacted with the condition $[F_1(1, 58) = 113.56, p < .0001; F_2(1, 42) = 103.22, p < .0001]$, and was much larger in the Foil than in the No-foil condition. The Target × Carrier interaction was also modulated by the condition $[F_1(1, 58) = 4.47, p < .05; F_2(1, 42) = 2.46, p = .12]$. No other effect or interaction was significant in both analyses.

Separate analyses were run on the Foil and No-foil conditions. In the No-foil condition, the Target effect was significant $[F_1(1, 28) = 28.87, p < .0001; F_2(1, 42) = 18.08, p < .0001]$, the Carrier effect was significant by subject only $[F_1(1, 28) = 14.33, p < .001; F_2 < 1]$, and there was no interaction $[Fs < 1]$. In the Foil condition, the Target effect was significant $[F_1(1, 30) = 286.44, p < .0001; F_2(1, 42) = 153.46, p < .0001]$, whereas the Carrier effect $[F_1(1, 30) = 21.12, p < .0001; F_2 < 1]$, and the interaction $[F_1(1, 30) = 6.79, p < .05; F_2(1, 42) = 1.79, N.S.]$ were significant by subject only. However, this interaction did not correspond to the expected syllable effect. A 24 ms advantage occurred for the cvc detection in cvc•cv carriers relative to cv•cv carriers (respectively, 538 vs. 562 ms). In contrast, there was no evidence of the counterpart effect, namely, no cv target advantage for cv•cv over cvc•cv carriers (respectively, 469 and 465 ms, a −4 ms effect).

In view of Dupoux's (1993) claim that the syllable effect can only be reliably detected for slow participants, we split the participant sample into three groups, as a function of their overall RT. In each condition, we considered the ten fastest and ten slowest participants, and assigned the rest of the subject sample to an intermediate subgroup. In the No-foil condition, there was absolutely no hint of an effect (net average syllable effect[3] of −3, 6 and −5 ms, all $Fs < 1$, for the fast, mid and slow subgroup, respectively). In contrast, in the Foil condition, there was some evidence for a speed effect (net syllable effects of 3, 36 and 21 ms), with a significant Target × Carrier interaction in the intermediate $[F_1(1, 10) = 5.62, p < .05]$ but not the slow subgroup $[F_1(1, 9) = 3.53, p < .10]$.

---

[3] As in Dupoux (1993), the net syllable effect was computed as the sum of the carrier effect for CV targets ($RT_{CV\ targets/CVC•CV\ carriers} - RT_{CV\ target/CV•CV\ carriers}$) and the carrier effect for CVC targets ($RT_{CVC\ targets/CV•CV\ carriers} - RT_{CVC\ TARGET/CVC•CV\ carriers}$).

Discussion

Despite the procedural differences and the use of pseudoword carriers, the latencies for the No-foil condition (grand mean: 404 ms) were approximately in the same range as those reported by Mehler et al. (1981, grand mean: 364 ms). One half of the participants had overall RTs below 400 ms. This at least suggests that the changes that we introduced in the experimental procedure did not lead to major differences in the processing strategies deployed by the participants.

However, we did not observe the expected crossover interaction that signals a syllable matching strategy. In none of the six cells (three carrier sets and two conditions) did the interaction emerge. Rather, the data were characterised by an effect of target length, with latencies to the shorter (cv) targets faster than those to the longer (cvc) targets. The effect of target length was more marked when catch trials were included, and it was generally smaller with cvc•cv than with cv•cv pseudowords. While the target length effect suggests that participants were using a phoneme-based matching strategy, hence taking more time to detect a match for the longer targets, the reduction of this effect for cvc•cv carriers is ambiguous. It could signal a syllable effect, or it could be due to differences in the rate of phonetic information transmission for the two types of carriers.

The presence of catch trials had a massive effect on all aspects of performance. Participants made frequent false detections on catch trials and showed a higher miss level when catch trials were included. Furthermore, latencies were about 100 ms. slower with foils than without. Despite the general lengthening of latencies however, no clear indication of a syllable effect was found. Hence, Experiment 2 aimed at rendering the experimental situation more similar to that of Mehler et al. (1981) by blocking targets in homogeneous lists, in conditions including catch trials.

EXPERIMENT 2

In Mehler et al.'s (1981) experiments, all targets were made up of the vowel /a/ and a liquid pivotal consonant. We hypothesised that the greater heterogeneity in target composition in Experiment 1 might have made it harder for participants to extract syllabic cues, since the variation would give them less opportunity to compare the phonetic quality of cv and cvc targets containing the same vowel. Furthermore, if the syllable effect depends on the presence of subtle allophonic cues to syllabification, existing only for certain categories of consonants, the mixed condition of Experiment 1 may have blurred the effect by forcing participants to switch between different processing strategies. Experiment 2 thus examined whether blocking of targets by vowel (Experiment 2a) or pivotal consonant (Experiment 2b) influenced the pattern of reaction times.

Method

Participants.   Thirty-two participants were tested in Experiment 2a and 29 in Experiment 2b. Recruitment conditions were the same as for Experiment 1.

Stimuli.   The same stimuli as in the Foil condition of Experiment 1 were used. In Experiment 2a, trials were blocked by vowel, and in Experiment 2b, they were blocked by consonant category. The trials were re-arranged into two blocks of four lists. Each list comprised three trials (a go trial, a no-go trial, and a foil trial) with each of the 8 cv targets and each of the 8 cvc targets that included the same vowel (or the same pivotal consonant class, in Experiment 2b) for a total of 48 trials per list. Each list included one half of cv•cv and one half of cvc•cv carriers. The corresponding lists for the other block were obtained by interchanging the paired carriers. The order of trials within lists was fixed and pseudo-randomised with the constraint that matched targets would not appear in immediate succession, and the order of the two blocks was counter-balanced across participants.

Results

Accuracy was slightly higher than that of the Foil condition of Experiment 1. There were 1.7% misses in Experiment 2a, and 1.4% in Experiment 2b. False alarms rates were 5.3% and 5.6% for the foils, and 0.1% and 0.2% for the target-absent fillers, in Experiment 2a and 2b respectively. As in Experiment 1, participants who had less than 95% correct responses were eliminated, leaving 31 participants for Experiment 2a and 27 for Experiment 2b. Mean latencies are displayed in Figure 2.

Experiment 2a.   As in Experiment 1, cv detection was faster than cvc detection. This 31 ms Target effect was highly significant [$F_1(1, 30) = 12.86, p < .0001; F_2(1, 42) = 12.73, p < .001$], and was modulated by the carrier structure, as indicated by a Target × Carrier interaction [$F_1(1, 30) = 5.01, p < .05; F_2(1, 42) = 3.87, p < .06$]. In addition, due to a slight advantage for cvc•cv carriers, the Carrier effect was significant by subjects [$F_1(1, 30) = 10.65, p < .005; F_2(1, 42) = 2.24, p = .14$]. Cvc detection was significantly faster in cvc•cv than in cv•cv carriers (respectively, 584 and 623 ms), but no corresponding advantage occurred for the cv targets (respectively, 573 and 571 ms for the cv•cv and cvc•cv carriers).

The three-way interaction (Target × Carrier × Pivotal Consonant) was significant in the subject analysis [$F_1(2, 60) = 4.0, p < .05$] and close to significance in the item analysis [$F_2(1, 42) = 2.26, p = .12$]. We thus analysed each set separately. For the liquids, there was a significant Target

× Carrier interaction [$F_1(1, 30) = 6.94, p < .02; F_2(1, 14) = 4.08, p = .06$] and no main effects. However, the 16 ms Carrier effect for cv targets failed to reach significance in a local contrast test. For the fricatives, both main effects were significant by subject [$F_1(1, 30) = 6.06, p < .02; F_2(1, 14) = 1.25$, N.S. for the Carrier effect; $F_1(1, 30) = 4.28, p < .05; F_2(1, 14) = 3.38, p = .09$ for the Target effect] and there was no

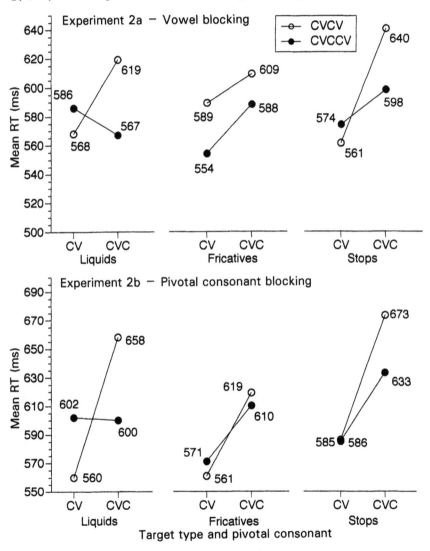

Figure 2. Mean latencies to CV and CVC targets for CVCV and CVCCV pseudowords, in Experiment 2a (Vowel-blocking, upper panel) and Experiment 2b (Consonant blocking, lower panel).

interaction. For the plosives, the Target effect [$F_1(1, 30) = 28.62$, $p < .0001$; $F_2(1, 14) = 13.70$, $p = .003$]   and   the   interaction [$F_1(1, 30) = 5.10, p < .05; F_2(1, 14) = 3.66, p < .08$] were significant.

Experiment 2b. The Target effect was highly significant [$F_1(1, 26) = 36.01, p < .0001; F_2(1, 42) = 36.49, p < .0001$], as well as the Target × Carrier interaction [$F_1(1, 26) = 78.33, p < .0001; F_2(1, 42) = 7.99$, $p < .001$], and the three-way interaction [$F_1(2, 52) = 4.75, p < .02; F_2(2, 42) = 2.13, p = .13$].

As in Experiment 2a, a clear crossover interaction appeared for the liquids [$F_1(1, 26) = 28.65, p < .0001; F_2(1, 14) = 13.59, p < .005$], together with a main Target effect [$F_1(1, 26) = 16.22, p < .0005; F_2(1, 14) = 11.29$, $p < .005$]. In addition, local contrasts indicated that the 42 ms cv•cv carrier advantage for cv targets was highly significant [$F_1(1, 26) = 10.19$, $p < .005; F_2(1, 14) = 10.35, p < .005$]. For the fricatives, only the Target effect reached significance [$F_1(1, 26) = 22.40, p < .0001; F_2(1, 14) = 12.65$, $p < .005$]. Plosives also showed a Target effect [$F_1(1, 26) = 41.72$, $p < .0001; F_2(1, 14) = 13.04, p < .005$], as well as a Carrier effect [$F_1(1, 26) = 6.56, p < .02; F_2 < 1$] and an interaction [$F_1(1, 26) = 5.33$, $p < .03; F_2 < 1$], by subjects only.

Subgroup analysis. For each experiment, we split the participant sample into three groups, as a function of their overall RT. As previously, we isolated the ten fastest and ten slowest participants, and assigned the rest of the sample to an intermediate subgroup. As Figure 3 illustrates, the results confirmed quite clearly Dupoux' s (1993) reanalysis.

First, in both experiments, the size of the syllable effect increased from the fastest to the slowest subgroup (35 ms, −26 ms, and 109 ms for Experiment 2a; 35 ms, 57 ms and 68 ms for Experiment 2b). Second, exactly as reported by Dupoux (1993), the most systematic change related to overall speed was in the size of the Carrier effect for cv targets. The slowest groups in both experiments were the only ones to show a sizeable advantage for cv•cv over cvc•cv carriers with cv targets (5 ms, −32 ms, and 27 ms for Experiment 2a; 1 ms, 5 ms and 42 ms for Experiment 2b). Finally, the average RTs for each group and each pivotal consonant showed a clear crossover interaction pattern only for the liquids.

Discussion

Overall, the data confirm and clarify the pattern observed in Experiment 1. As in the Foil condition of Experiment 1, a robust target effect was found, more markedly for cv•cv carriers than for cvc•cv carriers. In contrast however, performance appeared more sensitive to the nature of the pivotal consonant, as attested by significant three-way interactions. The target-blocking manipulation caused differences in latency patterns as a function of the pivotal consonant to emerge more distinctly. The major outcome of this manipulation was a clear crossover interaction for the liquid consonants. Although the interaction was significant in both blocked conditions, the net syllable effect was numerically larger in the consonant-

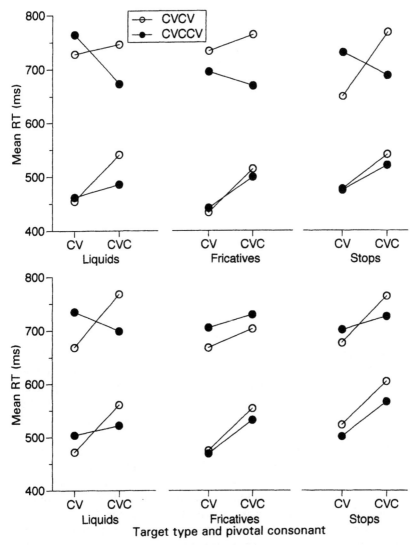

Figure 3. Mean latencies to CV and CVC targets for CVCV and CVCCV pseudowords, in Experiment 2a (upper panel) and Experiment 2b (lower panel), for the 10 slowest and 10 fastest participants.

blocking condition than in the vowel-blocking condition (100 ms vs. 68 ms). In addition, the carrier effect for the cv targets reached significance only in the consonant-blocking condition.

In sum, it seems that a syllable effect can only reliably be observed for liquid pivotal consonants. The complementary post-hoc analysis based on subjects' overall response speed provided further support for this conclusion. It showed striking similarities between our findings for the liquid set and the reanalysis of the original data by Dupoux (1993).

The present finding of a syllabic effect with liquids replicates Mehler et al.'s (1981) results, but at the same time demonstrates that the syllable effect does not generalise to most syllable structures in French. The fact that the diagnostic crossover interaction occurs only with liquids, and only under target-blocking conditions, argues against the strong hypothesis of a perceptual mechanism designed for the extraction of syllables. Rather, it lends support to the acoustic-phonetic interpretation proposed in the Introduction, which attributes the observed effects to the use of fine-grained phonetic information. To test this explanation further, the following experiment aimed at obtaining more information on the temporal location of phonetic information in the signal and its relation to RT patterns.

EXPERIMENT 3

Some of the findings from the previous experiments are consistent with a syllabic explanation. In particular, most conditions showed a cvc•cv advantage for cvc detection, which could be due to the syllabic match between the target and the initial syllable of the carriers. However, an alternative interpretation of that finding is that it reflects differences in the arrival of phonetic information in the signal as a function of syllable structure. According to this view, which we term the "phonetic throughput hypothesis", target detection latencies depend to a large extent upon the availability of the cues required for phoneme identification: the earlier these cues arrive the faster the detection response. Thus, one interpretation of the cvc•cv advantage for cvc targets observed here is that it mirrors in a relatively direct manner the differences in the rate of stimulus information accrual. Specifically, if the vowel and coda consonant information arrive earlier in cvc•cv than in cv•cv pseudowords, one could understand why cvc detection is faster for cvc•cv than cv•cv stimuli.

The aim of Experiment 3 was to collect data on the time-course of phonetic information, and to assess whether estimates of the temporal location of phonemes could account for the reaction time data from the previous experiments. To that end, two types of estimates were obtained. Acoustic-phonetic data were collected, through visual inspection of spectrograms as well as auditory analysis by one of the authors. Perceptual data were gathered in a phoneme gating experiment, in which participants were instructed to report what phonemes they had heard for successive gates of the carrier pseudowords.

Method

Participants. Twenty-one students from the University of Geneva participated in this experiment. Ten participants heard one list and eleven participants received the other.

Stimuli and Procedure. The 64 target-bearing carriers of the preceding experiments were used to construct a series of gates of increasing duration. The duration of the first gate was determined to correspond approximately to 3/4 of the duration of the initial consonant segment. Successive gates were created by incrementing the stimulus duration in steps of 15 ms up to the end of the carrier. The number of gates ranged from 10 to a maximum of 19. To limit each participant's contribution to about 1 hour, two experimental lists were prepared, each comprising an equal proportion of cv•cv and cvc•cv stimuli, selected so that paired cv•cv and cvc•cv pseudowords appeared in different lists.

The participants were required to write down what they heard as precisely as they could. Each trial consisted of an auditory warning signal, followed by the stimulus after a 500 ms delay. The inter-trial interval was set to 3 s to leave sufficient time for responding.

The temporal location of Vowel Onset and Pivotal Consonant Onset was also measured on spectrograms by a trained phonetician (C.M.), based on systematic phonetic criteria. The criterion used to identify vowel onsets was the appearance of the second formant. For liquids, the main criterion was the disappearance of the second formant, accompanied, for /l/, by an abrupt decrease in signal amplitude. For the stops (which were all unvoiced), the onset was located at the point where the two formants of the vowel disappeared. Finally, the appearance of noise and the disappearance of the second formant of the vowel indicated the onset of the (unvoiced) fricatives.

Results and Discussion

For each participant, we estimated the perceived location of the vowel as the duration of the first gate for which the vowel was correctly reported, and the location of the pivotal consonant as the duration of the gating stimulus for which the consonant was first correctly identified. We then used the results averaged across participants to compute two values for each carrier: an estimate of *vowel onset* (vo) location and an estimate of *pivotal consonant onset* (PCO) location relative to the beginning of the vowel. The first corresponded to the stimulus duration up to the beginning of the vowel, and the second was obtained by subtracting vo from the averaged stimulus duration up to the beginning of the consonant.

Phonetic analyses. The mean perceptual and phonetic estimates are displayed in Table 1. We ran analyses of variance with pivotal consonant category and carrier structure as factors to assess whether there were systematic variations in vowel onset and pivotal consonant onset location.

For the acoustic-phonetic measures, there were no significant effects for vo, although it was shorter for the cvc•cv carriers. In contrast, PCO was significantly shorter for cvc•cv than for cv•cv carriers [$F_2(1, 42) = 10.16$, $p < .005$], and varied according to the nature of the pivotal consonant [$F_2(2, 42) = 9.39$, $p < .0005$]. In addition, as the carrier effect was especially manifest for the liquids, the interaction came very close to significance [$F_2(2, 42) = 2.99$, $p = .06$].

For the perceptual data, similarly, no significant effects were obtained for vo, whereas PCO appeared to vary with carrier type [$F_2(1, 42) = 20.53$, $p < .0001$], pivotal consonant category [$F_2(2, 42) = 14.31, p < .0001$], and their interaction [$F_2(2, 42) = 4.40$, $p < .05$], due to a larger difference between cv•cv and cvc•cv carriers for the set with stop consonants. The large difference between perceptual and phonetic measures for the stops most likely stems from the criteria used in the latter. Acoustic-phonetic estimates were taken from the onset of silence, whereas gating data presumably indicate the location of closure release.

TABLE 1

Mean estimates of duration from stimulus onset to vowel onset (VO), from vowel onset to pivotal consonant onset (PCO), and total duration of the initial CV (CV), based on acoustic-phonetic measurements (upper panel) and on gating data (lower panel)

	CVCV carriers			CVCCV carriers		
	VO	PCO	CV	VO	PCO	CV
Acoustic-phonetic measures						
Stops	155	91	246	155	81	236
Fric	156	95	250	147	90	238
Liqu	150	127	277	124	95	219
Mean	154	104	258	142	89	231
Perceptual estimates						
Stops	190	206	396	184	126	310
Fric	176	148	324	169	127	296
Liqu	188	118	306	164	95	259
Mean	184	157	342	172	116	288

Thus, despite minor differences, the perceptual and acoustic-phonetic measurements agree in indicating that cv•cv and cvc•cv carriers do not differ much in the temporal location of the vowel information but show systematic temporal variations in the location of the pivotal consonant. According to both data sets, the consonant comes earlier in the cvc•cv pseudowords. This observation provides a natural explanation for the overall RT pattern, assuming that participants make their detection decision on the basis of the initial consonant plus vowel information when given a cv target, but wait for the pivotal consonant when receiving a cvc target. The following regression analyses aimed at testing the hypothesis that latencies were directly driven by phoneme throughput, by examining how durational variations across items predict the RTS.

Regression analyses.   One straightforward prediction is that detection times should vary as a function of the temporal location of successive phonemes, irrespective of the syllabic structure of the carriers. However, the time-course of phonemes is partly confounded with the structural factor, since PCO varies with carrier structure, as shown in the previous analysis of the temporal estimates. Hence, the finding that RTs vary with measures of phoneme location would not be sufficient to distinguish between a structural explanation and a phonetic explanation of the latency pattern.

To pit syllabic structure against phonetic throughput, we introduced a dummy variable (CAR) to code for carrier category (-1 for cvc•cv and $+1$ for cv•cv items). This predictor should best capture the part of item variability that is associated with the structural difference. Given the coding used, the carrier effect with cvc targets (cvc•cv faster than cv•cv) should translate into a positive contribution of the CAR predictor. Conversely, a carrier effect with the cv targets (cvc•cv slower than cv•cv) should lead to a negative contribution of CAR. The two questions of interest, then, were whether significant effects of syllabic structure (i.e., the CAR predictor) occur, when the contribution of phoneme temporal location (i.e., VO and PCO) is taken into account, and whether phoneme location predictors would account for some proportion of the variance, over and above the contribution of syllabic structure.

The phonetic throughput hypothesis assumes that perceptual mechanisms extract units of phonemic or subsyllabic size, and that participants make a detection response as soon as the phonetic information relevant to assess the target/carrier match has been processed. Hence a second prediction derived from that view is that reaction times should reflect the time-course of phonetic information to the extent that it is relevant to the decision. Thus, cv detection times should vary as a function of the temporal location of vowel onset, and cvc detection times should in addition be sensitive to the temporal location of the pivotal consonant.

We ran separate stepwise regression analyses for each of the four experimental conditions (Experiment 1, Foil and No-foil condition, Experiment 2a and 2b), target type (cv vs. cvc), and set of measurements (perceptual vs. acoustic-phonetic data). Each analysis used three predictors, the car dummy variable, the estimate of vowel onset location relative to the beginning of the stimulus (vo), and the temporal location of the pivotal consonant onset relative to the onset of the vowel (pco). The car predictor was forced first into the equation, and the two others were entered successively in order of decreasing contribution (with a .10 probability threshold). Table 2 displays the percentage of variance explained at each step of the regression and the parameters of the final regression equations.

Regarding first the analyses for cvc target detection (right section of Table 2), three main findings are worth noting. First, there is no effect of the car predictor, except in the vowel-blocking condition, with the acoustic-phonetic estimates. Second, all regression models demonstrate a systematic contribution of vo, which accounts for a large proportion of variance (from 46% in the No-foil condition up to 76% in the Foil condition). The value of the unstandardised vo coefficient in the regression models was generally very close to 1, meaning that the fitted relation was close to perfect (1 ms of input time accounts for 1 ms of response time). In the No-foil condition, the proportion of explained variance was clearly lower (around 50%), and the vo coefficient was reduced to about .5. Third, all regression models except one (No-foil condition with perceptual estimates) demonstrated a systematic contribution of pco, accounting for an additional 2–9% of explained variance (which corresponds to about 10–35% of the *residual* variance).

In summary, for cvc target detection, the best-fitting model is for the Foil Condition, with perceptual estimates. This model accounts for 85% of the rt variance. Thus, the mean rt can be predicted quite accurately from the resulting regression equation [rt = 300 ms (the constant) + time (in ms) to vowel onset + 1/2 the time from vowel onset to consonant onset]. Clearly, cvc detection is successfully explained by phoneme throughput, and there is little evidence to indicate that syllable structure plays any significant role.

The picture is different, and slightly more complex, in the case of cv target detection (left section of Table 2). Again, several observations are relevant. First, there was generally no effect of car, with the exception of the consonant-blocking condition, in which a marginally significant *negative* contribution was found. This finding mirrors the ANOVA results, but extends them by indicating that this syllabic structure effect cannot be

TABLE 2
Summary of stepwise regression analyses on the three sets of CVC·CV carriers ($n=48$)

Condition	Predictor	CV Target Detection				CVC Target Detection			
		R^2	Coeff.	SE Coeff.	Sign.	R^2	Coeff.	SE Coeff.	Sign.
Phonetic Estimates of VO and PCO									
No-foil	CARRIER	2.3	3.41	4.24	—	1.3	−1.55	4.26	—
	VO	34.5	0.32	0.07	.0001	47.3	0.43	0.06	.0001
	PCO	(35.8	0.21	0.21	—)	52.3	0.43	0.20	.04
Foil	CARRIER	0.0	−5.48	4.78	—	1.8	−1.87	4.86	—
	VO	50.6	0.51	0.07	.0001	78.5	1.03	0.07	.0001
	PCO	54.2	0.41	0.22	.07	82.5	0.72	0.23	.003
Vowel	CARRIER	0.2	0.42	5.89	—	8.0	13.43	5.01	.01
blocking	VO	12.5	0.24	0.09	.02	73.7	0.85	0.08	.0001
	PCO	(14.4	0.29	0.30	—)	(75.2	0.41	0.25	0.11)
Consonant	CARRIER	4.0	−9.97	5.36	.07	6.4	7.59	5.27	.16
blocking	VO	24.4	0.30	0.09	.001	75.3	0.94	0.08	.0001
	PCO	(24.8	−0.12	0.27	—)	77.9	0.56	0.25	.03
Perceptual Estimates of VO and PCO									
No-foil	CARRIER	2.3	3.32	4.24	—	1.3	1.51	3.82	—
	VO	34.7	0.33	0.07	.0001	54.7	0.45	0.06	.0001
	PCO	(37.6	0.15	0.10	.15)	(55.8	0.01	0.09	—)
Foil	CARRIER	0.0	−2.07	4.94	—	1.8	−6.90	4.82	.16
	VO	42.1	0.46	0.08	.0001	75.5	0.99	0.07	.0001
	PCO	(45	0.18	0.12	.14)	84.1	0.51	0.11	.0001
Vowel	CARRIER	0.2	0.10	5.73	—	8.0	6.42	5.98	—
blocking	VO	17.4	0.29	0.09	.004	66.1	0.80	0.09	.0001
	PCO	(17.5	0.00	0.14	—)	70.7	0.35	0.13	.01
Consonant	CARRIER	4.0	−10.2	5.23	.06	6.4	3.78	5.56	—
blocking	VO	27.9	0.33	0.09	.0004	71.8	0.90	0.08	.0001
	PCO	(29.2	0.12	0.13	—)	77.3	0.39	0.12	.002

Note: Lines between brackets and in italics correspond to non-significant (>.10) predictors, which were tested but not included in the equation.

reduced to variations in phoneme throughput. Interestingly, the CAR contribution appears to be related to the liquid set, since it completely vanishes if the same regression models are applied to the data for fricatives and stops only.

Second, all regression models indicate a significant contribution of vo, accounting for a substantial proportion of the variance (from 12% in the vowel-blocking condition to 54% in the Foil condition). However the contribution of vo was much less clear than for the cvc targets, especially for the two blocked conditions (respectively, 12.5 and 20.4% for vowel-

and consonant-blocking conditions with phonetic predictors; 17.4 and 23.9% with perceptual predictors). Again, this reduction is related to the liquid set. When the same regression model was applied to the data for fricatives and stops together, the proportion of variance explained by vo increased massively (respectively, 27.7 and 36.4% with phonetic predictors; 29.2 and 37.5% with perceptual predictors).

Third, as expected on the basis of the phonetic throughput hypothesis, in none of the eight regression models did PCO contribute significantly to CV target detection. This lack of contribution was not due to the link between PCO and carrier syllabic structure, since similar null effects were found in regressions in which the CAR predictor was not used.

In sum, in contrast to the results for CVC detection, the three variables considered are far from providing a full account of detection latencies for CV target detection. Neither the syllabic structure per se nor the temporal location of vowel information appears to constitute the most important driving factors in this condition. The regression findings corroborate the outcome of Experiment 2, indicating that liquids constitute a special case in showing a syllabic structure effect and much less influence of phoneme throughput. Clearly, other (as yet unidentified) factors need to be considered in order to explain CV target detection.

GENERAL DISCUSSION

The present research aimed at replicating the syllable effect first reported by Mehler et al. (1981) and to extend its generality to more varied stimulus materials than in the original study. In the first experiment, we used disyllabic pseudowords including liquids, fricatives, or plosives as pivotal consonant, and assessed the influence of catch trials. The characteristic crossover interaction was obtained in neither of the two conditions. In addition, in the Foil condition only, CVC detection was faster for the syllable-matching CVC•CV carriers than for the mismatching CV•CV carriers, but there was no indication of the opposite effect for CV detection. Experiment 2 used the same stimuli, but the targets were blocked either by vowel or by pivotal consonant. Different outcomes emerged as a function of the pivotal consonant category, and a clear crossover interaction was only obtained with liquids. In Experiment 3, we estimated the time-course of phonetic information in the carriers. Regression analyses showed that for CVC target detection, up to 85% of variance was accounted for by two temporal characteristics of the carriers, the location of the onset of the vowel and of the pivotal consonant, and there was no evidence that syllable structure played any significant role. In contrast, for CV detection, only the vowel onset location was predictive, and there was some evidence for a contribution of syllable structure.

Two additional aspects of the results deserve mention. The first concerns the influence of catch trials, in Experiment 1. Performance was markedly affected by the presence or absence of catch trials. Participants were much faster in the absence of catch trials, suggesting that they responded based on a match between the initial subsyllabic portion of the target and the carrier. When catch trials were present, they gave rise to about 5% of false alarms, indicating that participants could not always avoid such anticipatory partial match responses. Moreover, reaction times to shorter (cv) targets were faster than to longer (cvc) targets and this effect was larger in conditions including catch trials.

The second point concerns the analysis of the crossover interaction. We chose to decompose the interaction in terms of the local effects of carrier structure for each type of target. Several findings suggest that the two components of the interaction do not belong together, and may arise from different causes. The carrier effect for cvc detection (i.e., the latency advantage of cvc•cv carriers over cv•cv carriers) was generally present, and robust. It occurred for all pivotal consonant sets and it was not modulated by the blocking manipulation. Furthermore, the regression findings provide strong evidence that the cvc target effect is driven by the temporal characteristics of the carriers. In contrast, the carrier effect for cv detection (i.e., the latency advantage of cv•cv carriers over cvc•cv carriers) appeared labile and determined the lack of robustness of the interaction. It varied as a function of several factors: the pivotal consonant, the target homogeneity, and participant speed. Moreover, compared to cvc detection, the carriers' temporal properties explained a much smaller proportion of the variance, particularly in the regressions on target-blocking data, suggesting that other factors influenced the cv detection latencies.

In sum, with respect to the issues that led us to initiate this research, the present findings demonstrate that the syllable effect is limited to stimuli with liquid pivotal consonants, and that even for such stimuli, it is fragile. In our data, it only emerged when tested under relatively homogeneous target conditions, and even then, it was only apparent in the slowest participant subgroup. Taken together, the results provide a rather coherent picture. They are perfectly consistent with the initial findings (Mehler et al., 1981) and their reanalysis (Dupoux, 1993), and extend them to pseudowords. Indeed, we obtained a crossover interaction only in the condition closest to theirs, that is, with liquid pivotal consonants in blocked conditions. At the empirical level, the constraints that we have identified may provide a potential explanation for the elusive nature of the syllable effect (e.g., Kearns, 1994).

At the theoretical level, the present findings provide support for a subsyllabic/phonetic perceptual process and argue against the hypothesis of a syllable classification mechanism. In the Introduction, we contrasted two potential explanations of the syllable effect, a syllabic explanation and an acoustic-phonetic explanation. The syllabic explanation, endorsed by Mehler et al. and colleagues, assumes that the incoming signal undergoes an early process of syllabic segmentation and classification. The syllabic code resulting from this process serves to evaluate the match with the target. A weaker version of this hypothesis is the dual-coding proposal proposed by Dupoux (1993) and Sebastián-Gallés et al. (1992). In contrast, according to the acoustic-phonetic hypothesis, the perceptual process is based on smaller-sized units, and it delivers fine-grained phonetic information so that participants can continuously evaluate the phonetic and sub-phonetic match between the incoming signal and the target.

Several features of the present study favour the latter interpretation. Namely, the effect of catch trials on latencies and accuracy, as well as the predictive value of the carriers' temporal characteristics support the view that performance reflects in a quite direct way the incoming speech signal. Conversely, the fact that the syllabic effect is limited to one particular class of pivotal consonants seems hard to reconcile with the notion of a "bank of syllabic analysers" (Mehler, Dupoux, & Segui, 1990). A more parsimonious interpretation is that participants continuously attempt to match the phonetic features extracted from the incoming signal with their stored representation of the target. In some rather circumscribed conditions, however, the *syllabic* mismatch between the cv target and a cvc•cv carrier causes interference and delays the detection response. Of course, for this account to be complete, the reasons why this mismatch interference effect occurs only with liquid consonants, in target-blocking conditions, and for slow listeners remain to be elucidated.

One factor that might explain the special behaviour of liquids relates to potential ambiguities in the syllabification of the consonant clusters containing liquids. Obviously, all the clusters used to construct the cvc•cv carriers (except for the ambiguous set) were selected because they were considered heterosyllabic according to common descriptions of syllable structure (see, e.g., Dell, 1995). However, such categorical linguistic descriptions may not capture the finer details, and there is indeed evidence from explicit syllabification studies that not all clusters lead to consistent intuitions from listeners. Goslin and Frauenfelder (submitted) examined the agreement between five different syllabification algorithms for French, and compared the various solutions to (Swiss) French speakers' explicit syllabification of disyllabic pseudowords. Although the experiment did not include the exact clusters used here, the materials sampled from the four major phonetic classes (plosives, fricatives, liquids, and nasals), so that their findings provide at least an index of the probability of c•c syllabification for the present stimuli, with the additional advantage of stemming from exactly the same subject population. From their data, we computed that the proportion of c•c syllabification was around 90% for the three pivotal consonant sets used in the present study. Although it was slightly higher for the liquids than for the two other sets, it seems unlikely that such a minor difference could explain our findings.

A more plausible explanation, in our view, is the existence of acoustic-phonetic differences related to syllabicity, which have not been captured by the analysis of phoneme durations. In general, phonetic evidence suggests that spectral differences due to coarticulation, as well as other subtle timing variations are correlated with syllable structure (see Krakow, 1999). In the absence of any direct evidence indicating that such cues are perceptually more salient for liquid consonants in French, this account remains speculative, but we believe that it opens interesting perspectives for further research. It suggests more direct links between listeners' performance in RT tasks and the phonetics of syllabicity than have previously been assumed.

The second constraint, the influence of target blocking, suggests that the mismatch interference effect is conditioned by subjects' ability to build a richly specified representation of the target. When targets are mixed, participants have less opportunity to uncover relevant cues to discriminate between similar (i.e., matched cv and cvc) targets. So, although further evidence would be needed to substantiate this interpretation, the finding of a target blocking effect is certainly in line with the acoustic-phonetic account that we have proposed.

Regarding the influence of subjects' response speed, Dupoux (1993) and Sebastián-Gallés et al. (1992) assumed a race between two perceptual processes, one based on a syllabic routine and the other based on subsyllabic analysis. In their view, slow participants demonstrate a syllable effect because the (late) syllabic code has enough time to build up, and hence determines the response. Unfortunately, such a hypothesis fails to account for the two other constraints that we have identified here. In both experiments, slow participants tended to make fewer false alarms, but more misses than faster ones.

We speculate that these conservative participants require more than a phonemic categorical match and try to extract subtle subphonetic cues before making a go response. Accessing subphonetic detail and matching at that level may take more time than the analogous operations at the phonemic category level. Since it is at the subphonetic level that the mismatch between cv targets and cvc•cv carriers occurs, we can understand why the slow subjects show a detrimental effect in such trials. In a way, this account is similar to Dupoux's dual-coding proposal, except that the code requiring more time is assumed to be subphonetic rather than syllabic.

In conclusion, the main empirical contribution of the present study is the demonstration that the syllable effect occurs only in very circumscribed conditions, and that sequence detection latencies are in general directly determined by the time-course of phonetic information in the carriers. At the theoretical level, we propose a re-interpretation of the phenomenon, according to which it results from a combination of a phonetic effect, which explains the advantage of cvc•cv carriers for cvc detection, and a mismatch interference effect that occurs only when participants have ample opportunity to establish a refined and detailed representation of the target. Hence, we argue that the present findings are not compatible with the hypothesis of an early perceptual mechanism of syllabic classification, and furthermore, that the so-called syllable effect does not demonstrate the existence of such a mechanism.

Content, Dumay, and Frauenfelder (2000) have advanced further arguments against the hypothesis that syllables constitutes an early perceptual category. One argument comes from explicit syllabification studies. Contrary to the belief that syllable boundaries are clear and unambiguous in French, Content, Kearns, and Frauenfelder (2001) found that, when required to repeat the first part of bisyllabic words, French-speaking participants often included the intervocalic consonant, thus producing nearly as many cvc and cv responses. This result, which was recently replicated by Goslin and Frauenfelder (submitted), was observed despite the fact that our experimental stimuli were simple cv•cv words, for which phonological analyses unanimously assume a cv•cv syllabification. In addition, there was an asymmetry between syllable onset and syllable offset decisions. In contrast to the variation found for the repetition of the first part (i.e., offset decisions), participants nearly always included the consonant when required to repeat the second part of the words (i.e., onset decisions).

We take the explicit syllabification data to indicate that syllable onsets constitute reliable segmentation points in the signal, and we hypothesise that syllable onsets are used as privileged alignment points for lexical search in continuous speech recognition. In further studies, we have put this Syllable Onset Segmentation Hypothesis (sosh) to the test by investigating the processing of words embedded in multisyllabic carriers. We used the word-spotting task to examine whether a misalignment between a syllable onset and the target word onset delays the recognition of the word (Dumay, Frauenfelder, & Content, in press). According to sosh, the lexical cost due to word/syllable misalignment should be greater for final embedding, which corresponds to onset misalignment, than for initial embedding. This prediction was confirmed both by RT and error data. Onset misalignment (*zu•glac* vs. *zun•lac*) induced significant RT (93 ms) and error (7.3%) effects, whereas offset misalignment (*la•cluf* vs.

lac•tuf) revealed smaller and non-significant RT effects. Interestingly, our word-spotting findings bear a strong resemblance to results obtained by McQueen (1998) with Dutch, as well as Weber (2000) with English, thus substantiating our belief that the syllable onset segmentation strategy might constitute a general characteristic of speech processing. In sum, whereas the present research suggests that the precise assumptions that grounded the initial interpretation of the syllable effect were not correct, they certainly should not be taken as a rejection of the core idea that inspired Mehler et al.'s study, that syllable structure plays an important role in the perception of speech.

REFERENCES

Bradley, D.C., Sánchez-Casas, R.M., & Garciá-Albea, J.E. (1993). The status of the syllable in the perception of Spanish and English. *Language and Cognitive Processes, 8,* 197–233.

Cohen, J., MacWhinney, B., Flatt, M., & Provost, J. (1993). Psyscope: An interactive graphic system for designing and controlling experiments in the psychology laboratory using Macintosh computers. *Behavior Research Methods, Instruments, and Computers, 25,* 257–271.

Content, A., Dumay, N., & Frauenfelder, U. (2000). *The role of syllable structure in lexical segmentation: Helping listeners avoid Mondegreens.* Proceedings of the Spoken Word Access Processes (SWAP) meeting, Nijmegen: Max-Planck Institute for Psycholinguistics, pp. 39–42.

Content, A., Kearns, R.K., & Frauenfelder, U.H. (2001). Boundaries versus onsets in syllabic segmentation. *Journal of Memory and Language, 45,* 177–199.

Cutler, A., Mehler, J., Norris, D., & Seguí, J. (1986). The syllable's differing role in the segmentation of French and English. *Journal of Memory and Language, 25,* 385–400.

Dell, F. (1995). Consonant clusters and phonological syllables in French. *Lingua, 95,* 5–26.

Dumay, N., Frauenfelder, U.H., & Content, A. (in press). The role of the syllable in lexical segmentation in French: Word-spotting data. *Brain and Language.*

Dupoux, E (1989). *Identification des mots parlés. Détection de phonèmes et unité prélexicale.* Unpublished Ph.D. Thesis, Ecole des Hautes Etudes en Sciences Sociales, Paris.

Dupoux, E. (1993). The time course of prelexical processing: The syllabic hypothesis revisited. In G. Altmann & R. Shillcock (Eds.), *Cognitive models of speech processing* (pp. 81–111). Hove, UK: Lawrence Erlbaum Associates Ltd.

Frauenfelder, U.H., & Kearns, R. (1996). Sequence monitoring. *Language and Cognitive Processes, 11,* 665–674.

Goslin, J. & Frauenfelder, U.H. (submitted). A comparison of theoretical and human syllabification. *Language and Speech.*

Kearns, R. (1994). *Prelexical speech processing by mono- and bilinguals.* Unpublished Ph.D. Thesis, University of Cambridge.

Krakow, R. A. (1999). Physiological organization of syllables: A review. *Journal of Phonetics, 27,* 23–54.

McQueen, J.M. (1998). Segmentation of continuous speech using phonotactics. *Journal of Memory and Language, 39,* 21–46.

Mehler, J., Dommergues, J.Y., Frauenfelder, U., & Seguí, J. (1981). The syllable's role in speech segmentation. *Journal of Verbal Learning and Verbal Behavior, 20,* 298–305.

Mehler, J., Dupoux, E., & Seguí, J. (1990). Constraining models of lexical access: the onset of word recognition. In G.T.M. Altmann (Ed.), *Cognitive models of speech processing* (pp. 236–261). Cambridge, MA: MIT Press.

Mills, C. B. (1980). Effects of the match between listener expectancies and coarticulatory cues on the perception of speech. *Journal of Experimental Psychology: Human Perception and Performance, 3*, 528–535.

Norris, D., & Cutler, A. (1988). The relative accessibility of phonemes and syllables. *Perception and Psychophysics, 43*, 541–550.

Rietveld, A.C.M., & Frauenfelder, U. (1987). *The effect of syllable structure on vowel duration.* Paper presented at the XIth International Congress of Phonetic Sciences, Tallinn.

Sebastián-Gallés, N., Dupoux, E., Seguí, J., & Mehler, J. (1992). Contrasting syllabic effects in Catalan and Spanish. *Journal of Memory and Language, 31*, 18–32.

Seguí, J., Frauenfelder, U., & Mehler, J. (1981). Phoneme monitoring, syllable monitoring and lexical access. *British Journal of Psychology, 72*, 471–477.

Tabossi, P., Collina, S., Mazzetti, M., & Zoppello, M. (2000). Syllables in the processing of spoken Italian. *Journal of Experimental Psychology : Human Perception and Performance, 26*, 758–775.

Treiman, R., Gross, J., & Cwikiel-Glavin, A. (1992). The syllabification of /s/ clusters in English. *Journal of Phonetics, 20*, 383–402.

Weber, A. (2000). *The role of phonotactics in the segmentation of native and non-native continuous speech.* Proceedings of the Spoken Word Access Processes (SWAP) meeting, Nijmegen: Max-Planck Institute for Psycholinguistics, pp. 143–147.

Zwitserlood, P., Schriefers, H., Lahiri, A., & van Donselaar, W. (1993). The role of syllables in the perception of spoken Dutch. *Journal of Experimental Psychology: Learning, Memory and Cognition, 19*, 260–271.

APPENDIX

Carrier pairs used in experimental trials

Liquids		Plosives		Fricatives		Ambiguous	
CVCV	*CVCCV*	*CVCV*	*CVCCV*	*CVCV*	*CVCCV*	*CVCV*	*CVCCV*
daʀɛ	daʀke	ʃapi	ʃaptɔʀ	baʃɛl	baʃmi	kafõ	kafli
galuʀ	galtõ	fakɔʀ	fakty	tafi	tafno	pasɔk	pastad
fiʀu	fiʀnɛr	vipɔʀ	viptɛʀ	nifyʀ	niftaʀ	tifɛʀ	tiflas
dilo	dilmã	bikaʀ	biktuʀ	giʃe	giʃfɔʀ	ʀisaʀ	ʀistõ
vyʀõ	vyʀlɛt	dypal	dyptal	pyʃõ	pyʃkal	syfe	syfliʒ
gylaʀ	gylpõ	mykõ	myktɛl	lyfo	lyfni	bysaʒ	bystik
nuʀaj	nuʀtɛʀ	bupis	buptal	ʒuʃaj	zuʃti	gufal	guflyʀ
tuli	tulme	pukɛʀ	puktif	sufaʀ	suftik	ʒusɛm	ʒustɛʀ

LANGUAGE AND COGNITIVE PROCESSES, 2001, *16* (5/6), 637–660

Language-universal constraints on speech segmentation

Dennis Norris

MRC Cognition and Brain Sciences Unit, Cambridge, UK

James M. McQueen, and Anne Cutler

Max Planck Institute for Psycholinguistics, Nijmegen, The Netherlands

Sally Butterfield and Ruth Kearns

MRC Cognition and Brain Sciences Unit, Cambridge, UK

Two word-spotting experiments are reported that examine whether the Possible-Word Constraint (PWC) is a language-specific or language-universal strategy for the segmentation of continuous speech. The PWC disfavours parses which leave an impossible residue between the end of a candidate word and any likely location of a word boundary, as cued in the speech signal. The experiments examined cases where the residue was either a CVC syllable with a schwa, or a CV syllable with a lax vowel. Although neither of these syllable contexts is a possible lexical word in English, word-spotting in both contexts was easier than in a context consisting of a single consonant. Two control lexical-decision experiments showed that the word-spotting results reflected the relative segmentation difficulty of the words in different contexts. The PWC appears to be language-universal rather than language-specific.

The segmentation of a written text such as this one into its component words is a trivial task for the reader, because the writers have helpfully left empty spaces between the individual words. Speakers do not help listeners

Requests for reprints should be addressed to Dennis Norris, MRC Cognition and Brain Sciences Unit, 15 Chaucer Road, Cambridge, CB2 2EF, UK.

E-mail: dennis.norris@mrc-cbu.cam.ac.uk

Ruth Kearns is now with Procter & Gamble Technical Centres Ltd. We would like to thank Maarten Jansonius and especially Keren Shatzman for their help with the preparation and running of Experiments 2 and 4, and Antje Meyer for giving us the opportunity to conduct these experiments at the University of Birmingham.

http://www.tandf.co.uk/journals/pp/01690965.html   DOI: 10.1080/01690960143000119

in this way. Spoken utterances are continuous, and there are no completely reliable cues to word boundaries (Lehiste, 1972; Nakatani & Dukes, 1977). Therefore one of the tasks which the listener has to accomplish, in order to understand what the speaker is trying to say, is segmentation: dividing the continuous signal into its constituent words.

There are two main classes of solution to the problem of segmenting continuous speech. The first, and most general, solution is that adopted by the connectionist models TRACE (McClelland & Elman, 1986) and Shortlist (Norris, 1994). In these models, all possible lexical candidates consistent with any sequence of phonemes in the input compete, so that overlapping candidates inhibit one another. The competition process allows these networks to parse the input into a sequence of non-overlapping words.

The second strategy is to adopt a more explicit segmentation procedure in an attempt to capitalise on the available phonetic or phonological segmentation cues in the input. One such strategy that has received considerable empirical support is the Metrical Segmentation Strategy (MSS) of Cutler and Norris (1988). As applied to English, the MSS is designed to take advantage of the fact that the majority of content words in English begin at the onsets of strong syllables (Cutler & Carter, 1987). However, the MSS does not operate in the same way for all languages. The strategy is sensitive to the rhythmic structure of the listener's native language. In English the rhythmic unit is the foot, in French the syllable, and in Japanese the mora. There is now extensive evidence that listeners do indeed draw on their knowledge about the rhythmic structure of their native language in segmenting speech. This produces language-specific effects in segmentation (Cutler, Mehler, Norris, & Seguí, 1986, 1992; Cutler & Otake, 1994; Otake, Hatano, Cutler, & Mehler, 1993; McQueen, Otake, & Cutler, 2001; Sebastián-Gallés, Dupoux, Seguí, & Mehler, 1992). The rhythmic structure of language helps segmentation in the native language, for instance, but can lead to inappropriate listening strategies when the input is in a non-native language which has a different rhythm (see Cutler, Dahan, & Donselaar, 1997, for a review). A similar story can be told for phonotactic constraints. Phonotactic sequence constraints can be effectively exploited to segment the native language (McQueen, 1998), but again can be misleading when the input is in a non-native language in which the constraints are different (Weber, 2000).

One very powerful weapon in the listener's armoury was discovered by Norris, McQueen, Cutler, and Butterfield (1997). This is a constraint—the Possible-Word Constraint (PWC)—which disfavours interpretations which would leave a residue of the input which could not itself be exhaustively parsed into one or more words. The initial evidence for the PWC came from an experiment in which listeners were required to spot real words in short nonsense strings. Norris et al. found that words were harder to spot when the residue of the nonsense string was only a single consonant than when the residue was a syllable. Thus *sea* was harder to spot in *seash* than in *seashub*, and *apple* was harder to spot in *fapple* than in *vuffapple*. None of the residues—*sh, shub, f, vuff*—are in fact words of English. But *vuff* and *shub*, although they happen not to be members of the English vocabulary, satisfy all the phonological preconditions for membership and hence might well have been words. The two single consonants *sh* and *f*, on the other hand, could never themselves be viable candidate words. Norris et al. proposed that this constraint could provide a powerful method for inhibiting activation of words which are spuriously present in an utterance, and tested this by implementing the PWC in the computational model of spoken-word recognition Shortlist (Norris, 1994). In their implementation, the PWC works by penalising any candidate word which begins or ends at a point where there is no vowel between that point and a "known" boundary. Known boundaries are those locations in the speech signal where there is likely to be a word boundary, as determined by metrical information (Cutler & Norris, 1988), phonotactic information (McQueen, 1998) or silence (Norris et al., 1997).

Norris et al. (1997) presented simulations showing that Shortlist's ability to parse the input improved when the PWC was incorporated into the model. Furthermore, with the PWC, Shortlist was able to simulate a range of data including the metrical segmentation effects reported in word-spotting by Cutler and Norris (1988), by McQueen, Norris, and Cutler (1994), and by Norris, McQueen, and Cutler (1995) and in identity priming by Vroomen and de Gelder (1995).

An illustration of the potential value of the PWC can be seen by considering the utterance "they met a fourth time". This contains possible spurious occurrences of, for instance, *aim* (the**y m**et), *for* (**four**th), *I'm* (**time**) and *metaphor* (**met a four**th). But if these words were activated, each could be rejected by the PWC on the grounds that a single-consonant residue would inevitably be left unaccounted for. Thus *aim* leaves the initial sound of *they*, *I'm* leaves the initial *t* of *time*, and *for* and *metaphor* leave the final *th* of *fourth*; none of these residues could be parsed into words.

The PWC provides an integrated account of the use of both rhythmic and phonotactic cues. Rhythmic and phonotactic information, along with silence, all provide cues to the possible location of word boundaries. Furthermore, the PWC can make more effective use of these cues than theories which postulate that the input is explicitly segmented at possible segmentation boundaries. In contrast to the initial formulation of the MSS, or theories claiming that the syllable is a unit for lexical access (Mehler, 1981; Mehler, Dommergues, Frauenfelder, & Seguí, 1981; Seguí, 1984), the segmentation process does not need to begin by assuming that there actually are word boundaries at all of these locations. For example, the second syllable of the word *delightful* is a strong syllable, and there is a phonotactically determined syllable boundary between the second and third syllables. A mechanism that attempted to force word boundaries at these points might degrade word recognition by disrupting the processing of the intended word. However, the PWC operates only by eliminating word candidates which are misaligned with these boundaries. For instance, it penalises *lie* in *delightful* because a *t* would be unaccounted for between *lie* and the phonotactic boundary between the end of *delight* and the beginning of *ful*. But the PWC will not hinder recognition of aligned words, even where they have word-internal boundaries.

Although rhythmic and phonotactic information can be used in all languages, the precise implementation of these strategies is determined by the specific properties of individual languages. The PWC operates on the output of those language-specific segmentation procedures. As currently implemented, however, the PWC itself operates in exactly the same way for all languages. The PWC simply determines whether there is a vowel between the end of a word candidate and the nearest boundary. In other words, it makes use of the language-universal constraint that all words must have vowels. In nearly all languages of the world it is the case that a single consonant cannot form a lexical word. The current implementation of the PWC therefore reflects the fact that every component in the lexical parse of a stretch of continuous speech must contain at least one vowel. A given candidate word is only a plausible part of that parse if the residue of speech between the word's edge and a likely word boundary contains a vowel.

However, languages differ not only in their rhythmic and phonotactic characteristics, but also in what counts as an acceptable minimal word. In English, although function words can consist of a single reduced syllable (reduced forms of *the, a, to,* etc.), content words cannot. If the PWC is sensitive to this phonological property of English words, listeners should find it as hard to spot words embedded in weak-syllable contexts as in consonant contexts. If the PWC is a simple language-universal constraint, however, word-spotting should be much easier when the residue constitutes a weak syllable than when it is a consonant.

Furthermore, no English word can consist of an open syllable with a short full vowel. The word *se*, for example, with the vowel of *sell*, is not a possible word. There are six such lax vowels in English (those in the words *hat, bet, hit, book, hot,* and *hut*). Open syllables with long vowels are acceptable (e.g., *sea*) and closed syllables with short vowels (e.g., *sell*) are also fine. However, although *se* is not a possible English word, it would be a perfectly good word in French. French allows open syllables with lax vowels, as evidenced by words such as *thé* and *va*. In yet other languages, however, monosyllabic words of any kind are not well-formed words. In the Australian language Lardil and in the Bantu language Sesotho, for example, lexical words must have at least two syllables. The PWC could therefore be a language-specific constraint, one that reflects this linguistic variation. It is possible that the PWC is sensitive to the fact that in English, for example, an open syllable with a lax vowel is not a well-formed English word. If so, we would expect that if there was only a syllable like /sɛ/ as a residue between a candidate word and a likely word boundary in an ongoing parse of speech, that candidate would not be a plausible part of the parse.

The four experiments we report here address the question of the universality versus language-specificity of the PWC. The two critical experiments use the word-spotting paradigm, while two lexical decision experiments provide control data. If the PWC is language-universal, then a word will be hard to spot only if it is embedded in a context which could not be a word in any language. If the PWC is language-specific, however, then only contexts which could not be a word in the listeners' native language will make spotting embedded words difficult (even though the same contextual residues might be acceptable words in other languages). Both word-spotting experiments examine whether residues which contain vowels, but are not phonologically well-formed content words in English, behave like the syllables with full vowels studied by Norris et al. (1997), or whether they behave like non-viable consonant residues. The first word-spotting experiment examines syllables with the reduced vowel schwa; the second examines open syllables with lax vowels. Each of these experiments has a companion control experiment in which listeners were required to make lexical decisions to the words excised from the word-spotting stimuli. These control experiments enable us to determine whether any effects observed in the word-spotting experiments might be attributable to differences in the phonetic realisation of the stimuli in different contexts.

EXPERIMENT 1

If the PWC really is determined by a universal rather than language-specific notion of possible word, then we should expect word spotting to be easier for words in weak-syllable contexts than in consonant contexts. Weak-syllable contexts should behave just like the full syllable contexts in Norris et al. (1997). That is, spotting *sea* in /siʃəb/ should be easier than spotting *sea* in /siʃ/. But if the PWC is in some fashion language-specific, then English listeners should not treat syllables with weak vowels the same way as those with full vowels.

Method

Subjects. Twenty-four native speakers of English from the MRC Cognition and Brain Sciences Unit volunteer panel were paid for their participation.

Materials. The stimuli were derived from the following-context materials in Norris et al. (1997) by changing the vowels in their full-vowel syllabic contexts to schwa. So, for example, the target word *sea* could appear with either a following consonant context (e.g., /siʃ/) or a following weak syllable context (e.g., /siʃəb/). In the case of the following syllable contexts 11 of the 48 items retained exactly the same consonants (C*C) as in Norris et al. The remaining items were altered to avoid creating phonotactically illegal strings or strings that could be misheard as words, and to increase the variety of contexts. The experimental items are listed in Appendix A. There were 110 filler items; many of these had weak final syllables so that a final weak syllable was not a cue to the presence of an embedded word. There were also eight filler target words with following full syllables. As in Norris et al., half the target words were monosyllabic and half were bisyllabic. Target words only appeared with following contexts. Two experimental lists were constructed, each containing all the fillers, and all the targets, but with type of context counterbalanced over lists such that half the words on each list were in consonant contexts and half in weak syllable contexts.

Procedure. The materials were recorded onto Digital Audio Tape by a native speaker of English in a sound-attenuated booth. The stimuli were transferred to a computer and converted to stereo files where the speech was on one channel and inaudible timing marks were on the other. The two lists of stimuli were then transferred to a compact disc.

Listeners were tested individually in a quiet room; they heard the lists over headphones driven by a portable compact disc player. They were told they would hear nonsense words, some of which would contain real English words. They were asked to press a button as fast as possible whenever they spotted a real word, and to say aloud the word that they had spotted. Reaction Times (RTs) were measured from the offset of target-bearing items. Each listener heard a practice list, followed by one of the two experimental lists.

Results and discussion

Analyses of variance (ANOVAs) were performed on the latency and accuracy data. Four words were excluded from the analysis because they were missed by more than two-thirds of the subjects who heard them in either consonant or syllable contexts: *eager, tell, chain,* and *bother.* The results are summarised in Table 1.

The main effect of context was significant by subjects in the RT analysis ($F_1(1, 22) = 5.71, p < .03; F_2(1, 40) = 2.07, p = .16$) and by both subjects and items in the error analysis ($F_1(1, 22) = 16.21, p < .001; F_2(1, 40) = 17.20, p < .001$). The effect of number of syllables was significant in the RT analysis ($F_1(1, 22) = 9.35, p < .01; F_2(1, 40) = 5.72, p < .05$) but not in the error analysis ($Fs < 1$). There was also a significant interaction between context and number of syllables in the error analysis ($F_1(1, 22) = 18.24, p < .001; F_2(1, 40) = 11.27, p < .002$) but not in the RT analysis ($Fs < 1$). Although the error rates are lower than in Norris et al., the overall pattern, including the fact that the context effect in errors was larger in bisyllables, is very similar to the corresponding consonant and full-syllable conditions in their Experiment 1. In that experiment the overall context effect was 45 ms in RTs and 15% in errors, compared with 94 ms and 13% here.

The results of Experiment 1 are very straightforward: word-spotting is easier in weak syllable contexts than in consonant contexts. Furthermore, this difference is, if anything, marginally greater than the difference between the corresponding full-syllable and consonant contexts in Norris et al. (1997). There is therefore no suggestion that weak syllables violate the PWC. This suggests that the PWC operates according to language-universal principles.

EXPERIMENT 2

The differences observed in Experiment 1 involve comparisons between different versions of the same target words produced in different contexts.

TABLE 1

Mean reaction times (RTs, in ms, measured from target offset) and mean percentage error rates, in word spotting (Experiment 1) and in lexical decision to the same target words, Excised from their contexts (Experiment 2)

Target:	Monosyllabic		Bisyllabic	
Context:	CəC	C	CəC	C
Word spotting				
Mean RT	890	1001	789	866
Mean error	19%	22%	9%	32%
Example	seashəb	seash	sugarməl	sugarm
Lexical decision				
Mean RT	630	477	436	409
Mean error	14%	8%	4%	4%
Example	sea(shəb)	sea(sh)	sugar(məl)	sugar(m)

There is a possibility that the results could therefore reflect differences between the target words spoken in weak-syllable contexts and those spoken in consonant contexts, rather than an effect of the contexts per se. Experiment 2 was a control lexical decision experiment which addressed this concern. If the effect observed in Experiment 1 were due to the relative difficulty listeners had in segmenting the target words from their contexts, then there should be no difference in lexical decision performance on these target words when they are excised from their contexts and presented in isolation.

Method

Subjects.   Twenty-four native speakers of English, students at the University of Birmingham, were paid for their participation.

Materials.   Forty-four of the 48 targets words used in Experiment 1 were excised from their contexts using the Xwaves speech editor. Cuts were made at zero-crossings at the offsets of the final phonemes of the words. The word *eager* was not included since it had been excluded from the analysis of Experiment 1. Due to an error, the targets *usher, fool,* and *fun* were also excluded, instead of the targets *tell, chain,* and *bother* (which had also been excluded from Experiment 1). There were therefore 22 monosyllabic words and 22 bisyllabic words. These were counterbalanced over two lists, such that half the words on each list had been taken from consonant contexts and half from weak-syllable contexts. The words were presented in the same pseudorandom order in each list, mixed with 40 nonwords (20 monosyllabic and 20 bisyllabic), which had been excised from the Experiment 1 fillers.

Procedure.   Separate speech files were prepared for each item, and transferred to a portable computer running NESU experimental control software. These files were played over headphones directly from the computer's hard disk. Listeners were tested individually in a quiet room. They were asked to press a button as fast as possible whenever they heard a real English word, and (by analogy to the word-spotting procedure) to then say aloud the word they had heard. RTs were again measured from word offset. Each listener heard a short practice list of words and nonwords (also excised from Experiment 1 materials) and one of the two experimental lists.

Results and discussion

Two monosyllabic and two bisyllabic words were not included in the analysis (*tell, chain,* and *bother*, because they had been excluded in

Experiment 1, and *nether*, which was missed by two-thirds of the subjects who heard the version extracted from its consonant context). The mean latency and accuracy values for the remaining 40 items are given in Table 1.

The main effect of context in RTs was significant by subjects and items (words taken from consonant contexts were detected, on average, 90 ms faster than words taken from weak-syllable contexts; $F_1(1, 22) = 97.64$, $p < .001$; $F_2(1, 38) = 30.80$, $p < .001$), as was the main effect of word length (monosyllables were detected, on average, 131 ms more slowly than bisyllables; $F_1(1, 22) = 88.10$, $p < .001$; $F_2(1, 38) = 17.82$, $p < .001$). These two effects interacted ($F_1(1, 22) = 39.62$, $p < .001$; $F_2(1, 38) = 14.08$, $p < .001$); while the context effect was larger for monosyllabic than for bisyllabic words, pairwise comparisons showed that it was reliable in each case. The only effect which was significant in the accuracy analysis was the effect of target length: monosyllabic words were missed more often than bisyllabic words ($F_1(1, 22) = 17.21$, $p < .001$; $F_2(1, 38) = 4.80$, $p < .05$).

Words excised from consonant contexts (like *sea* from /siʃ/) were detected more rapidly than words excised from weak-syllable contexts (like *sea* from /siʃəb/). This is the reverse of the pattern observed in word spotting. The phonetic realiszation of the words in consonant contexts (particularly the monosyllables) was therefore better than that of the words in weak-syllable contexts. In spite of this difference in the quality of the words themselves, the targets in consonant contexts were harder to spot in Experiment 1. The difference in phonetic realisation of the words in the two contexts could therefore only have acted to weaken any effect of segmentation difficulty. Indeed, in a by-item Analysis of Covariance (ANCOVA) on the word-spotting RTs from Experiment 1 taking the lexical decision RTs as a covariate, the effect of context (which was not reliable in the original ANOVA) became significant ($F_2(1, 37) = 8.21$, $p < .01$). In a parallel analysis of the error data, the context effect in word spotting remained significant ($F_2(1, 37) = 13.18$, $p < .005$). Experiment 2 therefore confirmed that the advantage for words in weak-syllable contexts over those in consonant contexts in Experiment 1 reflects the relative segmentation difficulty of the words in these contexts.

EXPERIMENT 3

Experiment 1 revealed that weak-syllable contexts behave just like full-syllable contexts, despite the fact that weak syllables are not well-formed content words in English. This suggests that the PWC is language-universal rather than language-specific. Weak syllables, however, are well-formed function words. It therefore remains possible that the PWC is language specific, but that it is only concerned with whether the context could be any possible word in that language, irrespective of its status as a content or function word. A stronger test would be to determine if the PWC is sensitive to whether or not the context is a syllable which could not possibly be a word of any sort in the language. We can test this in English by using contexts consisting of an open syllable with a lax vowel. Such syllables can never be well-formed words in English.

Experiment 3 examined English listeners' ability to detect bisyllabic words with Weak-Strong (WS) or Strong-Weak (SW) stress patterns, in nonsense contexts which could or could not themselves form possible English words. For WS words, *perturb* for example, the contexts consisted of a single consonant (*sperturb*, /spətɜb/), a Consonant-Vowel (CV) syllable with a tense vowel (*dahperturb*, /dɑpətɜb/), or a CV syllable with a lax vowel (*dEperturb*, /dɛpətɜb/). If the PWC is language-specific, *perturb* should be harder to spot after /s/ and /dɛ/ than after /dɑ/, since only the latter residue is a possible word of English. If, on the other hand, the PWC is language-universal, *perturb* should be hard to spot after /s/ but easier after both /dɛ/ and /dɑ/, which could be words in some language.

For SW words (e.g., *echo*) the contexts were single consonants (*shecho*, /ʃɛko/) or CVC syllables, again one with a tense vowel (*fooshecho*, /fuʃɛko/) and one with a lax vowel (*foshecho*, /fɒʃɛko/). Single-consonant contexts should, again, be difficult. In this case, however, the two syllable contexts did not test whether the PWC is language-specific. Rather, they tested whether the difference between tense and lax vowels influences the location of perceived syllable boundaries. Lax vowels demand a closed syllable (*fosh*), which might lead to the segmentation *fosh-echo*. Detecting *echo* should therefore be easy in this condition, since the word is aligned with the syllable boundary after the /ʃ/ and the entire first syllable is a possible word. Tense vowels, however, allow an open syllable (*foo*), and, combined with the tendency of English to prefer maximal syllable onsets (Pulgram, 1970), this might lead to the segmentation *foo-shecho*. The target *echo* could therefore be as hard to spot in the tense vowel context as in the consonant context, since in both cases there is a single consonant between the beginning of the target and a likely word boundary (cued by the syllable boundary in *foo-shecho* and by the silence in *shecho*).

Method

Subjects. Thirty-six native speakers of English were paid for their participation. Participants were students at Girton College, Cambridge.

Materials and procedure. Forty-eight bisyllabic WS words (*perturb*) and 30 bisyllabic SW words (*echo*) were selected; none had other words embedded within them. The first syllables of the WS words consisted of a single consonant followed by schwa; the SW words all began with vowels. Twenty-four of the WS words were placed in three preceding contexts: a single consonant (*sperturb*); an open CV syllable with a lax vowel (*dEperturb*); and an open CV syllable with a tense vowel (*dahperturb*). It was not possible to find consonant contexts for the other 24 WS words (no phonotactically legal clusters could be formed with words beginning with voiced consonants, like *giraffe*, or those beginning with /s/, like *cigar*). These words were therefore only paired with tense and lax CV contexts. The SW words were also placed in three preceding contexts: a single consonant (*shecho*); a closed CVC syllable with a lax vowel (*foshecho*); and a closed CVC syllable with a tense vowel (*fooshecho*). In all strings, the only embedded real word was the intended target word. The items are listed in Appendix B.

The target-bearing items were divided over three lists, such that all of the SW words and the 24 WS words which had three contexts appeared on all three lists, with type of context counterbalanced over lists. The remaining target-bearing items (WS words with only two contexts) were also divided over the three lists; 16 of these words appeared in each list, each word appearing in only one context in a given list, with type of context counterbalanced over lists. Each list therefore contained 70 target-bearing items. A further 140 filler items containing no real English words were constructed. The fillers matched the target-bearing items in length and stress patterns; there were twice as many fillers with a particular number of syllables and stress pattern as there were target-bearing items with that structure. Each list contained all fillers, with target-bearing and filler items in pseudorandom order, such that there was always at least one filler between any two target-bearing items.

The materials were again recorded onto DAT by a native speaker of English in a sound-attenuated booth. The speaker attempted to minimise syllabification cues in the recording; medial consonants (/ʃ/ in *foshecho* and *fooshecho*; /p/ in *dEperturb* and *dahperturb*) were ambisyllabic, that is, were neither clearly syllabified in the first syllable nor in the second syllable. The procedure was otherwise identical to that of Experiment 1.

Results and discussion

ANOVAs were again performed on the RT and error data. An item was excluded from an analysis if, in any one condition in that analysis, it was missed by more than two-thirds of the subjects who heard it. The items excluded from the analyses involving the WS and SW items with all three types of context were: *canal, convert, lapel, reserve, angel, option, ever, ulcer,* and *usher.* Those excluded from the analyses of WS items with only Tense and Lax contexts were*: convert, lapel, reserve,* and *behave* (*canal* was included here because only the consonant context for this item failed the criterion). Mean RTs and error rates are summarised in Table 2.

Overall analyses. The first analysis involved the items which were presented in all three contexts: Tense, Lax, and Consonant. The means for the WS words which could be included in this analysis were: Tense, 388 ms and 13% errors; Lax, 446 ms and 10% errors; and Consonant, 501 ms and 27% errors (i.e., in this last case as in Table 2). The means for the SW items are those listed in Table 2. In these analyses, the effect of context was significant both in RTs ($F_1(2, 60) = 19.38, p < .001; F_2(2, 86) = 10.89, p < .001$) and in errors ($F_1(2, 60) = 15.31, p < .001; F_2(2, 86) = 12.42, p < .001$).

TABLE 2

Mean reaction times (RTs, in ms, measured from target offset) and mean percentage error rates, in word spotting (Experiment 3) and in lexical decision to the same target words, excised from their contexts (Experiment 4)

	Weak-Strong Target Contexts		
	Tense Vowel CV Syllable	*Lax Vowel CV Syllable*	*Single Consonant*
Word spotting			
Mean RT	423	448	501
Mean error	14%	15%	27%
Example	dahperturb	dEperturb	sperturb
Lexical decision			
Mean RT	271	262	
Mean error	7%	5%	
Example	(dah)perturb	(dE)perturb	

	Strong-Weak Target Contexts		
	Tense Vowel CVC Syllable	*Lax Vowel CVC Syllable*	*Single Consonant*
Word spotting			
Mean RT	511	466	607
Mean error	14%	10%	20%
Example	fooshecho	foshecho	shecho
Lexical decision			
Mean RT	313	301	321
Mean error	6%	6%	2%
Example	(foosh)echo	(fosh)echo	(sh)echo

Note. Weak-Strong words from consonant contexts were not included in Experiment 4.

No other effects in either RT or error analysis reached significance across both subjects and items. Planned comparisons between the three contexts for each type of word were then carried out.

WS words. Responses to WS words like *perturb* were faster ($t_1(35) = 2.12, p < .05; t_2(19) = 2.37, p < .05$) and more accurate ($t_1(35) = 5.36, p < .001; t_2(19) = 4.18, p < .005$) in the lax-vowel syllable contexts than in the consonant contexts. This result suggests that the PWC is a language-universal mechanism: CV syllables with lax vowels are not treated as impossible residues in English segmentation, like single consonants are, in spite of the fact that such syllables are not possible English words.

Responses to words like *perturb* were also faster ($t_1(35) = 3.79, p < .005; t_2(19) = 3.85, p < .005$) and more accurate ($t_1(35) = 3.51, p < .005; t_2(19) = 2.51, p < .05$) in the tense-vowel syllable contexts than in the consonant contexts. This result replicates the finding that words are easier to spot in syllabic contexts than in consonantal contexts, as predicted by the PWC. Listeners were also faster to detect WS words in syllable contexts with tense vowels than in syllable contexts with lax vowels ($t_1(35) = 2.61, p < .05; t_2(19) = 2.34, p < .05$). Note however that listeners were slightly more accurate in detecting WS words in syllable contexts with lax vowels than in syllable contexts with tense vowels. This difference suggests that there was a small speed-accuracy trade-off, though this difference was not significant ($t_1(35) = 1.17, p > .2; t_2(19) = 1.12, p > .2$).

We also conducted a second analysis, of all the WS words which appeared in tense and lax syllable contexts (i.e., the words in the previous analysis plus those words like *giraffe* which appeared only in syllabic contexts). In this analysis, the difference between tense and lax syllable contexts (of 25 ms, on average; see Table 2), was not significant (all Fs < 1). There was also no difference in error rates between these two conditions in this analysis (all Fs < 1). It therefore appears that there was no robust difference between these conditions, while performance in both was reliably better than that in the consonant condition.

SW words. Responses to SW words like *echo* were faster ($t_1(35) = 3.56, p < .005; t_2(24) = 3.68, p < .005$) and more accurate ($t_1(35) = 2.88, p < .01; t_2(24) = 2.33, p < .05$) in the lax-vowel syllable contexts than in the consonant contexts. This difference is again as predicted by the PWC, and replicates Norris et al. (1997). No other differences within the SW words were fully reliable. This means that while listeners were not reliably slower or less accurate in detecting SW words in tense-vowel syllable contexts than in lax-vowel syllable contexts, they were also not reliably faster or more accurate in this condition than in the consonant context condition. The fact that listeners were numerically slightly slower and less accurate in tense than in lax contexts suggests that there was some tendency for listeners to segment strings like *fooshecho* as *foo-shecho*, thus tending to make detection of *echo* as hard as in *shecho*. But, since the tense-vowel condition was also not reliably different from the lax-vowel condition, this tendency was not very strong. Contexts like *fosh* and *foosh* are both possible words, and there is no clear difference between these two conditions.

The principal result of Experiment 3 is clear. Listeners were able to spot words like *perturb* faster in CV syllable contexts with lax vowels than in single consonant contexts. This supports the claim that the PWC operates according to language-universal principles. Contexts which are possible words in some languages (CVs with lax vowels) should therefore be treated as acceptable residues in on-line speech segmentation in any language. For the same reasons which motivated Experiment 2, however, a control lexical decision experiment was run using the target words excised from the Experiment 3 materials.

EXPERIMENT 4

Method

Subjects. Twenty-five native speakers of English, students at the University of Birmingham, were paid for their participation. None took part in Experiment 2.

Materials and procedure. All 48 WS words used in Experiment 3 were excised from their syllabic contexts in the same way as in Experiment 2. The versions of the 24 WS words which had also been presented in consonant contexts were not used. In many cases it was not possible to find a splicing point which would produce a recognisable token of the word (for example, the words beginning with unvoiced stops, like *canal*, sounded as if they had voiced initial stops). The SW words were also excised from each of their three contexts (three of these words were excluded from the experiment: *ulcer* and *ever*, because they had particularly high error rates in word spotting, and *anchor*, to simplify counterbalancing). There were thus 48 WS words taken from tense and lax CV contexts, and 27 SW words taken from tense, lax and consonant contexts. The SW words were counterbalanced over three lists, such that each list contained nine words taken from each of the three contexts. The WS words were then counterbalanced over these three lists. Two of the lists each contained 24 WS words taken from each context. Two versions of the third list were made using the same counterbalancing of WS words (there were therefore four different lists, which could be treated either as three lists in the SW analysis or as two lists in the WS analysis). The words were presented in the same pseudorandom order in each list, mixed with 40 WS nonwords and 24 SW nonwords which had been excised from the Experiment 3 fillers. The only difference between the lists was the contexts from which the target words had been excised. The procedure was identical to that in Experiment 2. Each listener heard a short practice list followed by one of the four experimental lists.

Results and discussion

Three WS words were excluded from the analysis because they were missed by two-thirds of the subjects who heard them in one condition (*carafe*, *banal*, and *verbose*). The results for the remaining items are given in Table 2. Separate ANOVAs were performed for the WS and SW words. There were no effects either in speed or accuracy which were significant by both subjects and items, neither for the WS words nor for the SW words. There was therefore no reliable difference between words taken from the different contexts. SW words taken from consonant contexts were just as easy to recognise as those taken from either tense- or lax-vowel contexts. Most importantly, there was no difference between the WS words taken from lax-vowel CV contexts (e.g., *perturb* taken from *dEperturb*) and WS words taken from tense-vowel CV contexts (e.g., *perturb* taken from *dahperturb*). By item ANCOVAs on the word-spotting data for these two conditions from Experiment 3, taking the lexical decision data as covariate, confirmed this: neither the difference in RTs nor the difference in errors was significant. Any potential difference in word spotting performance between these two conditions was therefore not masked by any difference due to the phonetic realisation of the words in each of these contexts.

GENERAL DISCUSSION

The PWC treats CV syllables with lax vowels and syllables with schwa as nucleus in exactly the same way as syllables with full vowels. In other words, although only syllables with full vowels can stand alone and thus serve as well-formed content words in English, any type of syllable is a well-formed possible word in the sense that it constitutes an acceptable residue when appended to a candidate word. It appears therefore that the acceptability of such residue strings is not determined by the demands of a particular language. There are phonological constraints on the form of words acceptable in English, but syllables which violate these constraints are still acceptable residues for English listeners. Thus the definitive criterion for a viable residue in listeners' construction of an acceptable parse of continuous speech seems to be language-universal. A viable residue must be a syllable; but any syllable will do.

The present experiments were conducted in English. Psycholinguistics has a long and embarrassing tradition of claims for language-universality based on data from English alone. However, in this case the English experiments contribute the crucial cornerstone to an edifice built of converging data from many languages. For instance, further evidence that the PWC is indeed a language-universal strategy comes from a word-spotting experiment in Sesotho, a Bantu language spoken in Southern Africa. In Sesotho, any surface realisation of a content word must have at least two syllables. Cutler, Demuth, and McQueen (submitted) asked Sesotho listeners to spot words like *alafa* (to prescribe) in contexts such as *halafa* and *roalafa*. In the former, the single consonant context *h* is an impossible word and an impossible syllable; in the latter, the mono-syllabic context *ro* is a possible syllable of Sesotho but is not a well-formed Sesotho content word. Listeners spotted words significantly less rapidly and less accurately in the consonantal contexts than in the monosyllabic contexts. Thus even though *ro* is not a possible content word in Sesotho, this does not make it an unacceptable residue in Sesotho speech segmentation.

Similarly, McQueen and Cutler (1998) observed that Dutch listeners find it harder to spot words in preceding consonantal contexts (e.g., *lepel*, spoon, in /blepəl/) than in preceding CV contexts with schwa (*lepel* in /səlepəl/) or preceding CV contexts with a full vowel (*lepel* in /kulepəl/). As in English, weak syllables are not possible content words in Dutch; they are, however (again as in English), possible function words, and in this experiment were in the position (preceding a content word) which might have been filled by a function word. McQueen and Cutler's experiment thus suggests that a residue does not have to be a possible content word to be acceptable, but it leaves open the question of whether an acceptable residue must fulfil some potential role (e.g., as a function word) in the language in question.

These two experiments in Sesotho and Dutch motivate the same conclusion as the present English experiments: that the PWC is a language-universal strategy. But neither of them alone can fully make the case for this conclusion. From the Sesotho experiment we can conclude that it is not necessary for a syllabic residue to be a potential content word of the language; a monosyllable (which could in Sesotho be a morpheme, but not a lexical item) satisfies the relevant constraint. From the Dutch study, again, we conclude that potential content-word status is not required, since a syllable with schwa (which could in Dutch be a function word but not a content word) behaved just like a full syllable. The English data from the present experiments add the further important evidence that it is not even necessary that the syllabic residue be a viable stand-alone *syllable* of the language. Open syllables with lax vowels, such as /dɛ/, perform no function in English. They cannot be content words, they cannot be morphemes, they cannot be function words. Nevertheless they constitute residues which are acceptable to the PWC.

The stimuli used in the Dutch and English experiments with reduced syllable residues differ in one interesting respect. Whereas the Dutch stimuli had the residue before the target word, in the English stimuli the residue followed the word. With the following contexts used in Experiment 1, the onset of the weak syllable in /siʃəb/ would not constitute a "known boundary" from the perspective of the PWC (neither phonotactics nor the onset of a full syllable signal a boundary). The PWC will therefore not trigger until the "known boundary" determined by the silence at the end of the stimulus. One might, therefore, be tempted to believe that listeners could sometimes respond before the PWC was violated. If this were so one might not expect to see any evidence of a language-specific PWC if listeners responded too quickly.

However, the results from the Dutch word-spotting experiments with reduced syllable residues before the word make this seem unlikely. McQueen and Cutler included stimuli like *səbegin* (/səbəxɪn/) where the target word *begin* has a WS stress pattern. In these materials there was no "known boundary" at word onset. If the PWC were language specific, and schwa were not treated like a full vowel, then the word onset, and indeed every position up to the onset of the strong syllable, would violate the PWC. The word would violate the PWC well before it could be recognised. However, *begin* was spotted as easily in *səbegin* (/səbəxɪn/) as in *geebegin* (/xebəxɪn/; with a CV context with a full vowel) and *zasəbegin* (/zasəbəxɪn/; with a bisyllabic context including a full vowel and a schwa). The results for English stimuli with contexts following the words are thus the same as the results in Dutch with contexts preceding the words.

There is a second reason why it is unlikely that the possibility of listeners responding too rapidly in Experiment 1 led us to miss a language-specific effect. This follows from the differences in response time to monosyllabic and bisyllabic words. Monosyllabic words, presumably because they have less perceptual support, are responded to more slowly than bisyllabic words. If there were a language-specific PWC effect that was emerging later in time, then it should be more apparent in the more slowly identified monosyllabic words. However, although there was a marginally larger PWC effect of context for monosyllabic words in RTs, there was a substantially bigger effect in the opposite direction in errors. The fact that these effects go in opposite directions means there is no support for the idea that the PWC effect emerges only for slower responses.

It appears that the PWC operates only on the basis of very simple phonological information (the presence or absence of a vowel), and not on any higher-order knowledge about what constitutes well-formed words or even syllables in any particular language. Open syllables with lax vowels may constitute independent words in some languages. But they constitute viable residues for lexical activation even in languages in which they do not come into question as potential members of the vocabulary.

Some further recent results in Dutch are consistent with this view. Mauth (1999) has shown that single consonants which are inflectional morphemes in Dutch (the verbal third person singular -*t* and the nominal plural -*s*) are treated in segmentation in the same way as other single consonants which have no such morphemic status in the language. Dutch listeners found it as hard to spot words in morphemic consonantal contexts as in non-morphemic consonantal contexts. These results suggest that the PWC is not sensitive to the fact that in Dutch, the phonemes *t* and *s* are meaningful units; instead, it is a purely phonological mechanism which treats all vowel-less sequences as equivalent (and as equivalently unacceptable for the PWC's purposes).

The only remaining question left open by the current body of evidence on the PWC concerns a very small minority of the world's languages. It is claimed that some languages allow vowel-less syllables and words (see, e.g., Dell and El Medlaoui's [1985] analysis of Tashlhiyt Berber). If the PWC depends simply on the presence or absence of vocalic information in the speech signal, then it is unclear how it might apply in the segmentation of languages such as Tashlhiyt Berber. This question is currently being investigated in our laboratory.

If the PWC is indeed universal, then it could be of considerable value in language acquisition. Infants would not need to learn the relevant constraints for their own native language. If the PWC has the same form across languages, it could assist infants in their initial attempts to segment continuous speech and acquire their first words (Johnson, Jusczyk, Cutler & Norris, 2000; cf. Brent & Cartwright, 1996). Johnson et al. (2000) have recently shown that 12-month-old infants do indeed appear sensitive to PWC factors while listening to continuous speech. The infants were familiarised with lists of monosyllabic words (e.g., *rest*), and then heard passages of continuous speech containing words which had the familiarised words embedded within them. These matrix words were either mono-syllabic (e.g., *crest*) or bisyllabic (e.g., *caressed*). The infants looked longer in the direction of a loudspeaker playing the passages if the passages contained the bisyllabic matrix words (where there is a syllabic residue left after the embedded word is found) than if they contained the monosyllabic matrix words (where there is only a consonantal residue). That is, it seemed that they were able to recognise *rest* in the context of *caressed* but not in the context of *crest*. These results suggest that the PWC is a powerful weapon for speech segmentation in the infant's as well as the adult listener's armoury. Note that the continuous speech used in this experiment provides a more general test of the PWC than the isolated fragments of speech used in word spotting.

We began by asking whether the PWC is a language-specific or language-universal constraint on speech segmentation. The original demonstration of the PWC by Norris et al. (1997) compared consonant residues with syllable residues. This left open the possibility that the critical unit determining the viability of a parse might be either the minimal phonological word of a particular language, or the syllable as a phonological unit in general. The experiments reported here (and especially in combination with the findings of Cutler et al., submitted, and of McQueen & Cutler, 1998) provide a clear answer to this question. Segmentation is impaired when the residue between the end of a candidate word and the nearest known boundary is a consonant, but not when it is a syllable, regardless of whether the syllable is a possible word, of any kind, in the vocabulary of that particular language. The PWC is satisfied by any syllable, irrespective of whether or not the syllable in question might have a place in the language-specific vocabulary.

The simulations reported in Norris et al. (1997) used a modified version of the Shortlist model (Norris, 1994). The algorithm implemented in the model consisted simply of a penalty applied to any candidate word where the stretch of speech input between the edge of that candidate and the nearest known boundary did not contain a vowel. Our results suggest that this simple algorithm, with no special provisions for any particular vocabulary but applicable to all languages in the same way, is likely to be the correct characterization of the PWC. Of course, the boundaries which allow the PWC computations to be performed include phonotactic constraints on syllable structure and reflections of rhythmic structure, so that they themselves are dependent on the rhythmic and phonological characteristics of each language and thus are by no means language-universal. But although these boundaries can be determined in a highly language-specific way, the PWC which operates upon them does so in every language in the same way; it is language-universal.

REFERENCES

Brent, M.R., & Cartwright, T.A. (1996). Distributional regularity and phonotactic constraints are useful for segmentation. *Cognition, 61,* 93–125.

Cutler, A., & Carter, D.M. (1987). The predominance of strong initial syllables in the English vocabulary. *Computer Speech and Language, 2,* 133–142.

Cutler, A., Dahan, D., & Donselaar, W. van (1997). Prosody in the comprehension of spoken language: A literature review. *Language and Speech, 40,* 141–201.

Cutler, A., Demuth, K., & McQueen, J.M. (submitted). Universality versus language-specificity in listening to running speech.

Cutler, A., Mehler, J., Norris, D.G., & Seguí, J. (1986). The syllable's differing role in the segmentation of French and English. *Journal of Memory and Language, 25,* 385–400.

Cutler, A., Mehler, J., Norris, D.G., & Seguí, J. (1992). The monolingual nature of speech segmentation by bilinguals. *Cognitive Psychology, 24*, 381–410.

Cutler, A., & Norris, D. (1988). The role of strong syllables in segmentation for lexical access. *Journal of Experimental Psychology: Human Perception and Performance, 14*, 113–121.

Cutler, A., & Otake, T. (1994). Mora or phoneme? Further evidence for language-specific listening. *Journal of Memory and Language, 33*, 824–844.

Dell, F., & El Medlaoui, M. (1985). Syllabic consonants and syllabification in Imdlawn Tashlhiyt Berber. *Journal of African Languages and Linguistics, 7*, 105–130.

Johnson, E., Jusczyk, P.W., Cutler, A., & Norris, D. (2000). *12-month-olds show evidence of a Possible-word Constraint.* Paper presented to the 140th Meeting, Acoustical Society of America, November.

Lehiste, I. (1972). The timing of utterances and linguistic boundaries. *Journal of the Acoustical Society of America, 51*, 2018–2024.

Mauth, K. (1999). Morphology and the segmentation of spoken language. Poster presented at *Tutorials in Behavioural and Brain Sciences*, Ohlstadt, Germany, July 1999.

McClelland, J.L., & Elman, J.L. (1986). The TRACE model of speech perception. *Cognitive Psychology, 18*, 1–86.

McQueen, J.M. (1998). Segmentation of continuous speech using phonotactics. *Journal of Memory and Language, 39*, 21–46.

McQueen, J.M., & Cutler, A. (1998). Spotting (different types of) words in (different types of) context. *Proceedings of ICSLP 98, Sydney, Australia* (pp. 2791–2794). Rundle Mall: Causal Productions.

McQueen, J.M., Norris, D.G., & Cutler, A. (1994). Competition in spoken word recognition: Spotting words in other words. *Journal of Experimental Psychology: Learning, Memory, and Cognition, 20*, 621–638.

McQueen, J.M., Otake, T., & Cutler, A. (2001). Rhythmic cues and possible-word constraints in Japanese speech segmentation. *Journal of Memory and Language, 44*, 103–132.

Mehler, J. (1981). The role of syllables in speech processing: Infant and adult data. *Philosophical Transactions of the Royal Society, Series B, 295*, 333–352.

Mehler, J., Dommergues, J.-Y., Frauenfelder, U.H., & Seguí, J. (1981). The syllable's role in speech segmentation. *Journal of Verbal Learning and Verbal Behavior, 20*, 298–305.

Nakatani, L.H., & Dukes, K.D. (1977). Locus of segmental cues for word juncture. *Journal of the Acoustical Society of America, 62*, 714–719.

Norris, D.G. (1994). Shortlist: A connectionist model of continuous speech recognition. *Cognition, 52*, 189–234.

Norris, D., McQueen, J.M., & Cutler, A. (1995). Competition and segmentation in spoken word recognition. *Journal of Experimental Psychology: Learning, Memory, and Cognition, 21*, 1209–1228.

Norris, D., McQueen, J.M., Cutler, A., & Butterfield, S. (1997). The possible-word constraint in the segmentation of continuous speech. *Cognitive Psychology, 34*, 193–243.

Otake, T., Hatano, G., Cutler, A., & Mehler, J. (1993). Mora or syllable? Speech segmentation in Japanese. *Journal of Memory and Language, 32*, 258–278.

Pulgram, E. (1970). *Syllable, Word, Nexus, Cursus.* Mouton: The Hague.

Sebastián-Gallés, N., Dupoux, E., Seguí, J., & Mehler, J. (1992). Contrasting syllabic effects in Catalan and Spanish. *Journal of Memory and Language, 31*, 18–32.

Seguí, J. (1984). The syllable: A basic perceptual unit in speech processing? In H. Bouma & D.G. Bouwhuis (Eds.), *Attention and performance X: Control of language processes* (pp. 165–181). Hove, UK: Lawrence Erlbaum Associates Ltd.

Vroomen, J., & de Gelder, B. (1995). Metrical segmentation and lexical inhibition in spoken word recognition. *Journal of Experimental Psychology: Human Perception and Performance, 21*, 98–108.

Weber, A. (2000). The role of phonotactics in the segmentation of native and non-native continuous speech. In A. Cutler, J.M. McQueen & R. Zondervan (Eds.), *Proceedings of the Workshop on Spoken Word Access Processes* (pp. 143–146). Nijmegen: Max Planck Institute for Psycholinguistics.

APPENDIX A

Target-bearing items used in Experiment 1. The targets are spelled in standard English orthography; the contexts are transcribed in the International Phonetic Alphabet (IPA).

Monosyllables		Bisyllables	
Consonant	Schwa	Consonant	Schwa
tea/v/	tea/vəm/	mirror/f/	mirror/fəs/
plough/n/	plough/nəb/	feather/n/	feather/nəθ/
run/dʒ/	run/dʒəm/	ulcer/f/	ulcer/fəp/
pole/ʃ/	pole/ʃəb/	lager/f/	lager/fəd/
tell/θ/	tell/θəl/	heather/f/	heather/fəm/
fool/tʃ/	fool/tʃəl/	suffer/θ/	suffer/θək/
sun/tʃ/	sun/tʃən/	bother/n/	bother/nəm/
toy/n/	toy/nəθ/	cover/k/	cover/kəf/
chain/θ/	chain/θəb/	leather/n/	leather/nəd/
fun/tʃ/	fun/tʃəθ/	shiver/θ/	shiver/θəf/
doll/v/	doll/vəd/	quiver/n/	quiver/nəl/
shoe/m/	shoe/məf/	powder/m/	powder/məb/
spell/ʃ/	spell/ʃəb/	gather/m/	gather/məf/
dull/f/	dull/fəd/	eager/θ/	eager/θəb/
sea/ʃ/	sea/ʃəb/	ever/θ/	ever/θək/
oil/tʃ/	oil/tʃən/	anchor/θ/	anchor/θən/
vein/tʃ/	vein/tʃəl/	foster/n/	foster/nəθ/
boy/s/	boy/səl/	usher/f/	usher/fəm/
key/v/	key/vəm/	nether/f/	nether/fəθ/
smell/ʃ/	smell/ʃəs/	measure/m/	measure/məb/
knee/ð/	knee/ðəf/	tremor/f/	tremor/fəb/
bell/ʃ/	bell/ʃəf/	horror/θ/	horror/θəl/
zoo/θ/	zoo/θəb/	sugar/m/	sugar/məl/
gun/tʃ/	gun/tʃəθ/	weather/f/	weather/fəf/

APPENDIX B

Target-bearing items used in Experiment 2. The targets are spelled in standard English orthography; the contexts are given in IPA transcription

Weak-Strong triples (24)		
Tense	*Lax*	*Consonant*
/zi/canal	/zɛ/canal	/s/canal
/dʒaɪ/canoe	/dʒɛ/canoe	/s/canoe
/zɔʊ/carafe	/zɪ/carafe	/s/carafe
/gaʊ/caress	/gɪ/caress	/s/caress
/vɔ/cavort	/vɛ/cavort	/s/cavort
/vaɪ/collect	/vɒ/collect	/s/collect
/θɜ/command	/θɛ/command	/s/command
/vɔ/contain	/vʌ/contain	/s/contain
/laʊ/convert	/lɛ/convert	/s/convert
/tʃaɪ/convict	/tʃæ/convict	/s/convict
/laʊ/kebab	/lɛ/kebab	/s/kebab
/tɜ/lapel	/tʌ/lapel	/f/lapel
/lɑ/liaise	/læ/liaise	/b/liaise
/fu/mature	/fɒ/mature	/s/mature
/vɜ/morose	/vɛ/morose	/s/morose
/rɑ/neglect	/rɪ/neglect	/s/neglect
/dɑ/perturb	/dɛ/perturb	/s/perturb
/gɜ/possess	/gɪ/possess	/s/possess
/kaɪ/rebuke	/kɪ/rebuke	/ʃ/rebuke
/lɑ/regret	/lʌ/regret	/t/regret
/vɔʊ/reserve	/vɪ/reserve	/θ/reserve
/nɑ/resign	/nɛ/resign	/t/resign
/pɔɪ/resist	/pʌ/resist	/ʃ/resist
/tʃaɪ/result	/tʃʌ/result	/θ/result

Tense/Lax Weak-Strong items with no matching consonant item (24)

Tense	Lax
/vəʊ/banal	/vɒ/banal
/tʃaɪ/behave	/tʃɒ/behave
/lɑ/berserk	/lɛ/berserk
/rɑ/buffoon	/ræ/buffoon
/gɝ/cigar	/gɒ/cigar
/gaʊ/convey	/gɪ/convey
/dɔɪ/degree	/dʊ/degree
/gaʊ/demand	/gʌ/demand
/tʃɔɪ/dessert	/tʃɪ/dessert
/nɑ/deserve	/nɪ/deserve
/dʒaʊ/design	/dʒʌ/design
/nɔɪ/detect	/nɪ/detect
/pɔɪ/dissolve	/pɪ/dissolve
/vi/disturb	/væ/disturb
/hɔɪ/divorce	/hʌ/divorce
/tʃɔ/façade	/tʃɪ/facade
/gɝ/fatigue	/gɛ/fatigue
/kəʊ/gazelle	/kæ/gazelle
/tʃəʊ/gazette	/tʃɪ/gazette
/tʃaɪ/giraffe	/tʃæ/giraffe
/dʒaʊ/select	/dʒɪ/select
/dɝ/survey	/dɛ/survey
/nɑ/syringe	/nɒ/syringe
/gɝ/verbose	/gɛ/verbose

Strong-Weak triples (30)		
Tense	*Lax*	*Consonant*
/zəʊm/abbey	/zɛm/abbey	/m/abbey
/mɔɪz/absent	/mɛz/absent	/z/absent
/tʃəʊg/action	/tʃɛg/action	/g/action
/gɑz/ancient	/gɛz/ancient	/z/ancient
/gaʊz/angel	/gʌz/angel	/z/angel
/lɑθ/angle	/lɛθ/angle	/θ/angle
/nul/angry	/næl/angry	/l/angry
/fɔɪk/ankle	/fɛk/ankle	/k/ankle
/vəʊm/anxious	/vʌm/anxious	/m/anxious
/vɑf/apple	/vʌf/apple	/f/apple
/nɑθ/eagle	/næθ/eagle	/θ/eagle
/fuʃ/echo	/fɒʃ/echo	/ʃ/echo
/dəm/effort	/dɛm/effort	/m/effort
/kaɪv/equal	/kɪv/equal	/v/equal
/pɔɪf/extra	/pæf/extra	/f/extra
/gɑn/image	/gɛn/image	/n/image
/fuʃ/object	/fɛʃ/object	/ʃ/object
/nɜm/ointment	/nɪm/ointment	/m/ointment
/nɑdʒ/onion	/nædʒ/onion	/dʒ/onion
/sɑθ/option	/sɪθ/option	/θ/option
/fum/oven	/fɒm/oven	/m/oven
/dɑl/oyster	/dæl/oyster	/l/oyster
/kəʊs/ugly	/kɛs/ugly	/s/ugly
/vɑθ/uncle	/vɪθ/uncle	/θ/uncle
/vul/empty	/vɒl/empty	/l/empty
/faʊdʒ/anchor	/fɪdʒ/anchor	/dʒ/anchor
/ziθ/eager	/zɛθ/eager	/θ/eager
/dɔp/ever	/dʌp/ever	/p/ever
/lɔb/ulcer	/lʌb/ulcer	/b/ulcer
/dɑb/usher	/dɪb/usher	/b/usher

LANGUAGE AND COGNITIVE PROCESSES, 2001, *16* (5/6), 661–672

Lipreading and the compensation for coarticulation mechanism

Jean Vroomen

Tilburg University, Tilburg, The Netherlands

Beatrice de Gelder

Tilburg University, Tilburg, The Netherlands, and
Université Libre de Bruxelles, Brussels, Belgium

Listeners compensate for coarticulatory influences of one speech sound on another. We examined whether lipread information penetrates this perceptual compensation mechanism. Experiment 1 replicated the finding that when an /as/ or /aʃ/ sound preceded a /ta/-/ka/ continuum, more velar stops were perceived in the context of /as/. Experiments 2 and 3 investigated whether the same phoneme boundary shift would be obtained when the context was lipread instead of heard. An ambiguous sound between /as/ and /aʃ/ was dubbed on the video of a speaker articulating /as/ or /aʃ/. Subjects relied on the lipread information when identifying the ambiguous fricative sound as /s/ or /ʃ/, but there was no corresponding boundary shift in the following /ta/-/ka/ continuum. These results indicate that biasing of the fricative by lipread information and compensation for coarticulation can be dissociated.

A tacit assumption in psycholinguistic research has been that tasks involving the explicit identification and/or discrimination of phonemes (like phoneme monitoring or phoneme categorisation) tap much of the same processes as those involved in the implicit phonetic processing of natural speech. However, the idea that explicit phoneme categorisation directly reflects implicit phonetic processes may be too simplistic. In the present study, we indeed present results showing that explicit phoneme

Requests for reprints should be addressed to Jean Vroomen, Tilburg University, Dept. of Psychology, P.O. Box 90153, 5000 Le Tilburg, The Netherlands. E-mail: j.vroomen@kub.nl

The experiments were carried out as part of the PhD thesis of Vroomen (1992).

http://www.tandf.co.uk/journals/pp/01690965.html   DOI: 10.1080/01690960143000092

identification on the one hand, and so-called "compensation for coarticulation"—a process presumably at stake in the phonetic processing of natural speech—on the other, can dissociate.

Previously, it has been shown that ambiguous stops between /t/ and /k/ tend to be heard as /k/ after /s/ and as /t/ after /ʃ/ (Mann & Repp, 1981). The explanation given for this finding is that the perceptual system compensates for the coarticulation of the fricatives and stops which occurred in speech production. During production of a fricative-stop pair, the place of articulation of the stop is supposed to shift towards that of the fricative. A /k/ in the context of /s/ is thus more anterior than in a neutral context. The perceptual system compensates for this by adjusting the category boundary such that an "anterior" /k/ will nevertheless be heard as a velar /k/ when preceded by /s/. This effect has been replicated with an ambiguous fricative (henceforth /?/) midway between /s/ and /ʃ/ that was embedded in a lexical context biasing it towards /s/ or /ʃ/ (Elman & McClelland, 1988). More /k/ responses were obtained after christma? than after fooli?, as if listeners had heard /s/ in christma? and /ʃ/ in fooli?. Ever since, this finding has been taken as one of the prime examples of how high-order lexical information can affect phoneme perception, that is, of a proper "top-down" effect.

More recently, though, this picture has become more complicated. Pitt and McQueen (1998) argued that Elman and McClelland (1988) had confounded lexical context with transitional phoneme probabilities (TPs). Pitt and McQueen reasoned that an /s/ is more likely to follow /ə/ (as in christmas), and /ʃ/ is more likely to follow /I/ (as in foolish), and they argued that the results of Elman and McClelland should be attributed to this difference in TPs rather than to lexical biases. When Pitt and McQueen controlled words for TPs (e.g., as in juice and bush), they only found biases in the labelling of the fricative (listeners were lexically biased in that they tended to report bush when hearing bu? and juice when hearing jui?), but no subsequent shift in a /t/-/k/ continuum that immediately followed these words. In contrast, nonwords with TPs that biased the fricative either toward /s/ (as in /mi?/) or /ʃ/ (as in /neɪ?/) had an effect on labelling of both fricative and stop. Pitt and McQueen concluded that TPs rather than lexical effects were responsible for triggering the compensation for coarticulation mechanism observed by Elman and McClelland. They also argued that the dissociation between lexical bias on the fricative (bu? and jui?) with no accompanying shift in the /t/-/k/ continuum is a problem for TRACE (McClelland & Elman, 1986). This model has a single phoneme level that serves two functions, namely: (1) as output for explicit decisions about phonemes, and (2) as an intermediate processing stage between features and words. In such an architecture, biases in fricative identification and compensation for coarticulation should affect the same processing level, and so the effects should come and go hand-in-hand, without dissociation. In contrast, models like Merge (Norris, McQueen, & Cutler, 2000) are able to handle this dissociation because in Merge there is a distinction between phoneme decision nodes, which are lexically biased, and phonetic input nodes which are immune to lexical biases.

However, the TP-interpretation of the compensation for coarticulation data of Merge has also not been undisputed. Samuel (this issue) argues that the short monosyllabic words used by Pitt and McQueen (1998) may not have been potent enough to trigger a lexical top-down effect on compensation for coarticulation. He reports a lexical effect with long trisyllabic words while controlling TPs (i.e., bigram frequency). This finding is also in line with Elman and McClelland (1988; Experiment 3) who obtained a compensation for coarticulation effect with words in which differences in vowels (and hence TPs as defined by Pitt and McQueen) were explicitly controlled. A lexical effect on compensation for coarticulation may thus emerge with long, but not with short words.

One aim of the present study was a further attempt to dissociate biases on fricative identification from biases on the identification of the following stops. This dissociation has become important in the literature because it serves as evidence favouring Merge over TRACE (Norris et al., 2000). It seemed therefore important to show that the dissociation could also be found with materials other than short words controlled for TPs. We avoided the difficulty of using different TPs by combining the same auditory stimulus with lipread information. Fowler, Brown, and Mann (2000) conducted a study very similar to the present one. They used tokens of an auditory /da/-/ga/ continuum preceded by /al/ or /ar/. As originally reported by Mann (1980), the authors found that listeners identified ambiguous /da/-/ga/ syllables more often as /ga/ following /al/ than following /ar/. The same effect was found when instead of clear auditory /l/ or /r/, an ambiguous sound between /l/ and /r/ was dubbed on the video of a speaker saying /l/ or /r/ (a variant of the well-known 'McGurk effect'; McGurk & MacDonald, 1976). They observed that lipread information affected identification of the auditory ambiguous liquid, and more important, had an effect on identification of the following /da-ga/ continuum. Lipread information thus triggered compensation for coarticulation.

In the present study, we used the same methodology as in Fowler et al. (2000), but with fricative-stop tokens (an /a?/ as context token that preceded a /ta/-/ka/ continuum while dubbed on the video of a speaker saying /as/ or /aʃ/). The idea was that identification of the auditory ambiguous /?/ would be biased towards /s/ or /ʃ/ depending on the lipread information with which it was combined. The question was whether this bias in the fricative would trigger compensation for coarticulation so that an ambiguous stop between /t/ and /k/ would be heard as /k/ after lipread / s/ and as /t/ after lipread /ʃ/. If such an effect were obtained, it would show, as in Fowler et al., that lipread information penetrates early processes in speech perception. This would be in line with other evidence showing that lipread information can affect pre-phonetic processing stages (e.g., Green & Miller, 1985), and that, in general, there are cross-modal interactions at early stages of auditory and visual information processing (e.g., Vroomen & de Gelder, 2000a). Alternatively, if lipread information biases identification of the fricative, but has no effect on compensation for coarticulation, it would be evidence in favour of the distinction made in Merge (Norris et al., 2000) between implicit phonetic and explicit phonemic processes.

EXPERIMENT 1

To ensure that there were no stimulus confounds, we first wanted to replicate the finding that when an /as/ or /aʃ/ sound precedes a /ta/-/ka/ continuum, more velar stops are perceived in the context of /as/ if compared to /aʃ/.

Method

Subjects. Ten native speakers of Dutch took part in the experiment. None of them reported any problems with their hearing or sight.

Stimuli. A nine-step /ta/-/ka/ continuum was created that was preceded by /as/or /aʃ/. Natural tokens of /ta/, /ka/, /as/, /aʃ/, /asta/, /aska/, /aʃta / and / aʃka / were produced by a male native speaker of Dutch and recorded in a sound-damped booth. The speaker was also recorded on Sony U-Matic video for the audio-visual experiments. The auditory stimuli were low-pass filtered at 9.8 kHz, and then digitised at 20 kHz with a 12 bit analog-to-digital converter. The nine-step /ta/-/ka/ continuum was created by adding in proportion the amplitudes of the waveforms of the first 55 ms of a /t/ and /k/. The proportion of the /k/ increased from .2 to 1.0 in nine steps of .1 such that the /t/ endpoint contained .2 /k/ and .8 /t/, while the /k/ endpoint contained 1.0 /k/ and 0. /t/. The vocalic portion of the /ka/ sound was appended at the zero crossing of the so created stimuli.

From naturally produced /as/ and /aʃ/ tokens, the /s/ and /ʃ/ were cut out with the cut being made at a zero crossing. Then, the /ʃ/ was made to be of equal length as the /s/ by cutting out the final 64 ms, making each stimulus last 175 ms. The /s/ and /ʃ/ were appended at a zero crossing to the vocalic part of /as/ to make /as/ and /aʃ/ tokens. Finally, the /as/ and /aʃ/ tokens were prepended to the /ta/-/ka/ continuum with a 150 ms silence interval between them. The stimuli sounded natural and there were no discontinuities in the waveform audible as clicks. The stimuli were presented over two loudspeakers (Philips 420 car speakers with the peak amplitude set at 61 dB-A) in front of the subjects.

Procedure.   The stimuli were presented in two blocks of 90 stimuli each. Within each block, context sound (/as/ and /aʃ/) and token of the /ta/-/ka/ continuum was randomised. Each block was made up of five sequences of the eighteen possible combinations of context sound and token of the /ta/-/ka/ continuum.

Each subject participated in two sessions of 7 min each. Subjects pressed one out of four buttons to indicate whether they had heard /asta/, aska/, /aʃta/, or /aʃka/. The next stimulus was presented 2 s after a button press. As a warm-up, each block was preceded by nine different tokens.

Results and discussion

Figure 1 shows the identification functions of the /asta/-/aska/ and /aʃta/-/aʃka/ continua. The effect was exactly as predicted: an /as/ context increased the percentage of /ka/ responses compared with the /aʃ/ context.

Auditory *as* or *ash*

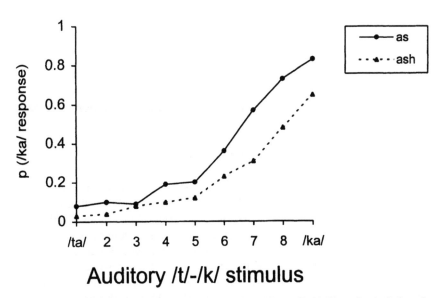

Figure 1.   The effect of an auditory /s/ or /ʃ/ sound on the perceived place of articulation of a following stop consonant.

The proportion of /ka/ responses was submitted to a 2 (context) × 9 (auditory levels) analysis of variance (ANOVA). As expected, identification functions rose from left to right as the target stimuli varied along the /ta/-/ka/ continuum, $F(8, 72) = 31.55$, $p < .001$. The effect of context was significant because more /ka/ responses were given when /as/ was the context than when /aʃ/ was the context, $F(1, 9) = 15.07$, $p < .001$. The interaction between context and the auditory information was significant indicating that the context effect was largest for the most ambiguous /ta/-/ka/ tokens, $F(8, 72) = 2.25$, $p < .05$. As can be seen in Figure 1, the most ambiguous part was near the /k/ endpoint of the continuum. This was mainly caused by three subjects who perceived less than 67% /k/ (i.e., 66%, 50%, and 50%) on even the most /k/-like stimulus (the /as/ context combined with the /ka/ endpoint). Individual analyses, however, confirmed that all subjects had the shift in the predicted direction. When a /ʃ/ was heard, the proportion of /ʃ/ responses (i.e., /aʃta/ plus /aʃka/) was .939 while it was .227 when an /s/ was heard, $F(1, 9) = 10.95$, $p < .009$. Thus, as expected, the heard context phoneme contributed to the identification of the fricative (a shift of 71.2%) and it shifted identification of the following stop. Experiment 1 thus replicated the basic compensation for articulation effect and shows that there were no confounds with the stimuli created for this series of experiments.

EXPERIMENT 2

Experiment 2 tested whether lipread information for the fricative can influence labelling of the fricative and whether, in addition, it affects labelling of the stop continuum.

Method

Subjects.   Ten new subjects drawn from the same population were paid for their participation.

Stimuli.   The nine stimuli from the /ta/-/ka/ continuum were now preceded by an /a?/. These sound tracks were then dubbed on the video of the speaker articulating either /aska/ or /aʃka/. The ambiguous /?/ was made in a similar way to the /ta/-/ka/ continuum, namely by summing the waveforms of a /s/ and /ʃ/. The tokens were spliced out from a naturally produced /as/ and /aʃ/ and they were made of equal length. By taking a proportion of .8 /s/ and .2 /ʃ/ a /?/ sound was made which was ambiguous between /s/ and /ʃ/. The rest of the /a?ta/-/a?ka/ tokens were exactly the same as in Experiment 1. The tokens were dubbed onto the video recording of the speaker saying /aska/ or /aʃka/. During the pronunciation of /s/ in /aska/, the speaker's lips were retracted, and during the pronunciation of /aʃ/ in /aʃka/, the lips were rounded. The pronunciation of the /k/ phoneme in the video recording was visually indistinguishable from /t/ since both phonemes belong to the same viseme cluster (i.e., a group of phonemes that are visually indistinguishable from each other; Walden, Prosek, Montgomery, Scherr, and Jones, 1977). Lipreading thus distinguished between /s/ and /ʃ/, but not between /t/ and /k/. The audio track was synchronised with the video at the onset of the initial vocalic portion of the stimuli. This resulted in natural looking stimulus events in which no desynchronisation of the audio track and video could be detected.

Procedure.   The stimuli were presented in 10 lists of random sequences of the 18 possible stimuli (nine auditory levels and two visual articulations). There was a 4 s pause between the successive stimulus events and a 10 s pause between successive sequences of 18 trials. Prior to testing, subjects were given 10 practice trials. Subjects were tested individually in a sound-damped booth. They viewed a 63-cm television monitor that presented both the auditory and visual dimensions of the speech stimuli. Subjects were seated at a distance of about 2 m from the monitor. The audio channel was set at a comfortable listening level with the peak amplitude at approximately 61 dB-A. Testing lasted about 20 min. Subjects were asked to respond orally whether they heard /asta/, /aska/, /aʃta/, or /aʃka/. Responses were written down by the experimenter.

Results and discussion

Figure 2 displays the proportion of /ka/ responses (i.e., the proportion of /aska/ plus /aʃka/ responses) as a function of the auditory levels, separately for the visual /as/ or /aʃ/ context. An ANOVA performed on the proportion of /ka/ responses indicated that the identification functions rose from left to right as the target stimuli varied from /ta/ to /ka/, $F(8, 72) = 169.05$, $p < .001$. The visual pronunciation of /as/ or /aʃ/ had a marginally significant effect on the identification of the /ta/-/ka/ stimuli, $F(1, 9) = 4.45$, $p = .064$. The interaction between the visual and auditory information of the stimuli was not significant, $F(8, 72) < 1$. However, although there was a small effect of the lipread context, it was in the opposite direction of what was expected. Instead of /as/, it was /aʃ/ that increased the proportion of /ka/ responses from .463 for the /as/ context to .483 for /aʃ/.

Performing a logit transformation on the data showed that the mean phoneme boundary in the /as/ context was 5.31 stimulus units while it was 5.15 in the /aʃ/ context, $F(1, 9) = 4.09$, $p = .074$. There was thus no phoneme-boundary shift towards the /ta/-end of the continuum when a visual /as/ pronunciation was seen. Individual analysis confirmed that only two out of ten subjects had a shift in the /ta/ direction.

Lipread *as* or *ash*

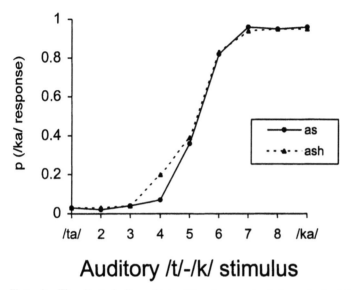

Figure 2.   The effect of a lipread /s/ or /ʃ/ on the perceived place of articulation of a following stop consonant.

An explanation for the failure of a visual /as/ to increase the proportion of /ka/ responses could be that the lipread information did not affect the identification of the fricative /s/ or /ʃ/. Since we asked our subjects to report both context and target stimulus, we were able to examine this. When an /s/ was seen, the proportion of /s/ responses (i.e., /asta/ plus /aska/) was .510 while it was .292 when a /ʃ/ was seen, $F(1, 9) = 8.14$, $p < .02$. Thus lipreading did indeed contribute to the identification of the fricative (a shift of 22%) , but not the stop. One might, however, argue that the effect of lipreading was too small for an effect to be observed on the following /ta/-/ka/ continuum, since only 61% of the context was correctly identified. We therefore tried to amplify the impact of lipreading in a second analysis by discarding all responses that were not in agreement with the lipread information. In the case a visual /s/ was seen, all responses with /ʃ/ were rejected (i.e., /aʃta/ and /aʃka /) and similarly, when a /ʃ/ was seen, all responses with /s/ (i.e., /asta/ and /aska/) were rejected. Thus, the lipread context was in this analysis always correctly identified. An ANOVA performed on these corrected measures indicated that the auditory variable was significant, $F(8, 56) = 99.28$, $p < .001$, but there was again neither an effect of lipreading, $F(1, 7) < 1$, NS, nor was the interaction significant, $F(8, 56) < 1$, NS. (Two subjects had to be discarded from this analysis because, on some steps on the continuum, the appropriate proportions could not be computed unless a division was made by zero.) The mean phoneme boundary was 5.31 stimulus units in the /as/ context, while it was 4.95 in the /aʃ/ context, $F(1, 7) = 1.53$, $p = .256$. Thus, the perceived fricative did not exert any influence on the phoneme boundary of the following /ta/-/ka/ continuum, even though in this analysis all subjects reported consistently /as/ or /aʃ/ depending on the context.

We were, however, still not satisfied with these results because in the latter analysis about 39% of the data had to be discarded. Moreover, it might be the case that coarticulatory effects would have been found if the /ta/-/ka/ tokens were more ambiguous since compensation effects are usually largest for the most ambiguous stimuli. In the final experiment, we therefore decreased the volume of the audio. It was hoped that this would boost the contribution of vision in the identification of the context and that the auditory information of the /ta/-/ka/ tokens would become more ambiguous.

EXPERIMENT 3

The same stimuli were used as in the previous experiment, except that the volume of the audio was lowered so as to increase the relative contribution of the lipread information.

Method

Subjects.   Seven new subjects, drawn from the same subject pool as before, were paid for their participation.

Stimuli and procedure.   The same as in Experiment 2, except that the volume of the audio was set at a level in which it became hard to distinguish /t/ from /k/ (the peak of the amplitude was at 51 dB-A).

Results and discussion

Figure 3 displays the proportion of /ka/ responses (i.e., the proportion of /aska/ plus /aʃka/ responses) as a function of the auditory levels, separately for the visual /as/ or /aʃ/ context. We first investigated whether subjects relied on vision in the identification of the context sound. The proportion of /s/ responses when /s/ was seen was .84, whereas it was .21 when a /ʃ/ was seen, $F(1, 6) = 39.23$, $p < .001$. Thus, lipreading contributed to the identification of the fricative (a shift of 63%) and the visual influence was boosted when compared with Experiment 2 (a 22% shift). Moreover, as

Lipread *as* or *ash*

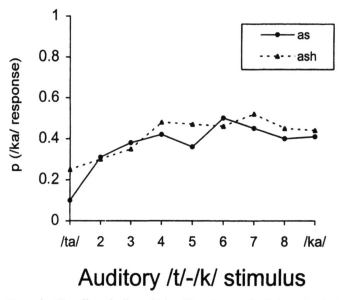

Figure 3. The effect of a lipread /s/ or /ʃ/ on the perceived place of articulation of a following stop consonant with the audio level at a low amplitude.

can be seen in Figure 3, identification of the /ta/-/ka/ tokens was much more difficult since the usual steep categorical identification functions were not obtained. However, there was again no effect of the visual information on the /ta/-/ka/ continuum. Lipreading an /s/ thus did not elevate the proportion of /ka/ responses.

An ANOVA performed on the proportion of /ka/ responses confirmed that the identification functions rose from left to right as the target stimuli varied from /ta/ to /ka/, $F(8, 48) = 3.16, p < .006$. The visual pronunciation of /as/ or /aʃ/ had a small and non-significant effect on the identification of the /ta/-/ka/ stimuli, $F(1, 6) = 4.12, p = .09$, but the effect was again in the opposite direction of what was found when /as/ or /aʃ/ were heard. When an /s/ was lipread, the proportion of /k/ responses was .39 whereas it was .44 when a /ʃ/ was lipread. (We report here only the responses in which the context was correctly identified. Including responses in which the context was incorrectly lipread did not change the results.) Thus, although we succeeded in increasing the contribution of vision and decreasing the quality of the /t/-/k/ tokens, there was still no effect of compensation for coarticulation.

GENERAL DISCUSSION

In the present study we showed that in a fricative-stop pair, lipread information biased identification of the fricative, but had no effect on compensation for coarticulation of the following stop. We thus observed a dissociation similar to the one reported by Pitt and McQueen (1998). They found that short words (bu? and jui?) biased identification of the fricative without consequences on labelling of the following stop. This pattern of results is accounted for by the Merge model (Norris et al., 2000) in which there is distinction between phonetic processes (biased by TPs) and phonemic decisions (biased by lexical information). On this account, lipread information would, like lexical information, affect phonemic decisions, but not phonetic processes.

This interpretation, though, is difficult to reconcile with Fowler et al. (2000) who found an effect of lipread information on compensation for coarticulation in a liquid-stop pair. It remains to be investigated whether the difference between our study and their study stems from the different phonemes that were used (fricative-stop versus liquid-stop). One possibility is that subjects may find it more difficult to distinguish lipread /s/ from /ʃ/ than distinguishing lipread /r/ from /l/. Fowler et al. obtained a 77% shift in identification of the liquid, whereas we obtained a 22% (Expt. 2) and 63% (Expt. 3) shift of the fricative. Although our lipread information was possibly weaker than in Fowler et al., our shifts are comparable with Pitt and McQueen (1998) who obtained TP-induced shifts of 17% and 37%, but who nevertheless obtained an effect on compensation for coarticulation. So at first sight, it seems that our fricative bias was within the range in which effects on compensation for coarticulation can be observed.

Despite these conflicting data about the stage at which lipreading affects speech processing, it is nevertheless clear that compensation for coarticulation can dissociate from labelling of the context phoneme. It shows that variables that affect explicit categorisation of phonemes may not affect processes involved in the phonetic processing of natural speech. There are other studies that have pointed out a similar contrast between processes involved in explicit phoneme identification and those involved in the processing of natural speech. From the neuropsychological literature it is known that the ability to identify CV syllables is a poor predictor of auditory comprehension deficits. On this basis, Hickok and Poeppel (2000) speculate that there is, akin to vision, a ventral cortical pathway for word recognition and a dorsal pathway for sublexical discrimination and identification. Norris et al. (2000) also make a strict distinction between phoneme units and decision units (for comments, see Vroomen & de Gelder, 2000b). Moreover, it is well-known that illiterates, Chinese, and dyslexics have problems with tasks requiring manipulation of speech segments at a subsyllabic level, while at the same time they have no apparent deficit in spoken word recognition (Bertelson, de Gelder, Tfouni, & Morais, 1989; de Gelder, Vroomen, & Bertelson, 1993). This all suggests that speech perception is less transparent than psycholinguistic tasks assume.

REFERENCES

Bertelson, P., de Gelder, B., Tfouni, L., & Morais, J. (1989). The metaphonological abilities of adult illiterates: new evidence of heterogeneity. *European Journal of Cognitive Psychology, 1*, 239–250.

de Gelder, B., Vroomen, J., & Bertelson, P. (1993). Effects of alphabetic reading competence on language representation in bilingual Chinese subjects. *Psychological Research, 55*, 315–321.

Elman, J.L., & McClelland, J.L. (1988). Cognitive penetration of the mechanisms of perception: Compensation for coarticulation of lexically restored phonemes. *Journal of Memory and Language, 27*, 143–165.

Fowler, C.A., Brown, J.M., & Mann, V.A. (2000). Contrast effects do not underlie effects of preceding liquids on stop-consonant identification by humans. *Journal of Experimental Psychology: Human Perception and Performance, 26*, 877–888.

Green, K.P., & Miller, J.L. (1985). On the role of visual rate information in phonetic perception. *Perception and Psychophysics, 38*, 269–276.

Hickok, G., & Poeppel, D. (2000). Towards a functional neuroanatomy of speech perception. *Trends in Cognitive Sciences, 4*, 131–138.

Mann, V.A. (1980). Influence of preceding liquid on stop-consonant perception. *Perception & Psychophysics, 28*, 407–412.

Mann, V.A., & Repp, B.H. (1981). Influence of preceding fricative on stop consonant perception. *Journal of the Acoustical Society of America, 69*, 548–558.

McClelland, J.L., & Elman, J.L. (1986). The TRACE model of speech perception. *Cognitive Psychology, 18*, 1–86.

McGurk, H., & MacDonald, J. (1976). Hearing lips and seeing voices. *Nature, 264*, 746–748.

Norris, D., McQueen, J.M., & Cutler, A. (2000). Merging information in speech recognition: feedback is never necessary. *Behavioral and Brain Sciences, 23*, 299–370.

Pitt, M.A., & McQueen, J.M. (1998). Is compensation for coarticulation mediated by the lexicon? *Journal of Memory and Language, 39*, 347–370.

Samuel, A. (this issue). Some empirical tests of Merge's architecture. *Language and Cognitive Processes, 16*, 709–714.

Vroomen, J., & de Gelder, B. (2000a). Sound enhances visual perception: Cross-modal effects of auditory organization on vision. *Journal of Experimental Psychology: Human Perception and Performance, 26*, 1583–1590 .

Vroomen, J., & de Gelder, B. (2000b). Why not model spoken word recognition instead of phoneme monitoring? *Brain and Behavioral Sciences, 23*, 349–350.

Vroomen, J. (1992). *Hearing voices and seeing lips: Investigations in the psychology of lipreading.* Unpublished doctoral dissertation, Tilburg University, Tilburg.

Walden, B.E., Prosek, R.A., Montgomery, A.A., Scherr, C.K., & Jones, C.J. (1977). Effects of training on the visual recognition of consonants. *Journal of Speech and Hearing Research, 20*, 130–145.

LANGUAGE AND COGNITIVE PROCESSES, 2001, *16* (5/6), 673–681

Phoneme-like units and speech perception

Terrance M. Nearey

Department of Linguistics, University of Alberta, Edmonton, Alberta, Canada

Decoene (1997) discusses two hypotheses concerning the relationship between stimulus properties and syllables in speech perception. The first, Decoene calls the *phonological hypothesis.* It is a compositional account whereby phonemes link directly to stimulus-properties, but syllables link to stimuli only indirectly through their phoneme constituents. This will be referred to as *perceptual phoneme factorability* below. Decoene's second hypothesis, the *integrative routine hypothesis,* is a more holistic account of syllable perception. Under it, basic stimulus-to-phoneme links can be supplemented by "... direct connections between syllabic units and certain stimulus features" (1997, p. 878). Other recent hypotheses about speech perception admit even more radical departures from phoneme factorability. For example, Goldinger's (1998) episodic lexicon posits direct links between word-sized symbolic units and the memory traces of individual utterances. Such a framework, in principle at least, allows for arbitrary stimulus-to-word links. This paper reviews certain systematic results from listeners' identification of monosyllabic words and nonwords in English. It is argued that these results arise naturally under the phoneme factorability hypothesis, but remain unexplained on more holistic 'large unit' accounts of word perception.

Allen (1994) reviews early work by Fletcher (1953), on the correct identification of naturally spoken nonsense CVCs in noise. This work shows evidence for a type of perceptual phoneme factorability: syllable scores can be extremely well predicted from the marginal correct

Requests for reprints should be addressed to: Terrance M. Nearey, Department of Linguistics, 4–32 Assiniboia Hall, University of Alberta, Edmonton, Alberta, Canada T6G 2E7. Email: t.nearey@ualberta.ca

This work was supported by SSHRC. Thanks to John Kingston for helpful comments.

http://www.tandf.co.uk/journals/pp/01690965.html   DOI: 10.1080/01690960143000173

identification of their constituent phonemes. Fletcher's summary of this behaviour can be stated as:

$$P_s = P_{C_1} P_V P_{C_2}, \tag{1}$$

where P_s is the probability of correct identification of an entire C_1VC_2 syllable and P_{C_1}, P_V and P_{C_2} are the marginal probabilities of correct identification of the constituent phonemes. In Fletcher's experiments the marginal P_{C_1}, P_V and P_{C_2} were nearly equal, so (1) can be approximated by

$$P_s = P_p^3, \tag{2}$$

where $P_p = (P_{C_1} + P_V + P_{C_2}) / 3$, the average correct identification rate of the three phonemes.

In a later study of the identification of CVCs in noise, Boothroyd and Nittrouer (1988) generalised Fletcher's formula to $P_s = (P_p)^j$. The value of j is referred to as the j-factor, estimated empirically by $\log P_s / \log P_p$. Boothroyd and Nittrouer (1988) found an average j value very near 3.0 for nonsense CVCs. The authors interpret j as an estimate of the number of informationally independent units that compose a syllable (see also Allen, 1994). When j is exactly 3.0, this is equivalent to the approximation (2) of Fletcher's phoneme independence model (1). The smallest possible value for a j-factor is 1.0. This will occur in the extreme case where there are only two kinds of trials: (i) the entire syllable (and, hence, each of its three phonemes) is perceived correctly, or (ii) the syllable and each of its phonemes are perceived incorrectly. In more realistic situations, the minimum of 1.0 will be approached when P_s scores are much higher than predicted from (1). The simulations discussed below illustrate how intermediate cases, between extreme holistic syllable behaviour ($j = 1.0$) and purely compositional phoneme behaviour ($j = 3.0$), may arise.

Intermediate values of j have also been found empirically. For example, for *real* CVC words included in their experiments, Boothroyd and Nittrouer (1988) found j to be only about 2.5. (Data in their appendix show $M = 3.05$, $SD = 0.14$ for nonwords and $M = 2.43$, $SD = 0.07$ for words across noise conditions.) This suggests that words are more holistically perceived than are nonsense syllables. However, Allen (1994) suggests that such deflation of the j-factor for real words may result from lexical redundancy or "context entropy". Such redundancy could arise from the statistical distribution of *symbols* (words and phonemes) in a way that is entirely stimulus-independent.

It is easy to construct a phoneme-based recogniser that achieves the independence benchmark j-factor of 3.0 for CVC syllables (see Nearey, in press-a, Appendix A). But perhaps such a result is also easy to achieve using a more holistic syllable-based recogniser; namely, one that relies on Decoene's "... direct connections between syllabic units and certain stimulus features" (1997, p. 878). If so, then *j*-factor results may have no bearing whatsoever on the 'size of units' issue. If, however *j*-factors near 3.0 are either impossible or very difficult to achieve with a more general CVC recogniser, then the case for strictly phoneme-based perception is strengthened considerably.

To explore this question, Nearey (in press-a) constructed "pseudo-synthetic" cue patterns for each of 1000 CVC syllables, with 10 possible segments in each phoneme slot. The recognition system was a Bayesian classifier incorporating parameters of the Gaussian distributions that were also used to generate the cue patterns for the virtual stimuli. These parameters were the means for each of the 1000 syllables and the standard deviations of a single (pooled over all syllables) diagonal covariance matrix (including variance due to the simulated channel noise discussed below). This classifier is capable of recognising arbitrary patterns corresponding to fully specified syllable templates and hence will be referred to as a *holistic syllable recogniser.*

(Note that marginal phoneme scores, P_{C_1}, P_V and P_{C_2} can be calculated for *any* syllable recogniser by simply assigning a unique (but possibly arbitrary) phoneme spelling to each syllable. Whether or not such a spelling bears any systematic relation to the stimulus properties of the syllable, phoneme identification scores are calculated with reference to the nominal phoneme spelling. Thus, if a presented syllable labelled as /pal/ was recognised as the syllable /pol/, the phoneme identification score can be represented as the ordered triplet [1 0 1]. The scores in each of the three phoneme slots are then averaged separately over all the words and over the nonwords in the set of trials to yield the marginal phoneme identification rates.)

The recogniser was tested with virtual stimuli generated by random trial-to-trial perturbation of a set of syllable means that were constructed by a simple synthesis-by-rule scheme based loosely on observed speech patterns. For the first such test, the cue patterns of those syllable means were constrained to be *acoustically phoneme factorable* in the sense defined below. Eight cues were manipulated. Four (*F*1 and *F*2 target frequencies of the vowel, and initial and final consonant voicing duration) had fixed values for each phoneme. Four others (initial and final 'dominant frequency' [spectral centre of gravity of burst for stops, *F*2 steady state for sonorant consonants], and *F*2 onset for initials and *F*2 offset for finals) embodied simple, systematic coarticulation effects. These followed locus-equation constraints (Sussman, Fruchter, Hilbert, & Sirosh, 1998) between vocalic and consonantal cues.

To illustrate a locus-equation constraint, consider the specification of the $F2$ onset cue for an initial /b/:

$$F2_{onset} (/b/) = a_{/b/}\ F2_v + b_{/b/}\ . \tag{3}$$

Here, $F2_{onset} (/b/)$ is the value of $F2$ at the onset of the transition into the vowel; $a_{/b/}$ and $b_{/b/}$ are consonant-specific (but vowel-independent) constants; and $F2_v$ is the value of $F2$ in the middle of the vocoid. A key feature of this rule is that its constants depend only on the phonemic identity of the initial consonant /b/. Although $F2v$ for any given syllable will ultimately depend on the phonemic identity of the vowel in that syllable, the rule specifying the initial $F2$ transition value does not make reference to the vowel category and a single consonant transition rule *applies to all phonemic vowel contexts*. Thus, the syllable patterns in the 8-dimensional cue space were constrained to lie in an orderly subspace consistent with simple constraints expressible at the *phoneme* level and are in this sense phoneme factorable.

Variations in signal-to-noise ratio in the experiments of Boothroyd and Nittrouer (1988) were approximated by adding simulated channel noise to the mean cue pattern for each syllable on each virtual trial. This noise consisted of random normal deviates, with increasingly larger variance simulating the successively noisier conditions. A random 13% of the CVCs were designated as real words (yielding approximately the ratio of real word to potential CVCs used by Boothroyd & Nittrouer, 1988).

Simulations showed that it was easy to obtain j values near 3.0 for nonsense syllables *when the means of the syllabic templates were phoneme factorable*; that is, when they were confined to the orderly subspace (of the full 8-dimensional cue space) imposed by constraints stated at the phoneme level. It was also relatively easy to simulate the reduced j-factor of 2.5 for real words by means of a word bias factor. This approach was inspired by Broadbent's (1967) work on frequency effects in word intelligibility experiments. The bias simply multiplied the stimulus-based likelihood of each simulated real word by a factor of 4.5, while non-words were left at their original values.

Thus, at least some phoneme-factorable stimulus patterns *can* lead to the target j-factor patterns using the holistic syllable recogniser. However, at least for the cases studied, the behaviour of the holistic recogniser is virtually identical to results produced by a phoneme-based recogniser applied to the same stimuli (Nearey, in press-a, Appendix A). It is hardly surprising that a holistic syllable recogniser produces target *j-factor* behaviour when its overall peformance is indistinguishable from a phoneme-based recogniser.

But suppose underlying cue-patterns are not perfectly compositional such that a conventional phonemic description captures a family resemblance among syllables, but there remains an irreducible residue of unique stimulus properties linked to each syllable. A recogniser with "... direct connections between syllabic units and certain stimulus features" (Decoene, 1997, p. 878) should be able to take advantage of this residue. Thus, syllable identification rates should be higher than predicted from marginal phoneme probabilities and, consequently, j-factors should be deflated toward their lower bound of 1.0.

Additional simulations showed that when the holistic recogniser is presented with stimuli containing even very small syllabic residues, j-factors are indeed markedly less than 3.0. Such residues were created by constructing syllable templates whose cue patterns were 'near misses' to exact functions of their phoneme constituents. This was done by starting with the pure phoneme-factorable patterns, but then systematically perturbing them by adding a random offset to each cue for each syllable template. Given these fixed (but no longer fully phoneme-factorable) templates, channel noise was again simulated by adding fresh Gaussian deviates to each template mean on each virtual trial. These simulations showed that even a *"soupçon* of syllabic *je ne sais quoi"* is sufficient to cause substantial deflation of the j-factor for both simulated words and nonwords. If factorable syllabic templates are perturbed by Gaussian random variates with a standard deviation of about 5% of the original ranges of the cues, the resulting template patterns are still very strongly correlated ($r > .97$) with those of the corresponding factorable model. Even in such a mildly "syllable-contaminated" case, j-factors are reduced by about 0.5 from the original condition, with a value of about 2.5 for nonsense and 2.0 for real words. Additional simulations were run with a larger fraction of syllabic residue. The means of the "20% syllable contaminated" models were still fairly strongly correlated with those of their factorable seed templates ($r > .78$). In this case, the j-factors are severely deflated, averaging roughly 1.5 for both words and nonwords. (Recall that the lower bound for the j-factor is 1.0.)

Although no analytic proof can be offered at this time, the above results suggest that general syllable-based recognisers may be able to achieve j-factor patterns similar to those found in human perception only when the input cue patterns are constrained to be phoneme factorable. It is logically possible that j-factor behaviour reflects production constraints independent of the architecture of the recogniser, as in the first simulations reported above. But if syllable cue patterns are factorable because of production constraints, then syllable-based and phoneme-based recognizers will exhibit similar behavior. The results summarised above suggest that a general syllable recogniser can achieve j-factor patterns found in perception experiments only when its added flexibility is superfluous; that is, only for stimulus patterns for which the more parsimonious phoneme-based recogniser is entirely adequate. Conversely, as soon as we move to cue patterns for which a syllable-based recogniser would have a systematic advantage, j-factors become severely deflated.

The j-factor results sketched above compute average correct identification rates of syllables and of phonemes over an entire listening condition. "Trading relation" experiments with synthetic syllables provide a second source of evidence for the perceptual adequacy of simple phoneme-based recognition models. These experiments track stimulus-response mappings for individual syllables. Mermelstein (1978) conducted an experiment with synthetic /bVC/ stimuli spanning the English words, bad, bed, bat, and bet by varying F1 frequency and the duration of the vocoid. Mermelstein's analysis indicated that a change in either cue affected perception of both the vowel and the final consonant. However, he also concluded that vowel and consonant choices were made completely independently of each other. Formally, $P_{VC_2} = P_V P_{C_2}$, which is compatible with Fletcher's factorability equation (1).

Whalen's (1989) analysis of his own similar *"bad-bet"* experiment shows that Mermelstein's hypothesis cannot fully describe the newer results. However, Nearey (1990) shows that a slight modification to Mermelstein's model accommodates Whalen's new data. Nearey's revised model also involves bottom-up evaluation of stimulus properties by phoneme-level elements. To this it adds small (stimulus-independent) biases favouring the specific VC combination patterns at and ed. Although they may have quite distinct ultimate causes (e.g., extrinsic allophony, compensation for coarticulation, etc.; see Nearey, 1990, 1992, 1997), these rhyme biases have essentially the same effect on classification as do the frequency biases of Broadbent (1967) or the real-word biases in the simulations of Nearey (in press a).

Nearey (in press b) shows that non-parametric j-factor analysis can be extended to trading relation experiments. Consider Whalen's bad-bet experiment. Because of the nature of the stimuli, the first consonant is always perceived as /b/, so $P_{C_1} = 1.0$ for $C_1 = $ /b/. In experiments with natural speech (e.g., Boothroyd & Nittrouer, 1988), probabilities are calculated only with respect to the "correct" syllable and are aggregated over all words (and again over all non-words) in a single noise condition. For synthetic continuum experiments, one can calculate the relevant quantities for each syllabic choice for each stimulus. Since response probabilities for C_1, V and C_2 vary greatly over stimuli, it is appropriate to define the relevant average phoneme probability, P_p', as the *geometric mean* of the probabilities of response to the constituent phonemes. This ensures that when (1) is true, $P_s = (P_p')^3$, where $P_p' = (P_{C_1} P_V P_{C_2})^{1/3}$, for arbitrary phoneme probabilities. (For numerical reasons, only syllables with response probabilities between .05 and .95

are considered. Cases where all but one of the marginal segment probabilities are 1.0 are also ignored, because then $j = log\ P_s\ /\ log\ P_p$' must equal 3.0.)

Applying these methods to Whalen's *bad-bet* data yields estimates of *j* of 3.19 for *bad*, 2.83 for *bat*, 2.86 for *bed* and 3.17 for *bet* (*SD*s ranged from 0.15 to 0.21). A *j*-factor of less than 3.0 indicates that word probabilities are relatively higher than predicted under phoneme independence (equation 1). The slightly smaller than 3.0 values for the words *bad* and *bet* (and the slightly larger than 3.0 values for *bat* and *bet*) are compatible with the pattern of diphone bias effects of Nearey's (1990) logistic model for this data.

Other continuum experiments show *j*-factors even closer to the theoretical independence value. Nearey's (1997) /hVC/ data show *j*-factors ranging from 2.83 to 3.11 over the 10 response syllables (*SD*s range from 0.28 to 0.32). In Massaro and Cohen's (1983) final experiment, a two-dimensional stimulus continuum spans the syllables /bla, dra, bla, dla/. The authors' own analysis suggests the need for a substantial bias term (implemented by their *contextual features*) against the phonotactically illegal */dla/. However, Nearey (in press-b) presents analysis of these data showing values that cluster tightly about the pure independence *j* = 3 curve. Numerical calculation yields *j*-factors of 2.94 to 3.06 over the four syllables (*SD*s ranging from 0.14 to 0.21). Nearey offers a tentative explanation for this apparent discrepancy with Massaro and Cohen's interpretation. This explanation involves admitting more complex *stimulus-to-phoneme relationships* than allowed for either by Massaro and Cohen's models or by Nearey's logistic models when the latter are constrained to use purely linear stimulus contrasts. Phoneme-based logistic models that add quadratic stimulus contrasts provide excellent fits to the classification data and predict (analytically) *j*-factors of 3.0 for all syllables (Nearey, in press-b).

One other continuum experiment shows larger deviations of *j*-factors from independence than the cases discussed so far. Whalen (1989) presents a second experiment spanning the words *sue, see, shoe,* and *see* in a two-dimensional cue space varying cutoff frequency of frication noise and *F*2 of a synthetic vocoid. Whalen demonstrates that these data also fail to meet Mermelstein's independence condition. Although the deviations in question are amenable to the same kind of diphone bias as in the *bad-bet* case (Nearey, 1990), the biases are considerably larger. This result is confirmed by a simple *j*-factor analysis of the raw data. Since the words in question are two segments long, the target *j*-factor for independence is 2.0. The values are nearly a full point larger for the syllables "shoe" (*j* = 2.50) and *see* (2.55) than for *sue* (1.55) and *she* (1.57; *SD*s range from 0.14 to 0.31 over all syllables).

The reasons for this relatively larger effect cannot be determined without further research. However, new simulations (analogous to those of Nearey, in press-a) with pseudosynthetic CVs based on this example show the general pattern of results can be readily obtained from a phoneme-factorable production model for certain stimulus configurations. Specifically, large biases and skewed j-factor patterns can be observed when (i) the two-dimensional cue space is first normalised by a linear transformation producing within-syllable covariance matrices that are unit diagonal in the normalised coordinates; (ii) syllable means formed the vertices of a parallelogram in the normalised coordinates (resulting from strictly additive effects of C and V on cue patterns); and (iii) those parallelograms deviate substantially from rectangles in the normalised coordinates. When the vertices lie on a rectangle, however, j-factors approach independence values, and best-approximating logistic models will not require bias terms. See Nearey (1992) for a discussion of the relation of the geometry of stimulus means to category boundaries of logistic models in some simple cases.

In summary, the hypothesis of phoneme factorability of syllable perception is compatible with a wide range of experimental data from speech categorisation experiments. Such factorability arises naturally from a phoneme-based recognition model. It is incumbent on proponents of more general syllable-based theories to demonstrate how factorability can plausibly arise in their own framework. The simulation studies sketched above suggest that factorability is a fragile phenomenon that does not arise naturally from a general syllable-based recognition model. It is possible to argue that apparent phoneme factorability in perception is merely a passive reflection of *production* constraints. But strict phoneme-based constraints on production outputs mean that no additional accuracy can obtain from a more general syllable-based model: phoneme-based recognition will work just as well. The postulation of extra entities (here, direct syllable-to-stimulus links) with no clear empirical consequences for recognition is certainly a violation of Occam's razor. It is also bad statistical modelling practice, as it typically leads directly to the problems of overfitting and undertraining.

REFERENCES

Allen, J. (1994). How do humans process and recognize speech? *IEEE Transactions in Speech and Audio Processing, 2,* 567–577.

Boothroyd, A., & Nittrouer. S. (1988). Mathematical treatment of context effects in phoneme and word recognition. *Journal of the Acoustical Society of America, 84,* 101–114.

Broadbent, D.E. (1967). Word-frequency effect and response bias. *Psychological Review, 74,* 1–14.

Decoene, S. (1997). The representational basis of syllable categories. *Perception and Psychophysics, 59,* 877–884.

Fletcher, H. (1953). *Speech and hearing in communication*. New York: Kreiger.

Goldinger, S.D. (1998). Echoes of echoes? An episodic theory of lexical access. *Psychological Review, 105*, 251–279.

Massaro, D., & Cohen, M. (1983). Phonological context in speech perception. *Perception and Psychophysics, 34*, 338–348.

Mermelstein, P. (1978). On the relationship between vowel and consonant identification when cued by the same acoustic information. *Perception and Psychophysics, 23*, 331–335.

Nearey, T. (1990). The segment as a unit of speech perception. *Journal of Phonetics, 18*, 347–373.

Nearey, T. (1992). Context effects in a double-weak theory of speech perception. *Language and Speech, 35*, 153–171.

Nearey, T. (1997). Speech perception as pattern recognition. *Journal of the Acoustical Society of America, 101*, 3241–3254.

Nearey, T. (in press-a). The factorability of phonological units in speech perception: Simulating results on speech reception in noise. In Smyth, R. (Ed.), *Festschrift for Bruce L. Derwing.*

Nearey, T. (in press-b). On the factorability of phonological units in speech perception. In J. Local, et al. (Eds.) *Papers in Laboratory Phonology VI*. Cambridge: Cambridge University Press.

Sussman, H., Fruchter, D., Hilbert, J., & Sirosh, J. (1998). Linear correlates in the speech signal: The orderly output constraint. *Behavioral and Brain Sciences, 21*, 241–299.

Whalen, D. (1989). Vowel and consonant judgments are not independent when cued by the same information. *Perception and Psychophysics, 46*, 284–292.

LANGUAGE AND COGNITIVE PROCESSES, 2001, *16* (5/6), 683–690

Mapping from acoustic signal to phonetic category: Internal category structure, context effects and speeded categorisation

Joanne L. Miller

Department of Psychology, Northeastern University, Boston, USA

INTRODUCTION

The early stages of speech perception are often characterised in terms of a perceptual mapping between acoustic signal and prelexical phonetic representations. Although early research focused on the abstract categorical nature of these representations, more recent findings have shown that phonetic categories are internally structured in a graded fashion, with some members of the category perceived as better exemplars than others (e.g., Kuhl, 1991; Miller, 1994; Oden & Massaro, 1978; Samuel, 1982). In this paper I present highlights from two recent investigations in our laboratory that examine this structure and its role in processing. The first focuses on how different types of contextual factors influence internal category structure and the second focuses on the role of internal category structure in speeded phonetic categorisation.

CONTEXT EFFECTS

A widespread finding in the study of speech perception is that the mapping from acoustic signal to phonetic category is highly context-dependent. One form this context dependency takes involves the boundaries between phonetic categories. Numerous studies have shown that both acoustic-phonetic factors and higher-level linguistic factors systematically alter the

Requests for reprints should be addressed to Joanne L. Miller, Department of Psychology, Northeastern University, Boston, MA 02115. E-mail: jlmiller@neu.edu

This research was supported by NIH Grant DC 00130 to J. L. Miller and by a Minority Fellowship from the Acoustical Society of America to Sean Allen. The author thanks Sean Allen and Larry Brancazio for their helpful comments on an earlier version of the paper.

http://www.tandf.co.uk/journals/pp/01690965.html   DOI: 10.1080/01690960143000065

location of such category boundaries along acoustic continua (see Repp & Liberman, 1987). Over the past few years we have been investigating whether one of these types of contextual factors, namely acoustic-phonetic factors, alters not only the location of phonetic category boundaries, but also which stimuli within a category are perceived as the best category exemplars. Our basic strategy for these studies has been to create extended speech series that deliberately include poor as well as good exemplars of a category, and ask listeners to rate the stimuli in terms of category goodness. The critical issue is how variation in a given contextual factor affects which stimuli along the acoustic continuum are perceived as the best category exemplars.

For example, in one of our early studies on the acoustic-phonetic contextual factor of speaking rate (Miller & Volaitis, 1989), we created two voice-onset-time (VOT) series. Each series ranged from short VOT values appropriate for /bi/ through longer VOT values appropriate for /pi/ to very long VOT values beyond those appropriate for /pi/. The /p/s with very long VOT values (which, for purposes of explication, we label */p/) sounded breathy and exaggerated. The two series differed from each other in speaking rate, specified by syllable duration. In a preliminary two-choice identification experiment, we found that as speaking rate slowed, the /b/-/p/ category boundary shifted toward longer VOT values, as expected from previous research. In the main experiment, which used a category-goodness rating task, we found that the location of the best-exemplar range within the category (defined as the range of stimuli receiving ratings that were at least 90% of that given to the highest-rated stimulus in the series; see Miller & Volaitis (1989) for details) shifted to longer VOT values with the slower speaking rate. In subsequent studies, we have found similar effects on best-exemplar location for other acoustic-phonetic contextual factors, including sentential speaking rate (Wayland, Miller, & Volaitis, 1994) and phonetic-feature context (Volaitis & Miller, 1992) (and see Hodgson & Miller (1996) for related findings). Taken together, these studies demonstrate that changes in acoustic-phonetic context can alter the location of the best exemplars of a category along an acoustic continuum.

In a recent investigation (Allen & Miller, in press) we asked whether a shift in best-exemplar location would occur if a higher-level linguistic contextual factor, rather than an acoustic-phonetic contextual factor, was manipulated. We focused on the higher-level contextual factor of lexical status, i.e., whether a sequence of phonetic segments forms a word of the language or a nonword. It is well known that lexical status affects category boundary location (Ganong, 1980). For example, if listeners are presented stimuli from the two VOT series *beef-peef* and *beace-peace*, they tend to identify stimuli with mid-range VOT values along each series so as to form a real word of the language, *beef* in the first series and *peace* in the second series. As a consequence, the /b/-/p/ category boundary is located at a longer VOT value for the *beef-peef* series than the *beace-peace* series. The question we addressed was whether the effect of lexical status is limited to the region of the category boundary, where there is ambiguity in category membership, or whether the effect pervades the category, altering which stimuli are perceived as the best exemplars.

To answer this question, we created two matched extended VOT series. One ranged from a word to a nonword (*beef-peef-*peef*) and the other ranged from a nonword to a word (*beace-peace-*peace*). In a preliminary two-choice identification experiment we found, as expected, that the /b/-/p/ boundary was located at a longer VOT value for the *beef-peef-*peef* series than the *beace-peace-*peace* series. In the main experiment, listeners were asked to judge the goodness of the initial consonant of each token from the two series as an instance of /p/ using a 1–7 rating scale. We expected to obtain non-monotonic goodness functions for both series. The critical question was whether the stimuli judged to be the best exemplars of the /p/ category would be shifted to longer VOT values for the *beef-peef-*peef* series compared to the *beace-peace-*peace* series.

The main finding, confirmed by statistical analysis, was that the change in lexical status did not shift the location of the entire best-exemplar range, as occurs with acoustic-phonetic contextual factors, but instead shifted only that part of the range bordering the category-boundary region. This is illustrated in the left panel of Figure 1. Initial inspection of the group functions (based on smoothed individual functions) revealed an overall difference in height between the functions, with the tokens receiving somewhat higher ratings when the /p/ was judged in the context of the word (*peace*) than the nonword (*peef*). To adjust for this height difference,

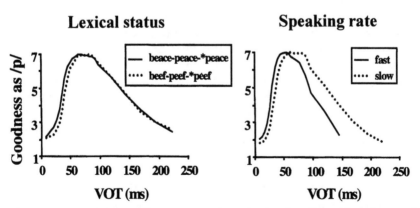

Figure 1. Normalised group goodness functions showing the effect of lexical status (left panel) and speaking rate (right panel) on the internal structure of the /p/ category. (Adapted from Figures 1 and 2 of Allen & Miller, in press.)

which is not relevant to our main question, we normalised the two group functions so that they both peaked at a value of 7, and it is these normalised functions that are shown in the figure. As can be seen, the location of the best-exemplar range remained relatively unchanged with the change in lexical status, a pattern which contrasts with the change in best-exemplar location that is found for acoustic-phonetic contextual factors, such as speaking rate. To ensure that this qualitatively different pattern was not due to some idiosyncrasy of our stimuli, we conducted a control experiment in which we altered the speaking rate of the stimuli in the *beace-peace-*peace* series, and tested a new group of listeners using the same procedures on the fast and slow versions of the stimuli. The normalised data, which are displayed in the right panel of Figure 1, show that the variation in speaking rate did alter the location of the entire best-exemplar range, as expected from our previous research, and statistical analysis confirmed this observation.

These findings suggest a dissociation between the effect of lexical status and the effect of acoustic-phonetic factors such as speaking rate on the location of a category's best exemplars. Acoustic-phonetic factors, but not the higher-order linguistic factor of lexical status, alter the location of the entire best-exemplar range of the category. We suggest that this dissociation derives from the listener's sensitivity to the differential effects of these contextual factors in speech production. Acoustic-phonetic contextual factors alter the production of the critical segmental information, and we propose that listeners take this variation into account by altering the location of the perceived best category exemplars. In contrast, lexical status does not alter VOT values in production: in a companion production study (Allen & Miller, in press) we found no systematic effect of lexical status on the VOT values of voiceless consonants in words (such as *peace*) versus matched nonwords (such as *peef*). Thus there is no systematic variation for the perceptual system to take into account and, as our perceptual data show, lexical status does not substantially alter the location of the best-exemplar range for the voiceless category in perception. Note that according to this proposal, although many contextual factors alter the location of the boundaries between categories, only those contextual factors that systematically change the way in which the critical segmental information is produced will substantially affect the location of the category's perceived best exemplars.

SPEEDED CATEGORISATION

The dissociation between different types of contextual factors reported above underscores the importance of considering the internal structure of categories, as well as the boundaries between categories, when studying phonetic perception. Accordingly, in a related set of studies (Miller & Cox, in prep), we have been examining how internal category structure, as reflected in category goodness ratings, affects how quickly listeners can map the acoustic signal onto phonetic categories during on-line processing. For this investigation, we created nine different extended VOT series, each based on a different word pair. For three of the series, the word-initial consonant was labial (as in the series *bat-pat-*pat*), for three it was alveolar (as in the series *den-ten-*ten*), and for three it was velar (as in the series *ghost-coast-*coast*). In a preliminary category-goodness rating task, in which listeners were asked to rate each token for the goodness of its initial voiceless consonant (/p/, /t/, or /k/) using a 1–7 rating scale, we obtained the expected non-monotonic goodness function for each series.

For the first of two speeded categorisation experiments, we selected tokens from each series that covered a wide range of VOT values and varied considerably in category goodness. We presented these tokens to three groups of listeners. Each group heard the tokens from the three series with a given place of articulation randomised together. The listeners' task was to decide as quickly as possible whether each word began with /b/ or /p/ (labial group), /d/ or /t/ (alveolar group), or /g/ or /k/ (velar group) and to indicate their response by pressing one of two labelled keys (e.g., B or P). The main question was how quickly listeners could perform this two-choice categorisation. On the basis of the literature (e.g., Pisoni & Tash, 1974), we expected that response time would be relatively slow for the poor voiceless category exemplars near the voiced-voiceless category boundary, and relatively fast for the best voiceless category exemplars. At issue was the response time for poor voiceless category exemplars with VOT values longer than those of the best exemplars. If response time is a direct function of category goodness, then response time for these stimuli should be relatively slow. However, if response time depends more on the position of the stimulus vis-à-vis the category boundary, then response time should be relatively fast in that these stimuli are far from the voiced-voiceless boundary and are clearly identified as members of the voiceless category.

Overall, similar findings were obtained for all nine stimulus series. Representative data are shown for one of the series, *den-ten-*ten*, in the left panel of Figure 2, where the response time function for the relevant stimuli (those ranging from the voiced-voiceless boundary region to the longest VOT values) is presented along with the goodness function for the series. The main finding across the nine series, confirmed by statistical analysis, was that response time was relatively slow for poor voiceless exemplars near the voiced-voiceless category boundary, but relatively fast for poor voiceless exemplars with long VOT values—overall, poor voiceless exemplars with long VOT values were categorised as quickly

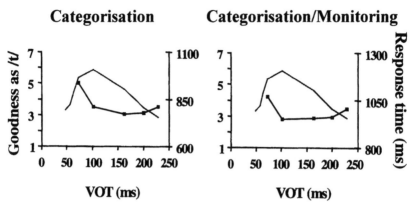

Figure 2. Group response time functions (thick lines with symbols) for the *den-ten-*ten* series from a categorisation task (left panel) and a categorisation/monitoring task (right panel). The group goodness function (thin line) from the preliminary category-goodness rating task is overlaid on the response time function in each panel.

as the best exemplars themselves. These findings provide support for the view that categorisation time is more dependent on position vis-à-vis the category boundary than on perceived category goodness.

Note that in the experiment just described listeners in a given group made two-choice speeded categorisation judgements on tokens that all had a single place of articulation. Given this design, it is possible that listeners were not fully analysing the poor exemplars with long VOT values, but simply quickly categorising them as voiceless by default, due to their breathy, exaggerated quality. To control for this possibility, we conducted a second experiment with new listeners using the same stimuli, but a task that involved monitoring as well as categorisation. Again, three groups of listeners were tested. However, this time each group heard the stimuli from all nine series randomised together. The listeners' task was to monitor for two initial consonants, /b/ or /p/ (labial group), /d/ or /t/ (alveolar group), or /g/ or /k/ (velar group). When they heard one of the target consonants they were to respond as quickly as possible by pressing one of two labelled keys (e.g., B or P); if the word did not begin with one of the target consonants, they were to refrain from responding. With this task, listeners could not use a default strategy of simply pressing the key corresponding to the voiceless consonant whenever they heard a poor exemplar that was breathy and exaggerated, as the task required listeners to analyse the stimuli for place of articulation as well as voicing. The question was whether with this new task, we would also find that poor exemplars of the voiceless category with long VOT values were categorised quickly. The answer was yes. Overall, response times were longer than in the first experiment (as to be expected, given the additional monitoring task), but the general pattern of response times was the same. The data for the *den-ten-*ten* series are shown in the right panel of Figure 2. Statistical analysis across the nine series confirmed that, as in the first experiment, response time was relatively slow for poor voiceless exemplars near the voiced-voiceless category boundary, but relatively fast for poor voiceless exemplars with long VOT values—overall, poor exemplars with long VOT values were categorised as quickly as the best exemplars themselves. Taken together, the data from the two tasks demonstrate that categorisation time is not a direct function of perceived category goodness. Instead, the time it takes to map the critical acoustic information onto a phonetic category appears to depend more on the exemplar's location in perceptual space vis-à-vis a boundary with a competing category.

SUMMARY AND CONCLUSIONS

The findings described in this paper provide additional support for the view that phonetic categories have a rich internal structure, and they provide new information on the role of this structure in speech processing. The findings on *context effects* show that although some contextual factors that alter the location of a phonetic category boundary also alter the location of a category's best exemplars, other contextual factors have a more limited effect, primarily confined to the boundary region. Of considerable importance will be to determine just which contextual factors affect the entire structure of a phonetic category, and which are limited to the boundary region. As noted earlier, we propose that the way in which a contextual factor alters the mapping between acoustic signal and phonetic category depends on the role of that factor in speech production; for further discussion of this point, see Allen and Miller (in press). The findings on *speeded categorisation* show that the speed with which a listener maps the acoustic signal onto a given phonetic category depends more on the exemplar's position in perceptual space vis-à-vis a boundary with a competing category than on its perceived category goodness. Thus even though listeners are exquisitely sensitive to fine gradations in category goodness, revealing richly structured phonetic representations, these differences in perceived category goodness do not translate directly into categorisation speed. The nature of the categorisation process that yields this response pattern remains to be determined. More generally, although many questions about the mapping between acoustic signal and prelexical phonetic representation remain unanswered, the current findings underscore the importance of considering both the boundaries between categories, and the graded internal structure of categories, when building models of the early stages of speech processing.

REFERENCES

Allen, J.S., & Miller, J.L. (in press). Contextual influences on the internal structure of phonetic categories: A distinction between lexical status and speaking rate. *Perception and Psychophysics.*

Ganong, W.F. (1980). Phonetic categorization in auditory word perception. *Journal of Experimental Psychology: Human Perception and Performance, 6,* 110–125.

Hodgson, P., & Miller, J.L. (1996). Internal structure of phonetic categories: Evidence for within-category trading relations. *Journal of the Acoustical Society of America, 100,* 565–576.

Kuhl, P.K. (1991). Human adults and human infants show a "perceptual magnet effect" for the prototypes of speech categories, monkeys do not. *Perception and Psychophysics, 50,* 93–107.

Miller, J.L. (1994). On the internal structure of phonetic categories: A progress report. *Cognition, 50,* 271–285.

Miller, J.L., & Cox, E. (in prep). Phonetic categories: The relation between perceived category goodness and categorization time.

Miller, J.L., & Volaitis, L.E. (1989). Effect of speaking rate on the perceptual structure of a phonetic category. *Perception and Psychophysics, 46,* 505–512.

Oden, G.C., & Massaro, D.W. (1978). Integration of featural information in speech perception. *Psychological Review, 85,* 172–191.

Pisoni, D.B., & Tash, J. (1974). Reaction times to comparisons within and across phonetic categories. *Perception and Psychophysics, 15,* 285–290.

Repp, B.H., & Liberman, A.M. (1987). Phonetic category boundaries are flexible. In S. Harnad (Ed.), Categorical perception: The groundwork of cognition. Cambridge: Cambridge University Press.

Samuel, A.G. (1982). Phonetic prototypes. *Perception and Psychophysics, 31,* 307–314.

Volaitis, L.E., & Miller, J.L. (1992). Phonetic prototypes: Influence of place of articulation and speaking rate on the internal structure of voicing categories. *Journal of the Acoustical Society of America, 92,* 723–735.

Wayland, S.C., Miller, J.L., & Volaitis, L.E. (1994). The influence of sentential speaking rate on the internal structure of phonetic categories. *Journal of the Acoustical Society of America, 95,* 2694–2701.

LANGUAGE AND COGNITIVE PROCESSES, 2001, *16* (5/6), 691–698

Why phonological constraints are so coarse-grained

Janet Pierrehumbert

Department of Linguistics, Northwestern University, Evanston, USA

Current models of speech perception are divided with regard to the status of "phonology", or general implicit knowledge of the sound patterns of a language. In the TRACE model (McClelland & Elman, 1986) the phonotactic and prosodic constraints of phonology are treated as epiphenomenal from regularities in the lexicon. In contrast, Norris (1994), Vitevich and Luce (1998) and Merge (Norris, McQueen, & Cutler, 2000) respond to a growing body of experimental literature indicating that low-level encoding of the speech signal (the level whose result is passed up to the lexicon for potential word matches) is sensitive to phonotactic and prosodic constraints. Here, I will explore the consequences of the assumption that the architecture of the speech perception system includes a fast phonological preprocessor (hereafter, an FPP) which uses language-specific, but still general, prosodic and phonotactic patterns to chunk the speech stream on its way up to the lexical network. By integrating such information, the FPP imputes possible word boundaries to particular temporal locations in the speech signal. An important question is what types of phonological patterns are candidates for being encoded in the FPP: Can the processing system exploit any statistical regularities whatsoever in the shape of words? Does absolutely any structural description which is logically possible in phonology provide a usable constraint? I will explore the causes and consequences of one observation about this issue, namely that viable constraints are coarse-grained. Although the logical apparatus of phonological theory would make it possible to state extremely fine-grained constraints (e.g., constraints containing complex and detailed combinations of features and structural positions), the constraints for which we now have linguistic or psycho-linguistic evidence are considerably simpler.

Requests for reprints should be addressed to Janet Pierrehumbert, Dept. of Linguistics, 2016 Sheridan Road, Northwestern University, Evanston, IL 60208, USA.
Email: jbp@northwestern.edu

http://www.tandf.co.uk/journals/pp/01690965.html   DOI: 10.1080/01690960143000218

The explanation advanced here depends on the tight connection between phonology and processing. That is, phonology impacts not only well-formedness judgements, but also patterns of allophony in production and strategies of chunking in perception. It follows that the different speakers of a language community need to have identical or highly similar phonologies. Otherwise, the allophonic patterns of the speaker would mislead the listener about how to chunk the speech stream, and nonrecoverable errors in lexical access would result. However, people do not all know all the same words. I will argue that the phonological constraints are coarse-grained with reference to the claim that the learning of phonology needs to be robust across variations in individual vocabularies. Phonological constraints must be coarse-grained because complex and detailed phonological descriptors are statistically unstable across differences in vocabulary, and cannot be learned reliably. This paper in no way exhausts the issue of statistical robustness, which has many other repercussions for learning; for example, see Johansson (1997) for repercussions in the area of morphology. Similarly, I take no stand on whether the coarse-grained character of phonology is innate or emergent in the cognitive system.

METHODS

The results presented here are calculations over phonological transcriptions and word frequency data from the CELEX English database (Baayen, Piepenbrock, & Gulikens, 1995). A list of 11,382 monomorphemic words in CELEX was compiled by linguistics graduate students working in the Ohio State University Phonetics Laboratory. It includes words which are coded in CELEX as monomorphemic, and words which are coded as having obscure morphology, but were judged by all three students to be nondecomposed. This list figures in the study as the community vocabulary of nondecomposible words whose nature determines what should receive a unitary parse by the FPP. The monomorphemic word set, as opposed to the full dictionary, is used because CELEX includes a large number of morphologically complex words and compounds (such as *bachelor's degree*) which have acquired specialised meanings. Such forms have internal word boundaries and should be excluded from the training set which defines constraints on simplex forms.

Individual vocabularies of various sizes were constructed from the list of CELEX monomorphemes by downsampling of the community vocabulary set. The downsampling is frequency-weighted because it is more likely that a child would learn a frequent word than an infrequent one. However, idiosyncratic experiences can permit a child to learn a rare word that few other children know. Words of count 0 in CELEX were assigned a count of

1, as otherwise they are unavailable as candidates for selection. Vocabularies of five different sizes were computed: 400, 800, 1600, 3200, and 6400 words, representing individuals at different levels of vocabulary development. For each vocabulary size, 20 different vocabularies were generated through independent random samples of the full set.

The maximal sample size computed was 6400 words, because a preliminary estimate of the age and educational level corresponding to inventory size suggested that only rather well-educated adults would know this many morphologically simplex words. This estimate was made by sending random samples of the word lists to two reading specialists. Very small vocabularies are of interest because even young toddlers have significant success in using string-spotting and language-particular phonological patterns to decompose the speech stream (see review in Jusczyk, 1997). The astonishing extent of children's early success in parsing speech should not, however, obscure the fact that many years are required to reach adult levels of performance. Error rates in segmental perception and production tasks are above adult levels until age 7 to 9 (see review in Barton, 1980). Allophony, stress/accent, and phonetic precision continue to develop from 6 to 12 (Atkinson-King, 1973; Chevrot, Beaud, & Varga, in press; Eguchi & Hirsh, 1969; Kent & Forner, 1980; Lee, Potamianos, & Narayan, 1999; Raimy & Vogel, 2000).

Four different phonological regularities were evaluated for each vocabulary size. (1) An extended form of the basic trochaic pattern of English. Results in Cutler and Butterfield (1992) show that the predominance of words with initial stress in English is exploited in speech perception to hypothesise word boundaries. Phonologically, this means that English has a trochaic foot structure (a strong-weak foot structure), and that a foot is positioned at the left edge of most words. A trochee yields a 100 stress pattern if positioned at the left edge of a trisyllable, and a 010 stress pattern if positioned at the right edge. Since languages can differ typologically on both foot structure and foot alignment (see Hayes 1994), both must be learned to yield the experimental findings. Here, I evaluate the learnability of the foot alignment for trisyllables, e.g., the learnability of the generalisation that 100 stress patterns are better than 010 stress patterns in English.

(2) The second phonological regularity evaluated was a set of junctural constraints on a nasal in coda position followed by an obstruent in onset position (hereafter, NO clusters). A set of experiments in Hay, Pierrehumbert, and Beckman (in press) showed that the frequencies of such clusters in the lexicon are gradiently reflected both in speech perception and in well-formedness judgments. Of the clusters used in Hay et al. (in press), five were selected for analysis: /n.t/, /n.s/, /n.f/, /m.f/ and /n.p/. These span the range of cluster frequencies. /n.t/ is the most frequent

NO medial cluster. /n.s/ is quite frequent and is judged to be highly well-formed, though not as highly as /n.t/. /n.f/ is not common, but is nonetheless more common within monomorphemes than across a word boundary. Accordingly, the FFP should not posit a word boundary. /m.f/ occurs in only 12 monomorphemic words. A decompositional parse wins statistically over a simplex parse and dictates the well-formedness judgement. Nonetheless, speakers may still have implicit knowledge that this cluster is a possible one. A monomorphemic loan word containing this cluster could probably be added to the English lexicon without reanalysis. /n.p/ is completely impossible except across a word boundary.

(3) The third phonological pattern evaluated was a statistical pattern which accurately describes the monomorphemes as a group but which appears excessively detailed as a phonological constraint set. This is a hybrid of the first two targets of investigation; a set of NO constraints specific to trisyllabic words with initial stress. The constraint set involves the same clusters as in the second calculation, but these clusters are now confined to the juncture between the first syllable, which is stressed, and the second syllable, which is unstressed. The ranking of the clusters is (in actuality) the same in the total monomorphemes set as the ranking for the five NO clusters without a stress constraint. If such a complex constraint were learnable, then it would be possible for a language to have a phonological grammar with co-occurrence restrictions for NO clusters which depended on the stress pattern of the word. Such complex constraints are not reported.

(4) Lastly, I evaluate the learnability of a regularity discussed in Moreton (1997): Word-final stressed /gri/ (as in *agree*) has higher frequency than word-final stressed /kri/ (as in *decree*). /gri/# is 45 times more common than /kri/# as a token frequency, but only twice as frequent as a type. This minor phonological regularity of English is of interest because Moreton's categorisation-bias experiment yielded a null result, contrary to hypothesis. This result requires scrutiny, because it contrasts with a large body of results indicating that phonotactic knowledge is stochastic. The phonotactic constraint in question combines a triphonemic specification with a less than typical stress template, hence it is similar in complexity to the hypothetical NO-plus-stress constraint.

The relative learnability of each of the four target patterns was calculated as follows: 20 independent random samplings of the community vocabulary were drawn for each of the five vocabulary sizes. For each individual vocabulary, the counts of the target patterns were established. The counts were ranked, with individuals viewed as agreeing in their grammars if they agreed in the ranking. If all 20 individuals have the same ranking, then the pattern in question is obviously learnable with estimated $p < .05$ of any error. Any disagreement in ranking means that agreement

TABLE 1

Partial results for learning of NO patterns. Absolute counts in an 800 word vocabulary for 4 individuals

Individual	/n.t/	/n.s/	/n.f/	/m.f/	/n.f/
1	14	6	3	1	0
2	12	6	4	0	0
3	9	9	1	1	0
4	11	12	0	0	0

among 20 individuals on that ranking cannot be assured, given the vocabulary size.

RESULTS

Stress regularity (1) is perfectly learned for all five vocabulary sizes. In even the smallest vocabulary size examined, the 100 pattern is more common than the 010 pattern in all 20 individual vocabularies. This highly robust bit of phonology has no phonemic specifications, and so all trisyllabic words can contribute to the size of the training set.

Example data on learning of the NO pattern (2) is given in Table 1. This table shows absolute counts for the five heterosyllabic NO clusters, over an 800 word vocabulary, for 4 of the 20 individual vocabularies. Individual no. 1 has five distinct counts which are in the same order as counts in the community vocabulary. Hence, this individual has learned the full ranking. For individuals no. 2 and no. 3, there are ties between cluster counts. Since the corresponding counts in the community vocabulary differ, individuals no. 2 and no. 3 show incomplete learning. Individual no. 4 presents a particularly deviant case. There is a three way tie amongst the less frequent clusters, and there are more words with /n.s/ than with /n.t/ (reversing the correct rank ordering).

Table 2 provides an aggregate measure of the extent to which individuals' vocabularies show the correct ranking, for all five vocabulary

TABLE 2

Mean Spearman rank correlations for NO clusters and NO clusters in strong-initial trisyllables

Vocabulary size	NO Clusters	NO clusters in strong-initial trisyllables
400	0.80	0.21
800	0.88	0.45
1600	0.98	0.61
3200	1.00	0.68
6400	1.00	0.93

sizes examined. It compares the learnability of NO rankings (2) with the learnability of the NO ranking as confined to the initial trochee of trisyllabic words (3). The aggregate measure of learnability is the mean of the Spearman rank correlation between the phonotactics of individual vocabularies and the phonotactics of the full community vocabulary. This statistic reaches a maximum value of 1.0 when all individuals learn the same ranking as the ranking in the full vocabulary.

Overall, the NO pattern displays a rather good degree of learnability (at 0.8) for even the 400 word vocabulary—indeed the examples in Table 1 are not representative, but were selected to illustrate bad as well as good outcomes. It reaches 1.0 at 3200 words and remains there for the next larger vocabulary. The learnability of the hypothetical NO-stress pattern is extremely poor for a small vocabulary, and even at 6400 words unanimity has not been reached. With 6400 monomorphemic words representing a high vocabulary level which not all adults achieve, this regularity is not viable as a shared constraint in the phonology of the community.

Turning now to the /gri/#—/kri/# contrast (4), the only relevant monomorphemic words listed in CELEX are *agree, degree, filigree, pedigree* and *scree, decree*. The complete CELEX also contains four complex forms with embedded *agree* or *degree*. In the simulation, only 90% of individuals with a 6400 word vocabulary had learned that /gri/# is better than /kri/#. This outcome occurred because some individuals acquired *scree* and *decree*, but not *pedigree* and *filigree*. In this particular simulation trial, the learnability was actually worse for a 6400 word vocabulary than for a 3200 vocabulary (for which 95% of individuals learned the generalisation). However, even at 6400 words, only 10% of individuals had all four /gri/ words in their vocabulary. Overall, the phonotactic generalisation hangs by the thread of a just a few distinct types. As discussed in Bybee (2001), the experimental and historical evidence suggests that small numbers of types, no matter how individually frequent each one may be, do not tend to project phonological generalisations. Moreton's failure to find a difference between word-final stressed /gri/ and /kri/ in speech perception thus suggests that they are not the subject of phonotactic constraints as such. Instead, their well-formedness is based on the well-formedness of their subparts as exhibited in more diverse positions.

DISCUSSION

The calculations just presented bear out the claim that phonological regularities can be uniformly learned by individuals with different vocabularies. A local regularity mentioning specific phonemes—a five way ranking of NO clusters—can be uniformly learned from 3200 words or less. This is 28% of the community vocabulary, a vocabulary consistent with the suggestion that phonotactics are learned by late childhood or early adolescence. A stress constraint involving a large temporal scale but no specific phonemes can be learned even more readily. The calculations also show that two complex patterns involving a combination of particular phoneme sequences with a specfic stress template are not reliably learnable even from an adult-level vocabulary. Thus, such constraints are not robust enough to use in bottom-up phonological encoding. The relationship of statistical reliability to complexity and vocabulary size appears to be in the right range to correspond to the positive and negative experimental results cited above.

These calculations exemplify a specific line of reasoning, and do not provide anything like an exhaustive survey of the relationship between granularity and learnability. The calculations presented in Hay et al. (in press) in fact presupposed without argument somewhat finer grained descriptions than used here. Noise in the experimental data makes it difficult to determine whether this detail assisted the fit by modelling knowledge more accurately, or impeded it by introducing statistic instability. More detailed experiments are needed to resolve this issue. The results of these calculations also suggest follow-up work in which individual variation in well-formedness judgements and speech perception is related to assessment of individual vocabularies.

REFERENCES

Atkinson-King, K. (1973). Children's acquisition of phonological stress contrasts. *UCLA Working Papers in Phonetics*, No. 25.

Barton, D. (1980). Phonemic perception in children. In G.H. Yeni-Komshian, J.F. Kavanagh, & C.A. Ferguson (Eds.) *Child phonology: Volume 2, perception* (pp. 97–116). New York: Academic Press.

Baayen, R.H., Piepenbrock, R., & Gulikens, I. (1995). *The CELEX lexical database (release 2) CD-rom*. Linguistic Data Consortium, University of Pennsylvania, Philadelphia PA.

Bybee, J. (2001). *Phonology and language use*. Cambridge: Cambridge University Press.

Chevrot, J.-P., Beaud, L., & Varga, R. (in press). Developmental data on a French sociolinguistic variable: the word-final post-consonantal /R/. *Language Variation and Change, 12*.

Cutler, A., & Butterfield, S. (1992). Rhythmic cues to speech segmentation: Evidence from juncture misperception. *Journal of Memory and Language, 31*, 218–236.

Eguchi, S., & Hirsh, I. (1969). Development of speech sounds in children. *Acta Octo-Laryngologica*, Suppl. 257.

Hay, J.B., Pierrehumbert, J., & Beckman, M.E. (in press). Speech perception, well-formedness, and the statistics of the lexicon. In R. Ogden, J. Local, & R. Temple (Eds.), *Papers in laboratory phonology VI*. Cambridge: Cambridge University Press.

Hayes, B. (1994). *Metrical stress theory: Principles and case studies*. Chicago: University of Chicago Press.

Johansson, C. (1997). *A view from language; Growth of language in individuals and populations*. Ph.D. dissertation, University of Lund.

Jusczyk, P. (1997). *The discovery of spoken language.* Cambridge, MA: MIT Press.

Kent, R., & Forner, L. (1980). Speech segment durations in sentence recitations by children and adults. *Journal of Phonetics, 8,* 157–168.

Lee, S., Potamianos, A., & Narayan, S. (1999). Acoustics of children's speech: Developmental changes of temporal and spectral parameters. *Journal of the Acoustical Society of America, 105,* 1455–1468.

McClelland, J.L., & Elman, J.L. (1986). The TRACE model of speech perception. *Cognitive Psychology, 18,* 1–86.

Moreton, E. (1997). Phonotactic rules in speech perception. Abstract 2aSC4, 134th Meeting of the Acoustical Society of America, San Diego, CA, Dec. 1–5.

Norris, D. (1994). Shortlist: A connectionist model of continuous speech recognition. *Cognition, 52,* 189–234.

Norris, D.G., McQueen, J.M., & Cutler, A. (2000). Merging information in speech recognition: Feedback is never necessary. *Behavioral and Brain Sciences, 23,* 299–325.

Raimy, E., & Vogel, I. (2000). Compound and phrasal stress: A case of late acquisition. Paper delivered at the Annual Meeting of the Linguistic Society of America, Chicago, Jan. 6-9.

Vitevich, M., & Luce, P. (1998). When words compete: Levels of processing in perception of spoken words. *Psychological Science, 9,* 325–329.

LANGUAGE AND COGNITIVE PROCESSES, 2001, *16* (5/6), 699–708

Access to lexical representations: Cross-linguistic issues

William D. Marslen-Wilson

MRC Cognition and Brain Sciences Unit, Cambridge, UK

An adequate account of "spoken word access processes" is going to require, if nothing else, a convincing definition of the notion "word". Without knowing what is being accessed, it will be hard either to construct a theory of how access is conducted, or to determine what are the appropriate tests of such a theory and its competitors. The nature of the account will differ, in fundamental ways, depending on whether what is being accessed is a stored representation of a word's acoustic-phonetic form, a decomposed representation of its constituent morphemes, or even a direct mapping to lexical semantic representations without mediation by any conventional form of phonological representation.

Put differently, we need a better understanding of the structure of the mental lexicon—what are its basic units of representation and analysis, and how are these organised in relationship to each other? Any attempt to resolve these questions is immediately confronted with the immense variety of lexical arrangements across languages. The research I summarise here represents one preliminary attempt to explore and describe this cross-linguistic variation. Do we find evidence for common underlying principles, that might place useful constraints on the notion "word" in the context of lexical access from speech? The results we have so far suggest that lexical systems are as notable for their differences as for their similarities.

Requests for reprints should be addressed to William D. Marslen-Wilson, MRC Cognition and Brain Sciences Unit, 15 Chaucer Road, Cambridge, CB2 2EF, UK.
E-mail: w.marslen-wilson@mrc-cbu.cam.ac.uk

I thank Harald Baayen for helpful comments on a previous version of this manuscript. This research was supported by grants from the UK MRC and ESRC.

http://www.tandf.co.uk/journals/pp/01690965.html   DOI: 10.1080/01690960143000164

STARTING POINTS

The constraints on space rule out any general coverage of research in this area. Accordingly, what I present here should be viewed as a status report for one particular program, working from a specific perspective. Its starting point is a view of lexical organisation developed initially in the context of English derivational morphology (Marslen-Wilson, Tyler, Waksler, & Older, 1994)—not because English has any special status but because English was the language that we first worked on. Derivational morphology, in a language like English, is the concatenation of a base form (a root or a stem) with one or more derivational affixes. These may be suffixes or prefixes, as in forms like *happiness*, analysable as {happy} + {-ness}, or *rethink*, analysable as {re-} + {think}. These derivational processes change the meaning, and often the form-class of the stem, and are generally thought of as generating new lexical items.

Our primary methodology for studying the representation of English derived forms has been the repetition priming technique, and our strategy is to use parallel tasks and contrasts, as far as possible, across the other languages we are looking at. The key assumption, in using priming to probe the structure of the mental lexicon, is that priming is obtained between morphologically related items if they both share the same lexical entry—if *darkness* primes *dark*, we assume this is because the prime *darkness* activates the underlying morpheme *dark*, and this facilitates the lexical decision response when *dark* itself is subsequently presented. This is in distinction to semantic priming, between pairs like *cello* and *violin*, where priming is assumed to involve interactions between two otherwise separate lexical representations.

For languages like English, where morphologically related words are typically also closely related in meaning and in form, the separation of morphological and semantic effects is not always straightforward. One way round this is to use versions of the priming task which are relatively insensitive to semantic effects, such as masked priming and delayed repetition priming. Using a variety of such techniques, we have developed a view of the English mental lexicon as a dynamic cognitive entity, distinguished by three core properties:

1. *Morphemic* and *decompositional*: The unit of representation is the morpheme, and complex words, where synchronically decomposable, are represented in terms of their constituent morphemes.

2. *Combinatorial*: The same morpheme combines with other morphemes across a morphological family; the morpheme {dark} in *darkness* is the same lexical and cognitive entity as the {dark} in *darkly*. Similarly, the {-ness} in *darkness* is the same as the {-ness} in *toughness*.

3. *Dependent on semantic transparency:* Compositionality is not assumed to apply across the board. Complex forms are only represented in decomposed, morphemic format if they are synchronically semantically transparent. The form *punishment* is semantically transparent and represented as {punish} + {-ment}. The form *department*, although superficially also complex, is semantically opaque. It cannot be represented as {depart} + {-ment} because this would give the incorrect semantics. Such words are represented as whole forms—in effect, as the single morpheme {department}. This means that English is viewed as only partially decompositional and combinatorial, and in this respect is similar to the AAM (Caramazza, Laudanna, & Romani, 1988) and Race models (Baayen, Dijkstra, & Schreuder, 1997) which also, but for different reasons, are built around a contrast between morphemically decomposed and whole-form representations of complex words.

The evidence for these claims about English comes from a set of priming effects, the most salient of which are the following:

Stem priming: This is the priming effect, found in masked priming and in immediate and delayed repetition priming (Marslen-Wilson et al., 1994; Marslen-Wilson & Zhou, 1999), between a semantically transparent complex form and its stem, as in prime/target pairs like *darkness/dark*. Critically, semantically opaque pairs like *department/depart* do not prime.

Affix priming: This is the priming effect between semantically unrelated prime-target pairs which share the same affix, as in *darkness/toughness* and *rebuild/rethink* (Marslen-Wilson, Ford, Older, & Zhou, 1996). This is strongest for productive affixes, and is interpreted as the combinatorial re-use of the same bound morpheme in both prime and target.

Suffix-suffix interference: This is the interference effect observed between semantically transparent pairs sharing the same stem but different suffixes, as in *darkness/darkly* (Marslen-Wilson et al., 1994; Marslen-Wilson & Zhou, 1999). The absence of priming between these highly semantically and morphologically related pairs is interpreted as inhibition between two affixes competing for linkage to the same stem.

The co-occurrence of these three effects we take to be diagnostic of a decompositional and combinatorial system. How far do we find similar effects in other languages?

POLISH

The first language we report on is Polish, a Slavic language with an exceptionally rich morphological system, and which also, like English, employs a concatenative derivational morphology, combining stems with sequences of prefixes and affixes. Unlike English, essentially all surface forms are morphologically complex, combining a bound stem with one or more suffixes. Thus the word *dziewczyna* "a girl" consists of a stem *dziewczyn-* and an inflectional ending *"-a"* which indicates the nominative singular feminine; the word *przybiegłam* "I run up" consists of the stem *"bieg-"*, the derivational-aspectual prefix *"przy-"* and the inflectional ending *'-lam'* which denotes the 1st person singular feminine past tense. In a series of studies, chiefly using delayed repetition priming tasks to reduce semantic effects, we have found a profile of results that is very similar overall to English (Reid & Marslen-Wilson, 2000).

Stem priming: We find strong stem priming in both simple and complex forms, ranging from pairs like *chodz-enie/chodz-i-ć* (walking/to walk) to highly complex forms like *bajk-o-pis-ar-stwo/pis-a-ć* (fable-writing/to write).[1] In the latter case, the shared morpheme (the stem {pis-}), is embedded in a multi-component complex form, and yet is able to elicit priming at a delay of 12 intervening items, under conditions where no priming is obtained between purely semantically related items, such as *dom/garaż* (house/garage) over the same delay.

Affix priming: We also find priming for pairs sharing the same affix, especially for more complex forms. In immediate repetition priming we find effects, on grouped analyses, for sets of pairs sharing derivational affixes, as in *kotek/ogródek* (a little cat/a little garden), sharing the diminutive suffix {-ek} or *kuch-arz/piłk-arz* (a cook/footballer) sharing the agentive suffix {-arz}. Affix priming effects come through as well in delayed repetition priming, using pairs like *roz-pakow-ywa-ł-em* (to unwrap, 1st person singular, masculine, past tense) and *roz-wałkow-ywa-ć* ("to flatten something using a rolling-pins"). These words share a derivational aspectual prefix {roz-} and the secondary imperfective suffix {ywa-}, and show strong priming even with 12 items intervening between prime and target.

Suffix-suffix interference: Polish shows strong interference effects of this type. Pairs like *pis-anie/pis-arz* (writing/writer) and *balon-owy/balon-ik* (balloon-like/a little balloon) show no priming at all in delayed repetition, despite the close morphological and semantic relationship between prime and target, and despite the fact that inflectionally related pairs, like *myśl-ę/myśl-e-ć* (I think/to think) show strong priming effects in the same experiment.

Semantic transparency: Finally, Polish shows strong effects of semantic transparency. As in English, there is no priming for semantically opaque pairs that historically shared the same stem, as in pairs like *jałowiec/jałowy* (juniper/futile). Unlike English, however, Polish also shows no priming

---

[1] Polish compounds like *bajk-o-pis-ar-stwo* form an interesting case, because, unlike the simple stem/stem English and Chinese compounds discussed later, they show evidence of decompositional representation. For more detailed discussion, see Reid (2001).

between pairs where the meaning of the prime, although semantically transparent, is not fully semantically compositional. In pairs like *wiąz-anka/wiąz-a-ć* (bunch/to tie), the word *wiązanka* is rated as being highly semantically related to the verb *wiązać*. Nonetheless, the meaning of the derived form is not compositional, in the sense that it is not fully predictable from the meaning of the stem combined with the nominalising affix {-anka}. Strict semantic compositionality may play a stronger role in determining representation than in English, although research is needed to clarify this.

The profile of results for the different kinds of priming relationships suggest that Polish and English have a great deal in common. Although they are very different languages in many important respects, they both fit an overall template that we interpret in terms of a morphemically organised, decompositional, and combinatorial mental lexicon.

ARABIC

Semitic languages like Arabic and Hebrew present a richly complex morphological system that is organised on fundamentally different principles to languages like English and Polish, with their concatenative morphological processes. Semitic languages, in contrast, employ a non-concatenative morphology, where the surface phonetic form is constructed by interweaving two or more abstract morphemes. In both Hebrew and in Modern Standard Arabic, the traditional analysis is in terms of a consonantal root, carrying semantic information, and a word pattern which specifies the syntactic category and the phonological structure of the surface form. Thus, for example, the triconsonantal Arabic root {ktb} with the semantic value of <writing>, combines with the word pattern {faʕala},[2] with the syntactic meaning of "active verb", to give the surface form *kataba*, meaning "write". The same root, {ktb} can combine with many different word patterns, in a highly productive system, to give a range of surface words with related meanings and differing syntactic properties, as in *kaatib* (writer), *maktuub* (written), *yaktubu* (he is writing) and so forth. Conversely, the same word pattern will combine productively with many different roots, so that, for example, {faʕala} combines with the root {ngl} <moving> to give the active verb form *nagala* "move".

These are highly abstract morphemes, that never surface as phonetic forms on their own, but whose presence is inferred on the basis of compelling distributional regularities. The question we investigated was whether, as already established for Hebrew (Frost, Forster, & Deutsch,

---

[2] This is the traditional representation of a word pattern, with the letters "f, ʕ, l" indicating the slots into which the consonants of the root will be inserted.

1997), there is evidence that these abstract entities function cognitively in ways comparable to stems and derivational morphemes in concatenative morphologies such as English. We cannot transpose exactly into Arabic the sets of priming contrasts that we employed for English and Polish, but there is a plausible correspondence between stem priming and root priming, and between affix-priming and word-pattern priming.

Root priming: Using cross-modal and masked priming techniques, we found clear evidence for priming between pairs that shared the same consonantal root (Boudelaa & Marslen-Wilson, 2000a). Given the role of the root in determining the semantics of the resulting word, we believe this is functionally comparable to stem priming in concatenative morphologies. Thus, for example, the prime /ʔidxaalun/ (inserting) speeds responses to the target /duxuulun/ (entering), where prime and target have in common the tri-consonantal root {dxl}. Strikingly, and quite differently from English and Polish, priming is just as strong when the prime is semantically opaque, as in the form /mudaaxalatun/ (interference), which also shares the root {dxl} with the target /duxuulun/, but where the meaning of the form is not synchronically predictable. This preservation of root priming under conditions of semantic opacity shows up consistently across all our experiments, and is also found for Hebrew, in comparable priming tasks (e.g., Frost et al., 1997).

Word pattern priming: While Arabic word patterns clearly diverge in important respects, their role in determining the syntactic characteristics of the surface form gives them some major functional characteristics in common with concatenative derivational affixes. Analogously to affix priming, we find significant effects in both cross-modal and masked priming, between pairs that share the same word-pattern but have different roots and different meanings (Boudelaa & Marslen-Wilson, 2000b). This holds both for the verbal morphology, as in pairs like /ħatˤˤtˤama/ and /farraqa/ (demolish/scatter), sharing the word pattern {faʕʕala), but also for the deverbal nouns, between pairs like /xudˤuuʕun/ and /ħuduuθun/ (submission/happening), sharing the word pattern {fuʕʕuulun} (with the meaning "deverbal noun, singular"). The absence of priming between forms like /suʒuunun/ and /ħuduuθun/ (prisons/happening), which have word patterns that are phonologically but not morphologically identical, demonstrates the morphological nature of the effects here, and rules out an account in terms of phonological overlap between prime and target.

These results for Arabic, and the comparable results for Hebrew, suggest strong support for a decompositional, combinatorial system, with abstract morphemes combining to produce the surface form, and being separated out in the process of recognition. The complete absence, however, of a semantic transparency effect in root priming, signals an apparent fundamental difference in the principles underlying the role of morphological combination.

Semitic non-concatenative morphology arguably plays an obligatory structural role in the generation of a surface form and its interpretation. This is not the case for concatenative morphologies like English, which link together already existing phonological entities. For these languages, morphological analysis is optional; the word still exists as a phonological form whether or not it is treated as a combination of morphemes or as an undifferentiated whole form (as is implicit in the interplay between whole-form and decompositional representation built into most current models of Indo-European morphology). For Arabic, there is not this option. Without morphological combination, weaving together consonantal root and word pattern, there is no surface phonological form.

COMPOUNDING IN CHINESE AND ENGLISH

The final set of comparisons involve compounding, a quite different procedure for word-formation, and where the starting point is Mandarin Chinese, rather than English. Compounding is a highly productive means of word formation in both English and Mandarin. Unlike derivational word formation, it does not involve the combination of a stem with an affix, but the linkage of two free stems—as in the English compound *houseboat*, made up of the two nouns *house* and *boat*.

The effect of this, in contrast to derivation, is that compounding is not fully compositional or combinatorial in nature. The meaning of a compound is never fully predictable from the meaning of its components. For example, although a *snowman* is a man made of snow, a *milkman* is not a man made of milk but someone who delivers milk (in the UK, at least). A *fireman*, however, is neither made of fire, nor does he bring fire to the house; rather he puts it out. There are many examples like this, and they all make the same point that the meaning of a compound is not reliably predictable from the combination of the meaning of its compounds. To know what a compound means, you need to know what it refers to. This is not true of synchronically transparent, productively generated derived forms. To know the meaning of *oiliness*, it is enough to know the meaning of *oily* and of *-ness*. The issue, that we addressed first in Mandarin and then in English, is whether this leads to a whole-word, rather than a decompositional and morpheme-based representation of compounds in the mental lexicon.

Compounding in Mandarin takes place in a functionally very different linguistic environment from English. Mandarin has essentially no derivational morphology, so that compounding is its only productive means of word-formation, under conditions where there is considerable pressure due to homophony at the syllabic level. Recent analyses suggest that around 70% of word types in Mandarin are bisyllabic compounds (Institute of Language Teaching and Research, 1986)

In a series of studies (Zhou & Marslen-Wilson, 1995) we addressed the issue of whether a morphemic account or a whole form account was appropriate. Mandarin seemed to be a plausible candidate for a morphemic account, because of the salience of individual morphemes in the spoken language and in the writing system. Extensive research using auditory-auditory repetition priming shows that such an account is not correct. Compounds are represented as separate lexical entries, and not as combinations of their constituent morphemes. This means that Mandarin, unlike the other languages we have studied, does not have a system of word-formation that is decompositional and combinatorial.

This raises the question of how English compounds are represented, which we investigated in a series of cross-modal experiments, looking at the priming relations between transparent (*bathroom*), opaque (*blackmail*), and pseudo (*shamrock*) compounds and their constituent morphemes (Zhou & Marslen-Wilson, 2000). Two results in particular seem hard to handle for a morphemic story. The first is that we did not find priming between the first and second constituents of a compound. Thus *bath*, for example, does not prime *tub*. This is quite inconsistent with the view that compounds are represented as strengthened links between their constituent morphemes.

The second finding is that shared constituents between transparent morphemes do not lead to priming unless the compounds as a whole are semantically related. Thus *headache* does not prime *headscarf*, even though they both transparently contain the morpheme *head*. In contrast, *teacup* does prime *teapot*. This is because these two compounds are strongly semantically related, whereas *headache* and *headscarf* are not. This is not consistent with a morphemic, combinatorial story, where the morpheme *head* is a constituent of *headache* and *headscarf* in the same way that *punish* is a constituent of both *punishment* and *punishable*. Indeed, on a strongly morphemic story, we might expect suffix-suffix interference for all these pairs sharing an initial morpheme, irrespective of overall semantic relatedness. The fact that we do not is further evidence for whole form representations of English compounds. In summary, compounding in Mandarin and English seem to be remarkably similar, reflecting in the same way the representational consequences of the unpredictability of the meaning of compounds.

OVERVIEW

Despite the small sample of languages studied, and despite the commonalities we see in the specific characteristics of a given morphological process across languages, we are nonetheless left with a wide range of lexical arrangements. Mandarin Chinese seems to lie at one extreme, with apparently no combinatorial procedures for word-formation, and with a lexicon made up of whole forms, in which compounds and the words that make up these compounds all have separate lexical representations. English has a similar system for compounding, but also has a decompositional system of word-formation and representation, reflecting the different processing requirements of derivational procedures that operate on a combinatorial basis, and that deliver predictable and compositional meanings.

In this respect English parallels the broad characteristics of a language like Polish, which has a much richer and more complex morphological system. Both these languages, in turn, share with Arabic (and Hebrew) a combinatorial and decompositional approach to lexical representation. In these Semitic languages, however, morphological representation appears to play a more fundamental structural role, so that no surface form can be produced without some underlying process of morpho-phonological combination. This delivers both the surface form, and its basic syntactic and semantic properties.

These differences in lexical representation, although reflecting only a preliminary sample of languages, and reflecting a single type of experimental approach, nonetheless suggest that unitary models of spoken word access processes may not be possible across languages. Although all lexical systems must share the same underlying cognitive and neural constraints on representation, process, and acquisition, these constraints seem to be sufficiently broad to allow different systems to be constructed on apparently quite different organisational principles.

REFERENCES

Baayen, R.H., Dijkstra, T., & Schreuder, R. (1997). Singulars and plurals in Dutch: Evidence for a parallel dual route model. *Journal of Memory and Language, 36*, 94–117.

Boudelaa, S., & Marslen-Wilson, W.D. (2000a). Non-concatenative morphemes in language processing: Evidence from Modern Standard Arabic. In A. Cutler, J.M. McQueen, & R. Zondervan (Eds.), *Proceedings of the Workshop on Spoken Word Access Processes* (pp. 23–26), Nijmegen, The Netherlands: Max-Planck Institute for Psycholinguistics.

Boudelaa, S., & Marslen-Wilson, W.D. (2000b). *On the use of word pattern morphemes in modern standard Arabic.* Paper presented at the 14th Annual Symposium on Arabic Linguistics, University of California Berkeley, March.

Caramazza, A., Laudanna, A, & Romani, C. (1988). Lexical access and inflectional morphology. *Cognition, 28*, 297–332.

Frost, R., Forster, K.I., & Deutsch, A. (1997). What can we learn from the morphology of Hebrew? A masked priming investigation of morphological representation. *Journal of Experimental Psychology: Learning, Memory, and Cognition*, 23, 829–856.

Institute of Language Teaching and Research (1986). *A frequency dictionary of Modern Chinese*. Beijing: Beijing Language Institute Press.

Marslen-Wilson, W.D., Ford, M., Older, L., & Zhou, X. (1996) The combinatorial lexicon: Priming derivational affixes. In G. Cottrell (Ed.), *Proceedings of the 18th Annual Conference of the Cognitive Science Society* (pp. 223–227). Mahwah, NJ: Lawrence Erlbaum Associates Inc.

Marslen-Wilson, W.D., Tyler, L., Waksler, R., & Older, L. (1994). Morphology and meaning in the English mental lexicon. *Psychological Review*, *101*(1), 3–33.

Marslen-Wilson, W.D., & Zhou, X. (1999). Abstractness, allomorphy, and lexical architecture. *Language and Cognitive Processes*, *14*(4), 321–352.

Reid, A. (2001). *The combinatorial lexicon: Psycholinguistic studies of Polish morphology*. Unpublished Ph.D thesis, Birkbeck College, University of London.

Reid, A., & Marslen-Wilson, W.D. (2000). Organising principles in lexical representation: evidence from Polish. In L.R. Gleitman & A.K. Joshi (Eds.), *Proceedings of the Twenty-Second Annual Conference of the Cognitive Science Society*. (pp. 405–410). Mahwah, NJ: Lawrence Erlbaum Associates Inc.

Zhou, X., & Marslen-Wilson, W.D. (1995). Morphological structure in the Chinese mental lexicon. *Language and Cognitive Processes*, *10*, 545–601.

Zhou, X, & Marslen-Wilson, W.D. (2000). Lexical representation of compound words: Cross-linguistic evidence. *Psychologia*, *43*, 47—66.

LANGUAGE AND COGNITIVE PROCESSES, 2001, *16* (5/6), 709–714

Some empirical tests of Merge's architecture

Arthur G. Samuel

Department of Psychology, SUNY Stony Brook, New York, USA

Norris, McQueen, and Cutler (2000) have put forth a model of word and phoneme processing—Merge—that they describe as purely bottom-up, yet capable of accounting for all of the findings in the literature that have previously appeared to require the positing of top-down mechanisms. They argue that Merge should be preferred to all interactive models, because it can account for the data at least as well, with less theoretical baggage.

In most respects, Merge is similar to other models of word and phoneme recognition. The initial level of processing, the "input phonemic" level, is similar to the input level in most other models (typically called the feature level; Norris et al. noted that this level could have been called the feature level in Merge). The top level of the model consists of lexical representations. As in models like TRACE (McClelland & Elman, 1986), each lexical representation competes with the others, via mutual inhibition.

What makes Merge unique is the characterisation and connection pattern of a set of representations called the "output phoneme" level, in which there are also mutually inhibitory connections. The output phoneme level receives input from the input phoneme level, and from the lexical level. Although this architecture includes connections from the lexical level to the phonemic, Norris et al. assert that Merge is purely autonomous. The crux of this claim is their characterising the output phoneme level as not really an integral part of the word perception system. Instead, it should be thought of as an almost artificial, task-specific construct, which the listener uses to meet the particular demands of an experimental situation.

Requests for reprints should be addressed to Arthur G. Samuel, Department of Psychology, SUNY Stony Brook, Stony Brook, NY 11794-2500. E-mail: asamuel@ms.cc.sunysb.edu

Support for this work was provided by NIMH grant R01-51663.

http://www.tandf.co.uk/journals/pp/01690965.html   DOI: 10.1080/01690960143000047

The output phoneme level was designed to meet two apparently contradictory goals: First, it should allow lexical influences to be seen in phonemic responses, because there are many demonstrations of this in the literature. Second, lexical influences should not truly affect phoneme perception, as this would be, by definition, an interactive model. In assessing this architecture, two questions arise: (1) Is this aspect of the model justifiable in principle?, and (2) Is the resulting model consistent with the data?

Norris et al. motivate the splitting of phonemic processes into input and output levels on several grounds. For example, they argue that in phoneme decisions it is important to incorporate mutual inhibition, whereas in early processing such inhibition is undesirable. Norris et al. acknowledge that a purely bottom-up model in which lexical information cannot in any way affect phonemic output (e.g., Race; Cutler & Norris, 1979), cannot account for the empirically observed lexical influences on phoneme decisions. Note that this second point is only justification for building in (top-down) lexical-phonemic connections; it does not motivate the separation of phoneme processing into different *levels*. Similarly, even if one accepts the arguable claim that inhibitory connections are good for decisions and bad for earlier processing, this again does not justify a split between phonemic perception and phonemic decision making. Instead, these arguments might justify the existence of an early feature analysis stage separate from a subsequent phoneme level (as in most models).

The critical question for Merge's architecture is what the output phoneme level is really like. Why is there a separate level for phonemes, and not for words? We must make decisions about words, and about many other constructs, depending on the task. So, if a subject is in a gender judgement task in French or Spanish, is there a gender output level? If so, then the output phoneme level really might not be an integral part of the word recognition system. Yet, this level is used to account for virtually every demonstration of lexical influences on phonemic processing. Critically, the model incorporates connections from the lexical level to the phonemic output level. Would there be such connections to nodes in a "gender output" level? If not, then it would seem that the output phoneme level is in fact a more integral part of the word processing system.

Rather than try to go through a case by case review of each observed lexical influence on phonemic output, it is instructive to consider findings that meet Norris et al.'s standard of showing lexical influences on phonemic processing, without the involvement of phoneme identification. In the compensation for coarticulation phenomenon, the perception of one phoneme is altered as a function of the preceding one, to compensate for effects of the earlier phoneme's articulation on the following one (Mann & Repp, 1981). Elman and McClelland (1988) argued (and Norris et al. have strongly affirmed) that because compensation is believed to be a relatively low-level process, if it were affected by lexical activation, then top-down influences would be implicated. They produced a fricative that was perceptually ambiguous (i.e., equally likely to be heard as /s/ or /ʃ/) and used that sound to replace the final fricative in words such as "foolish" and "Christmas". When these words preceded test stimuli whose initial phonemes spanned a /t/-/k/ or a /d/-/g/ boundary, the identification of the stop consonants shifted, replicating the compensation effect found when real fricatives precede these stops. In this case, the same physical sound (the ambiguous fricative) altered the perception of a *following* sound in different ways, depending on whether the lexical context of the fricative caused it to be heard as /s/ or as /ʃ/: Lexical activation produced an effect on phonemic processing, in the absence of any task-required phonemic identification of the fricative.

Norris et al. rely on Pitt and McQueen's (1998) study to save Merge from this apparent disconfirmation. Pitt and McQueen noted that the vowels preceding the final fricatives in Elman and McClelland's study were not perfectly matched, and that the transitional probability (TP) from these vowels to the following fricatives potentially could have driven the observed results. In a set of experiments in which compensation could potentially be driven by lexical factors alone (with TP controlled), or by TP alone (with no lexical influence, by using nonwords), they consistently found an effect of transition probability, but not of lexical factors. There are at least two procedural details that must be considered before favouring this null lexical effect over the positive results of Elman and McClelland. Unlike Elman and McClelland, Pitt and McQueen used context stimuli that were monosyllabic. These stimuli were sufficient to bias the report of the context item's final fricative. However, there may not have been enough time during the monosyllable's presentation for lexical activation to reach the level needed for compensation to occur. The second concern is that the null result for the lexical manipulation might just be showing that the test conditions were not appropriate. There was a critical difference between the lexical and the TP conditions. In the latter, the stimuli were nonwords, rather than words. With such nonwords, with a synthetic final fricative appended to real speech, the final fricative would not be very tightly bound to the nonword, leaving it free to be grouped with (and therefore affect) the /t/-/k/ items. Mann and Repp were very concerned about this sort of effect, and its potential influence on compensation.

Samuel and Pitt (2001) have recently shown that these concerns were well founded. They conducted a set of compensation experiments, using longer context words, and controlling for the perceptual grouping of the final fricative in the context words. All context words (e.g., "abolish" vs. "arthritis") were chosen to have the same vowel (/I/) preceding the final fricative, eliminating any TP confound. Samuel and Pitt found reliable compensation effects on the identification of the initial stop consonants of a "tame"–"came" test series. These effects cannot be accommodated within Merge's framework, as they show top-down lexical effects on the perception of the fricatives, which in turn produce compensation effects.

In addition to compensation, lexically driven selective adaptation effects could in principle disconfirm MERGE. As with compensation, adaptation involves a low-level, sublexical change in phonetic encoding (Samuel & Kat, 1996). Therefore, if the perception of a phoneme is determined via lexical influences, and that phoneme produces an adaptation effect on some other speech sound, the top-down lexical-phonemic influence cannot be attributed to the output phonemic level.

Samuel (1997) reported an adaptation effect that met exactly these criteria. Polysyllabic words with /b/ in the third syllable were selected (e.g., "inhibition"), along with comparable words with /d/ (e.g., "armadillo"). The /b/ and /d/ portions were removed, with the resulting stimuli used to produce two kinds of adaptors. Control stimuli were made by replacing the speech segments with silence. Experimental items were made by replacing the speech segments with white noise. Previous work has shown that replacement by white noise produces phonemic restoration. In contrast, listeners do not restore the missing stops in silence-replaced stimuli. Samuel found that the noise-replaced words produced reliable adaptation effects on the labelling of stimuli from a /bI/-/dI/ test series; the controls had no such effect. Thus, the lexically determined phonemes caused the predicted effect, with the silent controls demonstrating that this effect was not artifactual.

We have extended the lexical adaptation results in a new series of lexically mediated adaptation experiments (Samuel, 2001). These experiments use Ganong's (1980) phoneme identification paradigm to examine lexical-phonemic influences. Consider, for example, the words "bronchitis" and "demolish". In Ganong's technique, stimuli are made by varying the identity of one phoneme along some dimension. With "bronchitis" and "demolish", the variation is in the identity of the final fricative. In both cases, eight versions were produced, ranging from a clear /s/ at one end of the continuum to a clear /ʃ/ at the other end. The "Ganong effect" is that for ambiguous stimuli, phoneme identification is strongly influenced by the lexical context: A middle item is identified as "s" in "bronchiti_", but as "sh" in "demoli_".

This result by itself is not diagnostic with respect to system architecture: While McClelland and Elman could claim the effect is due to TRACE's interactive nature, Merge can use the lexical connections to the output phoneme level to fit the data. However, the two model types can be dissociated by bringing the lexical shift into the adaptation paradigm: The same physical sound is identified as /s/ in "bronchiti_", but as "ʃ" in "demoli_". In Merge, this effect is at the decision stage—there is no change in the actual perception of the fricative. In TRACE, however, the phoneme is *perceived* differently, due to the top-down lexical influences. Thus, interactive models predict that the lexically-determined phoneme should cause adaptation shifts in accord with the lexically-driven identity of the fricative. Merge cannot predict such shifts, without expanding the nature of the output phoneme level to the point of being a true phoneme level, because listeners make no judgements/outputs for the fricatives in "bronchiti_" or "demoli_".

Samuel reported the results of three conditions. The test series was an 8-step "iss"-"ish" continuum, made by adding together different proportions of naturally produced /Is/ and /Iʃ/ tokens. The adaptors are made from four words that end with /Is/ (e.g., "malpractice"), and four that end with /Iʃ/ (e.g., "diminish"). As in the compensation work, the words were chosen to have at least three syllables (to allow enough time for lexical activation to build), and to have the same vowel preceding the final fricative.

For all eight words, the final fricatives plus several vowel pitch periods were removed. In the control condition, these truncated words were used as the adaptors. These stimuli should not produce any differential adaptation effects, if the relevant information has in fact been deleted. In a second condition, an ambiguous fricative from the iss-ish test series was appended to all eight truncated words. If lexical information can alter the perception of phonetic information, this ambiguous fricative should be heard as, and adapt like, an /s/ after one set of words, and as an /ʃ/ after the others. Samuel found exactly this pattern of results.

A third condition was used to rule out any possible acoustic artifact as the source of the adaptation. The adapting words were re-recorded, intentionally mispronouncing each final /s/ as /ʃ/, and vice versa. In addition, most of the final /I/ was removed, and replaced by white noise. Finally, each final fricative was replaced by a neutral fricative. These stimuli produced reliable lexically mediated adaptation, under conditions that preclude any acoustic artifact. These results replicate Samuel's (1997) finding of lexically driven adaptation, and extend them by using a Ganong-task lexical manipulation, rather than phonemic restoration. In both cases, changes in phonemic processing were observed that were based on lexical activation, and did not involve any report of the lexically induced phoneme. Rather, the shift was a consequence of the perceived phoneme's effect on another speech sound.

Collectively, there is now sufficient evidence available to conclude that an accurate model of word recognition must include true top-down connections from the lexicon to phonemic codes. Links to an "output phoneme" stage will not be sufficient. Thus, although Merge is an interesting and clever model, it cannot account for the data. Instead, interactive mechanisms are called for.

REFERENCES

Cutler, A., & Norris, D. (1979). Monitoring sentence comprehension. In Cooper, W.E. & Walker, E.C.T (Eds.), *Sentence processing: Psycholinguistic studies presented to Merrill Garrett* (pp. 113–134). Hillsdale, NJ: Lawrence Erlbaum Associates Inc.

Elman, J.L., & McClelland, J.L. (1988). Cognitive penetration of the mechanisms of perception: compensation for coarticulation of lexically restored phonemes. *Journal of Memory and Language, 27*, 143–165.

Ganong, W.F. (1980). Phonetic categorization in auditory word perception. *Journal of Experimental Psychology: Human Perception and Performance, 6*, 110–125.

Mann, V.A., & Repp, B.H. (1981). Influence of preceding fricative on stop consonant perception. *Journal of the Acoustical Society of America, 69*, 548–558.

McClelland, J.L., & Elman, J.L. (1986). The TRACE model of speech perception. *Cognitive Psychology, 18*, 1–86.

Norris, D., McQueen, J.M., & Cutler, A. (2000). Merging information in speech recognition: Feedback is never necessary. *Behavioral and Brain Sciences, 23*, 299–370.

Pitt, M.A., & McQueen, J.M. (1998). Is compensation for coarticulation mediated by the lexicon? *Journal of Memory and Language, 39*, 347–370.

Samuel, A.G. (1997). Lexical activation produces potent phonemic percepts. *Cognitive Psychology, 32*, 97–127.

Samuel, A.G. (2001). Knowing a word affects the fundamental perception of the sounds within it. *Psychological Science, 12*, 348–351.

Samuel, A.G., & Kat, D. (1996). Early levels of analysis of speech. *Journal of Experimental Psychology: Human Perception and Performance, 22*, 676–694.

Samuel, A.G., & Pitt, M.A. (2001). Lexical activation (and other factors) can mediate compensation for coarticulation. Manuscript submitted for publication.

LANGUAGE AND COGNITIVE PROCESSES, 2001, *16* (5/6), 715–721

The source of a lexical bias in the Verbal Transformation Effect

Mark A. Pitt and Lisa Shoaf
Ohio State University, Columbus, USA

Comparisons of responses to words and pseudowords figure prominently in our efforts to understand how spoken words are recognised. This was apparent in many of the presentations at the SWAP meeting (e.g., Fowler & Brancazio, 2000; Frauenfelder & Content, 2000). Differences in responding to words and pseudowords are assumed to demonstrate the influence of lexical memory in the task at hand, from which we infer the structural and functional characteristics of the processing system.

Each task we use in this enterprise is often best suited to address a subset of theoretical issues. For example, phoneme detection and identification are used most often to examine issues about prelexical processing, such as whether there is lexical feedback and what the structure of phonetic categories is. Lexical decision and other word-based tasks tend to be used to explore the properties of lexical memory. So when a lexical effect is identified in an unfamiliar task, it is important to determine what we can learn about word processing from it. This has been the goal of our work into the origin of word-pseudoword differences in the Verbal Transformation Effect (VTE).

THE LEXICAL EFFECT

The VTE is an auditory illusion in which listeners report hearing illusory utterances after listening to a word repeat over and over at a rapid rate. Listeners respond on the fly, repeating illusory percepts into a microphone.

Requests for reprints should be addressed to Mark Pitt, Department of Psychology, 1885 Neil Avenue, Columbus, OH 43210-0222. E-mail: pitt.2@osu.edu

We thank Lyn Canterbury and Kalyani Subramaniam for help in scoring data. Rochelle Newman and Jean Vroomen provided constructive feedback on an earlier version of the manuscript. Sample stimuli are available at http://lpl.psy.ohio-state.edu.

http://www.tandf.co.uk/journals/pp/01690965.html   DOI: 10.1080/01690960143000056

Transformations are reported throughout a trial, with new ones being introduced and others being rereported, including the veridical (i.e., intended) word itself.

The first series of experiments (Shoaf & Pitt, submitted) focused on establishing the validity and reliability of the lexical effect in the VTE, and then probing the data further to identify its cause. Natsoulas (1965) was the first to study word-pseudoword differences in the VTE in depth. He measured the number of unique transformations (different verbal reports, irrespective of their frequency) that listeners reported, and found that pseudowords yielded more unique transformations than words.

We began by replicating and extending this finding to a wider range of stimuli under more controlled experimental conditions. Monosyllabic and disyllabic words and pseudowords were phonetically matched across conditions as closely as possible so that differences in performance could be attributable to differences in lexical status rather than to other properties of the stimuli. For the monosyllables, one or both consonants of an initial cluster were substituted (e.g., "skunk"–"swunk"). For the disyllables, this involved swapping the order of the two syllables (e.g.,"center"–"tercen"). Stimuli were presented binaurally over head-phones for 350 repetitions with an interstimulus interval (ISI) of 250 ms. Listeners (31) reported transformations into a microphone that were recorded onto cassette tape for later analysis.

For both the monosyllables and disyllables, listeners reported reliably more unique pseudoword transformations than word transformations. This effect was not due to a difference in the frequency with which transformations are reported to the two types of stimuli, as the total number of transformations was not consistently greater for pseudowords than words. Further analysis of the data provided insight into the cause of the lexical effect. Transformations were categorised as a function of whether they were reports of the veridical percept itself (i.e., the original utterance) or nonveridical percepts (i.e., word or pseudoword illusory transformations). When the repeating stimulus was a word (monosyllable or disyllable), it transformed back into the veridical stimulus reliably more often than when it was a pseudoword. However, nonveridical reports showed no such lexical bias, with illusory pseudoword transformations being more frequent than illusory word transformations. This finding, in addition to accounting for why fewer unique transformations are reported to words, suggests that lexical memory facilitates the veridical perception of the recycling stimulus. To understand the processes that underlie this lexical effect, it is first necessary to develop a better understanding of what causes verbal transformations. This was the objective of the following work.

CAUSES OF VERBAL TRANSFORMATIONS

One clue as to a cause of the VTE came from inspection of the transformations listeners reported to monosyllables that began with /s/ clusters, like "skunk" and "swunk". The /s/ was omitted in some of the transformations, such as "gunk" and "wunk". We hypothesised that these transformations were caused by the perceptual regrouping (i.e., streaming) of the acoustic elements that made up the word (Bregman, 1990). Repetitive presentation of the word caused the high-frequency frication corresponding to /s/ to split off from the remainder of the utterance and form its own perceptual stream. For example, /g/-initial transformations (e.g., "gunk") occurred 43% of the time, while there were no reports of /k/-initial transformations (e.g., "kunk"), which suggests that the phonetic significance of the closure interval between /s/ and the remainder of the word was eliminated upon regrouping.

If streaming causes some verbal transformations, then listeners' reports should exhibit properties typical of regrouping percepts. Furthermore, which elements of an utterance split off should depend on the acoustic properties of the stimuli. These ideas were tested in two experiments using similar stimuli but different tasks (Pitt & Shoaf, in press). The stimuli were CVC pseudowords in which the strength with which the consonants bind with the vowel was manipulated. In the Intact condition, the consonants were continuants and nasals, which should be most resistant to streaming given their acoustic similarity (e.g., both are periodic signals and occupy similar frequency regions; /lom/, /wɛm/). In two other conditions, consonants were used that were expected to be most susceptible to streaming (e.g., fricatives, affricates, stops). These consonants occurred only syllable-finally in the Final condition (e.g., /lodʒ/, /wɛtʃ/), and in both consonant locations in the I+F (Initial plus Final) condition (e.g., /podʒ/, /pɛtʃ/).

In the first experiment, instructions to participants were modified slightly to extract more information from listeners about what they were hearing in order to test the regrouping account. Listeners (13) were trained to report the transformation, then the number of perceptual streams they heard at that time, and finally the contents of the background stream if one was present. There were 250 repetitions and a 0 ms ISI. Listeners' reports clearly suggested that streaming is one cause of the VTE. Sixty per cent of the transformations included reporting the presence of multiple streams. Almost without exception, the transformation formed the foreground stream and included one consonant and the vowel. The other consonant was reported as belonging to the background stream. The frequency of such "streaming" transformations varied across conditions, being 38% more prevalent in the Final and I+F conditions than in the Intact condition. Across the three conditions, the consonants split off as a function of their relative cohesiveness with the vowel. In the Final condition, only the final consonant streamed off. When both consonants were not tied tightly to the vowel, as in the I+F condition, only one consonant tended to split off at a time (more often the final consonant), but there were reports in which both split off simultaneously, leaving the vowel as the only segment in the foreground stream.

Further support for perceptual regrouping being one cause of the VTE was obtained in the second experiment, which used a task that tested the streaming account indirectly, but which also enabled us to identify the portion of the stimulus that corresponded to the streaming transformation. Listeners (18) reported the first transformation, after which they isolated the portion of the stimulus that corresponded to the transformation by pressing buttons on a keypad that moved two cursors anywhere within the speech file. The stimulus continued to repeat at the same rate while the cursors were moved, but only the portion of the signal between the cursors was audible. Those portions outside of the cursors were no longer audible. Listeners had 200 repetitions during which to hear a transformation and isolate it. The only visual cues that were provided were numbers on a computer screen indicating how many cursor positions towards the centre of the file each cursor had been moved.

There was a high degree of consistency among listeners in the transformations that were reported and in where the cursors were placed. Two representative stimuli along with final cursor positions are shown in Figure 1. For stimuli in the Final condition (e.g., /loʤ/), listeners moved the endpoint cursor towards the centre of the file past the frication corresponding to /ʤ/. For stimuli in the I+F condition (e.g., /pɛtʃ/), listeners did the same, but some also moved the initial cursor inward, suggesting that the stop burst and some of the aspiration split off. Cursor placement in the Intact condition was far less so, with much more variability in cursor placement and few listeners completely eliminating the initial or final consonant. Across all conditions, the segments that were eliminated were the same ones that were reported in the background stream in the immediately preceding experiment. The data from both tasks provide strong converging evidence that suggests some types of verbal transformations are due to perceptual regrouping.

More recent experiments have asked what besides perceptual regrouping causes verbal transformations. They were designed to minimise the frequency of streaming transformations so that other regularities might emerge in the data that would provide clues as to the identity and characteristics of other perceptual processes that are responsible for the illusion. Streaming was minimised by using Intact stimuli (e.g., /nal/, /jim/) and slowing stimulus presentation rate (ISI of

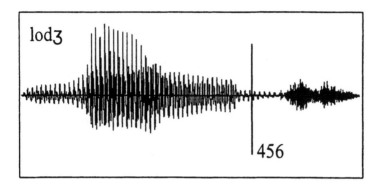

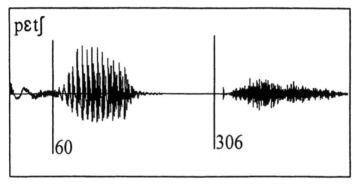

Figure 1. Waveforms of two stimuli. The vertical lines represent mean cursor positions measured in milliseconds from stimulus onset.

200 ms; 16 listeners) so that portions of each stimulus would be less likely to split off (Bregman, 1990).

This experiment succeeded in reducing the number of streaming transformations to 10%. The most frequent type of transformation (54%) was characterised by phoneme substitutions, with one or more veridical phonemes being replaced by a phonetically similar one. The remaining 36% were transformations back to the veridical percept. There was a great deal of regularity in the substitutions for both consonants and vowels. For the consonants, substitutions tended to change in place of articulation (e.g., /d/ for /b/ and /n/ for /m/). For vowels, front vowels tended to become lower and more backed (e.g., /I/ for /i/) and back vowels tended to be raised (e.g., /u/ for /U/). Satiation or fatigue of segmental representations may underlie this type of transformation. Repetitive presentation of an utterance may cause satiation, which leads to a slight shift in phoneme identity. Warren and Meyer (1988) and MacKay, Wulf, Yin, and Abrams (1993) have made similar proposals.

IMPLICATIONS FOR WORD PERCEPTION

Illusions can serve as windows into the processes that operate during veridical perception. By probing the causes of a verbal illusion like the VTE, one should be able to identify some of the processes involved in spoken word perception. The present findings suggest that perceptual regrouping and segmental satiation are two causes of the VTE. Both have been implicated in speech perception, so the present data reinforce these prior results (see Remez, Rubin, Berns, Pardo, & Lang, 1994; Samuel & Kat, 1996). That multiple processes appear to underlie the illusion makes the VTE a useful phenomenon for studying their simultaneous operation. Analysis of transformations across a range of testing conditions can identify these processes and demonstrate their interaction or independence. For example, the lexical effect could be driven by lexical processes influencing segmental satiation. Samuel's (2000) data showing lexical influences in selective adaptation, a paradigm which differs from the VTE only in *when* the effects of repeated presentation are measured, provide support for such a proposal. That regrouping and satiation act independently is suggested by the fact that streaming transformations have been found with and without phoneme substitutions.

The results showing that perceptual regrouping is one cause of the VTE suggest that lexical memory might also influence the strength with which the auditory elements of a word cohere. Nygaard (1993) found that lexical status influences the perceptual fusion of dichotically presented fragments of an utterance. It may well be that words which recycle transform back into the veridical percept more than pseudowords for the same reason: The lexical representation of the word may directly influence the perceptual organisation of speech and thereby serve as an anchor to stabilise perception. Put another way, lexical processes counter the effects of repetitive presentation that lead to streaming and help bind the acoustic elements of a word together. If this is the case, then words should yield fewer streaming transformations than pseudowords. Plans are underway to test this proposal. Finding such an effect would suggest that word perception involves more than processing the phonetic segments that make up a word. It also includes processes that assist in binding the acoustic elements of those segments together. Recent findings of Fowler and Brancazio (2000) demonstrating cross-modal lexical effects extend and reinforce this claim, so it is likely that word perception consists of multiple processes working in concert to match the acoustic signal with its representation in memory.

REFERENCES

Bregman, A.S. (1990). *Auditory Scene Analysis: The perceptual organization of sound.* Cambridge, MA: MIT Press.

Fowler, C.A., & Brancazio, L. (2000). Feedback in audiovisual speech perception. In A. Cutler, J.M. McQueen, & R. Zondervan (Eds.), *Proceedings of the Workshop on Spoken Word Access Processes* (pp. 87–90). Nijmegen, The Netherlands: Max Planck Institute for Psycholinguistics.

Frauenfelder, U., & Content, A. (2000). Activation flow in models of spoken word recognition. In A. Cutler, J.M. McQueen, & R. Zondervan (Eds.), *Proceedings of the Workshop on Spoken Word Access Processes* (pp. 79–82). Nijmegen, The Netherlands: Max Planck Institute for Psycholinguistics.

MacKay, D.G., Wulf, G., Yin, C., & Abrams, L. (1993). Relations between word perception and production: New theory and data on the verbal transformation effect. *Journal of Memory and Language, 32,* 624–646.

Natsoulas, T. (1965). A study of the verbal-transformation effect. *American Journal of Psychology, 78,* 257–263.

Nygaard, L. (1993). Phonetic coherence in duplex perception: Effects of acoustic differences and lexical status. *Journal of Experimental Psychology: Human Perception and Performance, 19,* 268–286.

Pitt, M.A., & Shoaf, L.S. (in press). Linking verbal transformations to their causes. *Journal of Experimental Psychology: Human Perception and Performance.*

Remez, R.E., Rubin, P.E., Berns, S.M., Pardo, J.S., & Lang, J.M. (1994). On the perceptual organization of speech. *Psychological Review, 101(1),* 129–156.

Samuel, A.G. (2000). Some empirical tests of Merge's architecture. In A. Cutler, J.M. McQueen, & R. Zondervan (Eds.), *Proceedings of the Workshop on Spoken Word Access Processes* (pp. 51–54). Nijmegen, The Netherlands: Max Planck Institute for Psycholinguistics.

Samuel, A.G., & Kat, D. (1996). Early levels of analysis of speech. *Journal of Experimental Psychology: Human Perception and Performance, 22,* 676-694.

Shoaf, L.S., & Pitt, M.A. (submitted). A test of node stability in Node Structure Theory. Manuscript submitted for publication.

Warren, R.M., & Meyer, M.D. (1987). Effects of listening to repeated syllables: Category boundary shifts versus verbal transformations. *Journal of Phonetics, 15,* 169–181.

LANGUAGE AND COGNITIVE PROCESSES, 2001, *16* (5/6), 723–729

Phonological variation and its consequences for the word recognition system

M. Gareth Gaskell

Department of Psychology, University of York, York, England

INTRODUCTION

This article examines possible solutions to the problem of form variation in the perception of speech. The form of a given word can change quite significantly in utterance context through processes such as reduction, assimilation, elision, and so on. Assimilation processes may be particularly influential for speech perception because in extreme cases they result in phonemic changes in the composition of a word (Koster, 1987). For example, assimilation of place of articulation in a phrase such as "lean bacon" causes the final coronal segment of *lean* to become more like /m/. This change may be partial, providing cues to two places of articulation, or more complete, with little or no residual information about the coronal place (Nolan, 1992). Complete assimilation causes phonological ambiguity—in *"leam bacon"* the surface segment could be a straightforward underlying /m/ or an underlying /n/ in its assimilated form—and this ambiguity must be resolved by the perceptual system.

PHONOLOGICAL CONTEXT EFFECTS

A critical factor in the resolution of this ambiguity is the contextual viability of any phonological change (Coenen, Zwitserlood, & Bölte, this issue; Gaskell & Marslen-Wilson, 1996). Place assimilation conforms to phonological rules or constraints regarding the place of articulation of the relevant segments. Gaskell and Marslen-Wilson (1996) examined the

Requests for reprints should be addressed to Gareth Gaskell, Department of Psychology, University of York, Heslington, York, YO10 5DD, UK. E-mail: g.gaskell@psych.york.ac.uk

The research discussed in this article was carried out in collaboration with William Marslen-Wilson.

http://www.tandf.co.uk/journals/pp/01690965.html   DOI: 10.1080/01690960143000128

effects of these constraints in a cross-modal priming experiment. They showed that an English word like *lean* in its assimilated form, when embedded in a phonologically viable context for assimilation (e.g., "*Sandra only eats leam bacon*"), facilitated lexical decision to the visual form of the unchanged word (e.g., LEAN) as strongly as an unassimilated prime. The same prime embedded in a context that violated the phonological constraints on assimilation (e.g., "*Sandra only eats leam gammon*") eliminated any facilitation. In German, Coenen et al. (this issue) also found that viable changes due to regressive place assimilation and progressive voice assimilation are tolerated by the perceptual system to a greater extent than unviable changes. However, the latter study found that noncanonical forms of words were never treated by the perceptual system as equivalent to canonical ones. Likewise, Bard, Sotillo, Kelly and Aylett (this issue) show that a range of phonological reductions elicited spontaneously result in reduced activation compared to citation forms. Nonetheless, in all these experiments, phonological changes in natural phonological contexts showed evidence of activation of the correct lexical form. Similar minimal changes in unnatural contexts did not appear to result in lexical activation (Coenen et al., this issue; Gaskell & Marslen-Wilson, 1996).

These results imply that the perceptual system compensates for alternations with reference to their surrounding phonological context. This compensation may develop gradually during language learning, through exposure to a range of variant forms (cf. the connectionist model of Gaskell, Hare & Marslen-Wilson, 1995). However it develops, the end product is sensitive to the phonological constraints involved in phonological alternations. In effect, the perceptual system applies these constraints in reverse to discern the correct underlying form.

PHONOLOGICAL VARIATION AND LEXICAL AMBIGUITY

The studies examined so far have only looked at the case where assimilation created nonwords in terms of surface form (e.g., *lean* → *leam*). In some cases, however, complete assimilation may create sequences that match words in their own right (e.g., *run* → *rum*). This second case generates a form of lexical ambiguity that occurs naturally in fluent speech (like lexical ambiguity for homophones), but involves two distinct lexical items. Here, I will discuss the recent findings of Gaskell and Marslen-Wilson (2001), who looked at the resolution of this ambiguity, again using cross-modal priming. Sentences with potential lexical ambiguities were created, which varied in terms of the word-final alternation (e.g., /rʌn/ vs. /rʌm/) and contextual viability of assimilation (e.g., /rʌm p.../ vs. /rʌm d.../). For the viable condition, the segment following the potentially assimilated word had a place of articulation that matched the alternation (e.g., "*rum picks*"). Thus, in the viable condition the phonological conditions were as expected if a word-final assimilation had occurred during speech production. These phonological constraints were contravened in the unviable condition by using following coronal consonants (e.g., "*rum does*"). The preceding contexts were neutral with respect to the suitability of the two prime words as continuations. A complete prime sentence might be "*I think a quick rum picks you up*", in which the critical prime (*rum*) was in some conditions ambiguous as to the underlying lexical item.

The visual forms of both relevant words (e.g., *run* and *rum*) were used as targets, enabling lexical activations of both words to be tracked. The target appeared at the offset of the prime word, in order to examine the immediate effects of phonological alternation, and participants made a timed lexical decision to the visual target. Facilitation of this decision by the related prime compared to an unrelated control condition is assumed to be a measure of the lexical activation of the prime. The overall results of this experiment supported earlier studies showing that the perceptual system is intolerant of even quite small deviations in the form of words (Coenen et al., this issue; Marslen-Wilson, Moss, & van Halen, 1996; although see Connine, Blasko, & Titone, 1993, and Connine, Titone, Deelman, & Blasko, 1997, for an alternative viewpoint). Despite the minimal difference between the lexical items involved, hearing "run" facilitated responses to *run* ($p < .05$) but not *rum*, and hearing "rum" facilitated responses to *rum* ($p < .05$) but not *run*. This was most noteworthy in the potentially assimilated condition, since contrary to previous results there was no evidence of compensation for assimilation, and no phonological viability effect as compared to the same token in an unviable context for assimilation.

A second experiment tested for any delayed compensation for assimilation by displaying the target words (this time just the targets such as *run* that end in coronal consonants) slightly later on in the presentation of the prime sentence (aligned with the vowel of the word following the critical prime word). Once again, there was significant facilitation for conditions where the prime was a direct match to the target ($p < .01$ in all cases), but no hint of any facilitation for the potentially assimilated condition.

SENTENTIAL CONTEXT EFFECTS

The first two experiments of Gaskell and Marslen-Wilson (2001) showed that if place assimilation results in a surface sequence that matches a lexical alternative, then in the absence of any sentential bias that alternative alone is activated. The influence of sentential context was examined in a third experiment, which used lead-in sentences that contained a pragmatic bias towards the coronal-final lexical item. For example, the neutral sentence "*I think a quick rum picks you up*" was preceded by the lead-in sentence "*It's best to start the day with a burst of activity*". This sentence had a theme that made the *rum* interpretation of the following sentence less plausible than the *run* interpretation.

The results again demonstrated the requirement for a close fit between incoming speech and lexical representation for successful lexical access. As before, primes that could not have been involved in assimilation only facilitated recognition of the lexical item matching the surface form of the speech, even when this lexical item was incongruent with respect to the preceding sentential context ($p < .05$ in all cases). Crucially however, the sentential context altered the activation profile when there was a surface alternation that could potentially have been caused by assimilation. Here, the recognition of both lexical candidates was significantly facilitated ($p < .05$), whereas previously only the item matching the surface form of the speech was facilitated (see Figure 1).

It seems, therefore, that a biasing sentential context can counteract the bottom-up perceptual preference for evaluating sequences such as /rʌm/ at face value, but only in tightly constrained circumstances. If the phonological context does not provide a suitable environment in which assimilation might have occurred, then /rʌm/ will be interpreted as the word *rum*, despite the preceding context that fits better with a lexical alternative. Only when phonological and sentential contexts are both suitable is there evidence of activation of a lexical item that matches the speech input at a more abstract level. Even in this case the perceptual system does not reject the lexical candidate that matches the speech in the surface form. Instead, both lexical items are activated, suggesting that at the relatively early point in time examined here, the lexical competition between these two items has not been resolved. Nonetheless, it seems that sentential factors play a critical role in ensuring successful communication for place assimilations that create lexical ambiguity (cf. Bard et al., 2001). This effect might usefully be termed interactive, in that sentential context appears to directly affect lexical activation, as measured by repetition priming. Nonetheless, the effect does not imply that feedback links are required in order to model the recognition process (Norris, McQueen, & Cutler, 2000), given a processing environment in which probabilistic contextual and acoustic information sources can both influence activation at the level of lexical content (Gaskell & Marslen-Wilson, 1997).

The results show a striking resemblance to studies of sentential context effects in lexical ambiguity (i.e., selecting the contextually appropriate

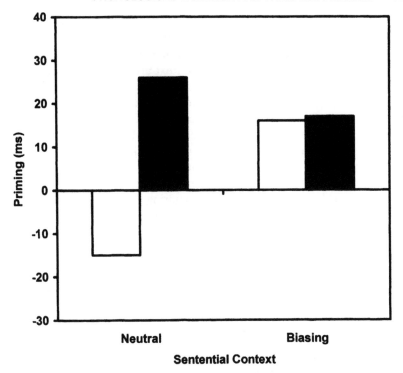

Figure 1.   The effect of sentential context bias on priming effects (test-control RT differences scores) for the potentially assimilated sentences (e.g., "I think a quick *rum picks* you up"). ■, noncoronal targets (e.g., *rum*); □, coronal targets (e.g., *run*). Results from Experiment 1 (neutral sentential bias) are on the left-hand side and from Experiment 3 (coronal sentential bias) on the right-hand side.

meaning of a word such as *bank*). The first experiment of Gaskell and Marslen-Wilson (2001) showed that in a neutral sentential context any ambiguities in spoken sentences such as "I think a quick rum picks you up" are immediately resolved by the perceptual system in favour of the words matching the speech in surface form, despite the presence of alternative interpretations involving assimilated speech. This unbalanced competition process is similar to lexical ambiguity resolution in the case of ambiguous words such as *port* with one dominant (i.e., frequent) and one subordinate (i.e., infrequent) meaning (Duffy, Morris, & Rayner, 1988). In these cases, a neutral context appears to result in the activation of the dominant meaning alone. The asymmetry in the case of ambiguity caused by assimilation is not a simple word frequency effect, but it may instead be a surface frequency effect, such that the occurrence of a word like *run* in its fully assimilated form (/rʌm/) is much less common than the canonical occurrence of a word like *rum*. Based on a simple analysis of a speech corpus, Gaskell and Marslen-Wilson (2001) estimated that less than 5% of spoken occurrences of words like *run* would be phonemically confusable with lexical neighbours due to place assimilation.

The correspondence with standard lexical ambiguity is strengthened when the effects of a biasing sentential context are taken into account. In cases where the phonological context makes the presence of an assimilated word viable (e.g., *rum picks*), a preceding context favouring the "subordinate" lexical entry provides a compensating source of evidence and results in the activation of two lexical items. This again bears strong similarities to lexical ambiguity experiments (e.g., Duffy et al., 1988; Tabossi & Zardon, 1993), which, when prior context favoured the subordinate meaning, demonstrated a more even competition between the alternatives. A constraining context favouring the subordinate meaning of an ambiguous word allowed access to the subordinate meaning without eliminating the activation of the dominant meaning.

These similarities in the resolution of naturally occurring ambiguity can be explained if the same mechanism underlies the resolution process in each case. Undoubtedly there is an important difference between the two situations, in that sentential context is generally unnecessary for choosing between distinct lexical items but necessary for identification of the relevant meaning of a word. This informational difference may explain why sentence context is often thought to play a more significant structural role in the selection of word meaning than in the identification of spoken words (e.g., Connine, Blasko, & Wang, 1994). However, when the informational circumstances are equated, by analysing examples of normal speech in which spoken word identification cannot rely solely on bottom-up information, we find the same kinds of sentential effects.

Thus, the task of resolving ambiguities caused by phonological alternations has proved to be a surprisingly complex one, involving the recruitment of information from a range of levels, from acoustic and phonological analyses through to sentential congruity.

REFERENCES

Bard, E.G., Sotillo, C., Kelly, M.L., & Aylett, M.P. (this issue). Taking the hit: Lexical and phonological processes should not resolve lexical access. *Language and Cognitive Processes, 16*, 731–737.

Coenen, E., Zwitserlood, P., & Bölte, J. (this issue) Variation and assimilation in German: Consequences for lexical access and representation. *Language and Cognitive Processes, 16*, 535–564.

Connine, C.M., Blasko, D.G., & Titone, D. (1993). Do the beginnings of spoken words have a special status in auditory word recognition? *Journal of Memory and Language, 32*, 193–210.

Connine, C.M., Blasko, D.G., & Wang, J. (1994). Vertical similarity in spoken word recognition—multiple lexical activation, individual-differences, and the role of sentence context. *Perception and Psychophysics, 56*, 624–636.

Connine, C.M., Titone, D., Deelman, T., & Blasko, D. (1997). Similarity mapping in spoken word recognition. *Journal of Memory and Language, 37*, 463–480.

Duffy, S.A., Morris, R.K., & Rayner, K. (1988). Lexical ambiguity and fixation times in reading. *Journal of Memory and Language, 27*, 429–446.

Gaskell, M.G., Hare, M., & Marslen-Wilson, W.D. (1995). A connectionist model of phonological representation in speech perception. *Cognitive science, 19*, 407–439.

Gaskell, M.G., & Marslen-Wilson, W.D. (1996). Phonological variation and inference in lexical access. *Journal of Experimental Psychology: Human Perception and Performance, 22*, 144–158.

Gaskell, M.G., & Marslen-Wilson, W.D. (1997). Integrating form and meaning: A distributed model of speech perception. *Language and Cognitive Processes, 12*, 613–656.

Gaskell, M.G., & Marslen-Wilson, W.D. (2001). Lexical ambiguity resolution and spoken word recognition: Bridging the gap. *Journal of Memory and Language, 44*, 325–349

Koster, C.J. (1987). *Word recognition in foreign and native language.* Dordrecht: Foris.

Marslen-Wilson, W.D., Moss, H.E., & van Halen, S. (1996). Perceptual distance and competition in lexical access. *Journal of Experimental Psychology: Human Perception and Performance, 22*, 1376–1392.

Nolan, F. (1992). The descriptive role of segments: Evidence from assimilation. In D.R. Ladd & G. Docherty (Eds.), *Laboratory Phonology II* (pp. 261–280). Cambridge: Cambridge University Press.

Norris, D., McQueen, J.M., & Cutler, A. (2000). Merging information in speech recognition: Feedback is never necessary. *Behavioral and Brain Sciences, 23*, 299–370.

Tabossi, P., & Zardon, F. (1993). Processing ambiguous words in context. *Journal of Memory and Language, 32*, 359–372.

LANGUAGE AND COGNITIVE PROCESSES, 2001, *16* (5/6), 731–737

Taking the hit: Leaving some lexical competition to be resolved post-lexically

Ellen Gurman Bard, Catherine Sotillo, M. Louise Kelly, and
Matthew P. Aylett

University of Edinburgh, Edinburgh, Scotland

INTRODUCTION

Natural variations in word pronunciation are not noise but information. Duration, prosodic prominence, vowel centralisation, and phonological reduction or assimilation can indicate whether a word stands alone or forms part of an utterance, whether it lies at the boundary of a major prosodic unit, is predictable in its context, or refers to a Given or a New entity.

Though this variation is related to high-level factors, most discussions of lexical access seem to assume that lower level processes—acoustic-phonetic processing, phonological representation in the mental lexicon, and lexical effects on phonological representations of input—simply overcome variations in natural pronunciation, assuring that the correct word is accessed and ultimately selected, with no shortfall in the process that demands the participation of higher level information. Many of the papers in this volume deal with the architectural detail of this view. This paper summarises work on spontaneous unscripted speech, where variations most naturally occur, which shows why any such approach is counterproductive.

Requests for reprints should be addressed to Dr E.G. Bard, Department of Theoretical and Applied Linguistics, University of Edinburgh, George Square, Edinburgh EH8 9LL, UK. E-mail: ellen@ling.ed.ac.uk

E.G. Bard, C. Sotillo, and M.P. Aylett, Human Communication Research Centre and Department of Theoretical and Applied Linguistics. Dr Aylett is now with Rhetorical Systems, Edinburgh. Dr Kelly is now in the Department of Psychology, University of Edinburgh.

This work was supported by the ESRC (UK)-funded Human Communication Research Centre and by EU BRA BR3175. This paper includes work reported at ICPhS99 and at SpoSS98.

http://www.tandf.co.uk/journals/pp/01690965.html   DOI: 10.1080/01690960143000100

The current assumptions, which we will call Plan A, effectively dissociate successful lexical access from the recovery of the information signalled by variable pronunciations. We will argue instead for a Plan B under which lower level lexical processes take the hit, in many cases failing to resolve lexical competition, and leaving scope for participation of the higher level information to which altered pronunciations are keyed. We will show that (1) natural variations in pronunciation do affect lexical access; (2) dealing with signalled information by other means would not be simple; (3) difficulties in lexical access promote dependence on discourse comprehension.

PHONOLOGICAL REDUCTIONS AND LEXICAL ACCESS

Effects of phonological assimilation (e.g. Coenen, Zwitserlood, & Bölte, this issue; Gaskell & Marslen-Wilson, 1996) are variable. Assimilations which are illegal in their context seem to block priming of the lexical item (Gaskell & Marslen-Wilson, 1996), while other assimilations usually do not. All these experiments, however, depend on read items whose general clarity might lead listeners to conclude that the careful speaker means what he says, so that /lim/ before *gammon* must be a new word. To test for effects of token and ambient speech quality, we examined words excerpted from their original contexts and manipulated both the articulatory quality of the words and the average quality of the stimuli.

Critical stimuli were tokens of the names of those landmarks in the HCRC Map Task Corpus (Anderson et al., 1991) (hereafter, MTC) which invited phonological reduction or assimilation (weak vowel reduction: *canoes, elephants*; nasal place-of-articulation assimilation, *pine grove*; d-deletion, *old mill*). Test (48) and control auditory primes (48) were matched as far as possible in length and frequency, with half of each from spontaneous running speech produced during the communication task and the other half tokens of the same words read in lists by the same speakers. Running speech primes were shorter than their list-read counterparts and were judged more assimilated by a panel of nine phoneticians. Experiment 1 fillers were all from spontaneous speech; Experiment 2 used the list-read forms of the same words. Subjects heard primes binaurally over headphones and made lexical decisions to letter strings presented at prime offset.

In both experiments, identity priming was robust: lexical decision was faster after either the spontaneous or the list-read prime (*elephants elephants*) than after unrelated words of similar quality (*waterhole elephants*). Only in Experiment 2, with clear list-read fillers, did reduced tokens prime less than their list-read counterparts. Yet in other experiments, those same reduced tokens proved less intelligible: in isolation they were correctly identified less often than their longer list-read counterparts (cf. Bard, Kelly, & Sotillo, 1998).

Robust priming indicates that all forms can access the intended lexical items. Effects of ambient speech quality, however, show that the course of lexical activation can be influenced by the general context in which it occurs. And ultimate failures of recognition demonstrate that phonology and the lexicon do not fully counteract acoustic deficits when resolving the competitor set. These results are difficult to explain under Plan A. Once access is made to a lexical entry, lexical and phonological information is supposed to be deployed to resolve competition with higher level information serving quite different purposes. Without such information, however, spoken word recognition does take the hit.

COMPLEX INFORMATION

Deaccenting

The difficulties for Plan A might turn out to be trivial if the differences in pronunciation can be analysed by simple additional processes. In the case of referring expressions, the bulk of the observed variation has been attributed to a simple distinction of referent status, with the prosodically prominent, accented introductory mentions of New entities being reliably longer and clearer than the non-prominent, deaccented second mentions of Given items (Hawkins & Warren, 1994). If so, variation in pronunciation of nominals could be represented via a single binary choice.

The New-accented and Given-deaccented contrast, however, is preponderant only where repeated mentions maintain their original sentence position and syntactic role (Terken & Hirschberg, 1994), as they do in many repetitive laboratory tasks. In more natural speech, however, successive utterances rarely serve the same communicative purposes and so should usually differ in structure and offer few opportunities for deaccenting.

Bard & Aylett (1999) tested this proposal on utterances containing 293 landmark names mentioned twice in the MTC. As predicted, pairs of utterances bearing repeated mentions had the same phrasal structure (sequence of NP, VP, PP) more often if they had the same communicative purpose (Dialogue Game Move: see Carletta et al., 1997), but such pairs were always in a minority. Classing each word as having non-boundary accent, boundary tone, or neither (Mayo, Aylett, & Ladd, 1997) and counting any move down this list as deaccenting, we found that accented-deaccented sequences were even rarer than random choice among the coding options would predict. Instead, over 70% of successive mentions were similarly accented. Even in these, the second mentions were significantly shorter and less intelligible in isolation than the first. Clearly, reduction in second mentions cannot be attributed solely or even largely to the accented/deaccented distinction. Hence binary coding of accent in perception would be of little use.

Control by listener knowledge: Lexical competition

Plan A might still be plausible if, as Lindblom (1990) has proposed, words are articulated clearly enough to be decoded by listeners with the aid of their other current knowledge. We examined two instantiations of this claim, one vis-à-vis lexical knowledge, the other vis-à-vis the listener's discourse representation.

The first instantiation suggests that reductions in pronunciation are less where lexical competition is greater, leaving acoustic and lexical information with a roughly constant chance of resolving competition in all cases. To test for such modulation, Sotillo and Bard (1998) examined MTC landmark names which invited assimilation of word-final alveolar nasals toward the labial (*seven beeches*) or velar (*pine grove*) initial consonant of the following word. First and second full mentions of the landmarks from running speech were compared to the list-read versions of the same names read by the same speakers. Words were classed by competitor set size under several definitions of the competitor set: (1) word-initial cohorts, (2) phonological neighbourhoods, and (3) a looser criterion which included virtually all identification responses, words sharing either the onset or the nucleus of the initial syllable and loosely matching the other (for example, *paint* for *pine*, *laddie* for *wagon*). Words were judged for assimilation by nine phoneticians. Overlaid with sufficient noise to avoid ceiling effects, all had been presented to naïve listeners ($n >$ 5) for identification during other experiments (Bard et al., 2000).

As usual, running speech forms were significantly less intelligible and more reduced than their list-read counterparts. The Lindblom model predicts more extreme reduction where lexical competition is less. Not even a trend in this direction was found.

Control by listener knowledge: Discourse

The second instantiation of Lindblom's suggestion involves tailoring speech to the listener's current knowledge of the unfolding discourse, with the key to the variation at a higher level, but still held by the listener at the time of lexical processing. To achieve this, however, the speaker must continuously update his or her own model of the listener's knowledge, an onerous task which is ignored in other domains (Horton & Keysar, 1996). Although speakers and listeners often share knowledge, Bard et al. (2000)

examined words produced in MTC contexts where speakers' knowledge could be shown to differ from listeners'.

Words from first and second mentions of MTC landmarks and their list-read control forms gave consistent results over four experiments. The listener's knowledge was irrelevant to the reductive effect of Givenness on duration and intelligibility. The effect was not blocked in introductory mentions to a second listener (speaker-Given but listener-New), or mitigated when the speaker had direct feedback about the listener's inability to see the named object, or enhanced when the speaker could infer greater knowledge on the listener's part. The Givenness effect on pronunciation seemed to follow only from what the speaker knew.

DISCOURSE COMPREHENSION

It appears that spoken words present perceptual difficulties which listeners cannot immediately resolve, because the key to resolving them is in the speaker's internal representation of the discourse. To make use of this information, the listener would need to recruit an account of the speaker's knowledge when intelligibility is lowest. In effect, this is Plan B.

To test the listener's behaviour, Bard, Cooper, Kowtko, and Brew (1991) used a variant of the primed probe recognition task (Fowler & Housum, 1987) in which a spoken monologue is interrupted by a pair of excerpted probe words, a prime and a target, and subjects are asked to decide if each has occurred previously in the interrupted speech. In the critical cases, the prime was either a first-mention token of a word, which had already been heard, or a second-mention token of the same word, which had not been heard at this point, but which would be reached in the monologue soon after it resumed. The critical target had been heard in some syntactic construction with the first-token prime in its original context. Fowler and Housum, however, found faster RTs to such targets after the second-mention primes. They attributed the effect to a binary perceptual process which classed deaccented second-mention primes as Given, thereby prompting reference back to the clause containing the first token.

Using workplace dictations, Bard et al. (1991) also asked for decisions on repeated words and on targets related to first tokens. Of the critical prime pairs, 25 were coreferential and 25 non-coreferential across mentions. Only coreferential pairs differed in length. Panels of judges, scanning the transcripts for words which would have to be mentioned again, selected the first mentions of the coreferential items significantly more often than first-mentions of non-coreferential, showing that the former were more important to the discourse. All prime and target words were presented to new subjects in two experiments, in the first exactly as recorded and in the second, overlaid with noise which, on pretest, had significantly reduced their intelligibility. Control trials included the same targets with previously heard but unrelated primes. Filler trials balanced combinations of previously heard and novel items, as well as relatedness of prime to target.

Fowler and Housum's binary explanation predicts that coreferential second tokens should prime most, for only these should signal Given status. In contrast, we predicted greatest priming for any coreferential prime with noise overlay. Degraded acoustic information should force listeners to recruit what they know of the discourse to the problem of recognising any primes, but the discourse, as we have seen, alloted a prominent role to the entities named by these coreferential words.

The results conformed to this prediction. Priming was significant only when primes were coreferential, but regardless of whether the prime was the first or the second mention. Added noise enhanced priming from either coreferential prime but decreased it for non-coreferential primes. For coreferential primes, variance in target RT was more strongly related to prime word characteristics (frequency, duration, RT, and distance of test from first mention) than to target word characteristics, whereas the reverse was true for the non-coreferential sets.

Under Plan A, all the primes should have been identified via acoustic and lexical information. Priming would have to be due to post-access discourse processing. If so, longer prime RTs, which could include access, selection, and such additional processing, should accompany shorter target RTs. In fact, prime and target RTs correlated positively: priming came with faster recognition of items important to the discourse. The association between degraded acoustic stimuli, increased discourse effects and fast recognition suggests that higher level information is intimately involved in the recognition of spoken words.

DISCUSSION

Overall, then, Plan A seems implausible. First, the acoustic material in spontaneously reduced word tokens activates the correct words, but degree of activation may reflect articulatory quality, and competition may not permit correct recognition. Lexical access does appear to take the hit. Second, alterations from "canonical" word pronunciation are not arranged in a way that is simple to decode by an ancillary mechanism. The degree of alteration is not keyed to the listener's lexical or discourse knowledge, but to the speaker's own view. Third, difficulty in recognising spoken words can enhance the use of discourse information for those items referring to discourse-prominent entities. As in the interpretation of pronouns in texts, items with important antecedents receive preferential treatment (Garrod, Freudenthal, & Boyle, 1994).

The results do support Plan B. Elegantly enough, graded difficulty in lexical access, keyed to the speaker's internal representation of discourse, furthers the listener's ultimate goal, comprehending the speaker's message.

REFERENCES

Anderson, A.H., Bader, M., Bard, E.G., Boyle, E., Doherty, G., Garrod, S., Isard, S., Kowtko, J., McAllister, J.M., Miller, J., Sotillo, C., Thompson, H., & Weinert, R. (1991). The H.C.R.C. Map Task Corpus. *Language and Speech, 34*, 351–366.

Bard, E.G., & Aylett, M. (1999). The dissociation of deaccenting, Givenness, and syntactic role in spontaneous speech. *Proceedings of the XIVth International Congress of Phonetic Sciences: Vol. 3.* (pp. 1753–1756). San Francisco, CA.

Bard, E.G., Anderson, A.H., Sotillo, C., Aylett, M., Doherty-Sneddon, G., & Newlands, A. (2000). Controlling the intelligibility of referring expressions in dialogue. *Journal of Memory and Language, 42*, 1–22.

Bard, E.G., Cooper, L., Kowtko, J., & Brew, C. (1991). Psycholinguistic studies on incremental recognition of speech: A revised and extended introduction to the messy and the sticky. *DYANA Deliverable R1.3B.* Edinburgh: University of Edinburgh.

Bard, E.G., Kelly, M.L., & Sotillo, C. (1998). Lexical access in spontaneous speech: Reduced forms prime less. In D. Duez (Ed.), *Proceedings of SPoSS* (pp. 93–96). Aix: ESCA, GFCP, & U. de Provence.

Carletta, J., Isard, A., Isard, S., Kowtko, J., Doherty-Sneddon, G., & Anderson, A. (1997). The reliability of a dialogue scheme. *Computational Linguistics, 23*, 13—31.

Coenen, E., Zwitserlood, P., & Bölte, J. (this issue). Variation and assimilation in German: Consequences for lexical access and representation. *Language and Cognitive Processes, 16*, 535–564

Fowler, C., & Housum, J. (1987). Talkers' signaling of "new" and "old" words in speech and listeners' perception and use of the distinction. *Journal of Memory and Language, 26*, 489–504.

Garrod, S., Freudenthal, D., & Boyle, E. (1994). The role of different types of anaphor in the online resolution of sentences in a discourse. *Journal of Memory and Language, 33*, 39–68.

Gaskell, G., & Marslen-Wilson, W. (1996). Phonological variation and inference in lexical access. *Journal of Experimental Psychology: Human Perception and Performance, 22*, 144–58.

Hawkins, S., & Warren, P. (1994). Phonetic influences on the intelligibility of conversational speech. *Journal of Phonetics, 22*, 493–511.

Horton, W., & Keysar, B. (1996). When do speakers take into account common ground? *Cognition, 59*, 91–117.

Lindblom, B. (1990). Explaining variation: A sketch of the H and H theory. In W. Hardcastle & A. Marchal (Eds.), *Speech production and speech modelling* (pp. 403–439). Dordrecht, Netherlands: Kluwer Academic Publishers.

Mayo, C., Aylett, M., & Ladd, D.R. (1997). Prosodic transcription of Glasgow English: An evaluation study of GlaToBI. *Proceedings of the ESCA workshop on intonation* (pp. 231–234). Athens, Greece: ESCA & U. of Athens.

Sotillo, C., & Bard, E.G. (1998). Is hypo-articulation lexically constrained? In D. Duez, (Ed.), *Proceedings of SPoSS* (pp. 109–112). Aix: ESCA, GFCP, & Université de Provence.

Terken, J., & Hirschberg, J. (1994). Deaccentuation of words representing Given information: contributions of persistence of grammatical function and surface position. *Language and Speech, 37*, 125–14.

Language and Cognitive Processes
Special Issue Subject Index

abstract lexical access code 472–473, 474, 491–505
access processes
  competition 469, 476–480, 507–534, 565–581,731–737
  feedback 469, 482–485, 486, 709–714, 715
  form-based processing 469, 486
  signal, lexical knowledge fit 469, 485, 731–737
  speech segmentation 469, 476, 480–481, 634–635, 637–660
activation-competition models 565–566
adaptation effects 484, 712–713
allophony 481, 692, 693
ambiguity 475, 484, 485, 492–493, 711–713, 724–728, 731–737
anticipation effect 558–559
Arabic 703–705, 707
artificial language-learning paradigm 483
assimilation effects 474, 535–564, 723–728, 731, 732

bottom-up inhibition 478, 583–607, 710

candidate words
  competition 476–477, 478, 479, 480, 507–534
  sentential context 486
categorisation, speeded 686–689
categorisation tasks 661–672, 678–680, 686–689, 711–714
category goodness ratings 684–686
Chinese 477, 705–706, 707
coarticulation
  compensation mechanisms 492, 661, 710–712
  fricative-stop compensation 482–483, 661–672, 710–712
  lipreading 661–672
  mismatch 519–523, 526
  word boundaries 472, 480
Cohort model 538, 541, 584, 594
competition 469, 476–480, 507–534, 565–581, 731–737
compound words 705–706
computational models 476, 478–479, 594–595, 605

context
  assimilation 536–537, 539–540, 552–557
  internal category structure 683–686, 689
  lexical 472, 485–486
  phonological variation 723–724
  sentential 485, 486, 725–728
  speech recognition 472, 485–486
continuous speech, segmentation 469, 476, 480–481, 634–635, 637–660
cross-linguistic studies 475–478, 493, 610–612, 638, 651–655, 699–708

deaccenting 733–734
density, neighbourhood 565–567, 572–580
discourse comprehension 735–736
Dutch 479, 485, 652–654, 664–672

entropy 574–580, 674
episodic representations 471, 472, 473
eye-tracking paradigm 479, 483, 507, 509–531

fast phonological preprocessor (FPP) 691, 692, 694
feedback 469, 482–485, 486, 709–714, 715
form-based processing 469, 474, 477, 485–486
French
  lexical selection 478, 583–607
  prelexical processing 492, 498–501
  segmentation 480, 481, 609–636
frequency 510, 559, 566, 676, 692
fricative-stop compensation 482, 483, 661–672, 710–712

German 474, 481, 535–564, 724
gestural model 537, 558

Hebrew 703–704, 707

inference processes 474, 475, 558, 559, 693, 723–729
inhibition
  bottom-up 478, 583–607, 710
  lateral 508–509, 525, 584, 604–605

inhibition—*cont.*
  lexical competition 469, 476–480,
    507–534, 565–581, 731–737
internal category structure 683–690
interpretation processes 469, 470,
  485–486

Japanese 472–473, 476, 491–503

language acquisition 475, 654, 691–698
lateral inhibition 508–509, 525, 584,
  604–605
lexical access
  abstract code 472–473, 474, 491–505
  competition 469, 476–480, 507–534,
    565–581, 731–737
  cross-linguistic issues 699–708
  feedback 469, 482–485, 486, 709–714,
    715
  mismatching information 477–481,
    486–487, 507–534
  phonological variation 474, 535,
    731–737
  representations 469, 474, 477,
    699–708
lexical activation
  context 724, 733
  mismatch 477–480, 507–508, 583–607
  sentential context 486
lexical decision studies 491–505, 508,
  527–530, 566–567, 637, 641–651,
  715
lexical knowledge
  phoneme identification 492, 493,
    583–607
  phonological variation 734–735
lexical representations
  morphological 469, 475–476, 699–708
  phonological 471–475, 535–564, 586,
    602–605, 691–698
  semantic 469, 475–476, 586–587,
    602–604, 699–708
lexical selection 486, 583–607
lexicon
  episodic representations 471, 472,
    473
  phonological constraints 691–698
  structure 699
  word representations 469, 471, 474,
    475, 477, 699–708
lip-reading 483, 661–672
liquid-stop compensation 671

Merge model 482–483, 509, 588, 663,
  671, 709–714

Metrical Segmentation Strategy (MSS)
  638, 639
mismatch effects 477–480, 486–487
  lexical selection 478, 486–487,
    583–607
  subcategorical 479, 507–534
  syllable detection 632, 633
  word recognition 507–534, 535, 538,
    552, 583–607
morphological representation 469,
  475–476, 699–708

neighbourhood density 565–567,
  572–580

parsing 693–694
perception, unit of 471–473, 480,
  673–681
perceptual processes
  compensation for coarticulation
    482–483, 492, 661–672, 710–712
  decision-making 486
  fast phonological preprocessor 691
  function 470
  mapping to lexicon 538, 610,
    683–690
  phoneme-like units 673–681
  phonological variation 535–564,
    723–729
  regrouping 717–718, 720
  subsyllabic/phonetic 631–634
phoneme monitoring 583–607
phonemes
  ambiguous 484, 492–493, 661–672,
    711–713
  factorability 673–680
  Merge model 709–714
  mismatches 478, 486–487, 507–534,
    583–607
  output representations 709–710, 714
  speech recognition role 471–472,
    473, 477, 661–662, 673–681,
    683–690
  substitution 575, 719
phonemic restoration 492, 712
phonetic category structure 683–690,
  715
phonetic throughput hypothesis
  624–630
phonological constraints 691–698
phonological representation
  constraints 474–475, 691–698
  in lexicon 471, 472, 473–475,
    535–564, 586, 602–605, 691–698

phonological representation—*cont.*
  variation and assimilation 535–564,
    723–729, 731–737
phonotactic knowledge
  prelexical processing 491–505
  spoken word recognition 565–581
  word boundaries 638, 639–640, 655
Polish 701–703, 707
Possible Word Constraint (PWC) 480,
    481, 637–660
prelexical processing
  fast phonological preprocessor 691
  lexical influence 469, 482–485,
    491–505, 709–714, 715
  selective adaptation 484, 712–713
  speaking rate 471–474, 684–686
prelexical representations 472, 473,
    477, 484–485, 673–681, 683
priming studies
  assimilation 539, 542–557, 723–729
  candidate word activation 476
  lexical representations 700–708
  mismatch 586–587, 603
  phonological variation 723–729,
    732–736

reductions 723, 732–733
rhyme 476–477, 485, 678
rhythmic structures 638, 639–640, 655

same-different judgements 568–574
second-language studies 477–478, 481
segmentation
  continuous speech 469, 480–481,
    637–660
  cross-linguistic research 476,
    610–612, 638, 651–655
  language-universal constraints
    480–481, 637–660
  syllable detection 480, 481, 609–636
selective adaptation 484, 712–713
semantically ambiguous words 475
semantic representations 469, 475–476,
    586–587, 602–604, 699–708
sentential context 485, 486, 725–728
Sesotho 652
Shortlist model
  lexical selection 478, 584, 585, 595,
    605
  speech segmentation 639, 655
speaking rate 471–474, 535, 559,
    684–686
spoken word recognition
  competition 469, 476–480, 507–534,
    565–581, 731–737
  context 472, 485–486

spoken word recognition—*cont.*
  major issues 469–490
  neighbourhood density 565–567,
    572–580
  phonological variation 474, 535–564,
    723–729, 731–737
  phonotactics 565–581
  prelexical processing 491–505
  speech segmentation 469, 476,
    480–481, 634–635, 637–660
  verbal transformation effect 715–721
spontaneous speech 731–737
streaming 717–720
sublexical effects 477, 566–567,
    579–580
subsegmental effects 479, 507–534
surface variation effects 474, 535–564,
    723–729, 731–737
Syllable Onset Segmentation
    Hypothesis (SOSH) 634–635
syllables
  recognisers 675, 676–678
  representations 613
  sequence detection task 609–636
  speech recognition 471, 673–681
  speech segmentation 480–481,
    609–636, 637, 639–641, 651, 655

tone information 477
top-down lexical effects 491–505, 587,
    663
TRACE model
  fricative stop compensation 482–483,
    662–663
  mismatch 478, 479, 507–531, 538,
    557, 585, 595, 605
  speech segmentation 638
  top-down connections 492–493, 587
trochaic structure 693, 696

Verbal Transformation Effect (VTE)
    484, 715–721
visual speech 483, 661–672
vocabulary 474–475, 692–697
Voice Onset Time (VOT) 472,
    684–689
vowel epenthesis effect 472–473,
    493–503

words *see* access processes; lexical
    access; lexical activation; lexical
    knowledge; lexical
    representations; lexical selection;
    lexicon and spoken word
    recognition
word spotting 637–660